Battis

Anne Hutchinson was a woman "of nimble wit and active spirit, and a very voluble tongue, more bold than a man" in argument, a woman with a decided religious instinct, a magnetic personality, and a peculiar talent for controversy. Written with verve and imagination, this book is an extraordinarily stimulating literary essay in intellectual history, which employs psychological and sociological insights that provide a fresh understanding of Mrs. Hutchinson's career and give her controversy with the Puritan Saints a new dimension in the history of colonial America.

This study examines the so-called Antinomian Controversy which Mrs. Hutchinson's doctrines aroused, seeks to explain why her views were so immoderately popular in some parts of the colony, and interprets the reasons for the ruling oligarchy's so energetically suppressing the movement.

In England, Mrs. Hutchinson came under the influence of the Reverend John Cotton, and when he migrated to the Massachusetts Bay Colony, she and her family soon followed. The newly formed Puritan colony was soon troubled by the heterodox opinions she held. During her early months in the colony, Mrs. Hutchinson was admitted to church membership, attended services regularly, and began to hold weekly women's meetings in her home to recapitulate the lengthy Sabbath sermons. But, increasingly, she drew a line of distinction between legalistic ministers who labored under a Covenant of Works and sanctified ministers who preached a Covenant of Grace. Her relatively permissive doctrine seems to have been most attractive to the affluent merchants and craftsmen of Boston, men who had been constrained in the performance of their entrepreneurial roles by the doctrine of responsible social organicism preached by the clergy and legislated by the gentry and yeomanry.

As Mrs. Hutchinson's following grew, the Puritan ministers and magistrates became progressively alarmed. It seemed to them that her tenets struck at the very nerve center of Puritan theology and social structure. They feared that her doctrine would elevate the individual conscience above all external authority and exempt the believer from conventional moral restraints. So church and state joined forces to suppress the heresy and to expel the Hutchinsonian faction from Massachusetts.

A close examination of Mrs. Hutchinson's career suggests that her mystical beliefs and her professions of divine revelation were in part the product of a psychological disturbance that became progressively delusional as the controversy developed. Dr. Battis has skillfully applied the behaviorial sciences to the field of historical research to produce a fascinating biography and a brilliant inquiry into the Puritan mind in action.

Emery Battis is associate professor of history in Rutgers University and a sometime off-Broadway actor.

SAINTS
AND
SECTARIES

The Institute of Early American History and Culture is sponsored jointly by the College of William and Mary and Colonial Williamsburg, Incorporated. Publication of this book has been assisted by a grant from the Lilly Endowment, Inc.

JOHN WINTHROP

SAINTS
AND
SECTARIES

Anne Hutchinson and the Antinomian
Controversy in the Massachusetts Bay Colony

EMERY BATTIS

PUBLISHED FOR
The Institute of Early American History and Culture
at Williamsburg, Virginia
BY The University of North Carolina Press · Chapel Hill

Manufactured in the United States of America

VAN REES PRESS • NEW YORK

FOR

My Mother

and Father

Preface

Every American who has survived the patriotic myths of the grade school history texts is acquainted with the name of Anne Hutchinson. Her heroic defiance of the Puritan autocracy has won the admiration of liberal minds and gained her acclaim as a notable champion of our religious liberty. Only in recent years has careful restudy of her doctrines suggested that perhaps there was much to be said for the viewpoint of her oppressors. This more balanced interpretation of Mrs. Hutchinson's controversy with the New England Saints was made possible by Perry Miller's penetrating analysis of the Puritan mind—a contribution for which all students of American history must remain deeply indebted to him.

It is not my purpose to remove any of the credit which is properly Anne Hutchinson's due. Indeed, although unconvinced that she was a conscious champion of any religious principles other than her own, I suspect that the most substantial strides toward religious freedom have generally been made, not by the dedicated and articulate proponents of that end, but rather by the strenuous endeavors of innumerable sectarians, such as she was, to gain religious freedom for themselves. In the long run religious heterogeneity and the force of numbers were more powerful persuaders than rational arguments in producing this great social change.

This book offers an account of a specific religious movement and its leader and of the circumstances which gave rise to that movement. In part, I have attempted to develop Professor Miller's conclusions along lines relevant to the Antinomian Controversy and to place them within the historical narrative of that event. Somewhat more originally—and perilously—I have sought to raise certain fundamental questions which have not hitherto been applied to the career of Mrs. Hutchinson and the tempest she aroused. Although the story has been frequently retold by professional historians and popular biographers alike, the narrators have been content to accept at face value Mrs. Hutchinson's own explanation of her religious experience. They have admitted her doctrine as a reasonable theological alternative to that espoused by the orthodox majority. They have further left the reader to understand that Mrs. Hutchinson's personality and powers of persuasion were sufficient cause to prompt the Bostonians to adopt the alternative she offered despite the manifestly dangerous consequences of such a choice. Perhaps this is the simplest and safest way of describing such an event. However, our present knowledge of individual and social psychology indicates that religious movements cannot be properly understood in these conveniently simple terms. Therefore, I have sought to explore in detail the personalities and motives of the individuals involved in this controversy. I have tried to determine what sort of person Mrs. Hutchinson was and what circumstances impelled her to press such radical conclusions. Further, I have tried to discover who these people were who took up her cause with such impassioned loyalty, what kind of people they were, what their backgrounds, needs, and attitudes were that they should make such a perilous commitment.

This search has led into realms of speculation which the cautious historian will enter only with trepidation. It has prompted the exercise of techniques which the untrained operator takes up at his peril. It is one thing to attempt to describe the psychological structure of an historical figure as it emerges from contemporaneous documents and accounts. It is quite another to pinpoint the factors in that person's experience which contributed most significantly to the organization of his personality structure and impelled him to pursue that course of action which made him historically interesting and important. Often such psychological determinants, unrecognized as such at the time, were never recorded and so remain forever lost to view. Although not a great deal is known about Mrs. Hutchinson before her arrival in Massachusetts there is enough to suggest that it is now possible to correlate the accessible data of her life experience in such a way as to provide a fresh understanding of her career. Indeed, with the data at our disposal it seems fruitless to continue to write of her as though she were a thoroughly normal person, motivated by normal impulses. The significant point is that Anne Hutchinson's religious views and her determination to carry them out were not the product of intellectualization in an emotional vacuum; they were part of a specific psychological response to a complex set of emotional pressures. From the available evidence I have sought to indicate the general outlines of that psychological configuration.

Midway in the passage of this work I received much encouragement and instruction from the pages of the Social Science Research Council's Bulletin No. 64 with its appeal for a more general application of the behavioral sciences in exploring the problems of history. When at last I had finished I drew still further assurance from Professor William Langer's presidential address before the American Historical Association. Deploring the want of "speculative audacity" in the field of historical research, he appealed for "new ideas, new points of view, and new techniques." If progress is made, he advised, "we must be ready, from time to time, to take flyers into the unknown, even though some of them may prove wide of the mark. Like the scientists, we can learn a lot from our own mistakes, and the chances are that if we persist, each successive attempt may take us closer to the target." I only hope that I have adhered to the spirit of these appeals and that my effort may bring us a little closer toward the center of this particular target.

Irrespective of success or failure, among the abiding pleasures of scholarly research are the obligations incurred along the way. From the very outset Professor Richard B. Morris of Columbia University and Professor Robert Handy of Union Theological Seminary have been continuously helpful and encouraging and their numerous critical suggestions have steered me safely around many a pitfall and booby trap. I am particularly indebted to Messrs. James M. Smith and Frederick A. Hetzel of the Institute of Early American History and Culture, and their assiduous corps of anonymous readers who explored this manuscript with glacial deliberation and thoroughness to recommend important revisions and to suggest the fundamental reorganization which was at last adopted. I would like also to acknowledge my gratitude to Paul Younge, M.D., Professor of Gynecology at the Harvard Medical School, who carefully examined the gynecological and medical data on Mrs. Hutchinson and offered a skillful diagnosis of her physical condition at the time of her trial and banishment. A generous grant from the Rutgers Research Council proved most helpful in working through the final stages of this enterprise.

Among my own colleagues at Douglass College my obligations are abundantly scattered. Professor Nelson Hanawalt has twice reviewed and revised the psychological speculations about Mrs.

Hutchinson. To Professor George P. Schmidt, I am much indebted for suggestions on the opening chapters, but even more for the warm encouragement and support which he supplied when energy and hope were at low ebb. The fruit of many stimulating discussions with Professors Harry Bredemeier and Richard Stephenson about the sociological implications of the Antinomian Controversy has inevitably found its way into these pages. Indeed, I cannot adequately express my gratitude to Dr. Bredemeier for his labors on the content of Chapter XVII in particular. The quantitative analysis of the Boston population was carried out under his patient direction, and at all times his incisive detailed criticisms and his wise general suggestions have been immensely valuable.

But in this endeavor, as in all things, my principal debt is to my wife, Elaine Cunningham Battis, whose imaginative insights and innumerable editorial suggestions and rewrites more properly entitle her to a credit on the title page of this volume. But for her wisdom and endurance and support this book might never have seen the light of day.

Douglass College
Rutgers
January, 1962

A Note About the Calendar
and Quotations

THE DATES in this book are all in the Old Style, according to the Julian calendar which was used in England and its colonies at the time these events took place. When, during Elizabeth's reign, Pope Gregory XIII had grandly annulled ten days in order to catch up with the true vernal equinox, the Protestant English, favoring pagan confusion over Popish common sense, rejected the change and clung for almost two centuries longer to the Julian irregularities.

I have chosen to retain the Old Style in order to simplify the task of those readers whose curiosity takes them back to the original sources, some of which, like the Winthrop *Journal* and the Massachusetts Records, remain quite generally and easily accessible. For those who wish to determine the New Style dates of any of the events described herein, it is necessary only to add ten days to the date given. Remember, too, that for the English of the seventeenth century the new year commenced, not on January first, but in the month of March, sometimes on the first day and sometimes on the twenty-fifth. I have sought to clarify this ambivalence by dating the chapter heads thus: January 1636/7, and so forth.

In the text quotations from seventeenth-century sources appear sometimes in their original form with archaic spelling and punctuation, and sometimes in modernized form. The latter are used because it was frequently necessary or more convenient to employ editions of seventeenth-century writings in which the forms had been modernized by later editors. The most notable examples of this usage are James K. Hosmer's edition of Governor Winthrop's *Journal*, Lawrence Shaw Mayo's edition of Thomas Hutchinson's transcript of Mrs. Hutchinson's trial before the General Court, and Charles Bell's edition of John Wheelwright's works.

Contents

Illustrations

SAINTS
AND
SECTARIES

I

Prologue:
"A Masterpiece of Women's Wit"

Late Summer, 1634

(i)

UNDER slatting lines and canvas, the *Griffin* lumbered heavily westward through the interminable dog days of August. Below deck, in the rhythmically shifting shadows of the great cabin, the Reverend Mr. Symmes paused thoughtfully in his remarks and frowned at the woman seated before him. The trip had not been an easy one: the blazing sun relentlessly parching deck and hull, the inescapable stench of cattle dung from the hold, the maddening clatter and chatter of innumerable small children, these had been enough to try the patience of any man.[1] But now to have this bold woman calculatedly ply him with cunning questions and raise doubts and disputations about the soundness of his teachings was irrefutably more than he need bear.

Symmes had been preaching to his fellow voyagers on love for one's neighbor as a means of evidencing a good spiritual estate. In our love we will "grow in grace," he reminded them, for we must strive always to lay up a "stock of grace."[2] Propriety had kept the woman silent as he lectured but the question period after his sermon abruptly unleashed her accumulated objections. His words,

1. John Winthrop, *Winthrop's Journal*, ed. James Kendall Hosmer, 2 vols. (New York, 1908), I, 134, hereafter cited as Winthrop, *Journal*.
2. "A Report of the Trial of Mrs. Ann Hutchinson before the Church in Boston, March 1638," in Charles Francis Adams, ed., *Antinomianism in the Colony of Massachusetts Bay, 1636-1638* (Boston, 1894), 328, hereafter cited as *Antinomianism*.

1

she bluntly suggested, bore a legal savor and did not correspond with her understanding of the doctrine. Clerical tempers must be held in check; Symmes sidestepped and parried deftly. Were not the words of the Apostle John precise and clear on this point: "We know that we have passed from death into life, because we love the brethren. He that loveth not his brother abideth in death." [3] What could possibly be more explicit? But the woman was not to be so readily pacified, and she brushed aside his citations with a cryptic hint that when they finally reached Boston the reverend gentleman would doubtless learn better. His efforts to penetrate her meaning proved fruitless and were at length cut off: "I have many things to say but you cannot bear them now." [4] Mr. Symmes was not the only person who could quote the Apostle John for his purposes.

Symmes had met Mistress Anne Hutchinson only once or twice before they had embarked on the *Griffin*, but he recalled that she had then spoken slightingly of certain clergymen well esteemed by him.[5] He remembered, too, that occasion on the ship a few days past, when she had ventured, with an air of mystery, to prophesy the date of their arrival in Boston. Thoughtfully he savored the rebuke he had then administered her pagan presumption.[6] But the rebuke had been plainly inadequate; steps must be taken to prevent the propagation of these questionable opinions. Symmes had not fled his Canterbury home and parish and turned his back on the errors of Old England to abet the breeding of yet more errors abroad. True, Mrs. Hutchinson's husband was a man of industry and good estate, well esteemed in the Lincolnshire countryside from which he had come. Indeed, Mrs. Hutchinson herself was reputed to possess redeeming qualities, but nonetheless heterodoxy was not to be endured, and besides, her impudent air of superiority was most unseemly in a woman.

3. "The Examination of Mrs. Ann Hutchinson at the court of Newtown," in Thomas Hutchinson, *History of the Colony and Province of Massachusetts Bay*, ed. Lawrence Shaw Mayo, 3 vols. (Cambridge, 1936), II, 373, hereafter cited as Hutchinson, *History*; I John 3:14.

4. "Court Examination of Mrs. Hutchinson," in Hutchinson, *History*, II, 373; see also John 16:12.

5. "Court Examination of Mrs. Hutchinson," in Hutchinson, *History*, II, 373.

6. *Ibid.*, 385.

(ii)

Amid the bustle of Thursday market in mid-September, the *Griffin* was sighted clearing Castle Island, borne under topsails and jibs into the broad harbor of Boston to make anchorage. The Great and General Court of Massachusetts, having fought and conquered the evils of tobacco and immodest dress, was in brief adjournment so that the deputies might return to their homes and harvest the crops which burgeoned in the fields.[7] But Governor Thomas Dudley, that "trusty old stud," was still on hand when Master Babb of the *Griffin* rowed ashore to deliver an ominous message.[8] "Charles, by the grace of God, . . . King," it announced, had commissioned his "right trusty and well beloved counsellour, William," Archbishop Laud, to regulate all plantations, with authority to call in patents, make laws, inflict punishments, and—dread note—remove governors.[9] This commission, an accompanying missive warned, was aimed particularly at Massachusetts, and even at that moment troops and ships were readying to bring the colonists under control.[10] How deep a flush must have risen on the grim, granitic features of Thomas Dudley as he steeled himself for the congenial task of organizing effective resistance: at last an enterprise adequate to the scope of his combative instinct. Those magistrates within call, Winthrop, Haynes, and Coddington, must be summoned together at once to provide counsel and formulate a plan of action that would be acceptable to the deputies when they reconvened on Wednesday next.

Meanwhile, Dudley did not allow external dangers to blind him to the threat of subversion from within. With mounting irritation, he heard the Reverend Mr. Symmes relate the substance of his encounters with Mrs. Hutchinson. The matter required careful scrutiny: unsound opinions were a noxious weed and must be rooted out at all costs. He would promptly convey these apprehensions to Mr. Wilson and Mr. Cotton, the ministers of the Boston church.[11]

On being apprised of the matter those two worthies—Cotton, only

---

7. Nathaniel B. Shurtleff, ed., *Records of the Governor and Company of the Massachusetts Bay* (Boston, 1853), I, 126-28, hereafter cited as *Colony Records.*
8. Gov. Belcher, quoted in Francis S. Drake, *The Town of Roxbury* (Boston, 1905), 242.
9. Hutchinson, *History,* I, 418-20.
10. Winthrop, *Journal,* I, 135.
11. "Court Examination of Mrs. Hutchinson," in Hutchinson, *History,* II, 370, 374.

a year in office, and Wilson now preparing to visit England—readily agreed that a close examination of the woman's opinions was called for. Cotton knew her—not well—but she had been an occasional attendant at his services in Boston in Old England. He had thought her devout and sound in her views, but still, they must not take chances.

The religious opinions of Mr. William Hutchinson were found quite inoffensive, and he was admitted to the fellowship of the church without demur.[12] His wife's application was scrutinized more narrowly, however. Mr. Symmes was requested to be on hand at the examination in order to substantiate his claims. But when Pastor Wilson queried Mrs. Hutchinson closely about the need of works as an evidence of salvation, she seemed to withdraw from her earlier position. What she had meant, she protested, was that the presence of grace must be plainly first in point of order.

Much impressed by her aptitude for doctrinal exposition, both ministers contented themselves that whatever discrepancy existed between her views and theirs was so slight as to be easily compassed and so they agreed to propose her to the church.[13] On Sunday, November 1, 1634, the day after Wilson had sailed for England, Mrs. Hutchinson stood before the Boston congregation and received the right hand of fellowship.[14]

(iii)

When Anne Hutchinson resumed her seat, a fully accredited member of the Boston church, Cotton doubtless dismissed the matter from his mind and turned back to the order of service. And Pastor Wilson, on shipboard, watching the rockbound coast of New England slip below the distant horizon, probably gave little thought to an episode that was now happily resolved. It would have been well for both had they reflected more precisely on the peculiar qualities of the newcomer; here was no ordinary woman. Could they have but momentarily disengaged themselves from their complacent assumption of masculine superiority, confirmed though it may have been by cultural and scriptural dictates, they might have observed that this dynamic personality bore a high potential for energetic, independent action, be it for good or ill. It was a fateful

12. Entry of Oct. 26, 1634, First Church of Boston, Records and Baptisms, 1630-1687, MS. copy in Massachusetts Historical Society.
13. "Court Examination of Mrs. Hutchinson," in Hutchinson, *History*, II, 374.
14. Entry of Nov. 2, 1634, First Church of Boston, Records and Baptisms, 1630-1687, Mass. Hist. Soc.

miscalculation on their part to assume that she would long remain the passive agent of masculine wills.

John Winthrop, Nestor of the Massachusetts Saints, sober Puritan though he was, had a keen and appreciative eye for a pretty face, even in those women he disliked. When he had dealings with a pretty woman, he took good care to note her comeliness in the pages of his journal, along with the more fundamental and mundane aspects of the case at hand. Although he found much else to remark in Mrs. Hutchinson, neither he nor his contemporaries thought her sufficiently beautiful to be worthy of comment. Indeed, when referring to Mrs. Hutchinson his descriptive powers were curiously limited to the angry reiteration of a single adjective. He seems to have reserved the word "fierce" mainly to describe the climate of New England and the temper of Anne Hutchinson. Although he fastened on her shortcomings and ignored her conspicuous virtues, so strenuously did he accentuate the fierceness of her temper, her manner, her carriage, her speech, and her countenance that there must have been substantial reason for concentrating on this particular attribute. Winthrop cites at least one public display of violent temper on her part, and others are deducible from the context of her history.[15] But from these same affective roots sprang also the superb courage with which she defended her views against overwhelming opposition and defied authority when it became blatantly unjust.

These qualities did not escape John Winthrop's attention; indeed they were soon brought forcibly to bear upon his security and peace of mind. "A woman of ready wit and bold spirit," he called her.[16] Winthrop's begrudging respect for that "ready wit" became, in due course, widely shared by his colleagues, who had like occasion to suffer its barbed thrusts. A woman of naturally good intelligence, raised in an English parsonage, she had been trained from childhood in Biblical exegesis, and in time developed a casuistical skill which enabled her to hold her own with the best theologians of her day. True, her emotional bent rendered her overly susceptible to some theological notions and shut her mind too firmly against others, so that she was, perhaps, unwarily drawn into a naive oversimplification of certain subtle and complex points of doctrine. But, within its limits, her mind was sharp and perceptive,

15. [John Winthrop], "A Short Story of the Rise, reign, and ruin of the Antinomians, Familists, Libertines, that affected the churches of New England..." [1644], *Antinomianism*, 157, 179.

16. Winthrop, *Journal*, I, 195.

and she was able to expound her ideas with great force and persuasiveness. John Cotton, even when he was at last impelled to condemn her bitterly on other counts, continued to speak admiringly of her "sharpe apprehension . . . ready utterance and abilitie to exprese [herself]." [17]

Mrs. Hutchinson's reliance on private meditations and her disinclination to accept the guidance of qualified religious teachers became a source of deep concern to John Cotton. Being well content with the rectitude of her own opinions, she clung to them with stubborn independence, regardless of the conflicting views of the clergy. "I have often feared the highth of your Spirit," Cotton later told her, "and being puft up with your owne parts." [18] Her intellectual independence and rigidity progressively gave rise to a critical and dogmatic temper, wherein she became too "sharply censorious of other mens spirituall estates." [19] Indeed the direction of her thought in her last years raises serious doubts about those claims which would make her a champion of religious liberty. With the passage of time she became increasingly intolerant of views which differed from her own.

But she had her warmer side as well. This could be amply testified by the many women she had tenderly nursed through sickness and attended at "Childbirth-Travells." And those of both sexes whose spiritual estates were uncertain eagerly welcomed her solicitude "and blessed God for her fruitfull discourses." [20] Gifted with a magnetism which is imparted to few, she had, until the hour of her fall, warm adherents far outnumbering her enemies, and it was only by dint of skillful maneuvering that the authorities were able to loosen her hold on the community. She was a woman who, through some impulse now obscure, sought an emotional outlet which seemed to resolve itself most effectively in the acquisition of power and influence over the lives and spiritual destinies of her fellows. Had she been born into a later age, Mrs. Hutchinson might have crusaded for women's rights or even wielded a hatchet for temperance's sake. But, for better or worse, her lot was cast in the seventeenth century, and her hand was to be felt in a theological tempest which shook the infant colony of Massachusetts to its very foundations.

17. "Church Trial of Mrs. Hutchinson," *Antinomianism*, 313.
18. *Ibid.*, 315.
19. John Cotton. *Way of the Congregational Churches Cleared* (London, 1648), 52.
20. *Ibid.*, 51.

II

Father and Husband

1578–1620

(i)

NORTH of English Boston, where the Lincolnswold dips down to meet the fens, the market town of Alford sits on a rolling foothill height. From Alford's edge one might look out mile on endless mile over flat and verdant fenny land, checkered with dikes and ditches, as far as the North Sea. Ringed about with smaller parishes and manors, Alford was their pocket metropolis, supplying a center of exchange and sociability.[1]

It was to Alford that the Reverend Mr. Francis Marbury had come to preach when he was released from Marshalsea Prison.[2] Young Marbury was a minister of the Gospel who bore his responsibilities with uncommon seriousness and integrity. The flux and growth of the Church of England in those days offered many irregularities to dismay the conscientious clergyman. Marbury's peculiar irritant was the ordination and appointment of clerics unread in Scripture and unfit to minister the cure of souls. A rash youth, armed with a caustic wit, he had hammered ceaselessly at this abuse. When at last his superiors could neither abate nor ignore his zealous protests, he was haled before the episcopal court of Bishop Aylmer. But even there he boldly pressed his cause and cast defiance in the grim faces of assembled divines.

"I come not to accuse but to defend," he declared, "but because

1. Reginald Dudding, *History of the Parish and Manors of Alford with Rigsby* (Horncastle, 1930), chap. 1, hereafter cited as Dudding, *History of Alford*.
2. Frederick Gay, "Rev. Francis Marbury," *Mass. Hist. Soc., Proceedings*, 48 (1915), 281.

you urge me for advantage, I say the Bishops of London and Peter-
borow and all the Bishops in England are guiltie of the death of
as manie soules as have perished by the ignoraunce of the Ministers
of their making whom they knew to be unable."

"Thou takest uppon thee to bee a Preacher," Aylmer stormed,
"but there is nothing in thee; thou art a verie Asse, an idiot, and a
foole—Thou art couragious, nay thou art impudent! By my troth I
thinke he be mad, he careth for no bodie."

"Sir, I take exception against swearing Judges," Marbury coolly
retorted. "I prayse God I am not mad, but sory to see you so out
of temper."

The Bishop blustered, Marbury stood fast, and so he was packed
off to Marshalsea, there to ruminate the hazards of contumacy.[3]

Now restored to a living and settled in Alford, Marbury wed
Bridget Dryden, daughter of John Dryden, Esq., of Canons Ashby
in Northamptonshire. In 1591, Anne, the second of their thirteen
children, eldest among their daughters, was born.[4] Shortly before
Anne's birth, Francis Marbury, still clamoring for an "able clergy,"
was again silenced by his superiors, removed from his post, and for
fifteen years thereafter remained at Alford without a ministerial
living.

(ii)

There are certain aspects of the family background and childhood of Anne Marbury Hutchinson that helpfully illuminate the
behavior of the mature woman. Conversely there are observable
qualities in the career of the mature Anne Hutchinson that help to
delineate the configuration of childhood influences which molded
the adult. Under any circumstances the stamp of a father's personality would have been deeply felt, and Francis Marbury was a
father of such a cast as to render his impress determinate. Marbury's demands on the world were as exacting as the demands he
imposed on himself. In a man of his vigor and assertiveness paren-
tal domination was natural. Being as well a man of high ideals and
precise scruples, he would have imposed exacting standards of behavior for his children. If he could scale these heights, why not
they?

3. Marbury's interrogation by the Bishop of London in "A parte of a register,
contayninge sundrie memorable matters, written by divers godly and learned in
our times—," *ibid.*, 281, 283 ff.

4. J. D. Champlin, "The Ancestry of Anne Hutchinson," *New York Genealogical
and Biographical Record*, 45 (1914), 23.

Anne was an imaginative and impressionable girl. In her father she found the magnetic center of her universe, and her love and fear of that ardent man became deeply ingrained in her being. Anne's longing for affection was unceasing, her admiration for her father knew no bounds. She was driven remorselessly by a hunger for his approval and by the fear that she could never satisfy his expectations. Consciously or unconsciously she modeled her attitudes and behavior on his. Little by little Marbury's salient traits —his obduracy and independent carriage, his contentiousness and high sense of principle—became part and parcel of Anne's own individuality. During these Alford years Anne imbibed from her rebellious parent, chafing in his enforced idleness, a lively sense of hostility toward established authority.

But the process of growth was not all passive assimilation. Though Anne yearned for the approval and guidance of a dominant personality, nonetheless her own vigorous will was emerging to contest the want and to assert itself. She struggled confusedly against her dependence, restlessly sought outlets for the affirmation of her own identity. Throughout her life this inner conflict was to persist, leaving omnipresent signs that despite her exterior vitality, Mistress Anne was the hapless victim of an obsessive personal insecurity. Her malaise proclaimed itself in little ways and large and in seemingly unrelated forms which were at last to conjoin and bring her notoriety and nemesis.

While living in Alford the Marbury children received religious training which accorded fully with their father's rigorous scruples. This was a God-centered household, whose members, dedicated to lives of piety, were habitually inclined to solve their problems by studious reference to the familiar and well-loved verses of the Bible. Indeed the whole cultural environment in which Anne Marbury matured was predominantly religious in its tenor. "Theology rules there," Grotius wrote of England in 1605.[5] That was the year the Marbury family left their Alford home to take up residence in London.

In 1605, Bishop Bancroft, urged on by the petulant orthodoxy of King James, swept some three hundred Puritan divines from their Anglican pulpits. In the desperate search for replacements, it was recalled that Francis Marbury, for all his stubborn dissidence, was at least clear of the Puritan taint, and he was appointed

5. Hugo Grotius, quoted in Winifred King Rugg, *Unafraid, A Life of Anne Hutchinson* (Boston, 1930), 21.

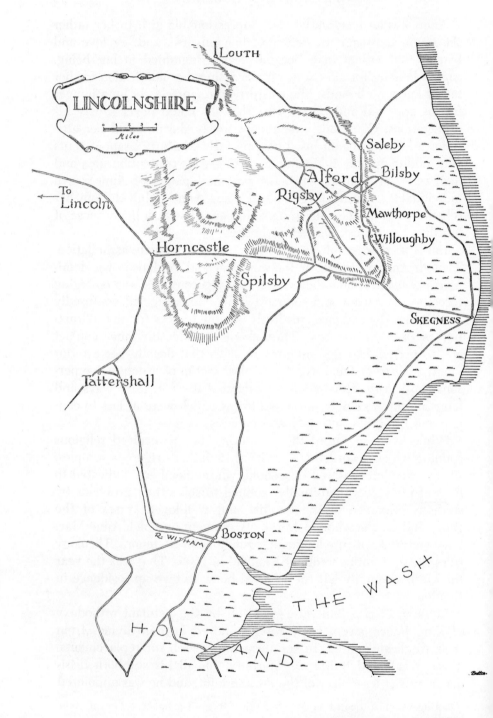

LOUTH

LINCOLNSHIRE

0 1 2 3 4
Miles

Saleby

Alford

Bilsby

Rigsby

To
Lincoln

Mawthorpe

Willoughby

Horncastle

Spilsby

SKEGNESS

Tattershall

R. WITHAM

Boston

THE WASH

HOLLAND

Batts.

to a church in London.[6] So off to the great metropolis the whole Marbury clan was transported, there to remain for the next six years. This time Francis Marbury managed to keep his doubts and cavils to himself, or possibly his ecclesiastical superiors saw fit to suffer them in silence. Whatever the case, Marbury held this new pulpit until his death in 1611.[7]

Although far from their familiar abode, neither the span of six years nor the distance of 120 miles had severed the Marbury ties with Lincolnshire. A year after Anne's father died, an old friend from Alford came down to London to claim her hand in marriage. Now twenty-one, Anne became the wife of William Hutchinson, and the eager couple journeyed back to Alford to set up a home of their own.

(iii)

Although Anne Marbury's parents had both descended from the lesser gentry, the Hutchinson family were tradespeople. For a brief period William's grandfather had attained the dignity of the mayoralty of Lincoln. When he died he left each of his sons a modest competence enabling them to establish themselves in trade. Edward Hutchinson, William's father, had set up shop as a mercer in Alford only a short time after Francis Marbury had assumed the vicarage of that town. Like his neighbor he proceeded to beget a conventionally large family, most of whose destinies were to become closely intertwined with that of their remarkable sister-in-law.[8]

The man Anne Hutchinson married offers a provocative study in contrasts and contradictions. William Hutchinson was a businessman of ample substance and ability, well able to provide for the material needs and comforts of his headstrong bride. The marriage gave every appearance of being a happy one. Each seemed thoroughly devoted to the other, and for his part Will Hutchinson adored the very ground that Anne trod. Without question or demur, he acquiesced in her every wish, regardless of the inconvenience or expense it cost, and at times the cost was enormous. One might well

6. John R. Green, *History of the English People* (New York, 1903), III, 62. In the spring of 1605 three hundred Puritan clergymen were removed from their livings for refusal to subscribe to the Canons of 1604 which required adherence to the prescribed rites and ceremonies of the Anglican church.

7. Champlin, "Ancestry of Anne Hutchinson," *N.Y. Geneal. and Biog. Record*, 45 (1914), 24.

8. Champlin, "Hutchinson Ancestry and Descendants of William and Anne Hutchinson," *ibid.*, 166.

believe that he provided his wife with all the affection, economic
security, and social prestige that any woman could ask. But despite
his attainments William Hutchinson appears to have been lacking
in those dynamic and positive qualities which Anne had found so
markedly present in her father. He was, as John Winthrop caustically observed, "a man of very mild temper and weak parts and
wholly guided by his wife." [9] This description could be dismissed
as the biased judgment of an unfriendly witness were it not amply
confirmed by similar comments from other contemporaries and by
Hutchinson's own admission that "he was more nearly tied to his
wife than to the Church." [10] Or to the whole community, he might
well have added. Passive and imperturbable by nature, lacking in
spirit and shrinking from disputation, he quietly followed where
Anne led him and accepted as his own the beliefs that she thrust
upon him. When she asked him to leave England for America he
did so; when she asked him to lay down his office on the principle
that visible ordinances were repugnant to the Word of God, he did
that too.[11] "The . . . [Hutchinson] family hath not been much inclined to subtilities," wrote Anne's brother-in-law John Wheelwright, "scarce any . . . have been sectaries." [12] During his married
life William Hutchinson cherished only one belief with any degree
of fervor; he was firmly convinced that his beloved wife was "a
dear saint and servant of God," and he dedicated himself unstintingly to the unenviable task of securing her happiness.[13]

The striking contrast between the personalities of Anne Hutchinson's father and her husband raises perplexing problems of personal
motivation and response. Could Anne have been attracted to William, the milder man, as a reprieve from the dominating qualities
of her father? Francis Marbury's mettlesome attributes, however
admirable Anne may have found them, could have left but narrow
scope for the expression of her own dynamic personality. The
household that had contained Francis and Anne Marbury must
have had the explosive potential of a powder magazine. With William it was different; he was devoted to Anne and swayed like a

9. Winthrop, *Journal*, I, 133.

10. *Ibid.*, 331.

11. *Ibid.*, II, 39.

12. John Wheelwright, *His Writings Including His Fast-day Sermon, 1637, and
His Mercurius Americanus, 1645,* ed. Charles H. Bell (Boston, 1876), 192, hereafter cited as Wheelwright, *Writings.*

13. Testimony of John Oliver before the church of Boston, in "Robert Keayne of
Boston, in New England, his Book, 1639," *Antinomianism,* 397.

reed before the pressure of her firm will. Indeed, in time, Anne may have felt that he swayed too easily. A little resistance would have given more zest to her yearnings. In place of the old tensions this new arrangement provided different and subtler complexities. In effect it left her sailing full before the wind without a rudder. The removal of her father's firm, directing hand, without adequate replacement, could well have drawn Anne into a progressively disturbing condition of emotional disorientation. Although she could not have understood or explained it, nonetheless Anne felt the lack and began obsessively to reach out in other directions for affective support and guidance.

But on the surface all seemed well. For twenty-two years William and Anne Hutchinson continued to live in Alford, establishing many close friendships and gaining the love and respect of their neighbors.[14] Like their parents before them they raised a large and lively family. Beginning with Edward, who was born in 1613, Anne gave birth to fifteen children, spaced at approximately seventeen-month intervals.[15] Anne's personal health and her techniques of infant care must have been excellent, for unlike most large families of that day, all of the Hutchinson children survived the prevalent dangers of parturition and infant disease. One child, William, born in 1623, died sometime before 1631, and, as was the custom, the same name was bestowed on another infant.

Throughout these Alford years the Hutchinson household appears to have been active and harmonious. As the family grew in size, a strong sense of solidarity developed which was to stand them in good stead at a later day. William's business prospered, swelling his income and giving him a status of some consequence in the community. As for Anne, despite the number of her dependents and the hardship of recurrent confinements, the vigorous young matron became more strenuously gregarious and restlessly sought new outlets for her boundless energy. Her compassionate and tender spirit inclined her to nursing the sick and in time she acquired great skill in the preparation of medicinal herbs and other domestic remedies so useful in an age that knew few trained physicians. Perhaps her aptitude explains the unusual hardiness and longevity of the Hutchinson brood. Certainly it rewarded her with the affec-

14. Cotton, *Way of the Congregational Churches Cleared*, 52.
15. Champlin, "Hutchinson Ancestry and Descendants," *N.Y. Geneal. and Biog. Record*, 45 (1914), 167-68.

tion and approval which her self-esteem so insatiably required. But there were other ways, less tangible and even more gratifying, by which Anne Hutchinson might affirm and dilate her own identity.

(iv)

A mature personal religion, like the web on a loom, is woven of a nubbly warp of external influence and a tensile woof of temperamental needs and responses, both so tightly interlaced as to be indistinguishable to all but the closest observer. During her rich and active life Mrs. Hutchinson felt the sway of a multiplicity of emotional and intellectual experiences which she weighed, qualified, and absorbed or cast off according to the growth and alteration of her personal needs.

The initial intellectual influence was that of her father, who was scrupulously insistent on a ministry sufficiently well educated to teach effectively the Anglican doctrine. At home and in church Anne first imbibed the fundamentals of Christian doctrine according to his understanding of them, and that understanding bore no taint of Puritanical deviation. On two occasions he had vehemently rejected aspersions of Puritanism and, indeed, had received his final appointment in part because he was reputedly free of the stigma of that sect.[16] On Anne's mother's side, the Drydens were known to be ardent Puritans and during her childhood she may have been exposed to Calvinist ideas through them.[17] But, inasmuch as her father was a vigorous and dominating personality as well as the qualified religious teacher of the family, any such influence must surely have been slight prior to the time of his death.

The Hutchinson connection did not weigh much in this respect. Several of Anne's brothers and sisters-in-law are known to have become Puritans, but they were unversed in theological subtleties and disinclined to engage in sectarian controversy.[18] Nor do the vicars of Alford seem to have exerted any decisive influence toward producing her mature views. Mrs. Hutchinson's only recorded reference to the Alford ministry was to indicate that in 1633 she was much troubled by the orthodox stand of the incumbent.[19]

16. Gay, "Rev. Francis Marbury," Mass. Hist. Soc., *Proceedings*, 48 (1915), 281; Rugg, *Unafraid*, 5.
17. Champlin, "Ancestry of Anne Hutchinson," *N.Y. Geneal. and Biog. Record*, 45 (1914), 24.
18. Wheelwright, *Writings*, 192.
19. Hutchinson, *History*, II, 384.

But there were near at hand richer sources of spiritual suste-
nance from which Anne Hutchinson could draw refreshment.
Twenty-four miles to the south, nearly a day's ride from Alford,
the renowned John Cotton held forth at St. Botolph's Church in
Boston. From him Mrs. Hutchinson drew the main lines of her doctrine, introducing by inference those embellishments which were
later to prove so embarrassing to Cotton and troublesome to the
Puritan authorities of Massachusetts.

It is not known when Mrs. Hutchinson first heard Cotton preach,
nor how long a period passed before she fully accepted his views.
Both had become settled in Lincolnshire at approximately the same
time. Within a very few years of his installation, Cotton's fame had
spread throughout the eastern counties and was surely known in
Alford. William Hutchinson, being a clothier, was doubtless drawn
early and often to the great sheep fairs and other markets of Boston, and occasionally Anne must have kept him company on the
long journey. The trip was tedious and tiring and could not have
been often undertaken by a woman whose field of activity was re-
stricted by domestic obligations and recurrent pregnancies. Nonetheless, the opportunity was present and even during the early
years of her married life reports may have piqued her curiosity to
hear the remarkable young vicar of St. Botolph's.

THE HUTCHINSON FAMILY

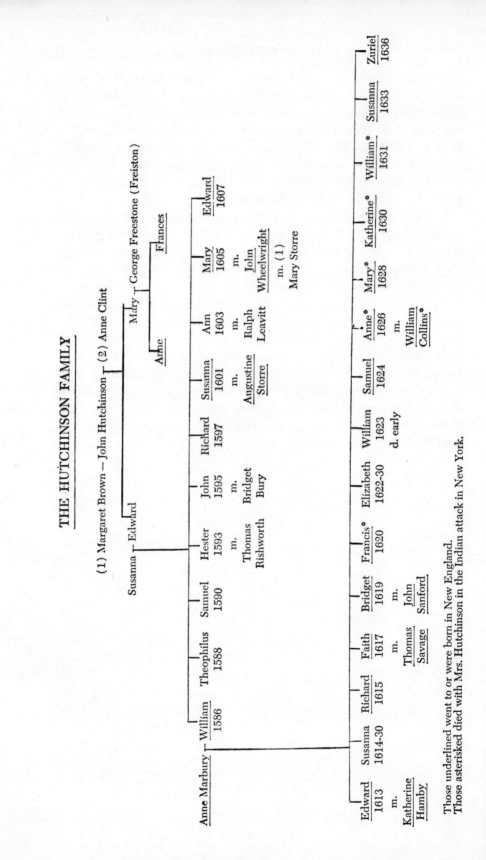

(1) Margaret Brown — John Hutchinson — (2) Anne Clint

Mary — George Freestone (Freiston)

Susanna — Edward

Anne   Frances

William 1586 | Theophilus 1588 | Samuel 1590 | Hester 1593 m. Thomas Rishworth | John 1595 m. Bridget Bury | Richard 1597 | Susanna 1601 m. Augustine Storre | Ann 1603 m. Ralph Leavitt | Mary 1605 m. John Wheelwright m. (1) Mary Storre | Edward 1607

Anne Marbury — William 1586

Edward 1613 m. Katherine Hamby | Susanna 1614-30 | Richard 1615 | Faith 1617 m. Thomas Savage | Bridget 1619 m. John Sanford | Francis* 1620 | Elizabeth 1622-30 | William 1623 d. early | Samuel 1624 | Anne* 1626 m. William Collins* | Mary* 1628 | Katherine* 1630 | William* 1631 | Susanna 1633 | Zuriel 1636

Those underlined went to or were born in New England.
Those asterisked died with Mrs. Hutchinson in the Indian attack in New York.

THE MARBURY FAMILY

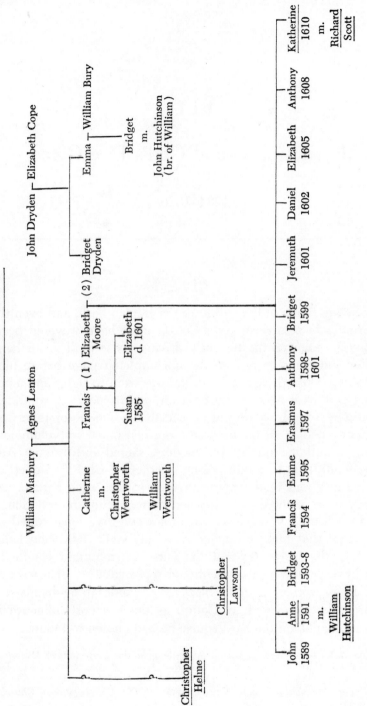

Those underlined went to New England.

III

Master Cotton and God's Free Grace

1584-1630

(i)

THERE are limits to the endurance of human flesh, and even the formidable resolve of John Cotton must have wavered occasionally and allowed the furiously driving goose quill in his hand to falter and come to rest on the uncompleted page before him. "Of making books there is no end," he was wont to sigh, "and much reading is a weariness to the flesh and spirit too." [1] A weariness indeed! Only death would put an end to the making of John Cotton's many books; all his life had been consumed by voluminous reading of authors, ancient and modern, sacred and profane. And to what end? That he might preach "a crucified Christ"—a doctrine of God's love and tender mercy, and so soften "such hard consequences as are wonted to be derived from absolute reprobation." [2]

As he reflected in such vein, Cotton's eye may have rested on the portrait that hung prominently on the wall of his bookladen study. [3] In the feeble light of the guttering midnight candle he could have perceived a conventional representation of a solemn-faced English clergyman in black gown and falling bands—Dr. Richard Sibbes—revered by Cotton as the foremost influence in directing him along the hard course he had chosen to follow.

1. Cotton Mather, *Magnalia Christi Americana, or the Ecclesiastical History of New England* (Hartford, 1820), I, 253, hereafter cited as Mather, *Magnalia;* Ecclesiastes 12:12.
2. Mather, *Magnalia,* I, 239; Cotton, *Way of the Congregational Churches Cleared,* 34.
3. Mather, *Magnalia,* I, 234.

While a student at Cambridge, Cotton had attended divine service with but perfunctory regularity and indifference. Not for him the homilies that might distract from scholarly endeavor. Then one day he attended a sermon preached by Dr. Sibbes, "wherein was discoursed the misery of those who had only a negative righteousness, or a civil, sober, honest blamelessness before men." Stricken by the implications of this doctrine, Cotton weighed the issue thoughtfully over many months and gradually came to discern the insufficiency of mortal man and the measure of his dependence upon God. With these "disconsolate apprehensions" Cotton became a "thoroughly renewed Christian," and henceforth directed his energies solely toward religious ends.[4]

A native of Derby, born in 1584, John Cotton was the son of Roland Cotton, a lawyer and strenuously devout Christian of that midland town. Indeed, so ardent was the elder Cotton in the exercise of his scruples that he often promoted the reconciliation of litigants, preferring the role of Christian peacemaker to any fees securable from litigation. These scruples must have imposed economic difficulties in furthering the formal education of his precocious son. Nonetheless, young John, at the age of thirteen, was admitted to Trinity College, Cambridge. Baccalaureate attained, on the strength of his considerable talents as a scholar of Hebrew he was received as a fellow at Emmanuel, an institution already notorious for the Puritanical leanings of its scholars. In his six years at Emmanuel, Cotton advanced quite rapidly through the positions of catechist, head lecturer, and dean. It was during this period that, influenced by Dr. Sibbes, he experienced his religious awakening and was diverted from secular scholarship to the priesthood. He was ordained in 1610, and two years later, at the age of twenty-seven, he became vicar of St. Botolph's Church at Boston, Lincolnshire.[5]

A gentle and mild-tempered man, not the least of Cotton's attributes was a Christian humility and spirituality that appears to have been denied many of his more vigorous brethren of the cloth: "the hardest of flints would have been broken on such a soft bag of Cotton." Indeed there were those who felt that he was excessive in his self-denial and humility. A portrait of Cotton leaves the impression of an introspective, almost timid man, illuminating the

4. *Ibid.*
5. For the facts of Cotton's life see John Norton, *Memoir of John Cotton* (Boston, 1834); Mather, *Magnalia,* I, 232-61; J. T. Adams in *DAB,* s.v. "Cotton, John."

complexity of mind and indecisiveness that almost incapacitated him at a critical point of his career. He was rather short and stout in figure. Long blond hair wreathed his sensitive, fair-complected face and ruddy cheeks; pensive blue eyes gazed nervously from under a broad, clear brow; blond mustache and tuft of beard strove to impart some element of virility to delicate, sensuous lips.[6]

A scholar and a man of God, Cotton shrank from human contacts, preferring the less abrasive companionship of his books and manuscripts. He seldom went abroad, choosing rather to spend "a scholar's day" of twelve hours in his study. But John Cotton was not to be stamped an ineffectual recluse. For all his solitary isolation, he was amiable in those personal relations he chose to maintain, and the size and ardor of his following suggest that he possessed an extraordinary kind of personal magnetism and persuasiveness. Like Anteus on his Mother Earth, Cotton in the pulpit, discoursing on God's word, found fresh strength and renewed assurance. His quiet, grave voice, clear and audible in the farthermost corners of the church, "had in it a very awful majesty," and his delivery was emphasized by "a natural and becoming motion of the right hand." [7] Hearers were much impressed by the prodigious memory which enabled him to repeat extended passages of Scripture without reference to the text.[8] He preached a Gospel of God's love and mercy, offering hope for those who would have faith and humble themselves before God rather than relying upon their own puny efforts. In his sermons he strove "to be understood by the meanest capacity." [9]

Perhaps it was here that his undoing commenced. The Puritan doctrine was complex and difficult, but Cotton compounded its complexities by probing recesses his colleagues had been well content to ignore. It was one thing to elucidate doctrinal subtleties in terms that trained theologians might follow and accept. But to expound them in language comprehensible to "the meanest capacity" was to beget ambiguities and open perilous vistas to even the most blameless of hearers. Mrs. Hutchinson's capacities were far from "mean," but to her understanding Cotton's sermons unfolded pre-

6. Mather, Magnalia, I, 252, 254. The portrait in the Connecticut Historical Society is reproduced in Samuel Eliot Morison, Builders of the Bay Colony (Boston, 1930).

7. Mather, Magnalia, I, 250, 251.

8. Edward Johnson, Wonder Working Providence of Sions Saviour in New England, 1628-1651, ed. J. Franklin Jameson (New York, 1910), 89, hereafter cited as Johnson, Wonder Working Providence.

9. Mather, Magnalia, I, 250.

cisely the mystical arcana her soul desired, and in terms that seemed comfortably consonant with Puritan orthodoxy. The key to those perplexities which so perturbed John Cotton and Anne Hutchinson lay deep in the murky recesses of the Puritan faith.

(ii)

Ever since the day of its founding, the Church of England had been troubled by reformers of one stripe or another. Changing times had pacified some only to breed others, and in desperation some of the most extreme had broken with the church and pressed "a reformation without tarying for anie." [10] But for the Puritans within the Church of England separation seemed only to beg the question: theirs not to flee the world but to make it over in the image God had ordained. So they stayed with the church and labored to purify it from within—to scatter its hierarchy and purge it of popish rites and remnants. It was given to the generation of John Cotton to plumb below the externals over which controversy had raged and to define essential Puritan doctrine, so that neither substance nor surface should be matters of doubt.

The task of the Puritan theologian was no light one. Perils were constantly latent in the metaphysical implications of his doctrine, and he must warily thread a tortuous path if he would guide his flock to safety and salvation. Two questions in particular plagued him, for on these the whole structure of his theology rested: What are the avenues of grace and what are the means of assurance? That is to say, how is man saved, and how does he *know* he is saved?

In defining the respective roles played by God and man in the great drama of salvation, the Puritan saw a radical disjunction which required all his logical skills to bridge. If man were conceded sufficient freedom to initiate or advance the process of salvation —if the creature were permitted to share the powers of the Creator—then grace was disparaged and divine omnipotence diminished. On the other hand, if God did all there loomed a fatalistic supernaturalism which palsied the self-determining power of the individual and destroyed all grounds for moral responsibility. The creature acted only as the Creator acted upon him and was in nowise accountable for his own performance.

The second question related to the nature of man's understand-

10. Robert Browne, *A Treatise of Reformation Without Tarying for Anie* (Middelburg, Holland, 1582).

ing: what does he know, and how does he know, and particularly what and how can he know of the supernatural? If knowledge could be said to derive exclusively from sensory experience, then man must be merely the reactive agent of an arbitrary and incomprehensible universe, capable only of mechanically reproducing the flow of phenomena outside his mind, and acting as those phenomena dictated. Conversely, if knowledge proved to be innate and intuitively comprehensible, if God dropped ideas into the mind independently of sensory experience, then education and the exercise of reason became meaningless, God's scriptural pronouncement superfluous, and the church unnecessary.

The root of the trouble lay with Calvin, from whom the Puritan fathers had drawn the essentials of their creed. The great Genevan had depicted an omnipotent deity in whose hands men were nerveless clay, totally incapable of performing any works pleasing to His eyes.[11] In the beginning God had arbitrarily predetermined the election of His creatures to eternal bliss or their assignment to endless perdition. Grace and doom alike were ineluctable and irresistible. Man was granted neither choice nor power of action in the matter of his ultimate disposition. Every possible avenue was closed against his participation. Even faith, the essential condition of salvation, was to be provided by God at the opportune hour. Although man's works were of no value in the sight of God, nonetheless he was invoked to strive mightily to attain that good of which he was destitute—but warned that without God's grace his strivings would be of no avail. To assume that they might be fruitful without divine intervention would be to limit the will of God and to throw contempt upon His majesty and omnipotence.

But this very omnipotence of God upon which Calvin had based his creed was the fixed rock over which his disciples so frequently stumbled. As long as God was omnipotent and acted in a manner which utterly disregarded logic and human needs, it was impossible to establish reasonable grounds for moral responsibility or individual assurance of election. If the infinite will of God controlled all things, how could they be sure that they were responsible for their own actions, and why should they not disclaim responsibility when they saw fit? If the infinite wisdom of God concealed from

11. William W. Fenn, "The Marrow of Calvin's Theology," *Harvard Theological Review*, 2 (July, 1909), 323-39; Georgia Harkness, *John Calvin, the Man and His Ethics* (New York, 1931); James Mackinnon, *Calvin and the Reformation* (London, 1936); Arthur C. McGiffert, *Protestant Thought Before Kant* (New York, 1915), chap. 5.

men the knowledge of their election and deprived them of the capacity to prove their fitness, how could they gain assurance?

Human frailty demanded assurance of some kind, and despite the remonstrances of Calvin, time was to prove that men would turn to the most convenient guarantee that grace was at hand. For some the soul was best informed of its regeneration by intuitional means, by the manifest presence of a "light within." The more hardheaded claimed that practical observance of the moral law provided more concrete evidence of salvation. A vast philosophic abyss lay between the two paths of assurance, but both expressed a universal need for certitude and security on the ultimate problem of man's existence.

(iii)

Over the years Puritan clerics tinkered assiduously with the problems Calvin had bequeathed them. In time they came to cite him with diminishing frequency, as gradually they evolved a theology which bore only token resemblance to that originally propounded in Geneva. But still Calvin remained the unseen referent of their thought, for they continued to be bound to the logic—but sought to evade the logical consequences of the predestination decree.

According to the Puritan version—the covenant or federal theology—God had made an agreement with Adam promising salvation and eternal life to him and his posterity if he faithfully observed the stipulation of divine law. This was the Covenant of Works. To facilitate obedience the law was inscribed on Adam's heart and breathed into his entire being. But Adam broke the law and fell from Paradise, and his faculties were then so crippled that fulfillment of the Covenant terms was no longer possible. Pitying man's sinful and helpless condition, God at last offered to Abraham new and milder terms, asking only a simple faith in the coming of Christ as his Redeemer. In return for this act of faith God imbued Abraham with His grace, the Divine Spirit which regenerates and strengthens the believer. Thus was Abraham enabled to fulfill the Covenant of Works. Thenceforth God undertook Himself to provide this simple and essential act of faith in Christ the Redeemer, for those whom He elected. This was the Covenant of Grace.

In expounding the Covenant terms the Puritan theologians attempted to make ethics logically deducible from grace, thereby incorporating moral responsibility into the Covenant. Although Adam had fallen, they pointed out, his faculties had not suffered irreparable deterioration. Faint "remains" of the divine image in man continued to glow weakly, unable to take positive action for good, but quite sufficient to differentiate good and evil and to allow man to make a choice between them.[12] With this advantage, the individual to whom grace was offered would be solely responsible for rejecting it and would thus have brought his own damnation on himself.

The Puritan depicted a God who was willing to accept man as a business equal in a contractual agreement. Assuming the initiative Himself, God freely offered His grace to all within hearing of the Gospel ministerially tendered. "Everyone that heareth the tender of the Gospel is bound to believe," John Norton preached. "All that hear it are equally capable of believing ... [and] whosoever believeth shall be saved."[13] Inasmuch as God stood ready to provide the essential belief for all hearers, all that was required of them was their voluntary consent. "Though God's grace do all," Richard Sibbes had warned, "yet we must give our consent."[14] Each man bore within himself sufficient light to guide him to the acceptance of grace and to know that rejection of it was tantamount to damnation. Whoever knowingly refused the offer must accept full responsibility for the condemnation which inevitably ensued.

Having bestowed on man a degree of freedom and self-determination that would have appalled Calvin, the Puritan clergy were still bedeviled by the problem of establishing a positive system of assurance. Persisting in the conviction that men were justified by faith and not by works, they were faced with the difficult task of determining whether or not faith was genuinely present in the believer. "Faith being as the root of all other graces, is more hidden than they are"; it lies concealed within the heart of the believer and offers no objective basis for confirmation.[15] In order to establish concrete evidence of the presence of saving grace, the Puritans found it necessary to make morality an intrinsic part of grace itself. They maintained that, although believers were no longer contractually bound by the Covenant of Works, God had not discarded this earlier compact but had carefully incorporated it within the

12. For the doctrine of "remains" see Perry Miller, *The New England Mind: The Seventeenth Century* (New York, 1939), 183 ff.; Perry Miller, "The Marrow of Puritan Divinity," Colonial Society of Massachusetts, *Transactions*, 32 (1937), 247-300.

13. John Norton, *The Orthodox Evangelist* (London, 1654), 195.

14. Richard Sibbes, *The Complete Works of Richard Sibbes, D.D.*, ed. Alexander B. Grosart (Edinburgh, 1863), VI, 8, hereafter cited as Sibbes, *Works.*

15. Peter Bulkley, *The Gospel Covenant or the Covenant of Grace Opened* (London, 1646), 233.

Covenant of Grace. "The husbandly jurisdiction of the law is taken away," [16] but it continues to serve as a guide for the deportment of Saints, "a schoolmaster to bring them to Christ." [17] The unregenerate naturally manifest a strong resentment of the commands of the law; "there grows a quarell betwene the heart and the Commandment, an exacerbation between them, and an enmity." But grace gently operates to remove this impediment: "The heart is softened and reconciled to God, it closeth with the Commandment, as the soft clay doth with the mold, and is ready to receive any impression." [18]

Grace, and grace alone, can bridge the awful gulf between sin and saintliness; with the gift of grace comes the beginning of morality. The powers within the believer that have slept since the Fall are reawakened and stirred into activity; the encrustation and mold which concealed the Law within the heart are wiped away, and burnished with new brilliance, it resumes its useful office as director of the soul.

God has by no means abandoned the decree. He still picks and chooses for election as He sees fit and without consideration of individual excellence. But in the Covenant He offers His assistance only to those who will consent to accept it. All that is expected of them is that they will try the powers God has given them: the way to gain assurance of grace is to give it a trial. "It is not so much the having of grace, as grace in exercise that preserves souls," wrote Sibbes.[19] The believer can now perform those works which were hitherto impossible, and in gratitude is called to give the proof of his regeneration. The works which he performs are not an absolute or causal condition of the bond, but rather consequent and declarative; the ability to perform them is a sure indication that the bond has been properly sealed. Although the root lies hidden, works are "the fruits of faith" which, "being seen do make known the tree from which they come." Sanctification does not precede justification, the gift is not contingent on the work, but sanctification flows easily and naturally from justification; it is a part of the gift of grace. "Therefore it is a warrantable and safe way for a man by and from his sanctification to take evidence of his justification, and of his estate in grace before God." [20]

16. John Cotton, *The New Covenant* ... (London, 1654), 124.
17. Bulkley, *The Gospel Covenant*, 57.
18. John Preston, *The New Covenant, or the Saints Portion* (London, 1630), 334.
19. Sibbes, *Works*, I, 191.
20. Bulkley, *The Gospel Covenant*, 29, 183.

For those who counted these as legal arguments, Thomas Shepard could only rejoin with somewhat ponderous humor, that very probably "the spirit of grace and sanctification runs very low in them; it is so little that they can scarce see it by the help of spectacles." These people, he maintained, are so devoid of grace and incapable of duties that they must simulate a faith to carry them to Christ. They "take Christ for a dishclout to wipe them clean again." [21]

Uneasily aware that their advocacy of man's freedom to act seemed to belie God's freedom to choose, the Puritan divines nonetheless encouraged believers to bend every effort to the proof of their regeneration. Though it is not possible to do everything they should, "yet this they doe . . . , they carry a constant purpose of heart to doe it. . . . They never come to give over striving to doe it." [22] The moral was driven securely home by Thomas Hooker: "You must not think to go to heaven in a feather bed; if you will be Christ's disciples, you must take up his crosse, and it will make you sweat." [23]

(iv)

One of the most pronounced characteristics of Puritan thought was its unflagging insistence on the primacy of reason and the need of rational self-control. In this respect they were thoroughly at one with their contemporaries. "Give me that man that is not passion's slave," Shakespeare had announced, and Jacobean England chorused a loud amen.[24] Of course the passions, imagination, and will were recognized as essential to the natural functioning of the individual, but if chaos were not to result, these faculties must be controlled by reason.

Anti-rationalist tendencies were anathema to all good Puritans. The imagination was a faculty whose hazards had been expounded in numerous texts and sermons. On this subject Sibbes had been quite explicit: "Imagination, of itself, if ungoverned, is a wild and raging thing." [25] Its normal function is to combine and present images to the mind for reasoned consideration, but without proper governance "it shapes things as it pleaseth," and circumventing the

21. "Sound Believer," and "Sincere Convert," in *The Works of Thomas Shepard* (Boston, 1853), I, 260, 108.

22. John Preston, *A Sermon Preached at the General Fast Before the Commons-House of Parliament* (London, 1633), 281.

23. Quoted in Miller, "Marrow of Puritan Divinity," Col. Soc. of Mass., *Publications*, 32 (1937), 288.

24. *Hamlet*, III, ii.

25. Sibbes, "The Soul's Conflict," *Works*, I, 180.

reason, sends its wild fantasies directly to the will for enactment. This is the faculty through which Satan attempts to produce havoc among the godly. When imagination and will overpowered judgment, the uses of reason were discredited, illiteracy upheld, and education—so vital to the Puritan scheme—was made to seem mere folly. Then were the "black-coates" of the "Ninniversity" spurned in favor of "one that speakes from meere motion of the spirit, without any study at all." [26] The sobriety and self-control which Puritan divines had so painstakingly inculcated were threatened by "silly women laden with their lusts." [27]

How then, were these unruly passions brought under the leadership of reason? Once again, only grace was capable of reviving reason and enabling it to direct the soul. Regeneration was the renovation of reason which gave it the power to grasp those universal truths which lay in the concrete data of the world and to order human faculties so that they co-operated in applying these truths to the betterment of a life on earth directed finally toward the glorification of God. "All the faculties of the soul being sanctified by grace," wrote Peter Bulkley, "they doe now ayme at one end, which is the doing of God's will. . . . The mind which was darkness before is now light in the Lord to know and understand the will of God . . . the judgement made to approve the good which is known, the will to desire and endeavor after the doing of it . . . the affections ordered aright to love the things which God loveth and hate the things which God hateth." [28]

This conclusion was not left unchallenged. A clamorous and growing wing of the Reformation insisted that true knowledge of conversion was gained only through the sudden ecstasy that accompanies the mystical infusion of grace. The Puritan clergy, British to the core in their empiricism, stoutly rejected this fanciful conclusion. Though God renders His grace strictly as He wills, the age of miracles is over, they protested, and He now sees fit to govern the universe by natural causation. The Puritans contended that grace, like all elements affecting physical bodies, was introduced by specific physical agents.[29] Vision was not miraculously bestowed upon the imagination, but was gradually insinuated into the mind by the external events or "means" chosen by God for that purpose.

26. Johnson, *Wonder Working Providence*, 127.
27. Roger Clap, "Memoirs," in Alexander Young, *Chronicles of the First Planters of Massachusetts Bay* (Boston, 1846), 359.
28. Bulkley, *The Gospel Covenant*, 178, 235.
29. Miller, *New England Mind: The Seventeenth Century*, 228.

The principal "means" was the preaching of the Gospel by the clergy. This hardheaded logic, however repugnant to sincere religionists, was inescapable if the Puritans wished to avert the spiritual anarchy that attended the vagaries of illuminism, or the "inner light."

The Puritans were obliged to be constantly on their guard against the intrusion of mystical enthusiasm and claims of prophetic power. It was conceded that man was gifted with an innate capacity to grasp the truth in things, but this was not to be construed as the possession of pre-existent ideas. The gift of prophecy was miraculous, but even the Biblical prophets could not prophesy whenever they pleased from an inexhaustible fund of innate knowledge but only when God moved them. Now the prophetic age was past, and the power of prophecy "falleth not under the compasse of creature-effects according to the order of second causes." [30]

The balance between illuministic and empirical extremes was at all times a difficult one to maintain, but the Puritans remained intensely aware that the peaceful pursuit of their way of life depended upon the success with which they reconciled these mutually exclusive modes of thought. In the event of uncertainty the unquestioned arbiter was always the Bible. "All parts of God's worship are by God alone appointed, in the word revealed, and thence to be fetched." [31] It could not be denied that latter-day prophecies, revelations, and illuministic insights impinged disastrously upon the sphere of that divine instrument.

(v)

John Cotton was a Puritan of the Puritans. One of the foremost of the covenant theologians, he had labored equally with the rest to construct and refine the new orthodoxy and with them risked persecution in his efforts to propagate the faith. But even orthodoxy suffers its differences of emphasis and extrapolation. The peculiar bent of Cotton's ministry had been drawn at the outset from the teaching of Dr. Richard Sibbes.

Seeking to win the regenerate to Christ, Sibbes had preached a gospel of human frailty borne up in the fullness of God's love and mercy. "What do the Scriptures speak," he asked, "but Christ's

---

30. Norton, *Orthodox Evangelist*, 263.
31. Thomas Hooker, *A Survey of the Summe of Church Discipline* (London, 1648), 6.

love and tender care over those that are humbled." He will be lifted up who is first cast down in the sense of his own helplessness. "A holy despair in ourselves is the ground of true hope"; in our weakness and misery, Christ will not refuse us, Dr. Sibbes reassured his listeners. "There are heighths and depths and breadths of mercy in him above all the depths of our sin and misery." [32]

Sibbes realized that moral obligation must be fulfilled, but he warned strenuously against the dangers of an undue emphasis on good works. All men, he noted, are the victims of "a natural kind of popery." [33] So great is man's need for assurance that he will find false comfort in his own works and thus, little by little, lose sight of his mortal limitations. But sureties firmer than any work of man are offered to him who sees his naked insufficiency and casts himself on God's mercy. Nor need he fear divorce from Christ for backsliding and errancy. Christ will not extinguish a faith which He has enkindled nor take back the grace which He has bestowed.

These charitable conclusions proved congenial to the mild and humane temper of John Cotton. They satisfied in him an intellectual comprehension of the frailty of human nature and a profound need to bestow and to receive compassionate understanding. The tenets of Richard Sibbes provided an adequate basis whereon Cotton could establish the benign tone of his own ministry. It is also likely that Sibbes' teachings offered Cotton a clue to the more fruitful understanding of that fountainhead of Puritan theology, the *Institutes* of John Calvin. Although most Puritan theologians had modified the rigorous logic of Calvinistic predestinarianism by the use of a more empirically comprehensible system of assurances, Cotton continued to regard Calvin as the master and cited his authority with more frequency than any of his colleagues. "I have read the fathers, and the schoolmen and Calvin too," said he, "but I find that he that has Calvin has them all." [34]

(vi)

That works were a handy token of regeneration was scarcely to be denied; there was much to be said for an arrangement which at once ensured personal probity and peace of mind. But Cotton

---

32. Sibbes, "Bruised Reed and Smoking Flax," *Works*, I, 38, 48, 43, 39.
33. "The Soul's Conflict," *ibid.*, 138.
34. Mather, *Magnalia*, I, 274.

could not bring himself to share his colleagues' enthusiasm for this facile strategem. To his mind it suffered two perilous shortcomings: first, it imputed to man capacities that were not properly his, and second, it was not necessarily reliable as a sign of election.

The covenanters, Cotton feared, by concentrating their attention on the supposition of man's effort, had beclouded the fact of man's errancy. John Cotton had looked out on the world and seen man helpless to achieve harmony within himself or within the social order without the gift of God's free grace. It was all very well to spur men to the proof of their election, but too often the ripest fruit of that endeavor was pride in one's presumed capacities —pride, the deadliest of sins, the leaven of conflict.

The likelihood of this outcome was increased by the Puritan disposition to place the initiative squarely on the believer, requiring him initially to recognize his mortal imperfections. It was man's awareness of his sinful nature, the clergy advised, that induced God to offer His divine aid. Regeneration was not precipitate and unforeseeable, they held, but was gently insinuated upon the elect in a series of logically successive phases. The initial term was probationary, a period of "preparative sorrow" wherein God modified the soul's resistance, disposed it to sorrow for sin and inclined it toward spiritual effort. Then must man bestir himself toward his regeneration: "The more wee indeavor, the more assistance and helpe wee find from him." [35] This effort and inclination was calculated to provide the believer with hope that he might shortly number himself among the saved, though the difference between man's "indeavor" and God's "assistance" might well perplex the curious legatee.

Even Dr. Sibbes was a devotee of the doctrine of "preparative sorrow." "Grace is little at first," he preached. "Nothing so little as grace at first, and nothing more glorious afterward; things of greatest perfection are longest in coming to their growth." Although Sibbes had denied that works in themselves could move God to exercise His favor toward man, he did, however inconsistently, assert that a recognition of our imperfections and a sorrowing for our sins will prompt God to have mercy on us. The "bruised reed is a man that for the most part is in some misery," he explained, "and by misery is brought to see sin the cause of it." It is

---

35. *Antinomianism*, 109. See Perry Miller, *The New England Mind; From Colony to Province* (Cambridge, 1953), 56, where Miller deals thoughtfully and at length with the problem of "Preparative sorrow."

in such bruised reed that Christ kindles His spark of hope, making it smoking flax, and on that flax He will continue to blow until it blazes brightly. But the reed must be bruised before the spark can ignite it.[36]

From Cotton's point of view the doctrine of "preparative sorrow" seemed at best a covenient device to whittle the predestination decree down to a size where man might seize on its rewards. It was the essence of Cotton's thought that he visualized a vast abyss between human nature and divine grace, a void that could be bridged only by God's will, not man's. The gift of God's grace, he contended, was absolute and gratuitous, bestowed without respect to either the virtues or the apprehensions of man, and implanted by means of an intimate union with Christ "before our faith doth put forth it self to lay hold upon him." [37] The act was unilateral and unqualified on God's part. At the moment of conversion the subject was without belief and without sorrow, either for his own sins or for the suffering of Christ. Christ must first "give himself in working faith, before faith can be there ... for man is as passive in his Regeneration as in his first generation." [38] It is God's free grace which engenders faith and with it all those resultant gifts and powers that mark a Christian.

Cotton's logic indicated that the "preparative sorrow" of the covenant theologians was not only a "work," but indeed, a form of evidence before the event—"a going aside to a Covenant of Works" he called it.[39] Any such "preparation" if it were not to be construed as calculated to influence God's decisions, must be subsequent, not antecedent to election. "If wee be active in laying hold on Christ, before he hath given us his Spirit," Cotton preached, "then we apprehend him before he apprehend us: then wee should do a good act and so bring forth good fruites, before wee become good trees; yea, and bee good trees before we be in Christ." [40] God's free grace is not a commodity for barter or blackmail but is promised apart from any preparation willfully made by man.

Cotton's insistence on the absolute and unqualified dispensa-

36. Sibbes, "Bruised Reed and Smoking Flax," *Works*, I, 49, 43.
37. Cotton, *Way of the Congregational Churches Cleared*, 41.
38. John Cotton, *The Covenant of Gods Free Grace Most Sweetly Unfolded* (London, 1645), 55, hereafter cited as *Covenant of Grace*.
39. John Cotton, *Sixteene Questions of Serious and Necessary Consequence propounded unto Mr. John Cotton of Boston in New England Together with his answers to each question* (London, 1644), 10, hereafter cited as *Sixteene Questions*.
40. John Cotton, *Gospel Conversion* (London, 1646), 39.

tion of God's grace put him at some disadvantage in grappling with the puzzle of assurance. Turning his back on the ingenious empirical stratagem of his colleagues, Cotton took a stand with Calvin who had said "If it must be determined by our works how the Lord is affected toward us, I admit we cannot obtain that object even by a very slight conjecture." [41] Even the unregenerate can obey the moral law, Cotton warned his parishioners, though their obedience is no better than a "legal reformation." This was possible because Christ had seen fit to dispense His benefits to mankind in two quite different forms. To the elect they had been offered in a Covenant of Grace wherein they were impelled by the spirit of Christ to perform His will. But to the unregenerate these benefits had been dispensed in a Covenant of Works, wherein they were induced by the fear of suffering the penalties of the law to lead lives that were at least morally correct. Those who had been reformed under this latter course, Cotton warned, do not make fit subjects for the Kingdom of Heaven, nor even altogether reliable ones for the community of man "for when a man hath been humbled under the spirit of bondage by the Terrors of the Law, he may never come to feel his need of Christ nor his own insufficiencie nor unworthinesse to receive him." [42] Such persons must be expected to turn from the law whenever its sanctions are withdrawn, and in their pride and in confidence of their autonomous state they may engender social conflict and subvert that harmony which it is God's purpose to maintain.

As a clergyman Cotton despaired of correctly identifying the elect solely on the basis of their good works or "sanctification." Even to the interested and careful observer, it seemed impossible to distinguish between moral effort which flowed from grace and that which was enforced under apprehension of the law; "a matter so narrow that the Angels in Heaven have much adoe to discern who differs; a work fitter for the Angels to cut the scantling in it, than for the Ministers of the Gospel." The most upright of Saints, Cotton maintained, cannot safely advance his sanctification as proof positive of his state of grace, unless justifying faith was plainly manifest beforehand. Justification is discerned sooner than sanctification, so if justifying faith remains but dark and indis-

---

41. John Calvin, *Institutes of the Christian Religion*, trans. Henry Beveridge (Edinburgh, 1845), III, ii, 28.
42. Cotton, *Sixteene Questions*, 9.

cernible, then sanctification will also be clouded with uncertainty and may be no more than a legal performance.[43] "For whilst I cannot believe that my person is accepted in justification, I cannot believe that my works are accepted of God as any true Sanctification." [44]

Cotton, whatever his confusions, remained true to the demanding logic of his doctrine. Sibbes, by minimizing the role of works as an evidence, had shifted perceptibly away from the federal theology and toward that of Calvin. Cotton had taken the final step—"even such a Calvinist was our Cotton." [45]

(vii)

The conversion experience, as Cotton understood it, was illuministic and nonempirical. The only satisfactory assurance of election lay in a noetic awareness of union with the Holy Ghost, the "witnesse of the Spirit it selfe." [46] Although sanctification necessarily followed justifying faith, its gifts or powers could not be seen or understood unless the believer had first seen Christ by faith, "the spirit of Christ enlightening his understanding in the knowledge of him." [47] By uniting Himself to the elect, Christ implanted faith and empowered the believer to put forth this new found faith to lay hold on Him and do His will.

However mystical or evanescent this sign may have seemed to the sturdily empirical minds of his clerical brethren, Cotton suffered no doubts about the impact or validity of the conversion experience as he had defined it: "The testimony of the Spirit is so clear that it may witness immediately." [48] Only after the believer was secure in the testimony of the Spirit was he free to advance his sanctification as a secondary evidence of his state of grace. With the free promise of grace, Christ's righteousness was imputed to the elect and his spirit quickened to the performance of holy duties —duties which were plainly seen to flow from Christ rather than from the terror of the law.[49]

43. Cotton, *Covenant of Grace*, 68, 74.
44. Cotton, *Sixteene Questions*, 8.
45. Mather, *Magnalia*, I, 250.
46. Cotton, *Sixteene Questions*, 5.
47. Cotton, *Gospel Conversion*, 23.
48. Cotton, *Sixteene Questions*, 6.
49. Cotton, *New Covenant*, 34, 64.

The power of Christ to work thus intimately in the believer raised some troublesome doubts about the nature of the Saint's union with Him. Cotton was occasionally open to the charge of ambiguity in defining this relationship. "We live, yet not we, but Christ liveth in us," he had said, leaving on the minds of the unwary the impression of a union so intimate that the elect was moved entirely at the behest of the Holy Ghost, without reference to any volition or power of his own.[50] On another occasion, he took particular care to remove any such doubts: "But we are not the same person with Christ, and therefore we have life not the very self same with him, but conformable to his and fashioned after the same image."[51] Although less satisfactory as a spiritual metaphor, this was inestimably safer as a theological conception.

Cotton did not patiently accept the notion that if Christ acts in man all the acts of man must be equally acceptable to Him. It was clear to him that even the elect were occasionally victims of error and backsliding. The Saints, he pointed out, were "free from the Covenant of the Law, but not from the Commandment of it." He emphasized the free promise of God's grace without reference to man's prior performance, but he stipulated clearly that after the original promise of God's grace obedience to the law was a necessary condition of salvation. Although he may have kept the mental reservation that the Saints were divinely empowered to fulfill the terms of the law, he was too much of a realist to believe that they were invariably inclined to do so. The law continued useful "to aggravate the sins of the elect upon their conscience," and to drive them "to feel their great need of Christ."[52] When the true believer sins, he repents and sorrows, not for fear of suffering the penalties of the law, but because he sees that "all his sinnes he hath committed have been a piercing and crucifying of Christ."[53] God will not deal lightly with such a sinner, Cotton warned; He will "school him thoroughly and make him sadly to apprehend how inworthily he hath made bold to abuse and imbeazle the treasures of the grace of God." But, though the Lord may be angered and may hide his face, "if a man know himself to be under the Covenant of Grace, then he doth not feare condemnation for his disobedience."[54] For the Saint to fear a divorce

50. *Ibid.*, 34.
51. Cotton, *Covenant of Grace*, 31.
52. *Ibid.*, 134, 37.
53. John Cotton, *The Way of Life* (London, 1641), 37.
54. Cotton, *New Covenant*, 134, 125.

from Christ because of his sins would be to deny the perseverance of Grace and to "go aside" to a Covenant of Works. Once elected the believer is as incapable of departing from a state of grace as he was helpless to initiate it. The Saint may torment himself for having pierced Christ with his sins, but the Covenant will remain unbroken and all breaches shall be pardoned "that they shall be remembered no more." [55]

Cotton's reliance on the immediate testimony of the spirit prompted a further significant deviation from federal orthodoxy. Being temperamentally disposed to credit intuitional stirrings as a sure witness of grace, he was impelled to press the intuitive faculty beyond its basic function of assurance. Although he denied the validity of prophetic or visual revelations "without or besides Scripture," he accepted the worth of intuitional revelations "such as are breathed by the spirit of God and are never dispensed but in a word of God"—that is, the intuitive perception of more profound connotations in the Scripture. Cotton professed to find authority for this conception in Paul's message to the Ephesians: "The Father of glory, may give unto you the spirit of wisdom, and revelation in the knowledge of him." But he was to find to his cost that such an interpretation was markedly at variance with the firmly empirical sentiments of his clerical brethren.[56]

In the main, however, Cotton adhered faithfully to the general theological pattern so painstakingly developed by the Puritan clergy. Such deviations as he made from the doctrinal position of his colleagues were generally matters of emphasis rather than radical rejection; emphases prompted partially by his peculiar emotional temper and partially by the factionalism with which he had to contend in his congregation. The main tenor of his teaching stressed God's love and mercy as revealed in the Atonement, and sought always to de-emphasize the efficacy of works on the one hand, and to modify the retributive quality of the predestination decree on the other.

(viii)

For twenty years Cotton preached from the high pulpit under the exquisite soaring lantern of St. Botolph's Church. At the

55. Cotton, *Covenant of Grace*, 13.
56. *Antinomianism*, 175, 176, 156; see also Hutchinson, *History*, II, 386; Ephesians 1:17.

outset of his ministry some apprehension was expressed about the ability of a youth to control so factious a congregation, and suspicions were voiced that he might introduce Puritanical notions. On the former score his critics need have had no concern. Soon after his installation Cotton energetically attacked and dispelled an Arminian faction which had threatened to convert the congregation to anti-predestinarian tenets. On the latter score, however, their fears were all too well founded, for Cotton moved implacably toward the Puritan extreme, carrying most, if not all, of his congregation with him. By 1615 the "unscriptural" forms and ceremonies had been removed or substantially modified, and, according to rumor, even members of more orthodox outlying parishes were attending services at St. Botolph's in order to escape the necessity of kneeling at communion.[57] Such bold nonconformism was bound to bring Cotton under a cloud, and for a short time he was silenced. Thereafter, however, having won the esteem and protection of Archbishop Williams, a prelate obligingly unexacting in his demands for conformity, Cotton remained long unmolested in the pursuit of his heterodox practices.[58]

The ministerial regimen which Cotton pursued while at old Boston staggers the credulity of ordinary mortals. One observer remarked a Sunday service of five hours comprising a sermon, psalms, the catechizing of children, then more psalms with an appended exegesis. Little wonder that at its conclusion "there were as many sleepers as wakers";[59] few possessed a stamina to match John Cotton's zeal. In addition to regular Sunday services, he lectured in the church on Wednesday mornings, Thursday mornings and afternoons, and Saturday afternoons, and he seems to have found time to promote the edification of a few select members with intimate lectures at his home every day. For his odd hours, in addition to study, there remained the further task of training delegations of students sent up each year from Cambridge to acquire a final polish at his hands.

Laboring thus diligently in this vineyard of souls, Cotton was fatefully drawn under the attentive scrutiny of Mistress Anne Hutchinson.

57. William Page, ed., *The Victoria History of the Counties of England: Lincolnshire* (London, 1906), II, 60.

58. Mather, *Magnalia*, 239.

59. Dudding, *History of Alford*, 146.

IV

"A Faire and Easie Way to Heaven"

Circa 1628–1630

(i)

FOR ANNE HUTCHINSON the journey from Alford down to Boston was a fitting prologue to the heavenly discourses of John Cotton. Mounted firmly on the pillion, she rode behind William they edged down the wold onto the narrow ribbon of road that stretched far into the boundless reach of fens. Hour by hour they jogged on, chatting perhaps of household problems or of purchases to be made and friends to be seen at Boston. But most of the long way there was little to do but watch the dumb sheep munching by the roadside, or the sea birds wheeling silently overhead, the quiet broken only by the horses' hoofs and the ceaseless lapping of water in the mere. Above, the overarching sky reached far out and down to the distant, low horizon like a great translucent dome of blue beneath which the travelers moved in solitude, sentient to the divinity which encompassed them. As they neared Boston the slender tower of St. Botolph's Church, needlelike, pierced the flat horizon and inching upward, beckoned them on.

Each visit to Boston probably lasted two or three days, during which time there was ample opportunity to hear Mr. Cotton preach. In addition to attending some of the frequent services in the great church, Anne may have furthered her knowledge of John Cotton and his teachings by participating in the meetings held daily at his house.[1] She must have seized every available opportunity, since the difficulties of the journey made it unlikely that

1. Mather, *Magnalia*, I, 238.

she could venture to Boston more than a few times each year. During this period Cotton does not seem to have known her at all well. He recognized her as an occasional attendant at his services and knew of her good reputation in Alford, but he was not ordinarily disposed to foster close relations with his parishioners, and it is improbable that he would single out a stranger for this distinction.[2]

Irrespective of the infrequency of her visits, Anne Hutchinson enthusiastically absorbed the rich content of John Cotton's sermons and in time became almost totally dependent upon his spiritual guidance. In time, indeed, Cotton came to fill a void Anne had but impatiently endured since her father's death. William's devotion was endearing, but his acquiescent spirit had left her to wander in troubled solitude through the uncharted reaches of her mind and imagination: most desperately she needed help in defining the scope and bearings of this interior universe. In Cotton's mind and manner she saw the authority she sought, a firm intellect to provide the mental direction that William had failed to provide, and yet a gentle disposition that would not inhibit her own spontaneity. Anne's acquaintance with Cotton at this time was not close, but a rapport was established which she rationalized into absolute dependence on his presence and teaching.[3] When his guidance was lacking, she was distraught and insecure; when he was again accessible, her uneasiness was dispelled and she confronted the world with renewed assurance. This trust became the mainstay of her existence, but the time was not distant when it would lead her into more desperate complications than even her febrile imagination could readily conceive.

(ii)

If, as seems likely, Mrs. Hutchinson was first introduced to Puritan doctrine by John Cotton, she was conditioned from the outset against the emphasis on good works implicit in the federal theology. In his determination to minimize the role of moral effort in the regenerative process, Cotton had established an equipoise of grace and works so delicate that the weight of a hair might upset the balance. He had not failed to mark either the social or the theological significance of moral behavior, but nonetheless he

2. Cotton, *Way of the Congregational Churches Cleared*, 50-51.
3. Hutchinson, *History*, II, 384-85.

had categorically insisted that the union with Christ was complete before and without any work or act of faith on the part of the elect. Those in a true state of grace bore within them an all-essential witness that was to be more closely regarded than works as an evidence of regeneration.

Anne Hutchinson's response to this doctrine was almost predictable in a woman of her curiosity and emotional susceptibility. She embraced it rapturously, and in her ardor conveyed its implications beyond Cotton's original design. Not only did she minimize his enjoinders to moral effort, but she concluded from his words that the gift of grace implied that actual indwelling of the spirit of the Lord mystically uniting the elect to Himself and relieving the mortal of the burden of his transgressions.

There were, to Anne's mind, too many "hypocrites" who masqueraded as the elect of God. A more unerring method was required for telling sheep from goats than federal theology provided, and what could be more conclusive, she thought, than an immediate awareness of God's presence in the heart of the believer. The elect gained true knowledge of their conversion by a mystical infusion of the Divine Spirit, an immediate personal union with the Holy Ghost, so clear as to render the additional evidence of sanctification quite superfluous. If the Saint felt the presence of God within his own heart, that was assurance enough—what matter how he stood in the world's account! Only those who experienced this inward witness of the spirit enjoyed the sureties of the Covenant of Grace. Christ completed the dispensation of the Covenant by assuming all transgressions unto Himself. The believer, imbued with the spirit of Christ, was freed from the shackles of the Covenant of Works as embodied in the moral law, and elevated by His grace above the demands of that code. Guided by the spirit within them, the elect were unerringly impelled to perform His will. "I live," Mrs. Hutchinson was wont to cite, "but not I but Jesus Christ lives in me." [4]

Substantially what Anne had done was to adopt Cotton's doctrine of assurance with rigorous literalism and push its logical implications to the farthermost limit. Cotton had been restrained by the Calvinist linkage of the Spirit with the Word. Mrs. Hutchinson broke that link. Thus Cotton went one way and Anne the other, despite the affinity between them. But much time would pass before either fully understood the cleavage in their views.

4. "Church Trial of Mrs. Hutchinson," *Antinomianism*, 328; Galatians 2.

(iii)

Anne Hutchinson may not have grasped the full purport of her theological conclusion, but she had verged perilously upon the heresy of Antinomianism. This disturbing heterodoxy was a reaction against the doctrine of good works and the idea of human participation in the regenerative process. In the effort to overthrow religious legalism and to enhance the Agent above the recipients of grace, some theologians had advanced the claim that Christians are freed from the moral law of the Old Testament by the new dispensation of grace proffered in the Gospel. Although the implications of this doctrine were far-reaching and often ominous, Antinomianism was essentially a theological *idea* and as such did not necessarily describe or prescribe any particular form of behavior. Indeed, differing conclusions and forms of behavior were drawn out of the doctrine by different exponents at different times.

The Church of the Middle Ages had been enabled to perform its great civilizing mission by incorporating moral observance into the core of its sacramental system. This arrangement provided powerful sanctions for the enforcement of Christian deportment and also offered the individual communicant concrete tokens of assurance. But in time the devout came to fear that morality was degenerating into perfunctory ritualism, with widespread adherence to the letter rather than the spirit of Christ's teachings. In the twelfth century some earnest believers, striving to demolish this ritualistic legalism, reminded their hearers that God's dispensation of grace had freed all Christians from the bonds of the moral law. The teaching of these spiritual reformers was often charged with innatist conceptions which propounded a mystical infusion of the Divine Spirit into the soul of the believer of such effect as to abolish the distinction between creature and Creator and preclude any possibility of the free operation of the human will. Then the recipient might stand above the law and freely transfer responsibility for transgressions to the charge of the indwelling Divine.

Most of these spiritual reformers maintained impeccable lives, but there were some who employed their doctrine to justify their own moral laxity and so exposed the whole movement to ecclesiastical censure. In the fifteenth century, after the failure of desultory efforts to control these groups, the weight of the Inquisition was thrown into an effort to crush them. But the seed had been sown and lay parturient within the earth.

Scarcely a century later conditions were again ripe for the emergence of popular enthusiasm of an Antinomian quality. Long-established convictions were breaking down, the old codes were disintegrating, and with the dissolution of the Church Universal, pious folk, hungering for spiritual certainty, were brought immediately face to face with their Maker. Luther's revolt raised the floodgate, and soon the plain of northwestern Europe was strewn with pietistic and enthusiastic sects. The epithet "Antinomian" was first specifically applied to the followers of John Agricola, a disciple of Luther.[5] With the best of intentions Agricola had drawn what seemed to be the logical conclusions from Luther's doctrine of justification by faith. But his cautious enjoinders and Luther's fulminations counted for nothing as ardent Germans perverted the teachings of Agricola into mystical tenets closely resembling those of the earlier spiritual reformers.

Among the radical sects which proliferated during the sixteenth century, there were sharper distinctions than is commonly recognized. Some were enthusiasts, finding religious guidance in the main, not from the Bible, but from a divine light within themselves. More often the sectaries were Biblicists, appealing to some favored section of the New Testament as authority for their actions. The Anabaptists, for example, were inspired by the Synoptic Gospel to strive in love and purity toward the Kingdom of God. A few of the sects were guided by special and bizarre meanings which they had professed to find in the Pauline Epistles. Quite distinct from these groups and most troublesome in the eyes of conservative Protestant and Catholic alike were the millenarian devotees of the Revelations of St. John. Unlike the Anabaptists, who had laid great emphasis on freedom of the will and faithful observance of the law, millenarians and enthusiasts shared a strong Antinomian tendency. A particular notoriety attended the millenarian disciples of Johann Bockholdt, or John of Leyden as he is better known to history. In their zeal the members of this sect acquired an ill repute that was unfairly applied to the whole radical wing of Protestantism. In the year 1635, obsessed by the need for bold action and dangerous risks in order to hasten the coming of the new era, they forcibly seized the cathedral city of Münster as a center for

<hr />

5. James Hastings, ed., *The Encyclopaedia of Religion and Ethics* (New York, 1908), I, 581; *The New Schaaf-Herzog Encyclopedia of Religious Knowledge* (New York, 1908), I, 91-92.

their prospective conquest of the world. Churches were plundered, women debauched, and all who refused to join their mission put to the sword. For over a century conservative men looked on all radical sects with fear and loathing, anticipating similar enormities wherever they appeared.[6]

The Family of Love, a perfectionist society, was destined to play a peculiarly influential role. Its founder, Henrik Niclaes, subject to ecstatic visions from his childhood, insisted that divine immanence implied a guiding light within and the impeccability of all believers. "There are some now living," he declared, "which do fulfill the law in all parts."[7] Although this smacked dangerously of Antinomianism and indeed was so construed by some of his followers and all of his enemies, Niclaes himself repudiated so radical an interpretation and stressed the importance of moral effort and fulfillment of the law. "No one is ever released from the law," he wrote; "the law is not abolished, it is fulfilled in love."[8] But the contrary implication remained for those who sought it, and for some it remained highly congenial.

(iv)

Millenarianism, enthusiasm, and Familism spread rapidly throughout the Netherlands and by dint of Spanish fire and sword were soon conveyed to the eastern counties of England. East Anglia and the Holland of Lincolnshire became a focal point for the arrival of heretical Lowlanders who spread their doctrines as assiduously as they plied their looms. By 1578 the Family of Love had acquired so large and clamorous a following that "the Privy Council saw fit to endeavour their suppression."[9] Efforts to crush the movement had only nominal success, and the numerous mystical tracts of Hendrik Niclaes continued to circulate underground, providing an important source of popular mystical and

6. Robert Friedman, "Conception of the Anabaptists," *Church History*, 10 (1940), 341-65; McGiffert, *Protestant Thought Before Kant*, 202; Ernst Troeltsch, *The Social Teachings of the Christian Churches*, trans. Olive Wyon (New York, 1931), II, 781; J. W. Allen, *A History of Political Thought in the Sixteenth Century* (London, 1928), 39; John Lothrop Motley, *The Rise of the Dutch Republic* (New York, 1853), I, 69.

7. Hastings, ed., *Encyclopaedia of Religion and Ethics*, IV, 183; Rufus M. Jones, *Studies in Mystical Religion* (London, 1923), 428 ff.; *New Schaaf-Herzog Encyclopedia of Religious Knowledge*, IV, 272.

8. Jones, *Studies in Mystical Religion*, 436.

9. Quoted in Margaret Lewis Bailey, *Milton and Jakob Boehme* (New York, 1914), 12.

Antinomian thought.[10] Meanwhile other sects flourished in their secret conventicles and kept alive the traditions of prophetic revelations and lay preaching.[11]

One place in particular seems to have become notorious as a center for erronists and enthusiasts of all stripes. A prototype of Rhode Island in this respect, the Isle of Ely in Cambridgeshire early acquired the repute of being a "land of errors and sectaries." [12] A group who were called Anabaptists came to light there in 1573 and were still much in evidence almost a century later when the revolution broke out. Familists were reported to "swarm and dayly increase in the Isle of Ely" [13] before 1590, and a century later the diarist Evelyn recorded them as being still active there.[14]

While Anne Hutchinson was still living in Alford she heard of these congregations and became much interested in them. Particularly was she impressed by a woman preacher who was active among them. Although she did not personally know this woman, and indeed never saw her, Mrs. Hutchinson "did exceedingly magnify her to be a woman of a thousand, hardly any like to her." [15] The woman's name is not recorded, but at that time she

10. Rufus M. Jones, *Mysticism and Democracy in the English Commonwealth* (Cambridge, Eng., 1932), 130.

11. Jones, *Studies in Mystical Religion*, 407 ff.

12. Thomas Edwards, *Gangraena* (London, 1646), Pt. II, 29.

13. Stephen Bernard Nutter, *The Story of the Cambridge Baptists in the Struggle for Religious Liberty* (Cambridge, Eng., 1912), 63; Jones, *Studies in Mystical Religion*, 406.

14. Evelyn's entry of June 16, 1687, is cited in Jones, *Studies in Mystical Religion*, 447.

15. Franklin B. Dexter, ed., "A Report of the Trial of Mrs. Anne Hutchinson Before the Church in Boston, 1638," Mass. Hist. Soc., *Proceedings*, 2d Ser., 4 (1889), 184. During the course of Mrs. Hutchinson's examination before the church of Boston, the Reverend Mr. Hugh Peter remarked to the assembly: "I would say this; when I was once speaking with her [Mrs. Hutchinson] about the woman of Elis [*sic*]; she did exceedingly magnify her to be a woman of a thousand, hardly any like to her, and yet we know the woman of Elis is a dangerous woman and holds forth grievous things and fearful errors." This reference to "the woman of Elis" has been variously interpreted as a classical or Biblical allusion, but in the succeeding sentence Mrs. Hutchinson refers to her as though she were a living, contemporaneous person: "I said of the woman of Elis but what I heard, for I knew her not nor ever saw her." This rather puzzling exchange is considerably illuminated by the following passage in Thomas Edwards, *Gangraena*, Part II, 29: "There are also some woman preachers in our times, who keep constant lectures, preaching weekly to many men and women. In Lincolnshire, in Holland and those parts [i.e., the parts about Holland in Lincolnshire] there is a woman preacher who preaches (it's certain), and 'tis reported also she baptizeth, but that's not so certain. *In the Isle of Ely (that land of errors and sectaries) is a woman preacher also.*" In indexes of English towns Ely is the only town which even approximates in sound or appearance the word, "Elis," and the identification seems reinforced by the fact that Ely had long been notorious as a gathering place for radical sectaries.

was presumably quite notorious, for the reference to her was made in terms that assume popular knowledge of the subject. Nor is it known whether the woman preacher was an Anabaptist or a Familist, but in any case, as far as the orthodox were concerned, she was "a dangerous woman and [held] forth grievous things and fearful errors." [16] Whatever the woman's doctrines may have been, they seem to have captured Anne's fancy, and may well have influenced or encouraged the pronouncement of her own heterodox notions. Mrs. Hutchinson was also impressed by the idea of lay preaching by women. Altogether the woman of Ely seems to have provided the Alford housewife with considerable food for thought.

There were at this same time a number of Anglican vicars who were also teaching doctrines of an Antinomian tone; men whose writings were to influence the radical sects of the Commonwealth period.[17] Indeed, their doctrines were more nearly in accordance with those of Mrs. Hutchinson than were the tenets of the Anabaptists or Familists, which approached her position obliquely at best. However, most of these uncanonical vicars were located in and around London, and there is no evidence to indicate that Mrs. Hutchinson had ever heard of their existence.

(v)

Exactly when Mrs. Hutchinson underwent her religious conversion none can say with certainty. The problem is complicated by the fact that her conversion was a complex and progressive development, passing through two or even more continuously overlapping phases. She seems to have moved first from the orthodox Anglican views in which she had been reared to the Puritan tenets of John Cotton. This conversion could have taken place at almost any time between 1615 and 1629, though circumstances suggest that it was probably nearer the latter date.

The second phase of her conversion, from the Cottonian tenets to her own extreme and mystical statement, seems to have occurred in 1630 or 1631. This development overtook her with great force and was attended by disturbing symptoms of which Mrs. Hutchinson has left a detailed description. The tenor of her account and other supporting evidence indicates that it could hardly have

16. Dexter, ed., "Church Trial of Mrs. Anne Hutchinson, 1638," Mass. Hist. Soc., *Proceedings*, 2d Ser., 4 (1889), 184.

17. Gertrude Huehns, *Antinomianism in English History* (London, 1951), 55 ff.

taken place more than two or three years before Cotton's departure for New England. The fervent temper of her religious activity in New England also suggests the relative novelty of her ideas. While in Massachusetts she proselytized and propagandized with the unfettered zeal of a neophyte. Had so ardent a belief been of long duration, she would have been prompted to similar action in Old England, which would have brought her notoriety, if not legal apprehension. But such was not the case; there is no suggestion of irregularity of doctrine or conduct on her part before she left England for the American wilderness.

V

"Thine Eyes Shall See Thy Teachers"

1629–1634

(i)

A SHUDDER OF APPREHENSION seized Protestant Europe as the third decade of the seventeenth century drew to its close. Gathering new force the Counter Reformation had swept in a flood tide over all Germany, threatening with destruction the hundred years' labor of Protestant reformers. Wallenstein's invincibles stormed northward to the Baltic shore, while the Emperor Ferdinand grimly plotted the establishment of a great Catholic Hapsburg Empire on the smoking ruins of the Lutheran faith. The liberties of French Protestants reeled under the blows of Cardinal Richelieu's armies. And at home in England Charles Stuart debonairly ascended the throne with his Catholic bride and flung challenge upon challenge at the Puritan-controlled House of Commons. Forced loans were exacted from the gentry and tonnage and poundage from the merchants. Those who failed to comply were cast into prison or suffered the loss of their goods, and the noisy protests of Parliament were silenced by dissolution which was to last eleven years. As if to demolish the Puritan dream entirely, William Laud, Archbishop of London and close counsellor to the King, staunch Arminian and implacable foe of Puritanism, now acted to impose a straitened conformity throughout the realm of England.

During these years Boston and the environing countryside of southern Lincolnshire suffered severe economic dislocation.[1] For

1. Page, ed., *Victoria History of Lincolnshire*, II, 279 ff.

some time the once flourishing wool trade had been slipping away, and Boston's prominence as a port declined. The Witham estuary was silting up; by 1628 only eleven smallish ships could be counted at its docks and moorings. To compensate for this loss of revenue, efforts were made to drain the fens in order to promote agricultural productivity. But this attack on the ancient modes of production had only led to more troubles, litigation about the rights to commons land, and riots calculated to prevent any change whatever. Wool prices continued their precipitate decline. The status of tenants and workers was threatened by the steady rise in rents, land values, and food prices, but the landlords' lot seemed to remain unimproved for want of venture capital with which to develop their holdings. Then, to crown all, in 1626 the King imposed a forced loan that seemed to threaten liberty itself.

There was much unrest in Mr. Cotton's congregation. Atherton Hough and William Coddington refused to submit to this unwarranted expropriation, and Cotton's patron, Theophilus, Earl of Lincoln, was lodged in the Tower for his resistance.[2] Mr. Cotton's more eminent parishioners were seen often together during those troubled days. Little groups stood about the churchyard after Sunday service, planning, plotting, nodding their heads earnestly in heated conversation. Or by twos and threes, cloaks pulled warmly about them, they jogged out the dusty road by sluggish Witham's edge, bound for the Earl's splendidly turreted mansion at Tattershall. There, in the great chamber they paced restlessly, or brooding before the massive carved fireplace, gazed ruminatively at the blaze which crackled and caracoled fitfully upward, as if expecting it, phoenix-like, to give birth to the conclusions they so determinedly sought.

Conspicuous among these projectors was bluff Thomas Dudley, late steward to the Earl, erstwhile warrior for the white plume of Navarre, and despite his years, still boisterous and bellicose in a worthy cause. At his side was Simon Bradstreet, his successor at Tattershall, a young Cambridge graduate, ardently suing for the hand of Dudley's daughter. Richard Bellingham, the Boston recorder, Alderman Thomas Leverett, William Coddington, and Atherton Hough were doubtless among their number. Isaac Johnson of nearby Sempringham, the husband of the Earl's sister and a

2. John Bruce, ed., *Calendar of State Papers, Domestic Series, of the Reign of Charles I, 1627-1628* (London, 1858), 72, 116, hereafter cited as *Cal. State Papers*.

devoted disciple of Mr. Cotton, was a ringleader of the group.[3]
As often as his labors permitted, Mr. Cotton himself was probably
an active participant in these sessions. At any rate he remained in
continuous communication with the leaders of the cabal during
the formulation of their plans. A more recent associate was a West
Countryman, John Humfry by name, who was then courting
another of the Earl's sisters. As treasurer of a languishing fishing
enterprise on the New England coast, Humfry was in a position
to offer these troubled gentlemen a way out of their difficulties.
From their conversations the Massachusetts Bay Company finally
emerged. Months passed as the plotters matured their design,
gained a royal charter which conveyed powers of government,
organized and then reorganized their leadership, and assembled
the personnel and equipment needed for so perilous an enterprise.
By early spring of 1630 all was in readiness for their departure.

In March John Cotton traveled to Southampton with his friends
to bestow a parting benison on the little fleet that lay in the harbor
waiting a fair wind for the new world. When he returned to Boston,
it was to enter a difficult interim period whose trials seemed calculated to season him for a new life. Scarcely had he settled down
when he was stricken with a tertian ague which laid him low for
weeks on end.[4] The same feverish ailment proved fatal to his
wife, Elizabeth. Weak with fever and prostrate with grief, Cotton
was removed from his Boston home to Tattershall, where the Earl
had invited him to spend a period of prolonged convalescence.
There he remained for nearly a year, slowly regaining his strength.
For some months thereafter he sojourned in London and traveled
extensively about the country before he was at last able to resume
the arduous labors of his pastorate. Not until 1632 did he return
to Boston, and then, striving to fill the well of his loneliness, he
took in marriage an old friend, Sarah Story, "a vertuous widow,
very dear to his former wife." [5]

(ii)

Cotton's extended absence from his Boston pulpit greatly dis-
tressed Anne Hutchinson. She had become dependent on his

3. "Last Will and Testament of Isaac Johnson," *Winthrop Papers* (Boston,
1929-47), II, 49.
4. A fever or ague characterized by the occurrence of a paroxysm every third day
(i.e., on alternate days).
5. Mather, *Magnalia*, I, 240.

spiritual guidance, and his illness now left a great breach in her life. She was not ready to avow that his doctrine was the true faith, nor had she yet arrived at the startling theological connotations that meditation would at last unfold. But to her mind Cotton's words had the ring of truth, and no other clergyman offered quite the same assurance; certainly not her Alford vicar, a man whose teachings left her much troubled in mind.[6]

Cotton had been away from Boston only a short time when a cruel fate suddenly lashed out at Anne Hutchinson. In September of 1630 young Susanna Hutchinson died. The fourteen-year-old girl, on the very threshold of young womanhood, was Anne's firstborn daughter and so assumed a particularly vital role in the taut pattern of her mother's emotional life. Sorrow pressed agonizingly on the distraught woman. Scarcely a month of mourning had passed when death struck again—this time seizing little Elizabeth, only eight years old and just beginning to become her mother's helper about the house. Perhaps both children had been stricken by the plague, which had ravaged London and was now pressing mercilessly northward. In another few weeks it was to decimate the population of Louth, but twelve miles above Alford, and in the fall of 1630 it may have passed through Alford on its relentless course.[7]

Doubt crowded on doubt as Anne strained for meaning in the universe that lurched senselessly around her: her children torn from her as she nursed their illness; John Cotton lingering endless weeks suspended between life and death. Why did God so pitilessly torment her? What had she done to warrant this affliction? The church of her father trumpeted a doctrine of works and retribution that seemed to publish her guilt to all the world. Why was there no one at hand to open the Scripture to her and help her find assurance of her innocence therein? Was there comfort somewhere in the teachings of Mr. Cotton, or must she abandon the Church of England and find consolation with the Separatists?[8]

As winter towered to its icy peak, Anne conceived once again and was stirred to exaltation and restless desires by the quickening of new life within her. Disconsolate at the loss of her children and unnerved by the bitter teaching of the church she withdrew

6. Hutchinson, *History*, II, 384.

7. Charles Creighton, *History of Epidemics in Britain* (Cambridge, Eng., 1891), I, 527.

8. Hutchinson, *History*, II, 383.

to the quiet of her chamber and kept "a day of solemn humiliation and pondering of the thing." [9] Now, with Cotton absent, she "had none to open the Scripture . . . but the Lord, he must be the Prophet." In the gloomy stillness of her room she felt the Spirit of God descend, bringing to her the words of the Apostle John: "Every spirit that confesseth not, that Jesus Christ is come in the flesh, is the spirit of Antichrist." [10]

The words spun senselessly through her mind. This was more puzzling than before, for did not all Christians—Papists as well as Protestants—confess that Christ was come in the flesh? Could it mean merely that the Turks were Antichrist? There was no solace here.

For twelve agonizing months Anne wrestled with her doubts. She was briefly tempted to turn to the conventional ministrations of the Anglican church for spiritual aid, but feared that by doing so she opposed Christ and walked in a Covenant of Works. Again and again she appealed to God for the light to comprehend His design, but she heard no answer. Then, with the coming of another winter, her faith and patience gained their satisfaction. The Spirit of God approached again and brought her the perception she had sought: "He that denies the testament denies the testator." The scales fell away from her eyes and she saw with God's pure light that the Antichrist dwelt in those who refused to teach the New Covenant—the Covenant of Grace. This revelation pointed most ominously at the ministers of the Church of England; it was they who bore within them the spirit of the Antichrist. Now she understood the inspired wisdom of Cotton's words and was able to know which was the clear ministry and which was the wrong, which "the voice of John [the] Baptist and which the voice of antichrist." [11]

(iii)

The fluent revelations of Anne Hutchinson, much as they may have bespoken the pattern of the Godhead, were even more revelatory of her own complex psychological structure. Like her colleagues in this terrestrial enterprise, she was impelled to invoke the unknowable divine in terms that satisfied not only her cultural preconceptions but the modifying force of her emotional needs.

9. *Ibid.*
10. *Antinomianism*, 173.
11. Hutchinson, *History*, II, 383-84; *Antinomianism*, 173-74.

Her religious professions, like theirs, often represented a rationalization of motives known only to her subconscious.

Close scrutiny of Mrs. Hutchinson's career reveals a pattern of psychological needs which were expressed in the concurrent and congruent roles of mystic, Antinomian, and religious agitator. It is not surprising that her psychological imbalance should resolve itself in religious formulas. She was raised and educated in a clerical household, and the cultural environment in which she moved was predominantly religious.

During her later years Mrs. Hutchinson appears to have suffered a dread of isolation and an exaggerated craving for moral support, a form of anxiety generally attributable to the lack of mental direction from a source where it is normally expected.[12] Students in the field of religious psychology cite many instances of women who have been tormented by fixed ideas and hysterical manifestations because their husbands have failed to guide their mental life. They engage in an obsessive search for a substitute mental director, and until he is found they suffer a profound horror of isolation. When a satisfactory director is located, the subject becomes almost entirely dependent upon his guidance and support; in his presence insecurity and uneasiness are dispelled, and problems are approached with renewed assurance. With a person of strong religious bent, such an influence could be exerted by a confessor or pastor or—given the proper set of stimuli—even the Deity. In union with a loving God the mystic seeks to attain peace, affection, self-assurance, and mental direction. "To realize the presence of the God of Love is the Mystic's method of securing the satisfaction of his essential wants." [13]

It has been observed that William Hutchinson seems to have lacked the power to provide adequate support and direction for his wife. The absence of this guidance, sharply felt after the firm influence of her father, apparently compelled Mrs. Hutchinson to turn elsewhere for affective support. In her extremely active social life she found the affection that enhanced her self-esteem. Mrs. Hutchinson was notably gregarious and her nursing activities brought ample rewards in gratitude and esteem. Also she suffered from a compulsion to verbalize her most errant thoughts, another

12. Pierre Janet, *Neuroses et Idees Fixes*, I, 465, cited in James Leuba, *Psychology of Religious Mysticism* (New York, 1929), 125.
13. *Ibid.*, 120.

unconscious device for the attainment of notice and approval.

More important, however, was her search for a substitute mental director. At first she was drawn to John Cotton, in whom she found a suitable symbol of authority who fulfilled the directional function without inhibiting her own expressiveness or spontaneity.[14] Later she was to form a similar attachment to Henry Vane, a young aristocrat who was for a time her neighbor in Massachusetts.[15] But even more to the point was her implicit reliance upon the elaborately detailed directions which she professed to receive from God. She claimed that her spiritual communion yielded revelations "as trew as the Scriptures" and professed that "she had never had any great thing done about her but it was revealed to her beforehand."[16] Here was a director for her mind with a vengeance! As a matter of fact, among authorities on the subject and even among the mystics themselves, claims of exterior visions and prophetic revelations such as Anne Hutchinson came to profess are not generally regarded as trustworthy evidence of union with the Divine Spirit.[17] The extremity of Mrs. Hutchinson's claims may have been the result of a pressing need for guidance and moral support.[18]

14. Erich Fromm, *Escape From Freedom* (New York, 1941), 178.

15. *Winthrop Papers*, IV, 25. After her banishment from Massachusetts, betrayed by Cotton, and left alone in the conspicuous and vulnerable role of religious leader of the Aquidneck colony, Mrs. Hutchinson's thoughts turned to Henry Vane, now back in England. Roger Williams told Winthrop that her "longings were great after Mr. Vane . . . [and that] if he came not to New England she must to Old England."

16. *Antinomianism*, 305; Hutchinson, *History*, II, 385.

17. Robert Thouless, *An Introduction to the Psychology of Religion* (Cambridge, Eng., 1923), 73.

18. Psychological investigation has disclosed that a strong egoism is one of the basic roots of mystical behavior. Leuba asserts that the mystics are "determined not only to be worthwhile, but to be recognized as such. . . . Their light shall not shine under a bushel." This tendency to self-affirmation is related to the basic frustration suffered in the absence of adequate mental direction. When the love relationship encounters an obstacle such as this, the libido is effectively blocked and is obliged to withdraw from its outward movement and settle back upon the ego, resulting in a strong tendency toward narcissism. The consequent insecurity must be relieved and the individual requires constant evidence of his self-importance. Persistent efforts are made to attract and hold attention. Approval of one's actions is essential and the capacity to arouse the emotional response of the public in token of such approval assumes primary importance. Leuba has observed this reaction in varying degrees in such diverse personalities as Francis of Assisi, Ignatius Loyola, and Saint Theresa. None of the mystics enjoyed a completely normal married life, most of them were consumed with a desire to shine, and many, in order to do so, laid disproportionately high value on their ability to play upon the emotions of the public. It is noteworthy that Harold Lasswell has found similar impulses operating under the same conditions in the lives of the political agitators he has studied. Leuba, *Psychology of Religious Mysticism*, 121; Harold Lasswell, *Psychopathology and Politics* (Chicago, 1930), 124 ff.

(iv)

There remains the possibility that Mrs. Hutchinson's mystical experience was initiated by more explicit and immediate needs than those cited; that a specific catalytic agent triggered the tensions created by these needs and directed them toward this particular solution. It seems not improbable that the deaths of her children provided a major impulse toward such a psychological expression. Not only would the emotional shock attending this double tragedy have been in itself traumatic, but the event would have been subject to interpretations that must have imposed a severe mental strain on the distraught mother. These children were undoubtedly under her care during their final illness. However much she may have sought to console herself with the belief that this was God's will, Mrs. Hutchinson could hardly have escaped the feeling that her own inadequacy was at least in part responsible for their deaths. She was a person who placed excessive demands on herself and was intent on the preservation of a favorable self-image; therefore, it would have been essential to her emotional quiet to minimize this hideous burden of responsibility or convert it to more favorable terms.

The situation was further complicated by the ambivalent interpretation the Puritans imposed upon such events. Bereaved persons who were fully confident of the innocence of the deceased and of their own state of grace could profess satisfaction that their loved ones had ascended to a just and enviable reward. But for those whose election was held uncertain, by themselves or by the community, a tragedy of these proportions was generally construed to be a clear manifestation of God's wrath. From whatever perspective the event is viewed, it gives the appearance of a traumatic experience, the meaning of which Mrs. Hutchinson was forced to convert to more reassuring terms. Wracked with unbearable doubt, the unhappy woman was in all probability driven forward on a restless and compulsive quest for certainty.

There is no way of knowing that Mrs. Hutchinson's initial mystical experiences occurred at this precise moment in her career, but it is known that they assumed a curiously delusional quality that might well fit these circumstances, and it would seem that the traumatic impact of this tragedy was adequate to their excitation. Her great personal need at this juncture would have been to organize a frame of reference within which she might reaffirm her self-esteem. Given the fact of her religious orientation, with its harsh emphasis on the correlation of human conduct and divine retribution, it would have seemed necessary that she obtain an assurance of God's love and support that transcended all considerations of guilt and punishment, or of effort and reward. Very often when an individual who is the victim of his own excessive demands persecutes himself for an act conflicting with his ideals and expectations, he may conclude that others similarly blame him. Incapable of flexible adjustment to the strains imposed by the situation, he is impelled to ascribe imagined attitudes and functions to their persons. He formulates "hypothetical relationships between himself and others and organizes them into a pseudo-community." [19] The pressure of self-esteem produces a convulsive attempt at exculpation and compensation for his feeling of guilt and inferiority, and a balancing delusion may be generated—one providing a sense of justification and even grandiosity. It seems possible that Mrs. Hutchinson, in this critical moment, may have created such a pseudo-community of imagined relationships to account for her dilemma: on the one hand the legalists, who presumably condemned her for her shortcomings, and on the other, the Deity, who accepted her despite the faults of which she felt secretly guilty. It has already been observed that her mystical locutions implied an intimate relationship with God superseding all legal conditions. She was assured that God would unalterably support her, and that her presumed persecutors—those who insisted on the legal correlation of conduct and retribution—would be forever cast down.[20] It was indeed a "most desperate enthusiasm." [21]

Succeeding developments may serve to confirm and expand this thesis. During the months following her tragic loss, Mrs. Hutchinson was succored by a physiological reinforcement of no slight value. During her hour of greatest need, when the loss of her children must have incurred a subsidence of self-affirmation, she became pregnant once again.[22] The physiological adjustment subsequent to pregnancy resulted in an exaltation that increased or pos-

19. Norman Cameron, "Paranoid Disorders," in Gardner Murphy and Arthur J. Bachrach, eds., *An Outline of Abnormal Psychology* (New York, 1954), 407-8; see also Roy M. Dorcus and G. Wilson Schaffer, *Textbook of Abnormal Psychology* (New York, 1950), 183.
20. Hutchinson, *History*, II, 383-84; *Antinomianism*, 173-74.
21. Hutchinson, *History*, II, 387. The words are Gov. Winthrop's.
22. Susanna and Elizabeth died in September and October 1630. Mrs. Hutchinson became pregnant again in January 1630/1; Champlin, "Hutchinson Ancestry and Descendants," *N.Y. Geneal. and Biog. Record*, 45 (1941), 168.

sibly even initiated a conviction of union with God transcending all legal considerations. In the lives of many of the mystics a marked periodicity has been frequently observed. It has been noted among female mystics that oscillations traceable to physiological causes are often the result of the exaltation accompanying pregnancy.[23] It was not by coincidence that hysteria derived its name from the uterine function, and this exalted state frequently occurs among pregnant women, mystical or otherwise. Among those of an extremely religious nature it is generally directed toward religious ends.

The pattern may be traced into Mrs. Hutchinson's future career. It was approximately during the period of a succeeding pregnancy, from July 1635 to March 1636, that she commenced her program of religious education and proselytizing in Massachusetts. The coincidence of pregnancies and religious exaltation did not escape the notice of her contemporaries. Several years later John Wheelwright spoke slightingly of the "strange fancies and erroneous tenets [which] possess her, especially during her confinement, where she might feel some effects too, from the quality of humours, together with the advantage the devil took of her condition attended with melancholy." [24] Wheelwright may also have remembered similar experiences which he had seen her undergo when they were neighbors in Lincolnshire.

(v)

The mystic type is not necessarily Antinomian, but among Antinomians there has been a strong tendency to mysticism. The mystic way varies widely, the course followed depending as much on the prevailing conception of the nature of God as on the temperament of the individual. Antinomianism, however, often entailed a conception of the nature of God which was intrinsically mystical and its more prominent exponents were almost invariably mystics. Mrs. Hutchinson was strongly inclined to mysticism; equally com-

23. Leuba, *Psychology of Religious Mysticism*, 90.
24. Wheelwright, *Writings*, 197. Melancholia and its attendant weakness was believed to expose the victim to the attacks of the devil who took advantage of this unguarded and hopeful disposition to slip deceptive fantasies into the brain, viz. *Hamlet*, II, ii:

> ... the devil hath power
> To assume a pleasing shape; yea, and perhaps
> Out of my weakness and my melancholy,
> As he is very potent with such spirits,
> Abuses me to damn me.

pelling motives seem to have led to her acceptance of Antinomianism.

The Puritan demand for rigorous self-examination greatly encouraged subjectivism, and the inadequate system of assurances laid down by Calvin aroused a cry for a surer knowledge of grace. Disregarding the attempts of theologians to straddle these delicate issues, Mrs. Hutchinson did not hesitate to travel the perilous road which stretched temptingly before her. Having chafed under the restrictions of the conventional theology, she pursued the mild illuminism of John Cotton to its highly subjectivist conclusions and arrived on the far side of orthodoxy with a solution at once intellectually and emotionally satisfying.

The neurotic individual, seeking protection against weakness and helplessness, strives for power and constantly endeavors to offset the feeling of being insignificant, a tendency which generally results in an assertive and domineering attitude.[25] In due course Mrs. Hutchinson would find broad scope for such an inclination in her activities as a religious teacher, malcontent, and dialectical opponent to the theologians of Massachusetts Bay. The Antinomian philosophy provided another such release. Theoretically, Antinomianism was a rejection of power by placing the human will in the hands of God, to be manipulated by Him as He saw fit. Practically, however, it amounted to an assertion of unqualified personal power and autonomy. The individual became a law unto himself and reserved the right to make all decisions affecting his actions without reference to the needs of the community. Such a philosophy offered incalculable advantage to a nature that was constantly striving to prove its own value. Like the timid child who courts danger in order to draw attention and establish proof of his own courage, Mrs. Hutchinson wrenched herself free of narrowly defined social obligations and determined to steer her own course. The very radicalism of the doctrine commended itself by contributing to that singularity with which she sought to win attention and approval.

(vi)

After her conversion to the Cottonian tenets, Mrs. Hutchinson was much given to critical scrutiny of the spiritual qualifications of the ministry. There was, however, one clergyman other than Cotton

25. Karen Horney, *The Neurotic Personality of Our Time* (New York, 1937), 166.

of whom she warmly approved. A mile or so east of Alford, in the hamlet of Bilsby, the Reverend Mr. John Wheelwright was installed as vicar in 1623, and it became apparent that he too preached a Covenant of Grace in very forthright terms.[26]

Shortly before his installation at Bilsby, Wheelwright had become a distant associate of the Hutchinson family through his marriage to Marie Storre, sister of the husband of Susan Hutchinson, who was Anne's eldest sister-in-law. So remote an affiliation with a clan so large may have left the young vicar comfortably beyond the range of Anne's formidable curiosity for a considerable period of time. But events conspired at last to bring him within the dubious web of her esteem. Around 1630, following the death of his first wife, Wheelwright was gathered into the more intimate family circle by his marriage to Mary Hutchinson, the youngest of Anne's sisters-in-law.[27]

So perceptive a spirit as Anne Hutchinson could not fail to observe that the Bilsby vicar was stamped with the seal of the Spirit. It was plain that he preached the New Covenant as clearly as Cotton did; perhaps less tenderly and poetically—brother Wheelwright's words often rang with a note of wry irony that may have eluded her rather humorless grasp—but the essence was identical.[28] For Anne, Wheelwright's office was largely to confirm and strengthen the conviction Cotton had ignited in her mind. Great as was her esteem for her brother-in-law, for Anne Hutchinson it was always Cotton's light which burned most brightly.

For a year or so, even with a defective ministry in Alford, Anne was able to garner spiritual riches to her soul's delight. The new infant in the well-used cradle by the fireside kept her hands busy and helped assuage her grief at the passing of Susanna and Elizabeth. With Mr. Cotton back at his old post in Boston and brother Wheelwright holding forth in Bilsby—and indeed often discoursing at her own table—she was content that God's sealed teachers were at hand to guide her. Fortified by their ministry, she spent long hours at silent meditation in her chamber or poring restlessly over the familiar pages of Scripture in search of more fruitful connotations. During these months God came often to her, bringing assurance of His support and stern declarations that all her persecutors

26. Dudding, *History of Alford,* 151; Edmund Wheelwright, "A Frontier Family," Col. Soc. of Mass., *Publications,* 1 (1895), 271.

27. Wheelwright, "A Frontier Family," Col. Soc. of Mass., *Publications,* 1 (1895), 271.

28. John Wheelwright, *Writings, passim.*

would be cast down and scattered.[29] So suggestible a nature as Anne Hutchinson's could not doubt the authenticity of these visitations nor long refrain from communicating their import to her family and friends. Each successive encounter was related to William and the children when all were assembled for evening prayers. The younger Hutchinsons stood in awe of their mother's comfortable intimacy with the Divine Spirit, and some of them were even encouraged to emulate these psychic prodigies. In an exemplary display of family teamwork, young Faith, though only seventeen, professed to have received supramundane communications confirming the authenticity of her mother's visitations.[30]

But in 1632 Anne Hutchinson's unstable paradise began to crumble. The first blow fell when brother Wheelwright was silenced by the authorities and removed from his ministry.[31] Within another year Mr. Cotton too had been driven from his pulpit by that relentless "tool of the Antichrist," William Laud, now Archbishop of Canterbury and prelate of all England.

(vii)

As summer waned to autumn in 1633, the *Griffin,* eight weeks out of England, beat its way toward the Massachusetts coast, bearing another two hundred souls to enrich or trouble the New English Zion. Conspicuous among her passengers were several eminent gentlemen, who were transplanting from old Boston to new. One of these was the Reverend Mr. John Cotton, and with him were two loyal parishioners, men of substance who had chosen to sacrifice the amenities of their Lincolnshire estates in order to share their pastor's exile in the wilderness. Thomas Leverett, "an ancient and sincere professor," a magistrate of Boston, had several times exercised his influence to prevent Cotton's displacement as a nonconformist, and had himself been reported to the High Commission for his stubborn refusal to bend a knee at the sacrament.[32] The other, Atherton Hough, former mayor of Boston, had established his mettle some years earlier by refusing to support the first royal loan of King Charles.[33] Now all three confronted the rigors of the new

29. *Antinomianism,* 173; Hutchinson, *History,* II, 383-84.
30. Hutchinson, *History,* II, 385.
31. Wheelwright, "A Frontier Family," Col. Soc. of Mass., *Publications,* 1 (1895), 271.
32. Winthrop, *Journal,* I, 110; Mather, *Magnalia,* I, 240.
33. Charles Henry Pope, *The Pioneers of Massachusetts* (Boston, 1900), 241.

world, perhaps anticipating the distinctions they might continue to enjoy, but surely little apprehending the turmoil in which they would become so soon involved.

Scarcely a year had passed after Cotton returned to his pulpit following the death of his wife when it had become apparent that the rigorous policy of Archbishop Laud would soon make his position at St. Botolph's untenable. Even the intercession of titled friends in court had been unavailing. Letters missive had been issued for his prompt appearance before Laud's Court of High Commission on charges of nonconformity.[34] Agents of the Archbishop had been on his trail and the port authorities alerted to prevent his departure from England. Warned by friends of the imminent danger of apprehension, Cotton had said farewell to his congregation, and doffing his clerical garb, fled to London. He had been joined en route by Thomas Hooker and Samuel Stone, who were similarly in flight from the Archbishop's men. Eluding their pursuers, who had been diverted to Southampton, the fugitive clerics had gone to Kent, where they were conveyed by small boat to their friends on the *Griffin*.[35]

The presence of so distinguished a clerical trio assured passengers ample distraction from the conventional boredom of an ocean voyage, and must surely have provided sufficient wind to waft them all to their destination in comfortable time. Every day at least one of the ministers preached, and on most days all three gave unstintingly of their homiletic talents. Midway in the passage, as if to signalize the reorientation of Cotton's career, a son was born to Sarah Cotton, his wife of a year, and was dubbed with disarming appropriateness, Seaborn.

Now John Cotton, scholar, recluse, and man of God, confronted the chilling realities of a primitive community insecurely poised on the edge of a vast wilderness. Bearing no arms and no armor but an unconquerable belief in God's everlasting love and mercy, the task before him was to sow that conviction in the New World. Whether the form and tenor of his beliefs would be as viable and applicable in an unsettled community as they were in one long established does not seem to have deterred him. The possibility that the heterogeneous, fast-growing population of New England might not share the theological sophistication he had so painstakingly inculcated in his Lincolnshire congregation seems not to have

34. *Cal. State Papers, Domestic, Charles I, 1633-34*, 480.
35. Mather, *Magnalia*, I, 242.

crossed his mind. Would the symbols he evoked have the same meaning as before? Would the Old World conceptions of Calvin and Sibbes fit the spiritual and ethical demands of the New World's turbulent growth? Would the delicate doctrinal equipoise of divine grace and human effort survive the buffetings of a frontier society where so high a premium was placed on freedom of the will? However subtle these distinctions may have seemed, they were soon to be the shoals upon which the state and church of Massachusetts almost foundered.

(viii)

Cotton's flight from England was a heavy blow to Anne Hutchinson. Disconsolate at the loss of her mentor, she despaired of finding another who preached the Gospel with equal understanding. She knew no minister in England to whom she could turn for guidance. At length "it pleased God to reveale himselfe ... in that of Esay 30:20": "And though the Lord give you the bread of adversity, and the water of affliction, yet shall not thy teachers be removed into a corner any more, but thine eyes shall see thy teachers." Strive as she might to go about her daily life as usual, the words nagged constantly at her mind; "thine eyes shall see thy teachers." Could God intend that she must follow her teacher to the end of the earth? The possibility lodged itself firmly in her brain. The prospect of the long and difficult journey was carefully weighed and the dangers of the new land fearfully pondered. But to remain in England seemed as perilous as to leave, for now the true faith was being relentlessly extinguished by the "Antichrist" in the Church of England. In her uncertainty God again revealed Himself, bringing her "a sure word that England should be destroyed." As for herself, He assured her that she need have no fear: "Though ... [you] should meet with affliction," the Voice told her, "yet I am the same God that delivered Daniel out of the lion's den, I will also deliver thee." [36] All doubt departed, and Mrs. Hutchinson concluded that her only course was to leave Alford and follow Mr. Cotton to New England. No argument or inducement would avail to alter her judgment. Nothing would suffice but that the large Hutchinson family sever its ancient ties with Lincolnshire and accompany their headstrong kinswoman to the distant shores of America that she might once again sit at Mr. Cotton's feet.

In the summer of 1633 the two Edwards, Anne's son, now a

36. Hutchinson, *History*, II, 384, 385; *Antinomianism*, 173, 174; Isaiah 30:20.

sturdy youth of twenty-one, and William's youngest brother, with his wife Sarah, sailed together for New England, presumably to prepare the way for the remainder of the family.[37] And in Alford, as summer waned to fall and winter, many Hutchinson hands busied themselves at the multitudinous tasks of preparation. There were clothes to be made and mended, stocks to be inventoried, deeds to be passed, and the uncertain contingencies of a whole new life to be curiously scrutinized and weighed. When at last spring returned Anne and William and their children left Alford for the last time and proceeded hopefully toward London across the fresh greenness of the Lincolnshire fen.

While awaiting embarkation the Hutchinsons remained at the home of Mr. William Bartholomew in London. This sojourn, however brief, allowed Mrs. Hutchinson ample time to air her theological fancies. In the excitement of the impending adventure Anne's spirit soared, and her tongue wagged incautiously. Mr. Bartholomew was doubtless impressed by the piety of this good woman who so earnestly informed him of her devotion to the renowned Mr. Cotton. The present expedition, he was apprised, was contrived solely that she might once again experience the ravishing joy of hearing Mr. Cotton preach.[38] But this scarcely had prepared him for what was to follow.

In the sticky heat of a London July, Anne and Mr. Bartholomew strolled together into the churchyard of St. Paul's Cathedral. Possibly she had been drawn there by the bookstalls clustered about the yard with the intent of seizing this last opportunity to purchase some theological books for spiritual comfort in the New World. Browsing through the tracts and sermons, her conversation turned to the Reverend Thomas Hooker. There is a man, Anne rashly ventured, whose spirit she did not like.[39] However, she had heard recently that in his farewell sermon he told his congregation of a startling revelation he had received from God. It seemed remarkable to her mind that so staunch a legalist as Mr. Hooker should profess to a revelation. Even more strange was the message it conveyed, which so strikingly confirmed her own persuasion. God had told Mr. Hooker that He "will destroy England and lay it wast, and that the people should be put to the sword, and the temples burnt, and many houses laid in ashes." Now was not this extraordinary!

37. *Colony Records*, I, 370; First Church of Boston, Records and Baptisms, 1630-1687, Mass. Hist. Soc.
38. Hutchinson, *History*, II, 385.
39. *Ibid.*, 385.

She was herself, Anne prattled on, "very inquisitive after revelations." Mr. Bartholomew's silence spurred her ahead. Indeed, "she had never had any great thing done about her but it was revealed to her beforehand." Observing her curiously, Mr. Bartholomew must have tried to fit this quaint irregularity into his artless comprehension of the Puritan faith. The effort no doubt failing, he kept his counsel, and they proceeded on their way.[40]

Toward the end of July 1634, the Hutchinsons and Bartholomews made their way to Thameside where the *Griffin* lay at her moorings, ready to set sail for New England.[41]

40. *Ibid.;* Mather, *Magnalia,* I, 310.
41. *Winthrop Papers,* III, 171.

VI

New England's Zion

Fall and Winter, 1634–1635

(i)

Boston was a town of troubles when Anne Hutchinson arrived there. And Boston's troubles but mirrored in small the growing pains which wracked the whole Bay Colony.

As the *Griffin* idled at anchorage in the Castle Island roadstead, Mrs. Hutchinson joined the throng of voyagers pressing against the high bulwark and with them gazed curiously across the fretfully lapping waters at the green and hilly town beyond. The broad inner harbor bristled with the masts and spars of vessels—Dutchmen, West Countrymen, Londoners—their sweaty crewmen laboring with noisy profanity to break out cargo from abroad or busily lading the pelts and pipestaves which the back country provided in such abundance. Now and again a cockleshell longboat or lighter would pull away from the mother ship and plough laboriously landward with its precious burden. As if impatiently reaching out to grasp these wares, Boston was thrust out into the harbor, not quite an island unto itself, yet a peninsula only by grace of the spare, tide-washed neck binding it tenuously to the mainland. Deferential to the carriers which were its only link to the old country, the town rudely turned its marshy back on the mainland beyond and fronted the broad harbor where its fortune lay. The lofty Trimountaine loomed heavily by the water's edge, cradling the town in its capacious lap. Nothing here to alarm the weary voyager. Green pastures, winding dusty roads, weathered cottages, their thatched tops refulgent in the later summer sunlight, betrayed no hint of the discontents that churned there, nor of factions forming, presently to seize on the traveler as a burning glass in which to focus their inquietude.

(ii)

The town that Anne Hutchinson now observed, though only four years old, was entering prematurely into its bumptious adolescence. Distinctive and enduring characteristics had already made their appearance. Nature had foreordained its woe and weal, stolen away the casual growth of pastoral youth, and untimely loaded on its back a thorny burden of metropolitan responsibilities. Blessed with an uncommonly snug and commodious harbor and ready access to the sea lanes of the North Atlantic, the town was destined to seize her fortune on the tide and breed a mettlesome race of mariners and merchants. But the force that wrought the splendid harbor had demanded equivalents. Wrested from the mainland and stripped of resources, Boston was isolated, ingrown, and barren, leaving its inhabitants more fuel for contention than for bodily warmth. Elbow room was lacking, room to thrash around in comfortably. Already men pressed eagerly against the town's watery limits, jealously conscious of their neighbor's holdings. Every lot was parceled out as guardedly as though it were the last.

The meandering streets of Boston conformed to the irregular topography of the peninsula. The Trimountaine, a three-topped range of hills thrust laterally athwart the center of the town, was the prime determinant of Boston's highway system. The High Street, main artery of the town, had with Puritan forthrightness taken its course due north from the Neck as though to bisect the peninsula equilaterally. Midway, the lofty Trimountaine loomed in its path, and the road veered northeast, then lurched crazily again to the northwest, following the shore line of the Great Cove. In consequence of this eccentric pattern Boston's streets and practically all of its approximately two hundred houses lay in the eastern sector of the town. Many dwellings were strung out the length of the High Street and its tributary lanes, but nearly half of them were concentrated in the quarter-mile square which lay between the Great Cove and the slope of Cotton Hill, easternmost of the Trimountaine range.[1]

1. "The Book of Possessions," Boston Registry Dept., *Records Relating to the Early History of Boston* (Record Commissioners of the City of Boston, *Second Report* [Boston, 1902]), 25, hereafter cited as "Boston Book of Possessions"; Nathaniel B. Shurtleff, *Topographical and Historical Description of Boston* (Boston, 1871), hereafter cited as Shurtleff, *Boston.*

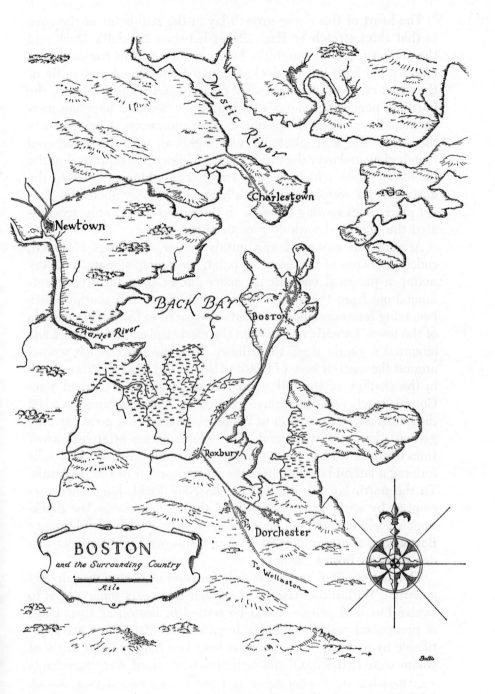

Mystic River

Charlestown

Newtown

BACK BAY

Boston

Charles River

Roxbury

Dorchester

To Wollaston

BOSTON
and the Surrounding Country

Mile

Battis

The heart of this dense growth lay at the mid-point of the cove in that short stretch of High Street between Bendall's Dock and the market place. Through the busy summer months the casks and crates piled high on the dock, the impatient squeal and rattle of the great crane as it querulously disburdened waiting vessels, the bustling, perspiring energy of laboring seamen and haggling merchants, all registered the pulsing beat of commerce. A few paces to the south the mud-plastered meetinghouse with its weathered thatch glowered over the market place in gloomy disapproval of the babble of trade which reigned there. The whine of saws in the dusty saw pit, roughhewn boards heaped carelessly about the market place, hogs rooting hungrily in the rutted streets only accentuated the urgent, disorderly growth of the town.[2]

Around this animated and untidy center, dwellings clustered, rudely innocent of ornament or paint, their long, sloping roofs denoting a practical concern for space rather than beauty. Streets fanned out from the market place, north, west, and south, houses becoming fewer and more comfortably spaced in the farther reaches of the town. Directly across from the market place the Prison Lane mounted a gentle slope to Sudbury End, the road which wound around the eastern base of Cotton Hill. At the head of Prison Lane in the shadow of the hill stood the home of the Reverend John Cotton, teacher of the church of Boston. Cotton's house marked the habitable western limit of the town; beyond that point lay only garden plots and wasteland. The Trimountaine stretched away from Cotton's yard to the Back Bay, a half-mile west, its three hills forming a lateral barrier across the western sector of the peninsula. To the north lay the gardens of the New Field, long since preempted by early arrivals. South of the Trimountaine lay Blackstone's Field and the common, both eagerly eyed by land-hungry Bostonians. Southernmost of all was Colburn's Field with its garden plots on Boston Neck.

The metropolitan and mercantile function of Boston was already apparent. Within the passage of another two years some eleven to twelve hundred people would be settled in Boston as their place of permanent residence. Three hundred and sixty-three are identifiable by name as adult males, at least two hundred and thirty of whom were married. Of the men about one-third were merchants

2. "Records of the Town of Boston, 1634-1660," Boston Registry Dept., *Records Relating to the Early History of Boston* (Record Commissioners of the City of Boston, *Second Report* [Boston, 1902], 10, 12, hereafter cited as "Boston Town Records, 1634-1660."

or craftsmen, most of them in the clothing or construction trades. Many of the rest were servants or laborers, performing a servile but essential function in a predominantly mercantile community.[3]

Only a short while before the Hutchinsons' arrival the townsfolk of Boston had made arrangements for the semi-annual election of selectmen to assume the responsibilities of municipal government.[4] As yet only freemen could have the vote in town affairs, and it was already established that only church members could become freemen.[5] The statistics of 1637 clearly indicate a trend that had developed from the outset. In that year 182 of Boston's adult males were church members, and of their number 160 had taken the freemen's oath and assumed the prerogatives of the franchise.[6] At least seventy-one of these freemen were ascertainably merchants or craftsmen, and doubtless a good many others might more tentatively be placed in that category.[7] The occupational structure and economic sentiments of the Bostonians were further indicated in those men who had been chosen for important public office. From 1634 through 1638 the town selectmen and deputies to the General Court were drawn from a small group of twenty-five men. Half of these men were merchants or members of closely allied professions. Ten men in particular were repeatedly chosen selectmen, holding that office for longer than one year, and of these at least six were merchants.[8] During the critical closing months of 1636 the freemen of Boston chose all three of their deputies and seven of the ten selectmen from the merchant class.[9] It was evident that the

3. Figures compiled from "Boston Town Records" and "Boston Book of Possessions" in *ibid.*; First Church of Boston, Records and Baptisms, 1630-1687, Mass. Hist. Soc.; Pope, *Pioneers of Massachusetts;* Charles Edward Banks, *Planters of the Commonwealth, 1620-1640* (Boston, 1930); James Savage, *A Genealogical Dictionary of the First Settlers of New England,* 4 vols. (Boston, 1860-62).

4. Samuel Drake, *The History and Antiquities of Boston* (Boston, 1857), 173.

5. *Colony Records,* I, 161.

6. *Ibid.,* 366-79; First Church of Boston, Records and Baptisms, 1630-1687, Mass. Hist. Soc.

7. "Boston Town Records, 1634-1660," 10, 12.

8. *Ibid.,* 1-38; Robert F. Seybolt, *The Town Officials of Colonial Boston* (Cambridge, 1939), 3-9. William Balston, William Brenton, John Coggeshall, William Hutchinson, Robert Harding, and John Sanford were merchants; Thomas Oliver was a surgeon; and the occupations of William Colburn, Thomas Leverett, and James Penne have not been determined.

9. Of the deputies, William Hutchinson, John Coggeshall, and William Brenton were merchants. Of the selectmen, William Hutchinson, Robert Keayne, John Newgate, John Coggeshall, John Sanford, and William Brenton were merchants. Thomas Oliver was a surgeon; William Balston was an innkeeper; and Thomas Leverett's occupation has not been determined. For a discerning discussion of the influence of merchants in the 1630's, see Bernard Bailyn, *The New England Merchants in the Seventeenth Century* (Cambridge, Mass., 1955), 16-44.

fortunes of the town were closely bound up with its mercantile endeavors and that any colonial policy which threatened those interests would encounter effectively concerted resistance.

(iii)

Indian summer lingered dry and hot through October.[10] In hay pasture and marsh field sweating men swung their scythes in plodding cadence, grimly intent on reaping every blade that Boston's niggardly soil would yield. Four years of New England had taught the colonists that the unseasonable heat of October was soon followed by November's biting winds and snow. Autumn in the Bay Colony was no time for pleasant dalliance.

For Anne and William Hutchinson these first weeks in Boston were occupied with the task of finding shelter. The town fathers had generously granted William a half-acre lot on the northwest corner of Sentry Lane and High Street. Not that it was so large—house lots were being apportioned in charily small parcels these days—but it was centrally located and surrounded by the homes of the "very best people" which suggest that the newcomers were held in considerable esteem.[11] Anne's sense of importance must have swelled as she stood on the site of her future home and surveyed her social prospects. Her next-door neighbors, up the narrow lane to Sentry Hill, were John and Mary Coggeshall, who had only recently moved into Boston from nearby Roxbury. A sober, responsible man of forty-three years, Coggeshall had already acquired a comfortable estate as a silk mercer and was now planning to diversify and expand his investments. His bearing and substance elicited such confidence that he had been promptly elevated to the substantial and variant dignities of deacon, town selectman, and deputy to the General Court. There was, nonetheless, despite his ecclesiastical appointment, some mistiness and irregularity in his doctrinal views which had prompted close examination by the clergy before he was admitted to the Boston church.[12] Whatever the present shadowy form of his heterodoxy, it was such as to render him susceptible to the theological importunities of his new

10. Winthrop, *Journal*, I, 137.
11. Thomas Lechford, *Notebook Kept by Thomas Lechford, Esq., Lawyer in Boston, Massachusetts Bay*, ed. Edward Everett Hale, Jr. (Cambridge, 1885), 317, hereafter cited as Lechford, *Notebook*.
12. Winthrop, *Journal*, I, 123.

neighbor, and in time to subject him to the influence of even more radical heresiarchs. But for the moment the determination of his views lay in the balance.

On the south side of the Sentry Lane stood the home of Atherton Hough, "gentleman," and his wife Elizabeth. A man of large estate and firm character, Hough was one of those bold disputants who had stood forth against the royal loan in '26. Late of old Boston where they had been members of John Cotton's congregation, Atherton and Elizabeth had faithfully followed that intransigent divine on his flight to the wilderness.

Facing about to the north, Anne would have confronted the newly established ordinary of Samuel Cole, Boston's first innkeeper.[13] A person of ample means, with a ready eye to the main chance, Cole was not above overcharging for his beer to line his purse and hopefully garnered what few additional farthings he might as "comfit-maker" to the self-denying people of Israel. However well or poorly his comfits may have sold, his wine and ale flowed freely enough to draw to the tap a spate of dubious and disorderly characters.[14] Albeit Mr. Cole was a church member of long standing, his ordinary would bear the close observance of law-abiding townsfolk.

Directly across the dusty and rutted High Street was the town spring. Fenced against the rooting and lapping of errant kine, it served as a vital communications center where housewives and servants gathered daily to draw water and gossip ample to their customary needs.

(iv)

South of this "spring gate" and diagonally opposite the Hutchinson property rose the commodious and austere dwelling of John Winthrop and his gentle wife, Margaret. A mainstay of the Puritan enterprise from its outset, Winthrop had been governor of the colony until unseated in a political upset only four months before the Hutchinsons' arrival. If ever a community can be said to have had its personification in a single individual, John Winthrop surely served that invidious function for the Massachusetts Bay Colony. During the formative years of the colony, its virtues and good intentions, its vices and shortcomings were as his. He was at once

13. "Boston Book of Possessions," 25; Lechford, *Notebook,* 51.
14. *Colony Records,* I, 155, 199, 208, 228; Pope, *Pioneers of Massachusetts,* 110.

its strength and also a considerable element of its weakness; its economic and intellectual vitality were in large part drawn from his blood and bone and so were its self-righteousness and bigotry. From 1629 to the day of his death twenty years later, Winthrop continued to play a dominant role in its government, and the twig was bent much as he inclined it.

It is tempting to speculate on that caprice which had impelled John Winthrop, alone of all the Puritan leaders, to confront his portraitist (and posterity) with a broad, open smile on his face.[15] That smile could hardly be described as infectious, or even altogether unself-conscious, but nonetheless, there it is, breaking all the rules of the game both by Puritan standards and those of the limner's craft. The finely arched brows raised in quizzical and strained amusement, the long, handsomely chiseled nose and heavy, pointed beard give him the air of a benign and waggish Svengali. Could such have been the image that this grave and humorless oligarch wished to have immortalized on canvas? Nowhere else is there a scrap of evidence to hint that he was given to robust merriment, or even to genteel levity. Time and again he passed through scenes of Rabelaisian drollery without a flicker of amusement, and barrelfuls of his public papers and private correspondence fail to betray any hint of wit or waggishness.[16]

John Winthrop was a complex individual and his motives are occasionally unfathomable. A tenderly devoted husband, a firm and affectionate father, a kindly and solicitous neighbor, he possessed in many respects a warm and magnanimous humanity. But he was a God-smitten man, and as he focused his soul on heaven, his lateral range of vision was narrowly contracted. Having suffered intolerable pangs before his own spiritual vocation was secure, he was possessed by a stern and self-righteous sense of dedication that would brook no impediment to the fulfillment of his dream of a new Zion.[17] He was not vindictive in the discharge of his duty, and he lacked the persecuting nature. One is occasionally horrified by the almost sadistic satisfaction some of his colleagues found in the pursuit of the unbeliever, but for Winthrop it was rather a stern, unpleasant obligation, which had been imposed on him by a just

15. See the frontispiece.
16. See p. 271 below.
17. "John Winthrop's Experiencia," *Winthrop Papers*, I, 154-60. For an excellent brief account of Winthrop, see Edmund S. Morgan, *The Puritan Dilemma, The Story of John Winthrop* (Boston, 1958).

God. When an enemy of the Puritan state had been defeated and removed, Winthrop was capable of magnanimity, and in some instances, of very warm and friendly feelings toward him.[18]

Winthrop, but lately squire of Groton Hall in Suffolk, was practiced in law and manorial administration and admirably qualified to assume the exacting demands of colonial governance. Brought up in the best traditions of the Tudor governing class and persuaded that God had bestowed on him a particular talent "for publick service," he was deeply conscious of the dignity and responsibility of his position.[19] He shared the inherited conviction of England's landed gentry that men were necessarily divided into the governors and the governed. In his lay sermon delivered to his fellow travelers while en route to New England, his sentiments on this score were lucidly set forth: "God Almighty in his most holy and wise providence hath soe disposed of the Condicione of mankinde, as in all times some must be rich some poore, some highe and eminent in power and dignities; others meane and in subieccion."[20] Firmly convinced that "the best part [of a community] was always the least, and of that best part the wiser part is always the lesser," he strongly distrusted democratic procedure and set himself against its introduction into Massachusetts.[21] The freemen of the Bay Colony, having entered into a covenant with God, had received from His hand powers of government, but in the interest of order and efficiency these were to be deputed by them to some properly qualified member of the community. Once a choice had been made the power to govern devolved entirely upon that person. "It is yourselves who have called us to this office," Winthrop reminded his constituents, "and being called by you we have our authority from God in way of an ordinance such as hath the image of God eminently stamped upon it." He made it clear that the liberty which men enjoyed was twofold. There was first that natural liberty which men held in common with beasts, "a liberty to do what he lists ... evil as well as good." But in His covenant God had dedicated the elect to lives guided by "federal or civil" liberty, a liberty which is "maintained and exercised in a way of subjection

18. See the continued correspondence with Roger Williams in *Winthrop Papers*, III.
19. "General Conclusions and Particular Considerations," *ibid.*, II, 126.
20. "A Modell of Christian Charity," *ibid.*, II, 282.
21. *Ibid.*, IV, 54.

to authority." [22] Resistance to duly constituted authority was universally regarded as the most heinous of all crimes. The Elizabethan forebears of the Puritans had looked upon rebellion as the "whole puddle and sink of sins against God and man," and in 1634 that conviction still persisted.[23]

Despite his insistence on the inherent superiority and prerogatives of the governing class, a vital aspect of Winthrop's political and social philosophy was his concern for the welfare of the "weaker sort." Although "the poore and despised [must not] rise upp against their superiors and shake off theire yoake," it seemed to him equally important "that the rich and mighty should not eat upp the poore." [24] The child of a medieval heritage and a manorial patrimony, Winthrop viewed the community as an organic whole wherein the fortunes of each were indissolubly bound up with the good of all: "A family is a little common wealth and a common wealth is a greate family." [25] His *Modell of Christian Charity* embodied a form of social organicism of which Aristotle or Aquinas would have well approved. "The care of the publique," he insisted, "must oversway all private respects . . . for it is a true rule that perticuler estates cannot subsist in the ruin of the publique." [26] As private citizen and as public official he strove conscientiously to support this dictum, giving unstintingly of his own estate and laboring to protect the interests of the "meaner sort" according to his best light.

At the outset the political structure of Massachusetts had been narrowly restrictive: a small and tightly closed oligarchy, headed by Winthrop, had effectively controlled all the channels of public power. Whenever the freemen clamored for additional powers, Winthrop had ceded them with the reluctance of a medieval baron surrendering his ancient prerogatives. Mounting resentment against Winthrop's administration came to a head in May 1634, when the freemen demanded a sight of the patent that they might know the full extent of their liberties. Realizing at last what had been withheld from them during the previous five years, they placed the whole system under review and proceeded to introduce sweeping reforms. So great was their indignation that in the ensuing election, despite John Cotton's imprecations on the rights of magis-

22. Winthrop, *Journal*, II, 238, 239.
23. Allen, *History of Political Thought in the Sixteenth Century*, 132.
24. *Winthrop Papers*, II, 282.
25. *Ibid.*, III, 424.
26. *Ibid.*, II, 293.

trates to tenure of office, Winthrop was overwhelmingly defeated and reduced to the status of an assistant "to admonish him thereby to look a little more circumspectly to himself." [27]

Although he had now been supplanted in the governor's chair by Thomas Dudley, Winthrop's solicitude for the welfare of the Bay Colony underwent no abatement, and his searching gaze continued to note each irregularity that might impede progress toward the perfection of the new Zion. Had Mrs. Hutchinson withdrawn to Salem or Ipswich her theological fancies might have escaped his notice for a longer time. But a whimsical providence had chosen to separate them only by the narrow, muddy width of the High Street; the sober guardian of orthodoxy on the one side, the curious and unsettled prober of divine intent on the other. Discovery and discord could not be long postponed.

(v)

Of course, William Hutchinson may not have commenced building his new house immediately. Very often newcomers, even among the wealthiest, had to content themselves with temporary quarters underground until the weather was propitious and workmen were available for construction. In such cases a cellar six or seven feet deep was excavated, lined with planking, partitioned, and roofed over, until, with the coming of spring, the superstructure could be erected over their heads or nearby. In August 1635, William had occasion to bring suit against a local bricklayer and three other laborers for charging excessive wages over periods ranging from six to thirty-six days.[28] This litigation suggests that the laborers had been engaged in the construction of the Hutchinson house. Pending its completion the family may have been quartered elsewhere —underground or sojourning with friends and neighbors.

Whatever the circumstances of its erection, the completed Hutchinson dwelling must have been a large one to accommodate so great a family. It was William's unenviable obligation to provide domicile for at least fourteen and possibly as many as nineteen people. In addition to himself and Anne, there were in the immediate family, Edward, twenty-two; Richard, who was nineteen; Faith and Bridget, now seventeen and fifteen; and Francis, an outspoken lad of fourteen. Sammy was ten, little Anne was eight; Mary was

27. Israel Stoughton to Dr. John Stoughton, 1635, Mass. Hist. Soc., *Proceedings*, 58 (1925), 458, 456.
28. *Colony Records*, I, 153.

six; and last came the small children, Katherine, William, and Susanna, who were four, three, and one, respectively.[29] The adults in the group seem to have also included Anne's sister Katherine Marbury, a spirited maid of twenty-four, and two spinster cousins of William, Anne and Frances Freiston, who were of his generation, perhaps in their middle forties.[30] There were two men servants: John Hord, a tailor, and Edward Dennis, who may have dwelt with the family at this time. The Hutchinson household appears to have had no maid servants; with so many able-bodied people on hand, such an addition may have seemed superfluous.

The house was doubtless similar to its neighbors in most essential respects: a large two-story wooden frame dwelling centered about a huge brick chimney from which fireplaces opened onto the larger rooms. The "foreroom" or parlor, with its low, brown-timbered ceiling, bare, whitewashed walls, and well-scrubbed floor, must have been spacious to accommodate the sixty to eighty persons who came to meet there in later days. A long table with stools or benches probably occupied the center of the room; in a conspicuous position would be the great chair where Mrs. Hutchinson held state, and in a corner the "best bed," hung about with curtains and valance.[31] Behind the parlor lay the kitchen, the cavernous maw of its blazing fireplace flanked with a profusion of pots and kettles. Elsewhere on the ground floor there was probably a side room or lean-to addition in which William kept his shop and wares, such being generally the custom among merchants of that time and place. In the yard a well-kept kitchen garden and small orchard would have filled some of the needs of their table, and beyond lay stables and sheds for the horses, cows, and pigs.[32]

(vi)

Scarcely were they settled before the family plunged into the buzzing life of the community. By the end of December all the adult members of the household, as well as Richard, Faith, Bridget, and Francis, still in their teens, had become members of the church

29. Champlin, "Hutchinson Ancestry and Descendants," *N.Y. Geneal. and Biog. Record*, 45 (1914), 167-68.

30. *Ibid.*, 165; entries of Nov. 9 and Dec. 28, 1634, First Church of Boston, Records and Baptisms, 1630-1687, Mass. Hist. Soc.

31. George Francis Dow, *Every Day Life in the Massachusetts Bay Colony* (Boston, 1935), 39 ff.

32. Lechford, *Notebook*, 156.

of Boston.[33] At the General Court of the following March—no earlier opportunity having presented itself—the freeman's oath was administered to William senior, Richard, and young Francis, and all were formally admitted to the privileges and immunities of the Company of the Massachusetts Bay. Francis Hutchinson, then only a boy of fifteen, was surely one of the youngest freemen in the colony. How he so prematurely attained this prerogative remains a puzzle, but being a youth of bold and contentious spirit—a chip off the old Marbury block—he may have made a reckless bid for the honor and, to the surprise of all, have not been denied. Edward, his more sober eldest brother, having preceded the family to Massachusetts by more than a year, had been admitted to church and freemanship in the summer before their arrival.[34]

However self-effacing and complaisant William Hutchinson may have appeared, the people of Boston soon recognized his worth. Two months after taking the oath, he was elected by his neighbors as their deputy to the General Court, and from that day forth his public life was continuously full. For a year and a half, he served as deputy, being further commissioned by the Court as appraiser and magistrate to settle small cases in the particular courts. In the spring of 1636 the freemen of Boston chose him as one of their selectmen, in which office he served four half-year terms.[35]

Meanwhile William's financial affairs also demanded his attention. The designation "Mr." was by no means exclusively an economic symbol, but most men so designated were affluent, and in Boston Mr. Hutchinson was looked upon as one of "the richer sort." William could count on Edward and Richard to manage the shop capably—both were skilled mercers. He needed the extra time to manage his new interests; a town meeting had awarded him a six-hundred-acre farm at Braintree, a property which soon came to be valued at approximately £400, and the General Court had granted him the possession of Taylor's Island in Boston Harbor.[36] The possibility of swelling his income by the sale of farm commodities or from rentals must have appealed to William, for he also purchased from Bray Rossiter about fifty acres of land in Dorches-

33. Entries of Nov. 2, 9, and Dec. 28, 1634, First Church of Boston, Records and Baptisms, 1630-1687, Mass. Hist. Soc.
34. *Colony Records*, I, 168, 170.
35. *Ibid.*, 145, 156, 175; "Boston Town Records, 1634-1660," 9-20.
36. "Boston Town Records, 1634-1660," 7, 8, 14, 19, 160; Lechford, *Notebook*, 69 ff., 101, 156, 317-18, 385, 390; *Colony Records*, I, 149.

ter, including tillage, pasture, and wood lots with two farmhouses.[37] But his shrewdest investment never paid off. Along with thirteen other Bostonians, William invested a small amount—perhaps little more than £12—in Bendall's Dock. The most frequented, if not the only, large docking facility in town, strategically located in the center of the Great Cove and equipped with a warehouse and crane, it was managed by Edward Bendall, an exceedingly clever and resourceful water dog. From a strictly economic viewpoint it was unfortunate that occurrences of a more spiritual nature interceded to bring about the dissolution of this little combination, and the whole promising enterprise was bought out for a mere £170.[38]

Wealth has its obligations as well as its rewards, and it was expected that those of "greater abilities" would contribute generously to worthy causes that lacked legislative support. By this means William came to be one of the first benefactors of the Boston Latin School and was further induced to lend £5 toward the building of the new fortification on Fort Hill. Although the latter donation was substantially the larger of the two, it should be observed that William, if not an enthusiastic champion of popular education, was essentially a man of peace, and what was more to the point, he knew the difference between a gift and a loan. There is, however, no record that the debt was ever repaid.

(vii)

The Hutchinsons' first winter in Boston was bitterly severe, the worst the colony had yet suffered. In November and December violent northeast tempests lashed at the shore, blanketing the town under a heavy mantle of snow from which there was no release before spring.[39] The harbor froze over repeatedly, gripping vessels at their moorings, preventing the passage of small boats, and imprisoning unwary venturers on the barren offshore islands. Those who dared to go afoot over the frozen harbor to Winissimet or Pullen Point were lucky if they received no more than an icy bath for their pains. A serious shortage of firewood was maddeningly aggravated by wasteful cutting in the small wood lots on Boston Neck.[40] Suffering these afflictions the common folk of Boston threatened to match the season's asperity with their own.

37. Lechford, *Notebook*, 157.
38. *Ibid.*, 69-74; Winthrop, *Journal*, II, 67-68.
39. Winthrop, *Journal*, I, 141, 143, 146; *Winthrop Papers*, III, 176, 177.
40. "Boston Town Records, 1634-1660," 4.

One Thursday evening in December William returned from town meeting to report that a minor revolution seemed to be at hand. The townsmen, chafing under their shortages, had refused to elect any of the "richer sort" to the land allotment commission. Although Boston was becoming a merchandising center, its inhabitants were still largely dependent upon their own agricultural output for subsistence. The scant thousand acres of the peninsula, much of it rugged and hilly, were scarcely adequate to the planting and grazing needs of the Bostonians. The land shortage had become a point of bitter controversy and a basis of class division. Tension had mounted earlier in the year, when the town acquired title to William Blackstone's extensive holdings south of the Trimountaine. John Winthrop and William Coddington hoped to reserve this land for the use of future inhabitants, and they also proposed to maintain a considerable portion as public common. Winthrop expressed fears that an overly generous distribution of land would aggravate the serious labor shortage by diverting workers into agricultural pursuits, and possibly Coddington and the merchant class hoped to prevent a development which would create new pressure to raise wages.[41]

At the town meeting on December 11 a majority of the freemen, "fearing that the richer men would give the poorer sort no great proportion," took advantage of the secret ballot to elect a land commission that would presumably be more sensitive to their interests. They chose an elder and a deacon (probably Oliver and Colburn) "and the rest of the inferior sort." [42] Coddington and the "chief men were left out" altogether and Winthrop was elected by so narrow a margin that he rose angrily before the meeting and refused to serve on the commission. At this point Mr. Cotton, who was of the conviction that "men of eminent quality and descent should enjoy more large and honorable accomodation," prompted the electorate to reconsider their action.[43] Apparently he persuaded the town meeting to accept his viewpoint, for they soon thereafter elected a new land commission which included Winthrop, Coddington, Bellingham, and Cotton himself.

In due course this reconstituted commission proceeded to allot

41. Winthrop, *Journal*, I, 143-44.
42. *Ibid.*, 143.
43. John Cotton, "An Abstract of the Lawes of New England," in Peter Force, ed., *Tracts and Other Papers Relating Principally to the Colonies in North America* (Washington, 1836-46, reprinted New York, 1947), III, No. 9, 147.

lands just as the commoners had feared they would. Colburn, Cotton, and Oliver, all members of the land commission, appropriated for themselves territories ranging from 100 to 250 acres; Winthrop, Bellingham, and Coddington had hitherto acquired even more expansive demesnes. But of the fifty-eight allotments made at Muddy River during this period, forty-two were only 20 acres or smaller.[44] A similar pattern was concurrently employed in the allocation of lands at Pullen Point and Rumney Marsh, where enormous tracts were dispensed to men who were among the twenty-five highest Boston officeholders.[45] The land policy seemed calculated to establish a class system on economic lines that would entrench the governing class in power.

A year later the selectmen took further steps to secure the position of the large property owners by preventing the unregenerate from acquiring property. An order was passed stating that land should be granted by the town only to those newcomers who were likely to become members of the church. At the same time it was decreed that present owners must not sell their houses or allotments to newcomers without municipal authorization.[46]

But now, in the winter of 1634, land was not the only commodity in short supply. From the outset there had been a pressing shortage of timber. The peninsula had been relatively bare of forest before the Puritans had arrived and by the fourth year of their habitation the shortage was acutely felt. With its rapidly expanding population lumber was urgently needed for housing. During the summer when immigration swelled and new construction took place, timber could be hauled from the mainland or sailed in from the harbor

44. "Boston Town Records, 1634-1660," 22-27, Muddy River allotments. Twenty-one men received 8 to 10 acres: Arratt, Beck, Biggs, Bourne, Brown, Courser, Davis, Denning, Elkin, Harker, Ines, Jackson, Johnson, Ormesby, Pemberton, Purton, Reade, Salter, Snow, Townsend, Turner, and Wilson; seventeen received 12 to 20 acres: Bates, Beamsley, Blacksone, Bulgar, Burchall, Cramme, Cranwell, Fitch, Heaton, Houlton, Mears, Mylam, Route, Scottow, Talmadge, Titus, Ward, Wardall, Walker, and Winchester; ten received 23 to 35 acres: Bendall, Bushnall, Dinely, Fairbank, Griggs, Pell, Pormont, Reynolds, Tappan, Woodward; two received 50 to 80 acres (Grosse, *Underhill); two received 115 acres (*Leverett, *Oliver); one received 160 acres (*Colburn); and one received 250 acres (Cotton). Asterisks indicate high officeholders.

45. *Ibid.*, 27-30, Rumney Marsh and Pullen Point allotments. One man received an unknown amount (Buttolph); one received 14 acres (Bates); twelve received 28 to 50 acres: Dyer, Faireweather, Gallopp, Gillam, Glover, Hudson, Matson, Maverick, J. Oliver, *Penne, Stidson, and Willys; nine received 60 to 112 acres: Cole, *Gibbons, *Harding, Hill, Marshall, *Newgate, Odlin, Pierce, and *Sanford; and eight received 161 to 314 acres: *Aspinwall, *Brenton, *Cogan, *Coggeshall, *Keayne, Tuttle, *Vane, and *Winthrop. Asterisks indicate high officeholders.

46. *Ibid.*, 5.

islands.[47] More difficult was the problem of satisfying the demand for fuel, particularly during the harsh and long New England winters. So desperate did their plight at last become that in the winter of 1637 Winthrop despairingly observed that Boston was nearly ready to break up for want of fuel.[48] There seemed also to be a chronic and irritating shortage of hay for winter fodder. Large quantities were required to supply all the livestock brought in from neighboring pastureland to winter in the barns of town, and the problem of transporting and storing sufficient quantities of the stuff must have been overwhelming.[49]

(viii)

Affairs in the colony at large were no less confused and embittered than those in Boston and at some points bore closely on the passage of events within the metropolis. During the early years of settlement the social and political structure of the colony had been largely determined by the purposes and philosophy of the original patentees. Although their exodus was partially motivated by economic exigencies, as they were frank to admit, their primary aim had been to establish a refuge for those of the Puritan persuasion.[50] To this end, they had arranged, contrary to precedent, to convey their whole government—charter and General Court—to the colony, remote from English authority. From the outset a small and tightly knit elite comprised of landed gentry, affluent merchants, and Puritan clergymen had arrogated the right to function as stewards for the community. They were now intent on maintaining independence from the mother country and political ascendancy over their own settlers so that the Puritan creed could be perpetuated with a minimum of interference.

Between and within these several groups conflict prevailed in what might be described as a pyramidal pattern. At the base were controversies between the Puritan elect and various elements of the unregenerate: royal and ecclesiastical authorities and rival claimants in England who sought to curtail the colony's prerogatives, or settlers within the colony who threatened Puritan control by overt challenge or by mere force of numbers. Midway in this

47. William Wood, *New England's Prospect*, quoted in Shurtleff, *Boston*, 41.
48. John Winthrop to John Winthrop, Jr., Jan. 22, 1637/8, *Winthrop Papers*, IV, 10.
49. Shurtleff, *Boston*, 41.
50. *Winthrop Papers*, II, 123.

pyramidal pattern a struggle persisted between the Puritan elite and the remainder of the freemen to determine who should attain political dominance within the colony. At the highest level there were conflicts within the governing elite itself, notably to determine the manner in which their power should be exercised.

The problem of the colony's political relationship with the mother country was most pressing. Indeed, by 1634, so exposed was their position that many domestic controversies were scrutinized and determined with reference to their impact on this relationship. The difficulty lay in the uncertain status of the patent granted to the Massachusetts Bay Company. In 1630, through the employment of rather dubious means, the patentees had succeeded in transferring their charter and company from Old to New England. When it was discovered that their patent conflicted with earlier grants made to John Mason and Sir Ferdinando Gorges, these men pressed claims against the Bay Company. Their cause was greatly advanced by the appointment of Archbishop Laud as head of the newly created Lords Commissioners of Plantations in General. Word reached Boston that the primary purpose of this commission was to introduce orthodox Anglicanism into Massachusetts and to bring the colony securely under royal control.[51] In January magistrates and ministers consulted earnestly to determine what course they should follow to avert the present danger. It was decided to "avoid and protract" as long as possible, and to employ all means at their command to convince English authorities of their loyalty to the Crown and their competence to maintain an orderly government. If all else failed they were determined not to accept a royal governor but "to defend [their] lawful possessions." Funds were raised and labor impressed for the erection of fortifications at the entrance to Boston Harbor.[52] But despite these warlike preparations the Puritans hoped to allay complaints against their government and avert interference by the Crown.

The threat to their charter raised afresh the troubled question of the Puritans' affinity to the Church of England. From the outset and for many years thereafter, despite all appearances to the contrary, the Puritans were adamant in their protestations of loyalty to the Anglican church, and they repeatedly denied the charge of separation from that body. At the hour of departure

51. Winthrop, *Journal*, I, 135.
52. *Ibid.*, 145, 134-35.

from England the leaders of the company had joined in a declaration which concluded: "[We] esteeme it our honour, to call the Church of England from whence we rise, our dear Mother, and cannot part from . . . [her] without much sadnesse of heart. . . . We leave it not . . . as loathing that milk wherewith we were nourished there, but blessing God for the parentage and education." [53]

John Cotton was less politic but equally firm in disclaiming separation. "Neither was our departure from them in those evill times, a Separation from them as no Churches, but rather a Secession from the corruptions found among them." [54] If the Puritans were to assert their policy of uniformity with any degree of consistency, it was essential that they maintain at least the outward show of loyalty to the church of their origin. It would further seem that if they were not Separatists, but loyal to the Church of England as they claimed, they were called upon to put down any attempts at separation which occurred in their midst.

But now a tempest whipped up out of Salem and threatened to scatter charter rights, anti-separatist claims, and all. Roger Williams, the new minister of Salem, was usually a gentle man in his personal relations, but he rode his convictions with a fierce temerity. Had he but remained settled in his beliefs an accommodation might have been reached, but he had a distressing way of peeling them off layer by layer, like the skins of an onion, to the discovery of progressively more alarming conclusions. He not only argued for separation and the independency of all churches but even denounced the Church of England as anti-Christian. What was worse, he rashly attacked the King's title to American soil and denounced the patents His Majesty had granted. And now he had altogether outdone himself by inciting Captain John Endicott of Salem, whose impulsiveness was legend, to mutilate the King's ensign on the supposition that the cross it bore was a popish symbol. There was no knowing what might ensue when word of this iconoclastic outrage drifted back to England.

Then the fulminations of Israel Stoughton brought attack from another quarter. The strenuously independent deputy from Dorchester pressed the cause of commonalty by challenging the primacy of governor and magistrates and denying their right to a veto power.[55]

53. *Winthrop Papers*, II, 234.
54. John Cotton, *Way of the Congregational Churches Cleared*, 14.
55. Winthrop, *Journal*, I, 137, 141, 142, 147.

Under these assaults the hardy oligarchs of Massachusetts did not so much as blanch. The peppery Endicott was severely admonished and disabled from holding office for a full year, and for Stoughton the same penalty was trebled. Roger Williams was haled to Boston to be queried, confuted, and chided by the ministers for the agglomeration of erroneous tenets he had spread on the wind.

But when, amidst these contentions, Mr. Hooker's Newtown congregation resolved to depart for the quieter pastures of the Connecticut valley, the Masters of the Bay sagged under the strain. The exodus of so goodly a company, it was feared, would take off much credit from the colony. "The removing of a candlestick is a great judgement which is to be avoid[ed]," Winthrop solemnly observed.[56]

And so, through the bitter winter domestic squabbles rose and were hastily suppressed or allayed, and rumors, requests, and warnings continued to flow from England. If the Puritans were to forestall royal interference and assure the future of their wilderness Zion, it behooved them to put their house in order and keep it so.

56. *Ibid.*, 132-33.

VII

"A Prophetesse Raised Up of God"

Spring and Summer, 1635

(i)

ANNE HUTCHINSON listened with thoughtful interest as William explained to her the precarious position in which the colony stood and the precautions which must be taken in order to secure their charter. William had already been drawn into the centers of authority, apprised of their problems and charged with significant responsibilities, so to him these were matters of deep concern. But Anne's world was a woman's world, not oblivious to the larger sphere, but in itself more compact and immediate, essentially concerned with primary needs and primary associations. Whatever might befall the charter or the King's colors, these matters could not intrude upon her obligation to establish her household—a task presently encumbered with unusual difficulties.

Not only had the Hutchinsons' late-season arrival left them without crops of corn and hay for the winter months, but the problem of clothing a large family against the rigors of New England winter was inexorable. Nonetheless, Anne found time to make the acquaintance of a broad circle of neighbors and place her nursing skills at their disposal. When the chests and trunks brought from England were at last unpacked and their contents laid out for use, Anne would have had special concern for the neatly wrapped and labeled packets of medicinal herbs and roots she had long gathered and learned so skillfully to apply. Tansy and catnip, pennyroyal, sage, and spearmint, suffusing their fragrant aroma throughout the room, summoned up recollections of the pleasure found in helping the sick—the heartwarming awareness of acceptance and approval and the sense of achievement and authority gained in sure knowledge of one's own competence.

In this new sphere there was ample scope for her solicitude and practice: subjected to extremes of weather, the hazards of the frontier, and an exuberant procreative urge, the people of Boston suffered a pressing need for whatever medical assistance they could find. In 1634 there were only three other practitioners on hand. The most highly respected of this group was Thomas Oliver, "a right godly man and elder of the church," who was "by his outward profession a chirurgeon." [1] Mr. Oliver, who had come early to the colony from Bristol in Gloucestershire, lived across the street from Mrs. Hutchinson on the north side of the Spring Gate. One of those of "greater abilities," he was a town selectman and land commissioner and played an influential role in local affairs.[2] Somewhat lower in social status, but nonetheless dedicated to his calling, William Dinely was a barber-surgeon, equally adept at pulling teeth, applying leeches, and trimming hair. A man of good report, Dinely was also a neighbor to Mrs. Hutchinson, having his home diagonally behind hers at the head of Prison Lane.[3] But the most colorful member of the local medical profession was Jane Hawkins, the midwife, "a poor silly woman" whose eccentric manner prompted rumors that she bore some familiarity with the devil.[4] Having been rejected for church membership, Goody Hawkins was pathetically eager to be accepted, and she unwisely ventured beyond her competence into the practice of "phisick," which, in her hands, combined large elements of quackery and faith healing. It was to her house that barren and credulous young wives of Boston secretly resorted, hopeful that her potions of mandrake oil might enable them to conceive and bear.[5]

To the charitable endeavors of this incongruous trio, Mrs. Hutchinson now added the commodity of her knowledge. In short time her neighborly solicitude had won her the affection and gratitude of a large part of the community. At the firesides and by the sickbeds of the women of Boston, she was on hand with com-

1. For Oliver's occupation, see Winthrop, *Journal*, I, 97; and the entry in John Hull's diary cited by W. H. Whitmore, "The Oliver Family," *New England Historical and Genealogical Register*, 19 (1865), 100.
2. "Boston Town Records, 1634-1660," 1-20.
3. *Ibid.*, 16, 24.
4. Wheelwright, *Writings*, 197.
5. Winthrop, *Journal*, I, 268; Cotton, *Way of the Congregational Churches Cleared*, 91.

fort and assistance whenever she was needed. Elizabeth Wardall, her old neighbor from Alford, would doubtless have been one of the first to know of Anne's skills and to solicit her aid when she was brought to bed of a son in early November. And perhaps, in January, Anne tramped across the snow covered backlot to assist at the delivery of Goody Brackett, the jailer's wife.[6] So, through the winter and into spring and summer there were babies aplenty and sickness besides, drawing Anne forth on her errands of mercy. Doors opened wide to her and her circle of warm friends and admirers expanded. The townsfolk were pleased to welcome her not only for her usefulness to the invalid or expectant mother but for her friendly concern about their spiritual welfare. Puttering industriously about neighbor kitchens or sitting by the patient's bedside, she inquired gravely into their soul's estate. The young wife confronting the uncertain perils of childbirth, the aged grandam measuring out her last days, were solemnly invoked to cast up their souls' accounts, to look into their hearts and find whether they had truly felt their everlasting need for Christ or attained any saving union with Him.

To her dismay Anne found that many of those she befriended—perhaps most of them—had long been trusting to their works as evidence of salvation. They professed that their souls had felt guilt and seen the desert of sin, and it was by dint of this knowledge that they had been impelled to pursue a Christian course. Mrs. Hutchinson was disturbed to find so many good women lying under a spirit of bondage. Gravely and patiently she would point out to the invalid in her charge that she was sadly enmeshed in a legal work which held out no hope of salvation. That little light it provided might, for a season, restrain from evil and constrain to the performance of known duties; it might even offer some "tastes and flashes" of spiritual comfort, but without the Lord Jesus Christ all gifts and graces would in the end "wizzen and vanish."[7] Without a sure sense of justification—an immediate witness of the Spirit—all our sanctification is no more than dust and ashes.

When at last the street door quietly closed after Mrs. Hutchinson, it was to leave behind a thoughtful, troubled woman, weigh-

6. "Boston Births, Baptisms, Marriages and Deaths," Boston Registry Dept., *Records Relating to the Early History of Boston* (Record Commissioners of the City of Boston, *Ninth Report* [1883]), 3, hereafter cited as "Boston Births, Baptisms, Marriages and Deaths."
7. Cotton, *Way of the Congregational Churches Cleared*, 51.

ing heavily the import of her words. The familiar world lurched and hung insecurely in the void as she groped uncertainly to find her bearing. By flickering candlelight the conversation was recounted to her husband, and point by point husband and wife probed and measured Mrs. Hutchinson's monitions, held them up against the known light of Gospel, weighed them against the familiar teachings of Mr. Cotton. At last, weary but exultant, they may have concluded that the three were as one, and thanked God that this good woman, their neighbor, had such light to bestow on them. And so, many good women were brought off from building their estate upon their own efforts, and by them their husbands too were invoked to re-examine the quality of their foundations and to come to realize how unsound were their expectations. By these means the word traveled from house to house, and these "private conferences did well tend to water the seeds publikely sowen." [8]

(ii)

Meanwhile, Anne went as usual about her daily tasks. With the coming of mild weather hearthfires were quenched in all but the great kitchen chimney, heavy overgarments were laid away for a season and one could venture more comfortably out of doors. Anne's household routines might now be pleasantly enlivened by the short walk, bucket in hand, to the Spring Gate. Crossing the street she could look down the Spring Lane between the rows of houses and out over the harbor where the earliest vessels from abroad soared with queenly dignity past Governor's Island. At the spring scraps of gossip were exchanged among neighbors, and Anne could pass on bits of information gathered from William, who had just assumed his seat on the General Court. It was common knowledge that the Court, proceeding as if by trial and error, had set aside Mr. Dudley and elected Mr. John Hayne to the governor's chair. In consideration of the heavy load of taxes which burdened the colony, Mr. Hayne's first gubernatorial act had been to forego the stipend of his office.[9] The expressions of gratitude at the Spring Gate may have been dampened by a wry observation that this was the least a man of his wealth might offer. Mary Coggeshall's new baby doubtless received its share of appreciative comment. Anne could speak for the skill with which Goody

8. *Ibid.*
9. Winthrop, *Journal*, I, 150.

Hawkins had administered the delivery, and perhaps breathed a hope that Mary now had a clearer view of her spiritual estate.[10]

As spring ripened to summer Anne herself became pregnant. It would not be easy this time; she was no longer a young woman. Now she was forty-four and the child forming within her would be her fifteenth in twenty-three years of marriage. Her experience in motherhood and the strength and resiliency of her body would help greatly and might somewhat allay her fears. But her heart stirred restlessly with inarticulate wants and drove her on to more strenuous trials of self-discovery and self-affirmation.

(iii)

On Sundays and Thursdays Anne scrubbed and combed her children and prepared to lead them to divine service. Just before the appointed hour, as young Arthur Perry marched jauntily up the High Street banging the drum that hung at his side, the houses of Boston disgorged their occupants in wonderful profusion.[11] Down lanes and paths townsfolk poured, singly, by couples and by clans, in compliant response to the noisly imperative summons, converging at last on the crude meetinghouse by the market place. So twice on Sunday and once on Thursday lecture day, the whole people of Boston, with a unanimity of action which hinted of coercion, attended the only devotional exercise authorized or permitted by the state.[12]

The meetinghouse stood on that short side street which marked the southern bound of the market place. A square, squat building, it was probably fairly large to have accommodated the thousand or more inhabitants of Boston in addition to numerous and frequent visitors and transients.[13] Mud-wattled exterior and thatched roof bespoke the urgent haste with which the Saints had sought to make adequate provision for their spiritual needs during the hectic early months of settlement. Gloomy without, severe and darkly illumined within, it was doubtless furnished with austere economy: row upon forbidding row of backless benches as hard

10. "Boston Births, Baptisms, Marriages and Deaths," 3.
11. "Boston Town Records, 1634-1660," 36; Johnson, *Wonder Working Providence*, 135.
12. *Colony Records*, I, 140.
13. Evarts B. Greene and Virginia Harrington, *American Population Before the Federal Census of 1790* (New York, 1932), 13; Carl Bridenbaugh, *Cities in the Wilderness* (New York, 1938), 6.

as death and God's retributive justice; at the front, opposite the entry, steps leading to a raised pulpit against the wall, a plain communion table below it, flanked on either side by seats to accommodate magistrates and deacons.[14] Over all a network of hand-hewn beams and rafters soared splendidly aloft to the pointed peak of the roof, providing a tentative and much needed note of grandeur. The temperature of this barnlike structure was entrusted to the regulation of Him for whose worship it had been constructed; chasteningly frigid throughout the winter, and during the summer parched with a heat appropriately reminiscent of that place they must soon come to but for His divine grace.[15]

Families entering the meetinghouse separated at the door, women to find their comfortless seats on one side and men on the other, all assuming place according to their status in the community. Brentons, Coggeshalls, and Hutchinsons well down front; Talmadges, Wilburs, and others of the middling sort perhaps comfortably midway, while those of "meane condition, and weake parts" craned their necks and strained their hearing from the rear of the hall.[16] Up front, by the pulpit, isolated in magisterial dignity, the Assistants, Winthrop, Coddington, and Bellingham, surveyed the solemn scene, while opposite them on the deacons' bench, sat Elders Leverett and Oliver along with sundry deacons. Above them all hovered the plump presiding genius of Master John Cotton, minister to the church of Boston.

Shortly after his arrival, a year and half before, Mr. Cotton had been ordained as teacher of the Boston Saints. Although John Wilson had been pastor of the Boston church since its founding, the community had grown sufficiently to require the services of two clergymen. Such an arrangement was customary among the larger Puritan congregations; a pastor "to attend by exhortation, and therein to dispense a word of wisdom," and a teacher "to attend unto doctrine, and therein to attend unto a word of knowledge." [17]

Cotton was warmly received in Boston and his teaching exercised a powerful effect on the community. Church membership

14. Winthrop, *Journal*, I, 219.
15. Dow, *Every Day Life in Massachusetts Bay Colony*, 227 ff.; Ola Winslow, *Meeting House Hill* (New York, 1954), 56-57; Sumner Powell, "Seventeenth Century Sudbury, Mass.," *Journal of the Society of Architectural Historians* 11 (1952), 3-15.
16. *Antinomianism*, 157.
17. Quoted from John Cotton in Babette May Levy, *Preaching in the First Half-Century of New England History* (Hartford, 1945), 6.

during the previous three years had remained virtually static. Then
suddenly, with Cotton's coming, many inhabitants professed conversion and sought admission to the church. Twenty-five were
accepted during a two-month period, and Cotton's first year as
teacher saw the admission of 117 new members, nearly doubling
the roster of the faithful. For the next two years membership
growth continued but at a rate more nearly proportionate to the
population increment of the period.[18] It seemed to John Winthrop
that it had "pleased the Lord to give special testimony of his
presence in the church of Boston, after Mr. Cotton was called to
office there." [19]

At the conclusion of Cotton's first year in the pulpit, and only a
few weeks after Mrs. Hutchinson's arrival, John Wilson took leave
of his congregation and returned to England to settle some family
affairs. For twelve months Mr. Cotton held forth in the pulpit
without rival, his misty statement of an already ambiguous doctrine
circulating throughout the community without check or qualifica-
tion. For twelve months Anne Hutchinson could luxuriate in the
rich discourse, soar heavenward on the winged words. Her cup,
it seemed, was full and running over.

Nor was this all. Since that distant day in England when Mr.
Cotton's illness had left her without spiritual guidance, her prayers
had not gone unheeded. Now even greater rewards seemed to flow
from the long hours of silent meditation when, with head bowed
over the worn Bible, she mused reverently on its profound enigmas.
It was then, she felt, that the presence of the Lord dwelt most
closely with her and gave her the light with which to comprehend
His word.

Mrs. Hutchinson's meditations may have strengthened her soul,
but they seem also—for the moment at least—to have marred her
reputation. In her indefatigable round of spiritual exercises, Anne
appears to have overlooked one observance held dear by her
fellow parishioners—the neighborhood prayer meeting. Indeed,
the more actively Anne pursued her nursing and missionary activities, the more conspicuous was her absence from these gatherings. Soon she became a target for local gossip. Some of her neighbors advanced the suspicion that she held such meetings unlawful
and without scriptural authority. Others rejoined that she was
too proud. Knowing Scripture as well as the teacher, how could

18. First Church of Boston, Records and Baptisms, 1630-1687, Mass. Hist. Soc.
19. Winthrop, *Journal*, I, 116.

she be expected to play so passive a role as these meetings required. So the rumors traveled until one of Anne's friends came to report the unfriendly talk.[20]

It may have been at about this time that Mr. Cotton came to visit her. He wished, he said, to deal with her quite candidly about her spiritual condition. He had heard of her work and was pleased that she had kept so many from building their spiritual estate upon their own duties. But he professed himself puzzled and dismayed that her faith seemed to have its source and strength, not from the public ministry, but only from her own private meditations. Although she had admitted the need for sanctification, he went on, she seemed scarcely able to discern it in herself. Her justification, however, she quite clearly discerned, and as freely announced. And last, did it not seem that she was perhaps "more sharply censorious of other mens spirituall estates and hearts, th[a]n the servants of God are wont to be?" Was it not better that God's children should be more concerned with judging themselves than others? [21]

Anne was disturbed by what she heard and resolved to take what steps she could to allay the rumors of the neighbors and the apprehensions of Mr. Cotton. But those who had thought that she was too proud may have been more nearly right than they could have suspected. It was not in Anne Hutchinson's nature to follow where she felt sufficiently sure of herself to lead.

(iv)

Anne's prodigious memory and keen mind were more than adequate to the task she now set herself. Had her judgment been equally sound she would have confined herself to the innocuous set pattern of the local prayer meetings. But her admiration for Mr. Cotton and her great need for self-expression prompted her to adopt the seemingly innocent course of repeating Cotton's sermons to a little congregation invited to her own house. That, at least, was professedly her original intention.

At first only a handful of women gathered in the Hutchinson parlor to hear these discourses, most of them housewives whose duties had kept them from attending the lecture of the preceding day.[22] Mary Dyer, the lovely wife of Boston's milliner, was one

20. Hutchinson, History, II, 368.
21. Cotton, Way of the Congregational Churches Cleared, 52.
22. Hutchinson, History, II, 370.

of the first to attend. A woman of naturally sweet disposition, but forward and courageous in support of her beliefs, Mrs. Dyer was to be one of Anne Hutchinson's staunchest supporters in the months to come.[23] When kitchen duties allowed, Anne's sister Katherine, would step into the room to listen, and young Bridget and Faith would come to hear Mr. Cotton's familiar words again. Goody Hawkins, crouching silently in glassy-eyed absorption, comprehended little that was said, but nodded in earnest approbation of the most abstruse points of doctrine. "Is that quite clear to you?" Anne solicitously asked her. "Oh, yes, very clear," old Jane joyfully rasped, delighted to find herself a center of attention.[24]

Jane Hawkins's innocence of theological niceties may well have been the pitfall into which Anne Hutchinson stumbled. At the meetinghouse women were expected, despite their incomprehension, to maintain a dignified silence. But in the informality of Mrs. Hutchinson's parlor, it was possible to allay doubts and satisfy curiosity. Anne was perhaps too eager to be helpful in the clarification of dubious particulars and, not incidentally, to display her formidable erudition. Thus she moved, step by treacherous step, from unadorned reiteration of Cotton's sermons to incautious exegesis of their doctrinal substance.

This was no chore for the unlettered or timorous. Cotton had been strenuously bent upon reducing the nominalistic quality of the covenant doctrine by reasserting the essential mystery of divine grace. At the same time he remained alert to the necessity of defining the moral implications of the covenant relationship. Consequently, to the unsophisticated or the doctrinaire, Cotton's sermons may often have seemed to argue by abatement. He was too guarded, too anxious to have the best of both worlds. The temptation for Anne to simplify, to construe, to hack away the empirical qualifier, proved irresistible. Called upon to expound dark places and resolve perplexing ambiguities, she dangerously advanced her own conclusions and too often labeled them as Cotton's own. Unhappily her views were not always identical with Cotton's and were seldom in accord with the earthbound views of his clerical brethren.

Anne did not unfold the whole of her mind in a day, nor was it necessary at the outset to strain or controvert Mr. Cotton's words in order to convey her point. To emphasize the salient and omit

23. Winthrop, *Journal*, I, 266.
24. Wheelwright, *Writings*, 197.

the extraneous would comfortably serve her turn. Nor is it likely that she was conscious of doing less than full justice to Cotton's beliefs.

The Hutchinson homilies were like a summons out of the wilderness to the good women of Boston, and they were drawn from far and near to the great house on the High Street. At first Anne's nearest neighbors and intimates in the congregation must have sought her out—Mary Coggeshall, Elizabeth Aspinwall, and Anne Leverett—or perhaps old acquaintances from Alford such as Alice and Elizabeth Wardall. In time they were joined by women from the farther reaches of the town.

Mr. Cotton, meanwhile, smiling beatifically upon this sedulous devotionalism, praised the Lord for the success of Mrs. Hutchinson's fruitful discourse.[25] It was deeply gratifying that one of his own flock should have the capacity to express his own views with such fervor and insight. Besides it was not a little delectable to find himself the subject of such intense admiration. Indeed, it seemed to all the Saints that they had good cause to be thankful for this happy change in their spiritual fortunes. It was surely providential, in the midst of wordly travail, that in one year the number of the elect should be doubled and that in the next they should receive the bounty of such heavenly discourse. Mrs. Hutchinson's coming was indisputedly a godsend to the town of Boston.

25. Cotton, *Way of the Congregational Churches Cleared*, 51-52.

VIII

"Divers Jealousies"

October 1635–May 1636

(i)

WITH THE COMING OF AUTUMN events took a threatening turn. Early in October the *Abigail* of London, nine weeks out of England, dropped anchor in Boston Harbor, bearing over two hundred passengers and a menacing smallpox infection.[1] The smallpox was brought promptly under control, but certain of the passengers proved less tractable. John Wilson returned on this vessel to assume his familiar place in Boston's pulpit; in his company came a curiously matched pair of voyagers, each of whom, in quite dissimilar ways, was to leave the stamp of his personality on the Bay Colony—and on the heart of Anne Hutchinson. The Reverend Mr. Hugh Peter, lately minister to the English congregation at Rotterdam, had fled Holland to escape the harassment of the English ambassador there.[2] Barrel-chested, swarthy, with eyes wide set, full lips, and pugnacious jaw, Master Peter was a creature of bewildering ambitendencies. His fertile imagination and demonic energy generated alternately within him a meddlesome, presumptuous spirit and crushing fits of melancholia. A "hot" preacher in the pulpit, he was nonetheless widely known for the cheery, jesting quality of his sermons. Although rigidly orthodox throughout most of his career, he ultimately acquired a reputation, however unfairly, as "an enthusiasticall buffoon preacher"

1. Banks, *Planters of the Commonwealth,* 161 ff.
2. Winthrop, *Journal,* I, 160.

and the champion of pietistic sectaries.[3] Mr. Peter had turned his flight to good account by coming to New England as agent for the Earl of Warwick to help organize the settlement of the lower Connecticut valley.

His co-agent in this enterprise was young Henry Vane, son of the Comptroller of the King's Household. Unlike the elder Vane, who took the world pretty much as he found it, trimming his sail to every prevailing breeze, young Harry was intensely idealistic. Dark eyes burned with dedication in his narrow, ascetic face, but the firm line of his patrician jaw was hopelessly betrayed by the sensitive incertitude of delicate lips. For all his dedication, Harry Vane suffered the inconclusiveness of a mind that had not yet come fully to terms with itself; strong in its negations, its affirmations were tentative and insecure. At the age of fifteen he had rejected the sacraments of the Anglican church and refused the vows essential to matriculation at Oxford. Since that time he had favored the Puritan doctrines, but even now, propelled by a strong mystical tendency, he was moving beyond the peculiar rigidities of the covenant brethren toward a religion of more inward experience. When Vane had first broached the idea of journeying to New England, his father had raged and Archbishop Laud had cajoled, both to no avail. Whereupon, the King himself intervened in Harry's favor, perhaps on the subtle assumption that a brief sojourn with the Saints might jolt the lad back to his sound Anglican senses. But the time for such a relapse had long since passed.[4]

On arriving in Boston, Vane was lavished with an attention that bordered on infatuation. The practical value of his immediate relationship to a prominent member of the Privy Council had not escaped the notice of his hosts. Influence at court was presently their greatest need. They promptly invited Harry to the inner circle of the elite and there, despite his tender years, he presumed to arbitrate a long-standing dispute between Dudley and Winthrop.[5] From the very outset Winthrop and Dudley had been at loggerheads on various matters of personal deportment and public policy. By the time Vane arrived, this discord seems to have become focused on a disagreement about the form and quality of justice to be meted out in an infant state. Winthrop thought it preferable to be lenient

3. Raymond P. Stearns, *The Strenuous Puritan, Hugh Peter* (Urbana, 1954), 35, 104; Edwards, *Gangraena*, Pt. II, 39; Bailey, *Milton and Jakob Boehme*, 110.

4. Winthrop, *Journal*, I, 162; James K. Hosmer, *The Life of Young Sir Henry Vane* (Boston, 1888), chap. 1.

5. Winthrop, *Journal*, I, 169 ff.

in the treatment of offenders, contending that "in the infancy of plantations justice should be administered with more lenity than in a settled state, because people were then more apt to transgress, partly of ignorance of new laws and orders, and partly through oppression of business and other straits." Dudley held a diametrically opposite view, and around this inflammatory issue factions had formed within the magistracy. Now the newcomers, Vane and Peter, sensing trouble, summoned the leaders of the opposing factions, and with Vane presiding, sought to establish a friendly agreement. The point at issue was submitted to the ministers to set down a rule. Cotton, Wilson, and Hooker pondered the matter overnight and concluded, in support of Dudley, that strict discipline was preferable in a young community. Articles were drawn to the effect "that there should be more strictness used in civil government and military discipline.... After sentence ... none shall intimate his dislike privately; or if one dissent, he shall sit down without showing any further distaste, publicly or privately." Winthrop thereupon conceded that he had "failed in over much lenity and remissness" and resolved thenceforth to adopt a stricter course.[6] And, indeed, so he did when the occasion presented itself.

(ii)

This meeting did not take place until January 1636, but the entire winter had been even more troubled than the preceding one. A proliferation of crises extended irritation to all corners of the colony. Roger Williams had at last overreached himself and was banished from the precincts of the Bay; but he left behind the infection of his opinions to divide and disturb the church of Salem. Saugus and Charlestown, too, were inflamed with controversy between pastor and parish. The Dorchester congregation had moved to Connecticut, and the people of Newtown were actively preparing their departure for those more commodious pastures.[7] The problem of Captain Endicott and the flag had been temporarily resolved by leaving the cross out of all regimental colors, but this ill-advised solution was soon to engender even greater complications.

But most exasperating were the shortages of food and the exorbitant prices charged by merchants and laborers, continuing

6. *Ibid.*, 170, 171 ff.
7. *Ibid.*, 168, 169.

problems which had long baffled solution and which, in their working out, were to touch strangely on the destiny of Anne Hutchinson.

From its earliest days the population of the colony had grown so rapidly that the supply of food, clothing, and housing could never keep pace with the demand. Indian corn, the staple agricultural commodity, had been subjected to price regulation in order that it might pass as currency, but corn prices, even under control, fluctuated considerably, ranging from ten shillings per bushel in 1631 to as low as three shillings per bushel in 1634. After 1634, a new surge of population growth brought a recurrence of the corn shortage and necessitated the imposition of export restrictions and the use of bullets as an additional form of emergency currency.[8]

For the regular and adequate supply of other commodities, the colonists were often at the mercy of factors beyond their ability to control effectively. Fabrics, tools, household utensils, livestock, and many other imported necessities were subject to exorbitant pricing by shipmasters and local merchants who were able to engross whole shiploads on arrival. Similarly, the costs of clothing manufacture and housing construction were largely determined by the continuing shortage of skilled workmen in those basic trades. Time and again Governor Winthrop interspersed his narrative of the colony's growth with indignant protests against oppression in wages and prices—the latter often double that which was charged in England.[9] Winthrop tactfully named no names but it was evident that many of the chief offenders were prominent Bostonians and his own near neighbors.

It soon became apparent that, if the colonial economy were not to collapse before it got underway, regulatory measures must be promptly introduced. For the institution of such controls, the colonial authorities possessed an adequate social philosophy and an ample body of legal precedent. The Assistants of the General Court during these formative years had been drawn almost exclusively from the ranks of the landed gentry.[10] The sole exceptions to this seem to have been William Coddington and Roger Ludlow,

8. *Colony Records*, I, 92, 137, 140; Winthrop, *Journal*, I, 64, 131.
9. Winthrop, *Journal*, I, 59, 112, 152, 169.
10. Of the seventeen men who served as Assistants between 1630 and 1637, fourteen laid claim to the titular dignity of esquire or gentleman, and all appear to have been holders of large landed estates. As noted, only Coddington and Ludlow professed to be merchants. See Pope, *Pioneers of Massachusetts*, 44, 64, 107, 145, 146, 157, 206, 213, 241, 247, 295, 332, 376, 437, 469, 508.

both of whom were merchants. The deputies too were predominantly men whose interests were primarily agricultural, yeoman farmers, or gentry.[11] Many of these men had come from backgrounds similar to that of John Winthrop and shared with him the organic social philosophy which he had so lucidly articulated in his *Modell of Christian Charity*. Like him they subscribed to the thesis that all "must be knitt together in this work as one man," and that "the care of the publique must oversway all private respects." [12] As a group they were intent on the success of their colonial project and were prepared to adopt vigorous measures toward that end.

Nor was the experience of these men confined to the realm of philosophic speculation. They had come but recently from England where those social ideals had assumed the concrete and legal form of civil intervention in the economic sphere. The disintegration of the guilds had prompted the Tudor state to assume, at least in principle, the responsibility for maintaining an equitable correlation of the earnings and expenditures of workers. By the end of the sixteenth century statutory controls of prices and wages had been nullified in their effect by the mounting inflationary spiral and gave way to periodic adjustment at the local level.[13] Justices of the peace were now authorized to regulate wage levels and commodity prices annually within their jurisdiction "according to plenty, scarcity . . . and the respect of the times." [14] While he was still in England, John Winthrop—and perhaps others among the colony magistrates—had thus become accustomed to the exer-

11. Between 1634 and 1637 there were 101 men who held the position of deputy to the General Court. Twenty-three of these men can be unquestionably identified as agriculturists of high or low degree; gentry, yeomen, or husbandmen. Fifteen were tradesmen of some sort and ten were craftsmen. Seven fall into other occupational categories; fishermen and so forth.

There are, therefore, 55 deputies of the 101 whose occupations are well established. Of the remaining forty-six it is difficult to speak with any authority. The records indicate that a substantial number of them held large amounts of land, and it seems a reasonable assumption that the great majority concentrated most of their energies and received most of their income from what was still the basic occupation of the outlying communities—agriculture. This compilation is based on a careful combing of Pope, *Pioneers of Massachusetts;* Lechford, *Notebook;* and the files of the *New Eng. Hist. and Geneal. Register.*

12. *Winthrop Papers*, II, 294, 293.

13. E. Lipson, *The Economic History of England* (London, 1948), III, 251, 252; R. H. Tawney and Eileen Power, *Tudor Economic Documents* (London, 1924), I, 371 ff.

14. Sir John Clapham, *A Concise Economic History of Britain* (Cambridge, Eng., 1951), 213; Wallace Notestein, *The English People on the Eve of Colonization* (New York, 1954), 219.

cise of this authority at each Easter session of the bench. Doubtless particularly fresh in their minds would be those regulatory measures which had been occasioned by the extortionate practices of East Anglian clothiers during the preceding decade.[15]

The gentry and yeomanry were warmly supported by the clergy in their opposition to mercantile profiteering. The Puritan ministers had long been outspoken in their criticism of unscrupulous economic dealing, sharing with their mentor William Ames the conviction that "to buy cheap and sell dear ... [was] a common vice, and much the worse for being so common.[16] In Massachusetts this viewpoint was most vigorously expounded by John Cotton when, in 1636, he was asked by the General Court to prepare a body of laws for the colony. On the problem of wages and prices Cotton was forthright and certain: "To the intent that all oppression in buying and selling may be avoided it shall be lawful for the judges in every town, with the consent of the free burgesses, to appoint certain selectmen, to set reasonable rates upon all commodities, and proportionably to limit the wages of workmen and laborers."[17] Some three years later when Robert Keayne, a wealthy Boston merchant, was accused of charging excessive prices, Cotton had further opportunity to set forth his views. Church and state had joined hands to chasten Keayne severely, and the unhappy man was not only fined heavily but came perilously close to being cast out of the church. Cotton seized the occasion to loose a blast from the pulpit against extortionate tradesmen and to provide the whole tribe of merchants with more sharply explicit directives for the conduct of their business.[18]

But long before this *cause célèbre* had so effectively dramatized the issue, the General Court had been laboring energetically to bring profiteers under control. Scarcely had they become settled in the colony before the magistrates were involved in efforts to work out an equitable system of wage and price controls. Initially their regulatory measures were calculated to limit the profits of construction workers whose skills were at a premium during this period of rapid population growth.[19] More general restraints were imposed

---

15. Lipson, *Economic History of England*, III, 252, 257.
16. R. H. Tawney, *Religion and the Rise of Capitalism* (New York, 1948), 180.
17. Force, ed., *Tracts Relating to the Colonies*, III, No. 9, 10; John Cotton, "Moses, His Judicialls," quoted in Richard B. Morris, *Government and Labor in Early America* (New York, 1946), 61.
18. Winthrop, *Journal*, I, 315 ff.; *Colony Records*, I, 281. See also Bernard Bailyn, "The *Apologia* of Robert Keayne," *Wm. and Mary Qtly.*, 3d Ser., 7 (1950), 568-87.
19. *Colony Records*, I, 74, 76, 77, 79.

in 1633, specifically including a ceiling on the wages which tailors might lawfully receive. This new measure stipulated that both donor and recipient should be impartially punished for overpayment. At its next sitting the General Court turned its attention to the problem of constantly rising prices. They now undertook to protect workers against the hardship of high price levels by imposing on all merchants a profit limit of four pence on the shilling. Within a year, however, much of the effect of this legislation was canceled out by the passage of a discriminatory enactment which repealed the penalties against employers for overpayment of wages. In consequence of this measure several employers were enabled with impunity to bring suit against workmen whom they had overpaid, and in each case excessively heavy fines were imposed.[20]

One of the chief causes of the continuing high price level was the sharply competitive bidding at the quayside for the cargo of incoming vessels.[21] In hope of reducing and stabilizing price levels, the General Court endowed on nine prominent merchants—one from each of the major towns—exclusive and original purchasing rights on all unassigned imports. Under the terms of this monopoly these men were allowed a 5 per cent resale profit.[22] However, the arrangement lasted but four short months, there apparently being no merchant in the colony who controlled capital resources adequate to enlarge on such a princely opportunity. The act was therefore repealed.

During the course of this economic struggle, the town and citizens of Boston necessarily played an important role. Most of the colony's merchants and many of its skilled craftsmen dwelt in Boston, and almost from the beginning Boston's wharves and market place had been the energizing centers of commercial activity. Any legislation calculated to inhibit the free flow of trade was bound to affect Boston's men of business. They did not consider themselves engaged in a philanthropic enterprise. They believed that the value of their goods and services should be determined by the prevalent need and the available means of compensation. It was difficult to avoid the conclusion that the regulatory measures of the Court had been aimed chiefly against the Bos-

20. *Ibid.*, 109, 111, 127, 153.
21. Winthrop, *Journal*, I, 152.
22. *Colony Records*, I, 142.

tonians.[23] Nor was confidence inspired by the insinuation that the spiritual condition of the tradesman was at best insecure.

But the traditions and philosophic outlook of the gentry were in the ascendancy and enjoyed the advantage of concurrence with the precepts of the church. It was the gentry and yeomanry who dominated the seats of power, formulated policy, and commanded clerical support. The merchants and craftsmen, although they controlled indispensable goods and skills, found themselves in a minority, cast in the role of public enemy and pitted against the substantial political strength of the agricultural community.

At last, in September 1635, the effort to regulate wages and prices took a new turn when all statutory controls were repealed. The magistrates, presumably seeking greater flexibility in their attack on the problem, now based their restraints on equity and proposed to deal with each case according to its merits and presumably their current state of mind.[24]

At this juncture, the people of Boston undertook to deal with inflation in their own way. A committee of three merchants—William Hutchinson, William Colburn, and William Brenton—was designated to draft a schedule of wages and prices. Whatever the result of their effort, it failed to satisfy John Winthrop, for three months later that disgruntled commentator observed that the merchants and seamen were continuing to sell "at most excessive rates (in many things two for one, etc.)." [25]

The most imaginative response to the difficult situation was advanced by Hugh Peter. Recognizing the need for an adequate capital base for the economic operations of the colony, he traveled energetically from town to town soliciting funds for the promotion of a fishing industry.[26] But this shrewd venture could at best promise long-term benefits, and present needs clamored insistently. At last, in February, the clergy proclaimed a day of fasting that the Saints might more concentratedly relish the full significance of their humiliations and suffering.[27]

23. *Ibid.*, 149; Winthrop, *Journal*, I, 152.
24. *Colony Records*, I, 150.
25. Winthrop, *Journal*, I, 169.
26. *Ibid.*, 168; Stearns, *Strenuous Puritan*, 92.
27. Winthrop, *Journal*, I, 175. For an excellent discussion of the commercial situation, see Bailyn, *New England Merchants in the Seventeenth Century*, 16-44.

(iii)

The Hutchinson household was also burdened with its own unique set of complications. In March Anne gave birth to another boy, Zuriel, which must for a time have curtailed her missionary efforts.[28] This additional responsibility was attended by other changes in the family. There would now be fewer workers, for Edward returned to England briefly to wed Katherine Hamby of Ipswich,[29] and Katherine Marbury, Anne's headstrong younger sister, having recently married Richard Scott, a Boston shoemaker, departed with him to join Roger Williams in Providence. At least one member of the Hutchinson household, it seems, could no longer accept the religious principles of the Bay Colony.[30]

Changes were taking place, too, in Mrs. Hutchinson's religious clientele. "A poyson does never insinuate so quickly nor operate so strongly as when women's milk is the vehicle wherein 'tis given," Cotton's grandson caustically observed many years later. Anne's cause had been taken up with extraordinary fervor by the distaff side and "these women, like their first mother, . . . soon hook'd in their husbands also."[31] So lively did masculine interest become that Anne was impelled to set up a second weekly meeting to which both men and women were invited. This additional session presumably met on Monday afternoon to recapitulate and dissect the sermon of the day before.

Anne could not fail to be impressed by the quantity and quality of the assemblage that was drawn every week to the house on the High Street. Sometimes as many as eighty men and women managed to crowd into the Hutchinson parlor to hear her comments on some particularly enigmatic passage of the preceding day. Some of these listeners, of course, were Hutchinson relatives, members of a rapidly burgeoning clan. Both Edwards and their wives would be on hand; and Faith with her new husband, Thomas Savage, the tailor; and young Bridget with hers, John Sanford, the ordinance

28. "Boston Births, Baptisms, Marriages and Deaths," 4.
29. October 13, 1636, Champlin, "Hutchinson Ancestry and Descendants," *N.Y. Geneal. and Biog. Record*, 45 (1914), 166-67.
30. John Osborne Austin, *The Genealogical Dictionary of Rhode Island* (Albany, 1887), 372. The later career of Katherine Marbury Scott was in some respects even bolder than that of her more famous sister. Not long after joining Roger Williams in Providence, she participated in founding the first Baptist church in the colonies and later became one of the first American Quakers. An active proselytizer for that sect, she defied the authorities of Massachusetts and suffered imprisonment and whipping for her boldness.
31. Mather, *Magnalia*, II, 516, 509.

expert, who was also a prosperous merchant and Boston selectman. (Bridget, it was common gossip, had made a particularly good match for one so young.) Some of Anne's disciples were old acquaintances from distant Alford, like Thomas and William Wardall and their wives, or Thomas Marshall, the ferryman. A good many were neighbors; the Coggeshalls, Atherton and Elizabeth Hough, and Samuel and Anne Cole, whose homes flanked the Hutchinson house on three sides. William Aspinwall of the blazing temper and unbridled tongue, bent on a restless quest of spiritual satisfaction came from a short distance down the street, and Thomas Oliver, Anne's fellow healer, walked from the Spring Gate. Others came from more remote parts of town; William and Margery Colburn, who lived on Frog Lane near the Neck, and William and Mary Dyer from Mylne Lane by the South Cove.

Here were some of the best and most important people in Boston. William Coddington, probably the richest man in the colony, certainly the only colonist who could yet afford a house of brick, was one of Anne's most faithful auditors. The attentiveness of this domineering autocrat must have been more than a little flattering to her. In time she would find him less complaisant. William Brenton and Robert Harding, prosperous merchants, were among Anne's followers, as were Edward Bendall, the dockman, William Balston, the innkeeper, and many more. These were all men who were well established in the community, among the earliest arrivals in the colony, dedicated church members and freemen of the Company. The concentration of wealth in Anne's parlor could hardly have escaped her notice, nor could she have failed to observe that here was also a goodly portion of the power elite of Boston and even of Massachusetts. Twelve of her adherents had served continuously on the board of selectmen, eight had been representatives to the General Court, and others were lesser officeholders. Her roster revealed some significant absentees, most notably Winthrop and Bellingham, but otherwise she could count among her adherents almost all Bostonians who were regularly elected to high public office.[32]

Attendance was not confined to any single social or economic group; rich and poor alike, magistrate and freeman, godly and "prophane" found spiritual succor in Anne's parlor. She welcomed not only proven members of the church but also a considerable

---

32. A detailed examination of Mrs. Hutchinson's following will be found in Chapter XVI and the relevant Appendices.

number of those who for various reasons sojourned outside the hallowed circle of elect. Wealthy merchants met on common terms with day laborers and servants such as John Compton and Matthew Jyans. Deacons and elders of the church rubbed elbows with Jane and Richard Hawkins, who had been denied admission to the church, or Samuel Sherman, who had not bothered to apply.

But poor and "prophane" comprised a slender minority among these convented faithful. Mrs. Hutchinson's compassionate and permissive doctrines had been received most warmly by Boston's men of business, merchants and craftsmen, who were either quite prosperous or at least moderately well-to-do. Indeed, the more successful they were in their earthly endeavors, the more enthusiastically they seemed to respond to her appeals. These were the men whose business methods had been under such continuous attack during the previous year. Being church members, they were confident that their professions of faith were as sound as those of their critics, and their state of grace as unassailable. But implicit in the running condemnation of their practices was the insinuation that the spiritual state of the businessman was wrapped in shadowy incertitude. The Puritan community regarded moral effort as an indispensable token of spiritual regeneration, but if an organic economic philosophy was held to be a basic component of the Puritan moral code, then it would seem that the tradesman's soul was indeed in a perilous state. This, at any rate, was the conclusion they had been left free to draw—unless they could choose to advance other tokens of election that did not bear so cruelly on their pecuniary interests. This alternative Mrs. Hutchinson had happily supplied by contending for the primacy of the Covenant of Grace, the essential witness of the Spirit. True assurance of grace, she insisted, was essentially a mystical experience preceding and precluding any consideration of moral effort on the part of the believer.

The leading merchants of Boston had not calculatedly adopted Mrs. Hutchinson's tenets with this mundane consideration in mind: the commitment was doubtless made without conscious awareness of related goals. But being only human it was essential to their psychological well-being that the framework of events and relations in which they were implicated should have meaning for them—such meaning as would confirm each man's sense of his own worth. The orthodox ideology had failed to satisfy this need, and Mrs. Hutchinson had unwittingly provided a felicitous conjunction. Although neither she nor her companions were disposed to abandon the basic moral pattern of the community, this altered perspective allowed greater latitude to define what was morally sound and what was not. Furthermore, it permitted them to rest confident in their regeneration despite all contrary claims founded on a paternalistic and organic philosophy.

(iv)

During the winter the scope and tenor of Mrs. Hutchinson's teachings had altered perilously. Hitherto her prelections had been generally in accord with those of John Cotton and between the two there was small room for controversy. Such differences as there may have been she refused to admit and he had failed to observe. But now John Wilson was back in the Boston pulpit and Wilson, Anne soon learned, was made of flintier stuff than Cotton.

A lean-faced man of equine aspect, with prominent nose, long jaw, and pursed lips, John Wilson viewed this world with an air of disapproving hauteur.[33] Now in his middle forties, Wilson seems to have been a crusty and formidable individual of dogmatic stamp and magnificently irascible temper. As pastor he bore responsibility for the moral guidance of the congregation, a role for which he appears to have been admirably cast. A "son of thunder," his "holy wrath" was strenuously exercised for the maintenance of strict discipline, wherein he had "a singular gift to the great benefit of the church." [34] The most sympathetic accounts of his pulpit manner only limn the portrait in more acid tones. One admirer leaves the impression that his voice was harsh and indistinct, while another makes apologetic reference to his stubbornly old-fashioned homiletics, comprised largely of exhortations to good behavior.[35] This formidable exterior was relieved by Pastor Wilson's whimsical

33. See the line engraving in Justin Winsor, ed., *Narrative and Critical History of America* (Boston, 1884), I, 713.

34. Mather, *Magnalia*, I, 312; Johnson, *Wonder Working Providence*, 67; Winthrop, *Journal*, I, 116.

35. Johnson, *Wonder Working Providence*, 67, refers to "thy thick utterance." Samuel Eliot Morison in *The Founding of Harvard College* (Cambridge, Mass., 1935), 173, interprets this as "plentiful utterance," as in "thick as leaves." However, *Webster's New International Dictionary* defines the archaic usage thus: "'thick' as 'thick utterance,' inarticulate, indistinct, muffled, dull." *The Shorter Oxford English Dictionary* gives "thick, of the voice, etc.; not clear; hoarse; husky; indistinct; inarticulate; also, of low pitch; deep; guttural; throaty." Mather, *Magnalia*, I, 283, ". . . preached more after the primitive manner, without any distinct propositions, but chiefly in exhortations and admonitions."

penchant for epistolary versification, rhymed letters "to all persons, in all places, on all occasions"—but only partially relieved, for the verse was at best doggedly pedestrian, and the content unwearyingly and sanctimoniously didactic.[36]

During the long course of his career in Boston, Pastor Wilson seems at last to have won the affection and esteem of his parishioners, but in 1636 he was widely unpopular and rapidly becoming more so. This unpopularity was perhaps attributable in part to the strictness of his teachings and in part to his violent and arbitrary manner. And unhappily for Wilson his astringent personality contrasted strikingly with the milder personal qualities of his partner in the Boston pulpit. Ill for Boston that Cotton should have his abode on the quiet, lonely hillside of the Trimountaine, while Wilson set up on his house beside the market place where little that transpired could escape his penetrating gaze.

When Wilson had returned to Boston in October, Anne was exposed to his teaching for the first time and saw at once the vast abyss which lay between his doctrines and her own. In the ordinary course of her meetings, she now analyzed Wilson's lectures as well as Cotton's, and commented on the startling discrepancies. To her mind the difference was appalling. Wilson's emphasis on public morality and evidencing justification by sanctification were, on the face of it, a reversion to the long-discarded Covenant of Works. It had been to escape that doctrine that Anne had fled England. Now there seemed no way of escape; her only recourse was to combat it with all the means at her command. She seethed with anger and resentment. Mr. Wilson did not have the seal of the Spirit, she informed her disciples; he was not an able minister of the New Testament; he deceived them to suggest that by adherence to the moral law they might take an active part in their own salvation.[37]

The audacity of her attack seems to have emboldened her adherents rather than deterred them. Opposition to Mr. Wilson became a convenient rallying point. His lectures stood in edifying contrast to Mr. Cotton's and the antithesis gave fresh cogency to Mrs. Hutchinson's disquisitions. Fervor for any cause is aroused by the immediate presence of its counterpart, and so the very solid substance of Mr. Wilson became a handy representation of the forces

36. Mather, *Magnalia*, I, 275; John Wilson, *Handkerchiefs from Paul*, ed. Kenneth Murdock (Cambridge, 1927), lxvii.

37. Hutchinson, *History*, II, 370.

of evil, the antagonist whose downfall would bring the true believers closer to their goal.

It soon appeared that Mr. Wilson was not alone in his erroneous teachings. Traveling into other towns on Sundays and lecture days, Anne found, to her infinite dismay, that of all the ministers in the colony, only Mr. Cotton was truly sealed and enabled to teach a Covenant of Grace. With the possible exception of Mr. Shepard, the new minister of Newtown, all the others were misguiding their flocks with a Covenant of Works.[38] She did not hesitate to announce this alarming conclusion to her coterie,[39] nor did she scruple at proselytizing in congregations outside Boston.

Mrs. Hutchinson's partisans outside the town were never very numerous by comparison with her local muster. Nonetheless, some very substantial citizens were drawn into her ranks, and the movement prompted grave misgivings among the ministers of those towns. Roxbury, being too near to escape the infection of neighbor relations, provided about twenty new disciples. Lieutenant Richard Morris, though a very stout soldier, failed to resist the contagion, and John Porter also succumbed, transmitting the fever throughout his family. From Roxbury the virus was conveyed to Newbury in the baggage of the influential and wealthy Mr. Richard Dummer on his removal thither. But for all his influence Mr. Dummer was able to garner no more than a brace of postulants in that remote outpost. In Charlestown, however, Anne's arcana luxuriated, bringing about two dozen converts into the fold, including some of the very best families, the Denisons, the Carringtons, and the Bunkers. Salem, too, though still dizzied by the whirlwind visitation of Roger Williams, provided about ten who shifted their allegiance to the more constant tenets of Mrs. Hutchinson.

Meanwhile, the High Street conventicles gathered fresh luster from the attendance of young Henry Vane. Soon after his arrival Vane's intense religiosity and mystical bent led him directly to the center of the Hutchinson coterie where he rapidly became one of Anne's staunchest champions. Vane and Cotton were attracted to each other from the outset, and the older man generously invited the newcomer to live in his home at the foot of Trimountaine. Vane accepted the offer and soon added a wing to Cotton's house

38. Cotton, *Way of the Congregational Churches Cleared*, 52.
39. *Antinomianism*, 162.

where he maintained residence for the duration of his stay.[40] In later years it was reported that Cotton, Vane, and Mrs. Hutchinson frequently met in Cotton's house for long discussions about the doctrine of free grace. These familiar colloquies, had they taken place, would doubtless lend a picturesque note to the unhappy story of Anne Hutchinson. Cotton, however, categorically denied that there were any such meetings; in view of his habit of seclusion and his rigorous study regimen, there seems no reason to doubt his word.[41] Although Vane was a frequent and loyal attendant at Mrs. Hutchinson's soirees, it seems unlikely that Anne often visited Cotton's home or had more than casual opportunity to talk with him about matters of doctrine. As Cotton himself belatedly recognized, had he seized opportunities to discuss theological problems with Mrs. Hutchinson, he would have seen in time the narrow but significant difference in their views and spared himself much later embarrassment.

In May Vane was elected governor of the colony. Unfortunately he had little but solemn deportment, personal charm, and social position to recommend him to that difficult post. Possibly the deputies gave him the governorship in the hope of using his influence in England to stabilize their position. If this was their purpose, the gamble did not pay off, for Vane proved to be as unstable as he was charming, and seriously lacking in executive capacity. But surely it was a great feather in Mrs. Hutchinson's cap to claim the governor as her disciple.

(v)

Once Anne had committed herself to oppose Mr. Wilson, the heterodoxy of her views could not remain long under cover. For a time Mr. Wilson had assumed that her meetings were in accord with the public ministry and had freely approved her efforts. But sooner or later, in so small and tightly knit a community, the difference of opinion must make itself known. It was probably in the late winter or early spring of 1636 that Wilson's eyes were at last opened to the divisions within his own congregation. In conversation with one of Anne's adherents he discovered that her doctrines were radically at variance with those of the orthodox clergy, and that she had quite deliberately undertaken to refute his teachings.

40. See Cotton's will in *New Eng. Hist. and Geneal. Register*, 5 (1851), 240.
41. Cotton, *Way of the Congregational Churches Cleared*, 88.

He did not divulge this disturbing news for some time thereafter, nor did he suggest that he bore anyone a grievance. Instead he preached with redoubled zeal against the errors he presumed Mrs. Hutchinson to be teaching, re-emphasizing the importance of works as an evidence of a sanctified estate.[42]

It was perhaps inevitable that Cotton, being closer to Mrs. Hutchinson in his opinions, should remain oblivious longer to the full purport of her teaching. Wilson chose not to confide his knowledge of the situation to Cotton; he may even have suspected him of complicity. The spread of Mrs. Hutchinson's doctrines had been attended by a general understanding that they were derived from Cotton himself, and that he remained her admiring patron. At last, one perturbed participant in Anne's gatherings saw that things were seriously amiss and reported his suspicions to the pastor of a neighboring church. This pastor, in turn, conferred with other clergymen and together they confronted John Cotton. They informed him that Mrs. Hutchinson was circulating dangerously corrupt tenets and that she and her disciples had even ventured to lay their heterodoxies at his door.[43]

Cotton promptly summoned Anne and several of her more conspicuous adherents. He repeated the accusations, pointed out the error of their opinions, and took them to task for too generously fathering their heresies on him. Anne and her followers indignantly denied all the charges. They had circulated no such opinions and had ascribed no such views to Mr. Cotton. Learning nothing in this quarter, Cotton resorted to spies in order to confirm his suspicions. Several women were asked to attend Anne's meetings and report on what she taught there. This proved fruitless, for Anne was either as innocent as she claimed—which seems unlikely—or suspected the mission of the newcomers and guarded her words accordingly.[44]

Poor Cotton, by now thoroughly bewildered, returned to his informants for further advice. Unfortunately, these well-meaning individuals could not produce the two sound witnesses which were essential in order to prefer charges against Mrs. Hutchinson. Indeed, the one good witness at their disposal was most reluctant to be known publicly as an informer. Lacking witnesses against the erronists, it was suggested that Cotton's best course would be to testify personally against the errors in question. Cotton seized upon

42. *Ibid.*, 58.
43. *Ibid.*, 39.
44. *Ibid.*, 52.

this counsel and undertook, in public and private, to make plain his strong distaste for the heterodox notions attributed to him.

This apparently only inflamed the issue. Hearing his repudiation, some of the orthodox in Boston taunted Anne's disciples with having falsely claimed Cotton's patronage. "Loe," they said (according to Cotton's report), "now wee have heard your Teacher bearing witnesse openly against those very points, which you falsely father on him." "No matter... what you heare him say in publick," the Hutchinsonians replied, "we know what hee saith to us in private." [45]

This was not true and Cotton properly resented their allegations. He was thoroughly earnest in his repudiation of the more radical doctrines laid to him, nor could he bring himself to believe that Mrs. Hutchinson was guilty of all the charges brought against her. At worst, it seemed, she had expressed confusedly certain ideas they held in common. He observed that it was not Mrs. Hutchinson, but "some of these Opinionists" who claimed private access to him and support for their doctrines.[46] There were, no doubt, those in the Hutchinson circle who had already gone well beyond Mrs. Hutchinson, as she had gone beyond Cotton in drawing fanciful conclusions from the doctrine of free grace. They may have assumed that their leader had the ear of Mr. Cotton, or may have been willing, in order to inflate their own prestige, to claim that she had such access. That Mrs. Hutchinson herself would have so claimed is unlikely. Although she was, perhaps, fairly certain of her own beliefs by this time, it appears that she was somewhat confused in relating them to Cotton's; she did not understand his mind as clearly as she supposed she did. But, despite her confusions, throughout the controversy, Anne Hutchinson bore herself with an integrity that belies any inclination to make claims which she knew to be untrue.

In any case, the issue at last came into the open in the summer of 1636. In the town of Boston the lines of division were clearly drawn; a firm majority of the church aligned in support of Mrs. Hutchinson, and a small but potent minority rallied around Mr. Wilson. With the exception of Mr. Cotton, that is, who hovered uncertainly between heaven and earth, of which party no man knew.

And so events stood when John Wheelwright arrived in Boston.

45. *Ibid.*, 40.
46. *Ibid.*

IX

John Wheelwright

June–October 1636

(i)

O N THE day Henry Vane was chosen governor of the colony, a vessel from England beat its way southward past the Isle of Shoals and Cape Anne towards Boston Harbor. Standing at the bulwark, straining for a glimpse of the land that was soon to be his home, was one whose coming was destined to fan the sparks of controversy into an uncontrollable blaze. The Reverend Mr. John Wheelwright presented an aspect of more than casual interest to the observer. The sturdy frame and athletic bearing of the clergyman oddly concealed the inner contradictions of his nature. On the playing field and in the pulpit, he had won a reputation for lively assertiveness. His combative agility on the football fields of Cambridge had reportedly made even young Oliver Cromwell flinch.[1] Although that incident had presumably occurred some twenty years before, the youth was father to the man; as a theologian, Wheelwright, driven by his contentious disposition, had persistently advanced doctrines that he knew were repugnant to his ecclesiastical superiors. But his placid features belied the militant report. Beneath the ample brow, large, lucent eyes, curiously commingling humor and sympathy, looked out on the world with cautious doubt, as if uncertain whether to hazard its trials. The irresolute half-smile which lingered about his lips was offset—perhaps concealment was the purpose—by the bold, upturned mustachios and narrow beard

1. "Letter to George Vaughan from Doctor Cotton Mather," Jeremy Belknap, *History of New Hampshire* (Dover, 1812), I, Appendix, 255.

then in vogue.[2] Although capable of zealous attachment to a worthy cause, Pastor Wheelwright's wry humor permitted him to mock the stubborn fantasies of zeal and encouraged him to regain his own sense of proportion when zeal threatened to become his master. In manner and in speech, he was ordinarily gentle and retiring,[3] and altogether he must have impressed the thoughtful observer as a man moderately and humorously suspicious of the busy world, but once in and committed to the contest, well able to sustain his part.

Now in the prime of life, Wheelwright stood poised between the chafing confinements of the Old World and the vast uncertainties of the New. Taken all in all, the past had not been grievously burdensome to John Wheelwright. Born forty-four years previously, the son of Robert Wheelwright of Saleby, he had apparently been brought up in moderately comfortable circumstances.[4] His childhood home on the northern rim of the East Lincolnshire fens was northernmost of a constellation of manors and parishes that lay on the compass quarters around the market town of Alford. Bilsby to the east, Mawthorpe and Willoughby directly south, Rigsby due west, and Saleby at the north—all within easy walking distance of Alford, which stood on an elevation at their center. In this cluster of villages John Wheelwright spent most of his life before leaving for New England; here he made his friends and raised his family and ministered to the needs of his parishioners. The life of the Alford countryside became deeply enmeshed in the life of John Wheelwright, creating affections and loyalties that time, distance, and adversity could not eradicate.

At the somewhat advanced age of nineteen, young John matriculated at Sidney Sussex College, Cambridge, and was admitted sizar, paying less and receiving rank and accommodations inferior to those of the well-to-do pensioners.[5] Sidney Sussex, founded in 1598, only thirteen years before Wheelwright entered, was the youngest of the Cambridge colleges, and one of the smaller, having scarcely more than a hundred students, scholars, and fellows altogether. Its master, Dr. Samuel Ward, a deliberate and penetrating teacher of divinity, was reported to have Puritanical leanings, so Wheelwright,

---

2. The portrait in the State House, Boston, is reprinted in Morison, *Builders of the Bay Colony.*

3. *Antinomianism,* 164.

4. Reginald Dudding, *History of Alford,* 151; Wheelwright, "A Frontier Family," Col. Soc. of Mass., *Publications,* 1 (1895), 271 ff.

5. Wheelwright, "A Frontier Family," Col. Soc. of Mass., *Publications,* 1 (1895), 271.

like many other Puritan divines, may have caught the proud infection while still an undergraduate.[6] Seven years later, the frolics and exercises of the underclassman, the "responsions" and "opponencies" of the sophister, the flintier and more purposive obligations of the bachelor all behind him, he received the coveted Master of Arts degree and stood ready to take holy orders. Bidding farewell to college "chums," like generations of Cantabrigians before him, he probably took "Hobson's choice" at that well-loved carrier's livery stable and, securely in the saddle, jogged across the great bridge over Cam, out onto the broad highway to the north.

Peterborough was his destination, on the southern flank of his native fenlands. In the draughty reaches of the great sprawling cathedral there, Wheelwright served out his probationary term as deacon, officiating at solemn ceremonies before the high altar.[7] A few short steps from where the neophyte reverently performed his office, hedged in by the massive piers of the choir, lay the earthly remains of Queen Catherine and Mary Stuart, hapless victims of royal intrigue and of England's restless growth. If ever he gave that tragic pair a passing thought, it was perhaps only to reflect that both were troublesome Papists whose fate was well deserved. The thought could hardly have struck him that those same relentless forces would one day use even John Wheelwright as their plaything, to send him packing on his distant travels, and to make of him an unwitting and unwilling agent of Britain's herculean urge to expand. But the time was not ripe for that; a period of preparation and of domestic felicity lay before.

In 1621, Wheelwright returned to the Alford country, there to wed Marie Storre, daughter of Bilsby's vicar. Soon after he succeeded to the benefice vacated by the death of his father-in-law,[8] and for nine years he served the people of Bilsby as their vicar, forming close attachments with his parishioners and gaining a reputation for his godliness and for the modesty of his preaching.[9] During that time he moved steadily closer to the Puritan principles that were then so stridently challenging the soundness of Anglican orthodoxy. His, however, was Puritanism with a difference. While his colleagues to the south sought to pluck some element of moral

6. David Masson, The Life of John Milton (London, 1877), I, 114, 118.

7. Wheelwright, Writings, 2.

8. Wheelwright, "A Frontier Family," Col. Soc. of Mass., Publications, 1 (1895), 271.

9. Antinomianism, 164.

responsibility from the harsh predestinarianism of Calvin, Wheelwright, like John Cotton, dwelt lovingly on man's utter dependence on God's free grace, and rejected any hint that man could
strive on his own behalf or that his work bore any merit in God's
eyes.[10] The subtle efforts of the revisionist theologians seemed to
him but a Covenant of Works, casting doubt on God's loving mercy.

After the birth of her third child, Marie Wheelwright found her
rest in Bilsby churchyard. Not long thereafter the bereft husband,
lacking a helpmate to raise his motherless family, married Mary
Hutchinson of Alford, a young woman fourteen years his junior.[11]
Mary was the youngest daughter of Alford's mercer, a member of
a large and congenial family already well known to Wheelwright.
The marriage proved to be a durable and affectionate one and
served to promote warm associations with other members of the
Hutchinson clan.

Suddenly, in 1632, the Bilsby benefice escheated to the Crown
"per pravitatem simoniae." [12] Exactly what brought this vacancy
about is not clear. The general impression shared by his contemporaries was that Wheelwright was silenced for his heterodox opinions: later antagonists, searching the vocabulary of abuse, never
once applied the charge of simony. Perhaps doctrinal reasons compelled his withdrawal, and by prearrangement, simony was inscribed on the record. Whatever the reasons, John Wheelwright
was reduced to the status of a private person, obliged to live as
best he could on the revenues derived from inherited lands.

Although Wheelwright lacked a regular pulpit his heterodox
views gained circulation and exerted an influence among the clergy.
Hansard Knollys, the vicar of nearby Humberstone, being troubled
in his soul turned to God for guidance and related that the answer
to his prayer came in these words, "Go to Mr. Wheelwright and he
shall tell thee and show thee how to glorify God in his ministry."
This divine counsel impelled the perturbed minister toward Bilsby
where he held numerous conferences with Wheelwright. "You cannot glorify God, either in the ministry or in anything else," Wheelwright advised him, "for you are building on works, not on grace."
So deeply was Knollys impressed by this counsel that thenceforth
he inclined toward the pietistic doctrines of the Baptists, a conclu-

10. Wheelwright, *Writings*, 165.
11. Wheelwright, "A Frontier Family," Col. Soc. of Mass., *Publications*, 1 (1895),
273.
12. "Through the irregularity of simony"; *ibid.*, 17.

sion which might have enjoined caution on Wheelwright could he have but foreseen it.[13]

At last Wheelwright decided that he must cast his lot with the Saints of New England. Many of his friends and relations had already settled in the Bay Colony. His brothers-in-law William and Edward Hutchinson, with their families, had sailed two years before, leaving the care of their widowed mother to Wheelwright. Denied a regular income, hedged on every side by constraints inhibiting the free exercise of his mind, John Wheelwright, with his wife, children, and the aged Susanna Hutchinson, embarked for New England in the early spring of 1636.

(ii)

John Wheelwright was warmly received in Boston. Not only was he a relative of the esteemed Mrs. Hutchinson, but he was widely presumed to share her views on the doctrine of free grace and the indwelling of the Holy Ghost. Her brother Wheelwright, Anne had assured her disciples, is a sealed and able minister of the Gospel.[14]

Wheelwright soon had occasion to gratify their warmest expectations. Not long after his arrival, he was called upon to exercise as a private brother at the Boston meetinghouse. As he ascended to the pulpit, the congregation was hushed in curious and hopeful suspense. Anne, in her place, glowed with confident pride. Gazing out over the stilled, expectant throng, Wheelwright addressed them in mild and persuasive tones.[15] The substance of his discourse was the nature of faith and the condition of the believer. When faith is at last bestowed, he told them, it is consummated by God with a real union between the believer and the person of the Holy Ghost. The believer, he continued, then becomes something more than a mere creature. As he quietly expounded these points, his hearers reflectively nodded their approbation or inwardly gave thanks to God for sending them another of His sealed ministers. But on the magistrates' bench John Winthrop stirred uneasily. These opinions and terms, he ruminated—"real union—the person of the Holy Ghost"—have no footing in Scripture.[16] To the unwary they may seem to open up a fair and easy way to heaven, but sooner or later

13. Nutter, *Cambridge Baptists in the Struggle for Religious Liberty*, 25.
14. *Antinomianism*, 174. See also Robert Baylie, *A Dissuasive From the Errours of the Time* (London, 1645), 57 ff.
15. *Antinomianism*, 164.
16. Winthrop, *Journal*, I, 197 ff.

they must incline all who carelessly imbibe them to sloth and moral negligence. He scowled apprehensively at the speaker, but resolved for the time to keep his counsel.

Wheelwright may well have been surprised at the adulation shown him by the friends and admirers of his sister Hutchinson. Although he was promptly taken over and regarded as one of the foremost of their company, he neglected to scrutinize precisely the conclusions which Anne had seen fit to extract from the covenant of free grace. Instead he too incautiously assumed that she was championing that covenant against an encroaching spirit of legalism. Presumably he was content to accept her description of the prevailing differences of opinion within the community, and unwisely failed to ask his fellow ministers their interpretation of the situation.[17] This omission on the part of a newcomer was bound to be deeply resented by the members of a fraternity that jealously guarded its prerogatives.

Emboldened by the sponsorship of the governor and an able, outspoken clergyman, the opinionists (as they were termed) now vigorously seized the initiative. "To communicate their new light" they sought to enlarge their influence within and beyond the limits of Boston. New arrivals in the colony were warmly welcomed and showered with courtesies and hospitality. In keeping with Mrs. Hutchinson's principles, her disciples advanced their cause in the most humble and loving manner. In all their actions they would appear "very humble, holy, and spirituall Christians, and full of Christ; they would deny themselves farre, speake excellently, pray with such soule-ravishing expressions and affections, that a stranger that loved goodnesse could not but love and admire them." [18] Listeners were lulled by the sweetness of the new jargon: "free grace," "gospel truth," "glorious light," and "holding forth of Christ" became the slogans and bywords of their campaign.[19] By their opponents, of course, these amiable devices were looked upon as the most hypocritical of "sleights."

Some of the Hutchinsonians adopted more combative techniques. Edward Johnson, just returned from England, was shocked to encounter "a little, nimble tongued Woman" who passionately upbraided that "company of legall Professors [who] lie poring on the Law which Christ hath abolished." She offered to lead Johnson to

17. *Antinomianism*, 200, 202.
18. *Ibid.*, 75.
19. Mather, *Magnalia*, II, 509.

one who would show him a way "full of such ravishing joy that he should never have cause to be sorry for sinne." "Come along with me," another one inveigled, "I'le bring you to a woman that preaches better Gospell then any of your black-coates that have been at the Ninniversity, a Woman of another kinde of spirit, who hath many revelations of things to come, and for my part . . . I had rather heare such a one that speakes from the meere motion of the spirit, without any study at all, then any of your learned Scollers, although they may be fuller of Scripture." [20]

But for a few months yet such incendiaries were in the minority, and proselytizing was carried forward in a temperate and peaceable manner.

(iii)

As the movement spread, the advocates of orthodoxy became much alarmed. They could find no place in their system of thought for a rival body of religious ideas; the Bay Colony "was not set up for tollerating times." [21] Nor were the Puritan fathers unique in this respect. The policy of lay and clerical authorities in Massachusetts reflected a virtually universal attitude toward irregular opinions in religion.

The ties that had bound all Europe to the Papacy, endowing monarchs and magistrates with the responsibility of enforcing Roman orthodoxy, had been abruptly severed by the Protestant revolt. But however drastic the change it had by no means introduced toleration into Protestant courts and vestries. The multiplication of beliefs had cast oil on the flames and carried intolerance and persecution to unprecedented extremes. Preconception contended with reality as the European world strove to tame the buoyant energies of the seventeenth century within the tattered net of medieval principles. Although diversity was the omnipresent and confusing reality, men clung for dear life to the comforting illusions of unity and uniformity. There was scarcely a soul who did not look with horror upon the toleration of doctrines different from his own. Among the various state churches, intolerance was further intensified by the introduction of patriotic sentiments and the demands of national security. Formerly the chief purpose of religious persecution had been to save the immortal soul of the heretic from damnation by forcing him to recant. In the sixteenth century heresy

20. Johnson, *Wonder Working Providence,* 134, 127.
21. *Ibid.,* 30.

began to assume the nature of a civil crime, and heretics were persecuted to prevent them from polluting the mind of the commonwealth with their errors, or to secure the state against the insidious encroachment of foreign ideologies.

In this atmosphere Puritanism struggled to maturity with the conviction that in order to survive it must defend itself against heterodoxy. Puritan intolerance has been made notorious by the violent fulmination of such zealous divines as Nathaniel Ward. "To authorize an untruth, by a toleration of State," Ward wrote, "is to build a sconce against the walls of Heaven, to batter God out of his Chaire ... polypiety is the greatest impiety in the world. To say that men ought to have liberty of conscience is impious ignorance." [22]

Actually the problem of toleration among the Puritans was considerably more involved than first appearances indicate. As always, the primary source of their contentions was the Bible. Deuteronomy provided the classic statement of the treatment to be meted out to unbelievers, and served as a convenient text for innumerable fire-breathing sermons. "If thy brother ... or thy son, or thy daughter, or the wife of thy bosom, or thy friend which is as thine own soul entice thee, saying, Let us go and serve other gods ... thou shalt not consent unto him, nor hearken unto him.... But thou shalt surely kill him; thine hand shall be the first upon him to put him to death." [23]

This injunction was given new force by the introduction of a social arrangement that the Puritans had made peculiarly their own. The "community of elect" was a derivative concept, Hebraic in intent, Aristotelian in effect, but given pragmatic value as an efficient instrumentality for the creation of a stable and prosperous society under adverse conditions. The medieval and ultimately Aristotelian tenor of their political thought is evident in Winthrop's *Modell of Christian Charity*. Winthrop envisioned the future colony as a highly organic community of interdependent beings who thought and functioned as a single unit. There was general agreement that any form of dissent from the common aim was not to be tolerated. Organicism and intolerance were further heightened by the Puritans' deliberate efforts to emulate the mores and strong in-group loyalty of the ancient Hebrew tribes and to adopt as their

22. Nathaniel Ward, "The Simple Cobler of Aggawam in America," Force, ed., *Tracts Relating to the Colonies*, III, 8-9.
23. Deuteronomy 13:6, 8, 9.

own the Hebraic claim of spiritual aristocracy. The society must
not only function as a unit, but in order to do so must remain
narrowly exclusive in content. Each Saint in the small circle of
elect became responsible, not only for his own way of life but, in
large part, for that of his fellows as well. They were God's chosen
people and as such held their spiritual fortunes in common. "The
eyes of the world are upon us because we professe ourselves to be
a people in Covenant with God, and . . . if we walk contrary to the
Covenant . . . we (of all men) shall have the greater sinne." [24] This
heavy obligation entailed not only constant self-examination but
also the close and continuous scrutiny of one's neighbor's opinions.
"We must labour to observe what is amisse in one another, and
labour to purge out all our corruptions; thus mutually to help one
another." [25]

Above all it was essential to prevent the admission of unbelievers
bearing the deadly contagion of heretical ideas. Just as communi-
cable diseases are subject to quarantine, so "unsound and corrupt
opinions, and practices . . . more infectious than any plague sore"
must be sent from "the common ayre of the countrey by banishment." [26] Inasmuch as church and state were mutually dependent,
the logic of their argument demanded that heresy be treated as a
civil offense. The Puritans repeatedly insisted that they did not
claim power over men's consciences; the nature of election was
such that they could hardly coerce the unregenerate into acceptance of their beliefs. In theory, "quiet heresy," such as made no
attempt to entice others from the orthodox faith, was to be left
undisturbed. But "heresy turbulent . . . in conjunction with teaching lyes in the name of the lord, or with disturbance of publick
order" was regarded in an altogether different light.[27] The deliberate circulation of heterodox opinions calculated to undermine the
established church or to set up a rival organization was considered
to be a breach of the peace and, under some circumstances, a seditious attack upon the security of the state. The offense was pun-
ishable "according to the quality and measure of the disturbance
caused." Before passing sentence, the offender was subjected to

24. Bulkley, *The Gospel Covenant*, 388.
25. Cotton, *Covenant of Grace*, 10.
26. John Cotton, "A Reply to Mr. Williams His Examination; and A Answer to
the Letters sent to him by John Cotton," Narragansett Club, *Publications*, 1st Ser.,
2 (1867), 27.
27. John Norton, *The Heart of N-England Rent at the Blasphemies of the Present
Generation* (Cambridge, Mass., 1659), 52.

admonition with full confidence that "the Word of God is so clear, that he cannot but be convinced in conscience of the dangerous error of his way." If argument failed to persuade the hapless culprit, he was then cut off from the community "not for cause of conscience, but for sinning against his own conscience." [28] In the face of defenses as impermeable as these, dissenters were doomed to go down in defeat.

As yet, the issues in Boston were not so clear as to demand such extreme remedies. A doctrine so ambivalent as that of the Puritans, so perilously balanced between the antitheses of nominalism and realism, posed a standing invitation to misconstruction and distortion. The present need, it seemed, was to leash the opinionists and bend their tenets back to the orthodox frame. So Pastor Wilson preached more vehemently than ever the need of evident sanctification, and the ministers of neighboring towns, Weld and Eliot of Roxbury, Symmes of Charlestown, Shepard of Newtown, labored to contain the incursions that had been made in their congregations. But John Cotton, balanced perilously on the razor's edge of his own subtle distinctions, failed to give satisfaction to either camp.

(iv)

John Winthrop observed these developments with mounting concern. Affairs of state were as turbulent and unsettled as ever. The recent death of Captain John Mason, patentee of the Council for New England, had allayed threats from that quarter, but now the colony was menaced in several new directions. Shipmasters had protested the refusal to fly the King's ensign with its idolatrous cross. One mariner, having noisily abused the colonists as traitors and rebels, was seized and cast into jail, a move that precipitated tumult among the sailors in the town and harbor. At last, after much debate, Vane and Dudley conceded that the colors might be flown at the Castle Island fort without reflection on the probity of the Saints. Winthrop, however, having curiously absorbed the iconoclasm of Roger Williams, demurred and refused to partake in the capitulation.[29]

The intrusion of the Pequot tribe into the territory around Narragansett Bay had for some time boded ill. In July the Pequots had

28. John Cotton, *Controversie Concerning Liberty of Conscience in Matters of Religion* (London, 1649), 7, 8.
29. Winthrop, *Journal*, I, 181, 182.

sounded their defiance of the white man with the barbarous murder of John Oldham, a trader from Watertown. Oldham was a "mad
jack" at best, whose passing would doubtless be mourned by few.[30]
But the murder signaled the Pequots' determination to exclude the
English from their hunting ground and seemed to require prompt
retaliation. An expedition under John Endicott harassed the Indians
for a spell, but served mainly to stir up the bee's nest, prompting
Governor Bradford of Plymouth to protest the needless provocation
of war.[31]

These perils, however ominous, were external in origin, and
could be dealt with by diplomacy or force as the occasion required.
More menacing to Winthrop's mind was the worm that gnawed
within their vitals and threatened to turn the Saints against each
other. Sitting at his desk one evening in October, Winthrop frowningly contemplated the blank page of the notebook that lay open
before him. This was a fresh volume in which but a few pages had
been marred by the vigorous scratches of his penmanship. Only a
few days before he had filled up and set aside that journal in which
he had chronicled so painstakingly all that had befallen the colonists since leaving England. Now those six years of hardship were
on trial. Yet the afflictions they had endured did not matter; it was
the dream they had cherished which was all important—the vision
of a city upon a hill where God's chosen Saints might demonstrate
to future generations of men how He desired them to live.

Now this new Zion was threatened with destruction at the hands
of a meddling woman who should have confined her enterprising
spirit to the chores of her kitchen. Winthrop had slight patience
for women who "meddle in such things as are proper for men,
whose minds are stronger." [32] He dipped his quill into the ink, and
after a moment's thought drove it with deliberation across the
blank page: "One Mrs. Hutchinson, a member of the church of
Boston, a woman of ready wit and bold spirit, brought over with
her two dangerous errors: 1. That the person of the Holy Ghost
dwells in a justified person. 2. That no sanctification can help to
evidence to us our justification. From these two grew many
branches; as, 1. Our union with the Holy Ghost, so as a Christian
remains dead to every spiritual action, and hath no gifts nor graces,

30. Nathaniel Morton, New Englands Memoriall, ed. Howard J. Hall (New
York, 1937), 56-58.
31. Winthrop, Journal, I, 183 ff., especially 186, 194.
32. Ibid., II, 225.

other than such as are in hypocrites, nor any other sanctification but the Holy Ghost himself."

He paused, the other branches presently eluding his troubled mind, then added as an afterthought: "There joined with her in these opinions a brother of hers, one Mr. Wheelwright, a silenced minister sometimes in England." [33]

On Sunday, October 23, two days after making this entry, Winthrop was disquieted by a more ominous development. The Hutchinsonians were pressing resolutely to force Wilson's withdrawal or at least counteract the effect of his legalistic preachments. During the service one of the faction rose in the meetinghouse and suggested that John Wheelwright be called as an additional teacher to the church of Boston.[34] As a decision was not immediately required, Winthrop saw that there was time and occasion to crush this project in the bud. The ministers of the Bay had become alarmed by the situation in Boston and had requested a meeting with the General Court to determine the extent of Mrs. Hutchinson's influence. The Court was to reconvene on the following Tuesday, and such a conference might well provide opportunity to unmask the heterodoxy of the newcomer and force Cotton to declare himself on one side or the other.

At nine o'clock on the morning of the twenty-fifth the Court was called to order. After dealing with a few minor legislative matters, the deputies turned their attention to the grave-faced elders.[35] A spokesman for the clergy recited their perplexity in the face of conflicting rumors. If they could but "know the certainty of these things," they might jointly adopt a course of action with respect to the Boston church. For a while the discussion ranged at large, but gradually it settled on the precise meaning of these doctrines maintained so obscurely by Cotton and Wheelwright. Both men were present in the Court and can hardly have been surprised by this turn of events. Did they believe, someone asked them, that sanctification was any help to evidence justification? Both ministers readily acceded to this point, Mr. Cotton firmly reminding his brethren that he had delivered that doctrine plainly in public many times. But, he added warily, no sanctification can be an evidence without a concurrent sign of our justification.[36] Whatever his col-

---

33. *Ibid.*, I, 195 ff.
34. *Ibid.*, 197.
35. *Colony Records*, I, 181.
36. Hutchinson, *History*, I, 51; Winthrop, *Journal*, I, 196.

leagues' perplexities, Cotton suffered no doubt that the essential witness of salvation lay in the immediate testimony of the Spirit. So eager were the ministers to claim him for their own that they slurred over the qualifier and professed their agreement on this issue.

Proceeding to the baffling problem of the indwelling of the Holy Ghost, they met a broad diversity of opinion. Mrs. Hutchinson, they were reminded, had insisted that the union of the believer with the Holy Ghost was a personal union. Governor Vane, from his seat at the head of the table, asserted that he too gave faith to such a union. Mr. Cotton demurred. He professed his belief in the indwelling of the Holy Ghost in the elect, but such union, he held, could not admit "a communication of personal proprieties"—the actual indwelling of the spirit of the Lord in the soul of the believer. Mr. Wheelwright declared his willingness to accept the same interpretation. As the ministers stripped off and examined the successive layers of meaning in this problem, they found to their dismay that it was impossible to reach a firm agreement among themselves. Some accepted the mildly innatist view of Cotton and Wheelwright; others, following Pastor Wilson and Mr. Winthrop, rejected the idea of divine immanence in any form.[37] Doctrinal unity was urgently required if the erronists were to be brought under control, and the elders were alarmed to find that on this crucial issue they could not achieve a meeting of minds. So the meeting adjourned without any clear resolution of their problems. Cotton was still straddling the doctrinal fence, and Wheelwright gave every appearance of being at least as sound in doctrine as some of his colleagues.

This trial and confirmation of their new champion may have encouraged the Hutchinsonians to proceed to the fulfillment of their design. On the next Sunday, at the conclusion of the service, one of the "opinionists" moved for resolution that John Wheelwright be called as a teacher to the church of Boston. Instantly John Winthrop was on his feet with a challenge. He would not consent to this call, he whipped out. Anger and resentment were barely concealed in his voice. The effect was magnetic. All eyes in the meetinghouse were fastened on the angular, bearded face, as he lashed out his objections. The church, he proceeded, was already well furnished with able ministers whose spirits were known to them and "whose labors God had blessed in much love

37. Hutchinson, *History*, I, 51; Winthrop, *Journal*, I, 196, 201.

and sweet peace." There being no urgent need, he professed it unwise to hazard the concord of the church by calling one whose spirit was unknown to them. Mr. Wheelwright, he sardonically reminded the congregation, had but lately put forth doctrines of an exceedingly dubious nature. Had he not held that the persons of the Holy Ghost and the believer are united, and what was worse, that after such union the believer became something more than a mere creature? [38]

Near Winthrop, on the magistrates' foreseat, Henry Vane coiled himself in magnificent juvenile indignation. Now he sprang. He marveled at Mr. Winthrop's words: Vane neither cared nor was able to hide his bitterness. Had not Mr. Cotton, he went on, only recently bestowed his approval on brother Wheelwright's doctrine? Innocence unvarnished in Vane, to assume even yet that Cotton was held a fount of orthodoxy: Cotton himself was by no means so confident. As the congregation hopefully searched his benign countenance for ratification, he adroitly sidestepped the issue by professing uncertainty about Wheelwright's meaning. Once again the sea of heads shifted in expectant concentration. Mr. Wheelwright rose and gently accepting Winthrop's charge, deftly restored his mangled terms to their proper and meaningful context. Winthrop, now on the defensive, stumbled and hedged, but gave not an inch. Mr. Wheelwright was indeed a godly and able man, he conceded, but he could not assent to the nomination of one who was apt "to raise doubtful disputations." Lacking unanimity, as required for such actions, the proposal thereupon collapsed and was abandoned.[39]

This effort having failed, an alternate resolution was advanced for the present accommodation of Mr. Wheelwright. A number of the church of Boston, notably William Coddington, William Hutchinson, Edmund Quincy, and Atherton Hough, had recently acquired large allotments at Mount Wollaston, ten or twelve miles to the south.[40] Farming and developing these properties had kept the owners and their families away from Boston over long stretches of time, and to their dismay had deprived them of adequate means of worship. Numerous meetings had been held that fall in hope of organizing a church there.[41] The plan to call Mr. Wheelwright to the Boston church having been frustrated, it was now proposed

38. Winthrop, *Journal*, I, 197.
39. *Ibid.*
40. "Boston Town Records, 1634-1660," 6, 7, 10, 14.
41. Winthrop, *Journal*, I, 190.

that he assume the more modest demands of the ministry at Mount Wollaston. Winthrop and Wilson would have doubtless preferred a more remote assignment. At Wollaston, surrounded by the ring-leaders of the Hutchinson faction, Wheelwright could continue to feed them ambiguous and disruptive fancies for conveyance to Boston. But better Wollaston than Boston meetinghouse, so no dissent was offered and the motion carried. The meeting over, the congregation shuffled down the aisles toward the open door, some glowering resentfully, the bolder muttering their determination to admonish their late governor for his unseemly behavior.

The next afternoon Winthrop was summoned before an indig-nant congregation assembled in the meetinghouse and asked to apologize for his attack on Wheelwright. Not readily intimidated, the hardy oligarch proceeded instead to enlarge on his criticism of the previous day. He told them that he had visited brother Wheel-wright with the resolution to remove or confirm the disparity of their views. The result of this interview, he stated, was a renewed conviction that Wheelwright's opinions were dangerously unsound. If, as Wheelwright contended, there was a real union with the person of the Holy Ghost, then it was an inescapable conclusion that the believer was more than a mortal creature; he must indeed become God-man—even Jesus Christ himself. "Now," Winthrop dryly observed, "[I] leave the church to judge whether this is agree-able to the doctrine of the church or not." Turning to Wheelwright, he earnestly beseeched that they might forbear the use of such terms as "real union" and "person of the Holy Ghost." These, he asserted, were of human invention, lacking scriptural basis or prim-itive usage, and their continued employment could only promote disputation and estrangement. For his part, he concluded, he did not propose to dispute the matter; but should any brother wish to see the light by which he walked, he would be pleased to impart it to him. "How this was taken by the congregation, did not ap-pear, for no man spake to it." [42]

42. *Ibid.*, 198 ff. Herein altered from third person to direct quotation, as indi-cated by the use of brackets.

X

"The Jarring Sound of Rattling Drums"

November–December 1636

(i)

THROUGHOUT the fall and winter the war of words raged on. "For the peace sake of the church, which all were tender of," the debate was mainly confined to writing. Letters, protests, propositions, and declarations flew to and fro with such zealous animosity that soon the peace of which all were so tender was reduced to shreds and tatters.[1]

At one point the epistolary combat was diversified by a lively confrontation of members of the Boston and Newtown congregations. The Bostonians submitted to this conference a draft of five propositions reaffirming their conviction that the believer was a passive agent in the initiation of faith and that sanctification was no evidence without a concurrent apprehension of justification. They appealed to their neighbors from Newtown to write out their differences on these points. Mr. Shepard's flock felt compelled to acquiesce in these propositions, but after heated debate they professed to see other and more serious areas of controversy. Thereupon they withdrew from the conference, drafted a roster of fifteen heterodoxies perilously entertained by the Boston congregation, and submitted this list to the magistrates. Irate at this apparent lack of good faith, the Bostonians composed a rebuttal, which concluded with a ringing affirmation of their primary article of faith: "that the immediat Revelation of the Spirit [comes] . . . in an absolut promise of free grace perswadeinge the soule of his interest

1. Winthrop, *Journal*, I, 201; *Winthrop Papers*, III, 328 ff.

125

in Christ, and that this is the infallible certaine evidence of our Justifyed estate." [2] And so the epistolary barrage was resumed with redoubled energy.

As the controversy mounted in intensity, the glare of criticism seems to have shifted from Cotton and Wheelwright to Governor Vane who had openly professed opinions more radical than those of the two ministers. Finding himself under attack by almost the entire Bay clergy, the young executive faltered and impulsively sought some means of escape from his thorny eminence. The arrival of letters reporting the tangled condition of his private affairs in England seemed to offer a way out. He confided these reports to Winthrop and Dudley, his fellow councilors, pointing out that the business required his prompt departure. Those two dignitaries, masking their satisfaction with appropriate expressions of regret, zestfully seized on his offer, and a special session of the General Court was promptly summoned.

On Wednesday, the seventh of December, Governor Vane called the Court to order. When all were at last quietly attentive, he briefly explained his dilemma and asked their consent to his prompt departure. Mr. Winthrop rose and helpfully attested to the urgency of this move. The deputies were nonplused by the awkward and unprecedented situation. A brief recess was proposed in order to weigh their decision more carefully. Before this motion could be acted on, one of the Assistants took the floor and piteously bewailed the loss of so good a governor during such trying times. This display of loyalty shattered Vane's uncertain composure, and collapsing in boyish tears, he sobbed out the real reasons for his departure. God's judgment would be upon them, he feared, for these differences and dissensions in their midst. Dolefully he protested the scandalous imputations which had been leveled at him, as though he had been the sole cause of all their troubles.

This hysterical disclosure placed the situation in a new and sobering light. Now the deputies, each in his own way, measured the implications of Vane's proposal anew. His allies in the Hutchinson circle, of whom there were at least seven in the Court, remained eager to maintain him in a position where he might effectively champion their cause.[3] Those who would have been relieved to see him out of office now realized that his departure under such

---

2. *Winthrop Papers*, III, 324-26.
3. *Colony Records*, I, 184-85. These were Coddington, Dummer, Coggeshall, Colburn, Brenton, Spencer, and Scruggs.

conditions could create a furor in the English court and spell future trouble for the colony. Thereupon, the antagonists united in their determination to refuse his petition and to keep the youthful waverer among them for the present.

Stunned by this blow to his hopes, Vane hastily recovered his self-control. He apologized for his passionate outburst, but asserted that his former reasons remained valid grounds for a prompt departure. It seems likely that by now the majority of the Court would have been well content to see the last of their unstable chief executive, as long as his withdrawal was construed in terms which did not reflect on the colony. Even his warmest supporters among these imperturbable Israelites must have suppressed with some difficulty their doubts concerning a leader who was so facile of his emotions before a public assembly. So with respectful silence which spared the embarrassment of a formal declaration, they registered their assent. After some further debate, it was agreed to hold new elections on the fifteenth of the month and the Court stood adjourned until the following Tuesday.[4]

News of Vane's defection promoted a flurry of excitement in Boston. The congregation was alarmed at the prospect of losing their champion. A number of them concluded that he must be persuaded to remain and a committee was delegated to inform the Court "that they did not apprehend the necessity of the governor's departure upon the reasons alleged." With supple vacillation, Vane avowed himself an obedient child of the church and succumbed to their will. When this fresh change of heart was announced, it was decided as a matter of convenience to cancel the plan for an interim election.[5] Vane resumed his chair of office and for the remaining five months of his term of office, the precarious political imbalance of the colony continued.

At that same eventful session of the Court, William Hutchinson —also at the church's request—was excused from assisting as a magistrate at the particular courts.[6] William had not been on hand to witness Vane's embarrassed attempt at escape. At the town meeting of the previous Saturday, William Colburn had been elected interim deputy from Boston to replace Mr. Hutchinson.[7] The reasons for this substitution are indeterminate. However de-

4. Winthrop, *Journal*, I, 201-2; *Colony Records*, I, 185.
5. Winthrop, *Journal*, I, 203.
6. *Colony Records*, I, 185.
7. "Boston Town Records, 1634-1660," 14.

voted to his wife, William may have been reluctant to continue in an office where he must so exposedly do battle for her cause. William seems to have cherished tranquillity in a way that Anne could have scarcely understood.

(ii)

Hugh Peter glowered menacingly at the pocked and rutted road which wound before him. December frost had hardened wagon tracks and hoofprints into treacherous snares about and around which his horse now cautiously picked its way. Plodding along the road to Boston, Master Peter had many problems to engage his mind. There was much to be done at Salem and this fresh summons to attend the General Court was an unwelcome distraction. His ordination as minister to the Salem church was little more than a week away. That office promised to hold more than its fair share of complications. The dissensions sown by Roger Williams still grew rankly in Salem and now eleven of his stubborn adherents were seeking to withdraw regularly into their own church. The enforced leisure of this journey would have allowed Hugh—who was seldom so long inactive—an opportunity to hammer out in his mind the new covenant of the Salem church; a stratagem designed to excommunicate automatically all those who still adhered to Williams's separatist position.[8]

But these preoccupations would not have dulled Master Peter's understanding of the more serious dissensions which raged in Boston. Nor could they have dimmed his conviction that he was qualified above most men to deal effectively with such problems. Hugh Peter's self-confidence was resolutely galvanic. The news of Vane's hysterical attempt at escape could hardly have come as a surprise to him. Having worked and lived in close quarters with Vane, the youth's instability and impetuosity would not have eluded Peter's perception. That it differed only in kind from his own peculiar infirmity was a matter of small moment to one so rocklike during his lucid intervals. But it was nonetheless disturbing to him that those opinions had at last come to infect and rot the very heart of their government. Mrs. Hutchinson's table talk plainly lay at the root of the trouble, so she must be curbed, and that promptly. And it seemed equally imperative that Mr. Cotton declare his views in precise, unclouded terms.

8. Stearns, *Strenuous Puritan*, 110-11.

When Peter arrived in Boston, there was yet a day or so before he and his fellow ministers were to confer with the members of the Court. The clergymen resolved to make the best of this time by conducting their own preliminary inquiry. On Monday, December 12, they met with John Cotton and queried him narrowly about the reported differences in their views. They bluntly reminded him of his responsibility for the troublesome parishioner who had caused the dissension. Some of them impatiently urged that it was now time for the magistrates to take her case in hand. Cotton protested that such procedure was not according to God, and begged them to pursue some other course for the present. It was at last agreed that they should confront her themselves and strive to reach an understanding. An interview at Cotton's house was arranged, perhaps for that same afternoon, and a messenger was sent to summon her into their presence.[9]

(iii)

With troubled and uncertain mind, Anne Hutchinson turned the corner into Prison Lane and trudged up the hill toward the little house which huddled in the shadow of Trimountaine. Passing the gloomy pile of the prison house, she came at last to Mr. Cotton's doorstep and knocked apprehensively at the great timbered door. In a moment it swung open and Mr. Cotton reassuringly admitted her into the warm parlor. The dancing firelight fitfully revealed a cluster of black-garbed figures, their stern, forbidding faces turned curiously toward her. Hugh Peter was in the forefront, exuding his customary ineradicable pugnacity, and near at hand was Thomas Shepard of Newtown, frail and pasty-faced as always, his benign features now worn with a widower's grief.[10] Gaunt, gray Nathaniel Ward stood thoughtfully by, his indignant, lacerating humor lurking but slightly beneath the urbane exterior. Thomas Weld and John Eliot of Roxbury were also there, intemperate zeal and gentle piety uncomfortably linked in ministerial harness. She saw her old combatant of the *Griffin*, Zachariah Symmes, now minister of Charlestown; and nearby a man unknown to her, the Reverend George Phillips of Watertown. Mr. Wilson, the chief victim of her strictures, had tactfully withdrawn to a far corner, apparently pre-

9. Winthrop, *Journal*, I, 203; *Antinomianism*, 170; Hutchinson, *History*, II, 372-73.
10. Johnson, *Wonder Working Providence*, 136.

paring to take notes on the conference. In the midst of this stern company, Anne must have found comfort in the familiar faces of Mr. Wheelwright and the two ruling elders, Leverett and Cogge-shall, both good friends and loyal supporters.[11]

Doffing her cloak, Anne moved warily to the seat that was offered her. Pinioned there by the hostile eyes of the clergymen, she glanced uneasily from one grim face to another. A numb wave of fear surged through her and spun its eddies out to the farthest corners of her brain.[12] Suddenly Mr. Peter's voice crashed noisily about her. They had summoned her, she heard him saying, because of reports that she had condemned their ministry. It was said that she had denied they taught a true ministry of the Gospel. His passion soared with each fresh allusion to their outraged dignity. How did their doctrine differ so greatly from that of Mr. Cotton, he thundered.[13] Stunned by the magnificent diapason of his vehemence, Anne fumbled weakly for a defense. Unable to piece one out under the continuing assault, she lapsed into helpless silence. The pack closed in. "[Why do you] cast such aspersions upon the ministers of the country?" Weld snapped at her. "Though we [are] poor sinful men and for ourselves we [care] not[,] but for the precious doctrine we [hold] forth we [cannot] but grieve to hear that so blasphemed." [14]

Frustrated by her refusal to answer, Peter changed his weapons. "I pray answer the question directly," he appealed to her, "as fully and as plainly as you desire we should tell you our minds. Mrs. Hutchinson we come for plain dealing and telling you our hearts." [15] Anne took courage from this conciliatory note. A passage from the Book of Proverbs flashed through her mind and she murmured it reassuringly to herself, "The fear of man bringeth a snare, but whoso putteth his trust in the Lord shall be safe." [16] Turning to Mr. Peter, she declared that she would deal with them as plainly

11. Hutchinson, *History*, II, 372, 374, 377, 380, 381, 383.

12. *Ibid.*, 379. In her testimony before the court Mrs. Hutchinson stated, "When I came unto them, they urging many things unto me and I being backward to answer at first, at length this scripture came into my mind 29th Prov. 15. The fear of man bringeth a snare, but whoso putteth his trust in the Lord shall be safe."

13. *Ibid.*, 372, 381. The dialogue that follows stands *as it was remembered* by the participants a year later at Mrs. Hutchinson's trial, so it is presumably at best only an approximation of their actual words at that time. Transposition from indirect to direct quotation has been employed where it seemed reasonably legitimate and has been indicated by the use of brackets.

14. *Ibid.*, 373.

15. *Ibid.*, 375.

16. *Ibid.*, 379, 381.

as she could. Peter seized the tender and plunged ahead. "What difference do you conceive to be between your teacher and us," he rapped out. Anne mounted her conviction and drove it resolutely forward. There was a wide and broad difference between Mr. Cotton and themselves, she affirmed, for they did not hold forth a Covenant of Grace as clearly as he did. Peter was unsatisfied and pressed her more closely—but wherein did they differ? They did not hold forth the seal of the Spirit as Mr. Cotton did, she informed him.[17]

"Where is the difference there?" another impatiently queried.

"Why," Anne was soaring in her element, "you preach of the seal of the spirit upon a work and he upon free grace without a work or without respect to a work, he preaches the seal of the spirit upon free grace and you upon a work."[18]

Cotton flushed uncomfortably. "[I] could have wished that [you] had not put that in," he protested.[19] It pained him, he told her, that she should put comparisons between his ministry and theirs. But Anne was not to be so put off: she found the difference even if he did not.

"Why cannot we preach a covenant of grace?" one of the others asked her.

"Why," she replied, "because you can preach no more than you know. You may do it in your judgment," she patronizingly offered, "but not in experience."[20] Warming to the subject, she illustrated her point by likening the astonished ministers to the Apostles before the resurrection of Christ.[21] "As the apostles were for a time without the spirit so until they had received the witness of the spirit they could not preach a covenant of grace so clearly."[22]

"What do you conceive of such a brother?" Peter interposed, indicating one of their number.

"He [has] not the seal of the spirit," Anne was prompt to assert.[23]

Mr. Shepard displayed a lively interest in her claim that they could not be able ministers of the New Testament before they were sealed. What exactly did she mean? Anne reminded him of a sermon he had preached on lecture day wherein he taught the

17. *Ibid.*, 372, 375, 381.
18. *Ibid.*, 381.
19. *Ibid.*, 373.
20. *Ibid.*, 381-82.
21. *Ibid.*, 372, 373.
22. *Ibid.*, 381.
23. *Ibid.*, 372, 373.

means by which a Christian may gain assurance of God's love. It was this sermon which had confirmed her suspicion that he was not sealed.

"Why [do you] say so?" Shepard mewed.

"Because you put love for an evidence," Anne judicially announced.

Observing the venturesome liberality of her condemnations, George Phillips thought to trick her into an embarrassing libel. Although he knew she had never heard him preach, he slyly asked her opinion of his ministry. The ruse apparently succeeded, for Anne's mind was firmly closed to the possibility that any but Cotton and Wheelwright, of those present, could be adequately sealed.[24]

For the moment the ministers were less concerned with their respective states of grace than with the terminological chaos which Mrs. Hutchinson had introduced. They were frankly puzzled by her use of the expressions "witness of the spirit" and "seal of the spirit." The terms were often loosely, and sometimes interchangeably, employed to mean either immediate assurance of salvation or the sanctification that distinguishes and confirms the faithful.[25] In either case, it was requisite that the usage be defined, and this Mrs. Hutchinson had sadly neglected to do. If she had meant to deny that her inquisitors were sealed in the latter sense, then here was indeed cause for clerical indignation. Cotton himself, although he ordinarily forbore such usage, had understood her to refer to the seal of the Spirit as "the full assurance of God's favour by the holy ghost." His colleagues, by no means so certain, were in a frame of mind to explore every phrase minutely for its offensive connotations. Having bandied the subject back and forth at such length as to preclude all hope of mutual understanding, confusion was compounded by the suggestion that they substitute the terms "broad seal" and "little seal."[26]

"If you will have it so be it so," Nathaniel Ward laconically grunted.[27] It was Mr. Ward's experience that the imperfections of man could be manifested in curious ways. Some of his humorless colleagues, however, made a mental note to query Mr. Cotton more precisely on this controversial issue.[28]

Its energy spent, the inquisition drew to a close. But the loquac-

24. Ibid., 373, 374.
25. Cotton, Sixteene Questions, 4-5.
26. Ibid.; Hutchinson, History, II, 382.
27. Hutchinson, History, II, 382.
28. Cotton, Sixteene Questions, 4-5.

ity of its victim was by no means exhausted, and the ardors of debate seem only to have replenished her self-assurance. Cornering Mr. Weld by the window, where he sat writing, she proceeded to favor him lengthily with an amplification of her views.[29]

Meanwhile the ministers conversed quietly as they cloaked and muffled themselves against the winter's cold. Mr. Cotton rendered his departing guests effusive apologies for the unkind comparisons made by his tactless parishioner.[30] His colleagues seemed not to take the matter so ill, however. Some avowed that in the future they would not so credulously accept all the reports they heard. Others shrugged it off and said they would speak no more about it. Nonetheless, the ruling elders were charged to look more closely to Mrs. Hutchinson's deportment.[31]

But the business continued to prey uncomfortably on their minds. The more they pondered what they had heard, the darker it seemed.[32] That evening, or early the next day before the Court was to convene, some of the ministers met again—this time without Mr. Cotton. This self-appointed delegation carefully drafted "sixteene questions of curious and necessary consequence" dealing with areas in which Cotton's views appeared to differ from their own. Among other things, they besought him to clarify that bewildering aggregation of spiritual "seals" which they had so lately encountered. The completed questionnaire, a formidable instrument, was then submitted to Cotton with a supplication that he respond as precisely and freely as he could.[33]

(iv)

On Thursday afternoon the Court reconvened.[34] The legislative docket was heavy and probably kept the deputies within the frigid confines of the meetinghouse until darkness and hunger at last forced an adjournment. New enactments were passed "for preventing the immoderate expence of provisions brought from beyond the seas."[35] A reorganization of the militia was prompted by the immediacy of the Indian menace. The entire military force was

29. Hutchinson, *History*, II, 381.
30. *Ibid.*, 372.
31. *Ibid.*, 372, 382.
32. *Ibid.*, 382.
33. Winthrop, *Journal*, I, 203; Cotton, *Sixteene Questions, passim.*
34. *Colony Records*, I, 185-86.
35. *Ibid.*, 186.

now grouped into three regiments under Colonels Winthrop, Haynes, and Endicott, with Governor Vane as chief general "for the time being." Before adjournment it was moved and passed that the colony should observe a day of fasting and humiliation on the nineteenth of January.[36] The reasons for this observance were generously manifold: "The miserable estate of the churches in Germany, the calamities upon our native country, ... the dangers of those at Connecticut, and of ourselves also, by the Indians" —but most importunately and pointedly—for "the dissensions in our churches."[37]

During the discussion a passing reference was made to the energetic policy the ministers had now adopted. Astonished by this disturbing turn of events, Governor Vane expressed displeasure that the clergy should have proceeded "without his privity."[38] Although his remark prompted no immediate debate, it did not pass unobserved.

The next day, before the conference of ministers and deputies was held, Cotton preached a sermon in the meetinghouse. Eager to promote a reconciliation of the contending parties, he conceded that evident sanctification could serve as an evidence of justification. Elaborating a theme dear to the heart of his mentor, Richard Sibbes, he went on to affirm that a true desire for sanctification was in itself a form of sanctification. Indeed, "if a man were laid so flat upon the ground, as he could see no desires, etc., but only as a bruised reed, did wait at the feet of Christ, yet here was matter of comfort for this."[39] But even this conciliatory gesture was soon to become fuel for the mounting flames.

The meeting that followed swept the combatants beyond the point of easy reconciliation. When insults and abuse—overt or covert—were freely exchanged, when principle became narrowly identified with personal self-esteem, then dispassionate scrutiny of the real issues was no longer possible. Vane opened the meeting by informing the ministers and deputies that they had been summoned once more to discover and pacify "the difference among the churches in point of opinion." Then Mr. Dudley rose and made an appeal for the candid expression of opposing views, a curiously uncharacteristic sentiment that promptly loosened Vane's impulsive tongue. He would be content to accept Dudley's counsel,

36. *Ibid.*, 187.
37. Winthrop, *Journal*, I, 208.
38. *Ibid.*, 203.
39. *Ibid.*, 204.

but, Vane intimated, might not this course be supererogatory, since the ministers were already "about it in a church way." Hugh Peter lunged to the ministers' defense. With due respect but compelling bluntness, he informed the Governor that "it had sadded the ministers' spirits that he should be jealous of their meetings or seem to restrain their liberty." [40] Too late Vane saw that he had blundered into a hornets' nest. He hurriedly ventured an awkward apology for the impulsiveness of his speech. Peter observed the retreat and pressed his advantage relentlessly. Before Vane had come to the colony, he pointedly remarked, the churches had been comfortably at peace with each other. The Governor ignored the unjust implication of this challenge. "The light of the gospel brings a sword," he hotly retorted, "and the children of the bondwoman [will] persecute those of the freewoman."

Peter reconnoitered and shrewdly aimed his next blow to undermine the emotional appeal of Vane's heroic stance. Assuming a tone of patronizing solicitude, he appealed to Vane to "consider his youth and short experience in the things of God." Above all he should seek to govern his careless propensity to "peremptory conclusions." Vane's defenses now thoroughly demolished, Master Peter broadened his assault on the ramparts of heterodoxy. Both in the Low Countries and in New England, he recalled, dissensions such as these originated in three principal causes: "Pride, new notions lift up the mind, . . . idleness, . . . [and ungrounded knowledge]." [41]

Having thus seized the initiative, the champions of orthodoxy proceeded with a degree of candor that should have given grim pleasure to old Thomas Dudley. As Peter's withering fire died away, Pastor Wilson stepped into the breach and delivered "a very sad speech of the condition of our churches." This hortatory effort, to judge from the ensuing repercussions, must have been in the main a waspish tirade against the majority of the church of Boston, delivered in but scarcely veiled terms. But Wilson gravely overreached himself when he insinuated that perhaps Mr. Cotton was partially responsible for the dissension. In example, he made reference to the sermon which Cotton had delivered just that day. Knowing full well what the answer must be, he pointedly raised the question whether any of those forms of sanctification that

40. *Ibid.*, 203-4.
41. *Ibid.*, 204. The Rev. William Hubbard in *History of New England* (Cambridge, 1815), 290, provides the third point but neglects to offer the source of his information.

Cotton had adduced could provide sufficient evidence of election without a concurrent sight of justification. Cotton was honestly obliged to concede that to his mind they could not, in which opinion Vane supported him, and so his attempted reconciliation was perverted into an additional source of grievance. In conclusion, Wilson's speech was apparently moved to represent the sense of the meeting and as such was approved by all the magistrates and ministers present with the notable exceptions of Vane, Coddington, Dummer, Cotton, and Wheelwright.[42]

John Cotton was ordinarily a man of sweet and placid disposition, not easily stirred to anger. That afternoon, when he left the meetinghouse, Cotton was boiling with indignation. Nor was he alone in his distress. As news of Wilson's "sad speech" spread throughout the town—subject, no doubt, to the amplification and distortion that normally attend such reports—resentment seethed and coiled from door to door, at last to explode in an enraged demand for expiation. A delegation, headed by Cotton, was formed to call on Mr. Wilson and admonish him for his uncharitable insinuations. Wilson received his visitors and, hearing out their protests, blandly rejoined that he had seen no breach of rule. He had been summoned to the Court with his fellow ministers, and had been requested to deliver his mind freely and directly. What he had said was of general application and common knowledge. Queried as to the intent of his remarks, Wilson flatly denied that they were directed mainly against the members of his own church. This denial his accusers found hard to credit, and so they departed, sorely vexed and determined to push the matter to a more satisfactory conclusion.

On Saturday, December 31, the Saints once again filed into the dreary glacial waste of the meetinghouse. Bundled to the ears and with footstoves aglow, they huddled on their hard, unyielding benches and nerved themselves for a fresh assault on the offending pastor. Summoned to rise, that proud priest, like a common prisoner at the bar, faced his unruly flock to hear the charges preferred against him. As soon as the formalities were under way, Governor Vane launched the attack against Wilson and pressed him bitterly for his offenses. One by one other members of the congregation stood in their places and flung reproaches at the unhappy parson. Wilson bore this humiliation with quiet dignity, responding soberly to each of the accusations brought against him. But the outraged crowd refused to accept his excuses and a majority hotly demanded a vote of censure. Cotton, who had followed the chase with more restraint than his parishioners, hastily intervened to ward off the fatal blow. He protested that, lacking unanimity, a formal motion of censure was out of order. Having averted the ultimate indignity, he turned upon his hapless colleague and administered a grave exhortation which partially allayed the vindictive temper of the congregation.

The next morning Pastor Wilson, if not chastened at least enjoined to caution, preached a Sunday sermon of such conciliatory tone that at its conclusion Governor Vane was prompted to rise and give public witness of his approval.[43]

Wilson's "sad speech" and the abortive attempt to censure him and bring about his expulsion from the Boston pulpit signalized the finality of the breach between the pastor and most of his congregation. Now the Hutchinsonians, emboldened by their numbers and solidarity, seized the offensive and sallied forth from their private conventicles to attack and discredit the orthodox doctrines at regular church services. "Now the faithfull Ministers of Christ must have dung cast on their faces, and be no better than legall Preachers," Winthrop mourned. The question period that ordinarily followed each lecture was now dominated by zealous sectaries who plied the minister with questions calculated to destroy confidence in his teachings. "You might have seene halfe a dozen Pistols discharged at the face of the Preacher," continued Winthrop's lament, "(I meane) so many objections made by the opinionists . . . against our doctrine delivered, if it suited not their new fancies." When Wilson rose to preach or pray, Mrs. Hutchinson and her more dedicated followers flaunted their disdain by boldly stalking out of the meetinghouse. Most of these protestants being women, the bewildered males of the Wilson coterie had no choice but to accept at face value the personal reasons advanced for their abrupt departure.[44]

Although Pastor Wilson was the favorite butt of this abuse, the sport was by no means confined to him or to Boston. The more venturesome of the factionists attended lectures in outlying settlements and seized the opportunity to abash and put to rout other

43. *Ibid.*, 204-5.
44. *Antinomianism*, 81, 82; Cotton, *Way of the Congregational Churches Cleared*, 61.

ministers who preached a Covenant of Works. Throughout the colony pastors were beleaguered with "epistles of defiance and challenge" refuting the doctrines delivered from their pulpits. Any ministers who taught by "syllogisme" or rational exposition of the Scriptures rather than by the immediate "motion of the Spirit" were set down as "Popish Factors . . . Pharisees . . . and Opposers of Christ himselfe." [45]

And so the bitter words flew back and forth throughout the cold winter months, "and it began to be as common . . . to distinguish between men by being under a covenant of grace or a covenant of works, as in other countries between Protestants and papists." [46] As rancor mounted, applications for membership in the church declined. Few people dared to submit their spiritual qualifications to the searching crossfire of the bitterly contending parties. At last, on January 8, the church rolls were closed, and for a year no new members were received into the church of Boston.[47]

45. *Antinomianism*, 82, 81.
46. Winthrop, *Journal*, I, 209.
47. Entry of Jan. 8, 1635/6, First Church of Boston, Records and Baptisms, 1630-1687, Mass. Hist. Soc.

XI

"Behold the Bed That Is Solomon's"

January 1636/7–May 1637

(i)

JOHN WINTHROP had not lightly assumed the exacting role of defender of the faith. The bitter controversy in Boston pressed him on the path toward his own Gethsemane. Through agonizing days and nights, Winthrop probed his spiritual estate and tearfully suffered the "beame of wrath" God had aimed at his soul. At last, in mid-December, he testified, "the Lord Jesus shewed himselfe and stood between that wrath and my soule," and he found afresh the spiritual light that had waned in his sight since his first discovery of it some twenty years before.[1] On January twelfth—his fiftieth birthday—the gaunt and bearded Puritan secluded himself at his desk, and in that process of self-mortification which afforded the Puritan mind such comfortable assurance of its inherent superiority, he poured out an anguished account of his religious experience from his youthful days to the present. The burden of this relation confirmed his belief that grace and works were inextricably interwoven in the working out of God's design for his Saints.[2]

The intensity of his spiritual rebirth freshened Winthrop's determination to convey his perceptions to his fellow townsmen, in the desperate hope that he might allay further contention. Unhappily his most earnest efforts brought him little but renewed frustration. A blunt letter to Cotton elicited a reply which, how-

1. Robert C. Winthrop, *Life and Letters of John Winthrop* (Boston, 1869), II, 161.
2. *Winthrop Papers*, III, 338 ff.

ever "loving and gentle" in tone, indicated that the recipient remained quite unmoved by Winthrop's pious calculations. At about this same time, Winthrop drafted two long theological essays, copiously larded with scriptural documentation. The first had been prompted by the new opinions which had broken out in the church of Boston, "that a man is justified before he believes; and that faith is no cause of justification." [3] In reply Winthrop now offered a "Declaration" expounding his conviction that faith must precede justification and is in part a cause of it. The second paper, his so-called "Pacification," contained seven propositions designed "to quiet and still those tumults" in the church of Boston.[4]

In anticipation of a theological imprimatur, Winthrop submitted these weighty disquisitions to the scrutiny of Pastor Wilson, who in turn conveyed them to Thomas Shepard. After studying them carefully, Shepard breathed relief that he had intercepted the documents before they were circulated at large. So many doubtful arguments had Winthrop advanced, that it seemed to Shepard "a good hand of providence" had intervened to prevent their delivery.[5] And irrespective of their merits, he questioned the wisdom of protracting the epistolatory debate, "it being an easy thing for a subtile adversary to take advantages at woords." [6] Gagged by his own allies, Winthrop abandoned his attempts at theological disputation and sought thereafter to gain his ends within the more congenial accommodation of the political arena.

Similarly intent on pacification according to his own light, John Cotton grappled assiduously with his "sixteen questions of serious and necessary consequence," which the ministers had submitted to him. The answers he returned can have provided his inquisitors small consolation. For the most part Cotton persisted in his fundamental beliefs and merely seized the occasion to reiterate opinions he had previously expressed. Most significantly, for the purposes of the debate, he clung to his conviction that "the testimony of the Spirit is so clear that it may witness immediately." [7] Although conceding that such testimony must be attended by an enlarged capacity for good works, he nonetheless maintained that the testimony is valid in and of itself without respect to its fruit. As for santification, it was, he admitted, a true evidence of justification "a

3. Winthrop, *Journal*, I, 206.
4. *Winthrop Papers*, III, 327, 328-29.
5. *Ibid.*, 329.
6. *Ibid.*, 327.
7. Cotton, *Sixteene Questions*, 6.

posteriori," but without a direct and concurrent witness of the Spirit, it was not a sure ground of "Primitive Comfort" for the soul.[8]

Through long pages of theological argument, Cotton labored to confirm his persuasion that as long as justification remains dark and uncertain, apparent sanctification cannot be applied as an evidence of grace. To find one's hope solely in the performance of good works, he insisted, is to go under a Covenant of Works. Hewing to the line of thought marked out for him by Dr. Sibbes, Cotton contended there were saving graces "not sanctifying, but . . . wrought before Sanctification," that may bear adequate witness to a safe estate. A man who recognizes his insufficiency and need of Christ, who seeks and waits for him "in every Ordinance and Duty," is already truly justified, even though he may be unaware of his state of grace.[9]

Like Winthrop, Cotton was also concerned with the problem of the role and order of faith in the process of salvation. On this point he was prepared to agree with the main body of orthodox opinion that faith did provide assurance of salvation. But, his interrogators were warned, faith must not be regarded as an autonomous effort on man's part to win his salvation. Faith could provide conclusive assurance of election only in so far "as it revealeth the free grace of God offered and applyed in Christ Jesus." [10]

(ii)

Thursday, the nineteenth of January, had been set aside by the Court as a solemn day of fasting and humiliation. Throughout the colony the occasion was observed in every church. In the afternoon the people of Boston, their senses whetted with cold and hunger, huddled in the barren confines of their meetinghouse to hear Mr. Cotton lecture on a text from Isaiah: "Behold, ye fast for strife and debate, and to smite with the fist of wickedness: ye shall not fast as ye do this day, to make your voice to be heard on high." With long and cogent argument, Cotton strove to allay conflict and promote reconciliation within the community.[11] When at last he drew to an end and stepped down from the pulpit, Mr. Wheelwright was called forward to prophesy as a lay brother. Mounting

8. *Ibid.*, 7.
9. *Ibid.*, 10.
10. *Ibid.*, 7.
11. *Ibid.*

to the pulpit, Wheelwright placed on the lectern before him a manuscript so bulky as to suggest that he had devoted considerable time and thought to his remarks. "Matthew, the ninth chapter, verse five," he announced his text, "—but the days will come when the bridegroom shall be taken from them and then they shall fast." [12] God's people fast, Wheelwright told the attentive congregation, because God is angry at them for their sins, and has removed Himself from their presence to show His displeasure. "Then cometh in all matters of mourning and fasting, all misery followeth from the absence of Christ." How might they restore the Lord Jesus Christ to their midst: what course should they take to keep Him among them? "We must all prepare for a spiritual combat," he exhorted.[13] His voice swelled and clattered among the rafters: [14] "Behold the bed that is Solomon's; there is three-score valiant men about it, valiant men of Israel, every one hath his sword in his hand, and being expert in war, hath his sword girt on his thigh. . . . They must fight, and fight with spiritual weapons, for the weapons of our warfare are not carnal, but spiritual . . . we must all of us prepare for battle and come out against the enemies of the Lord. And if we do not strive those under a covenant of works will prevail." [15] At these last words some among his audience must have stirred uneasily. Despite his injunction against the use of carnal weapons, his imagery was ominously suggestive; coupled with the intimation that those under a Covenant of Works were in some way the enemies of the Lord, there could be no mistaking the bent of his discourse.

In order to prevail in this combat—"for fight we must," he reiterated—the faithful must contend for the doctrine "that neither before our conversion nor after [are we] able to put forth one act of true, saving spiritual wisdom but we must have it put forth from the Lord Jesus Christ, with whom we are made one . . . we are not able to do any work of sanctification, further then we are acted by the Lord, nor able to procure our justification but it must be the Lord Jesus Christ, that must apply himselfe and his righteousness to us." [16] Nor would he allow that any work of righteousness in man might constitute an adequate assurance of faith. To the objection that it might seem uncharitable to condemn many of the

12. *Antinomianism*, 203.
13. Wheelwright, *Writings*, 153, 160.
14. *Ibid.*, 224; *Antinomianism*, 203.
15. Wheelwright, *Writings*, 160.
16. *Ibid.*, 162-63.

"wondrous holy people" who feel obliged to lean upon their works for assurance, his retort was hot and sweeping: "Brethren, those under a covenant of works, the more holy they are, the greater enemies they are to Christ." Although the children of God should ordinarily be meek in their deportment, when dealing with God's enemies the meekest of Saints must courageously strive to beat them down by "the sword of the spirit, the word of God." [17]

He paused in his argument to postulate the objection that such a course might "cause a combustion in the Church and Commonwealth." The purport of this suggestion was not lost upon his audience. "I must confesse and acknowledge it will do so," he answered his own objection, "but what then, did not Christ come to send fire upon earth?" [18] Even though strife and contention may ensue, it cannot hurt God's children to see the Gospel held forth clearly. "If we mean to keep the Lord Jesus Christ, we must be willing to suffer anything . . . if we will overcome we must not love our lives, but be willing to be killed like sheep; it is impossible to hold out the truth of God with external peace and quietness." [19]

In conclusion, he took care to warn his hearers against succumbing to the behavioral extremes implicit in the Covenant of Grace. "Let us have a care," he enjoined them, "that we show ourselves in all manner of good conversation—let us carry ourselves that they may be ashamed to blame us. . . . And let us have a care that we give not occasion to others to say that we are libertines or Antinomians, but Christians." [20]

If brother Wheelwright had sincerely designed to promote reconciliation within the congregation he had adopted a curiously perverse means of doing so. Not only had he implied that most of the ministers and magistrates were under a Covenant of Works, inasmuch as they had failed to accept the doctrines which he and Mr. Cotton held forth, but he had adjured the congregation in the most provocative and inflammatory words, to persist unrelentingly in their support of these doctrines. In extenuation of his discourse, it might be ventured that Wheelwright may not yet have understood how far Mrs. Hutchinson's doctrines were from his own. But he was nonetheless aware of the fact that the opinionists had been accused of libertinism and Antinomianism. His warning in this respect was well made, but it suggests a knowledge

17. *Ibid.*, 168, 169.
18. *Ibid.*, 170.
19. *Ibid.*, 172.
20. *Ibid.*, 174.

on his part that should have prompted a more judicious approach to the entire problem. If he felt bound by principle to reject conciliatory measures and to refuse compromise, he should have frankly stated his mind when he was first asked to address the congregation. Instead, he had chosen in this passionate outburst—passionate both in content and delivery—to unloose another bombshell on the unhappy town of Boston.[21]

How the champions of orthodoxy immediately reacted to this fresh assault on their cherished convictions is not clear. In his account of the Fast Day proceedings, John Winthrop—who was by now hypersensitive to every move in the struggle—made no comment on Wheelwright's sermon. Its implications could scarcely have eluded him, but for the moment he apparently saw fit to keep his counsel and bide his time.

Unhappily the rigors of a day of fasting afforded the good folk of Massachusetts little more than empty bellies. Despite their pious intentions the controversy continued its rancorous course. Scarcely two weeks had passed before it was deemed necessary for Cotton and Wilson to unite in reassuring a shipload of departing voyagers that, appearances to the contrary, all was well in the Bay Colony. Alert to the possibility that news of these disturbances might retard the wave of immigration, Cotton counseled the travelers to carry back to England word that this debate was only "about magnifying the grace of God." One party, he pointed out, sought "to advance the grace of God within us, and the other to advance the grace of God towards us." He tactfully refrained from pointing out that a vast abyss separated the two. So, he concluded, should they meet any in England who were searching for grace, Massachusetts was the place where, one way or another, they would surely find it.[22]

Cotton suffered the common plight of the peacemaker: his best efforts at pacification seemed doomed to invite dispute. Mr. Wilson in turn informed the voyagers that, to the best of his knowledge, all the ministers had sought to advance the free grace of God in justification—adding pointedly, "so far as the word of God required." He then proceeded to fan this spark of contrariety by expounding the necessity and uses of sanctification. John Winthrop later remarked that few could find any difference between the views of the two preachers. But the members of Boston church

21. *Winthrop Papers*, IV, 414; Wheelwright, *Writings*, 224.
22. Winthrop, *Journal*, I, 209.

saw the difference, and they were grievously offended by Mr. Wilson's speech.[23]

(iii)

Winter's end summoned the deputies from barn and shop back to affairs of state. On March 9 the General Court convened in the Boston meetinghouse. The legislators had scarcely time to become uncomfortable on their merciless benches before it was apparent to all that "these new opinions" would once again inflame their debates.[24]

Almost at once the proceedings fastened on Wheelwright's Fast Day Sermon with a determination and tenacity which hinted at the dexterous manipulation of a master politician. Although John Winthrop had confided to his diary no opinion on Wheelwright's sermon, he was not a man to lack opinions or to be reluctant to act upon them. From his viewpoint it was clear that Wheelwright's remarks had been made with malicious and destructive intent. It seemed to him that the newcomer had deliberately employed the occasion of a public holiday to incite the people of Boston against the authority of church and state. Nor did Winthrop lack company in this lurid interpretation of events: other highly placed individuals were equally disturbed by Wheelwright's remarks, and were similarly resolved that the time was ripe to place a check on the factionists. As individually, or perhaps collectively, they weighed the implications of this new development, it can scarcely have escaped the observation of these gentlemen—of Winthrop and Dudley, Endicott and other orthodox stalwarts—that Pastor Wheelwright had placed a weapon in their hands that would cut through the legal impediments and ambiguities that had hitherto restrained them. Wheelwright's sermon was, by their reckoning, an actionable offense, a contempt of authority tending to sedition. It seems not unlikely that they plotted beforehand a legislative strategy to bring about Wheelwright's conviction.

The proceedings of the Court were initiated with a request that Mr. Wheelwright be summoned from his home at Mount Wollaston to vouch for certain passages in his sermon. Pending his arrival, the Court consulted with the ministers to clarify some ambiguities in the church-state relationship that might inhibit effective action against the erronists. In answer to one query, which hinted that

23. *Ibid.*
24. *Ibid.*, 210.

the orthodox leaders were preparing a blast against the Hutchinsonians, the clergy agreed that no congregation might publicly
question a statement made by a deputy during the regular proceedings of the Court. This opinion secured a freedom of debate which
placed Winthrop in particular comfortably beyond the reprisals
of the Boston church. The ministers further agreed that the Court
might proceed "without tarrying for the church" in all cases of
manifest error and heresy that seemed to threaten the security
of the state.[25]

Thus fortified, the champions of orthodoxy singled out the
hitherto inconspicuous figure of Stephen Greensmith as a likely
object on which to try their legal arsenal. Greensmith, an itinerant
lumber dealer, had rashly observed that all the ministers but
Cotton, Wheelwright, and "as he thought, Mr. Hooker," taught
only a Covenant of Works. The Court promptly displayed its disagreement by imposing on the imprudent Mr. Greensmith a
staggering fine of £40 and required him to acknowledge the error
of his ways before every congregation in the colony.[26] Thus emboldened the legislators turned their guns on bigger game.

Immediately on being summoned, Pastor Wheelwright had
come up to Boston. At the moment of his arrival, the deputies
were intent upon the task of clarifying and expanding their authority in his case, so Wheelwright was obliged to cool his heels
over the weekend until they were prepared to deal with him. On
Monday morning, he was summoned to the meetinghouse. A copy
of his sermon was produced and he was asked to avouch certain
passages that had been found offensive. In response Wheelwright
submitted to the Court his own true copy of the sermon, whereupon
"he was dismissed very gently" and asked to stand ready to return
when they should need him.[27]

The Boston deputies observed these ominous preliminaries with
dismay. Even with Governor Vane presiding over the assembly,
they had been helpless to stem the tide of resentment that
threatened to engulf Mr. Wheelwright. Fearing that the Court
aimed to subject Wheelwright to an inquisitorial harassment,
Coddington and Coggeshall enlisted the support of his friends and
admirers throughout Boston. When the Court assembled on Tuesday morning, it received a petition signed by over forty members

25. *Ibid.; Antinomianism*, 193.
26. *Colony Records*, I, 189; Winthrop, *Journal*, I, 211.
27. *Antinomianism*, 193.

of the Boston congregation. The petitioners suggested that, as freemen, they were entitled to be present when the Court sat "in causes of judicature." They further inquired whether the Court had authority to proceed "in cases of conscience" without first referring them to the church.

The Court made short work of this appeal by inscribing on the back side of the petition the claim that it was their indisputable right to hold preliminary hearings behind closed doors. As to the church's title to prior jurisdiction, it was portentously intimated that the present action was regarded as somewhat more serious than a "matter of conscience." [28]

Mr. Wheelwright was again summoned into the meetinghouse, and the doors were locked behind him. The Court had examined his sermon, a spokesman informed him, and wished to question him about some apparently offensive passages in order "to cleare his meaning." Wheelwright eyed his inquisitor warily: had he been called before them as one presumed guilty, or as innocent, he inquired. Neither, was the reply, but as "suspected onely." Who then, he demanded, were his accusers? His sermon, the spokesman retorted, adding that since it had been acknowledged by him, the Court might now proceed ex officio. This last expression brought Wheelwright's friends to their feet in noisy indignation. Was the assembly about to become a Court of High Commission, they protested, that it might oblige a defendant to incriminate himself? After much heated discussion, the demonstrators were quieted and Wheelwright persuaded to submit to interrogation.

"Before his Sermon," he was asked, did he "not know, that most of the Ministers in this jurisdiction did teach that doctrine which he in his Sermon called a Covenant of works?" Wheelwright refused to answer. Once again the hall rang with protests that the Court sought to ensnare him—to make him accuse himself. Seeing the bent of the interrogation, Wheelwright now declined to accept further questioning and so, for the present, he was dismissed.[29]

Called back to the meetinghouse that afternoon, Wheelwright found that the ministers had also been summoned to attend. The doors were opened to the public, and the hall was soon jammed to overflowing with sympathizers and curious onlookers who had abandoned shops and fields and daily chores to observe the proceedings. Mr. Wheelwright was summoned to the front of the hall

28. *Ibid.*, 193 ff.
29. *Ibid.*, 194-95.

and requested to take a seat beside the other ministers. His sermon
was once again produced and several passages which had given
particular offense were read aloud. Wheelwright acknowledged
and justified his authorship of these excerpts. The examiners
pressed him closely. Was it his meaning that any of the ministers
or other Christians of this colony were under a Covenant of Works,
they asked. Wheelwright's guard was up: he had meant only such
ministers as could be shown to fit the description which he had
provided.

Seeing that they could not easily draw him into an admission that
would suit their purpose, his prosecutors proceeded to examine
witnesses about another of his sermons. By this diversion they
apparently hoped to lay at his door a definition of the Covenant
of Works so broad as to include most of the church members in
the colony. But the effort soon led the prosecution into doctrinal
matters beyond their jurisdiction or comprehension and it was at
last abandoned.[30]

Baffled at the impasse, the Court appealed once more to the
clergy. Was it the opinion of those reverend gentlemen that they
did "walke in and teach such a way of Salvation and evidencing
thereof" as brother Wheelwright had termed a Covenant of Works?
The ministers hesitated to answer so weighty a question without
careful deliberation. So the offending document was placed in their
hands for closer study and the Court adjourned until morning.[31]
A single evening sufficed to produce agreement among all the
ministers that they did indeed teach such a way of salvation as
Wheelwright had impugned in his sermon. All, that is, except
Mr. Cotton, who was either not consulted or, more probably, refused to be drawn into a judgment which was by implication
directed against himself as well as Wheelwright.[32] When the Court
reconvened the following morning, the eleven ministers returned
an affirmative answer. It was then moved that Mr. Wheelwright
be declared guilty of sedition and contempt.

From the first day of meeting, this session of the Court had
been embittered by harsh and angry words. Again and again Governor Vane had resorted to obstructive tactics in his efforts to
protect Greensmith and Wheelwright. Although Wheelwright had

30. *Ibid.*, 199.
31. *Ibid.*, 200.
32. Cotton, *Way of the Congregational Churches Cleared,* 59.

no great following outside of Boston, a considerable number of deputies questioned the wisdom of adopting drastically punitive measures against the erring parson. During the last two days of debate, Vane and Coddington had managed to hold a slender majority against conviction. But now the weight of clerical opinion swayed the uncertain minds of two of the magistrates and after summation of the testimony on this final day, the verdict was carried against Wheelwright.[33]

Flushed with victory, the orthodox majority pressed its advantage resolutely, denying a request that the dissenting vote be inscribed on the record. The rebuffed minority refused to accept defeat in silence. A protestation was drafted by their leaders and tendered to the Court, justifying the defendant as a faithful minister of the Gospel and condemning the Court's proceedings against him. Throughout the debate Winthrop, Dudley, and Endicott had marshaled their forces with consummate skill. Now aware that they had seized on a nettle, they maneuvered to postpone further struggle until their position was rendered more secure. The first step in the counterattack had been successful beyond all hopes: there was time for that which must follow. Accordingly, it was agreed that sentence on Wheelwright should be deferred until the next Court. A motion was made from the floor that Wheelwright should be silenced pending sentence. The suggestion was judiciously referred to the ministers, and they, in turn, reluctant to propose a course which might invite defiance, suggested that the problem be submitted to the judgment of the Boston congregation.[34]

In the early hours of this session, the Court had enacted that proxies would be admissible at the annual Court of Elections. Although the Hutchinsonians expressed hope that this might help their cause, it would seem rather to have guaranteed substantial majorities for orthodox candidates from outlying districts where Mrs. Hutchinson's opinions had not caught hold. Now, as the Court drew to adjournment, it was proposed that the forthcoming elections should be held in Newtown, a safe remove from the inflamed passions and influence of the Bostonians. Governor Vane stubbornly refused to put this motion to a vote. When the question was put to Deputy Governor Winthrop, he also tactfully declined to move

33. Joseph B. Felt, *Ecclesiastical History of New England* (Boston, 1862), II, 511.
34. *Antinomianism*, 201; Winthrop, *Journal*, I, 212.

the disadvantage of his own community. Mr. Endicott, however, was more than pleased to oblige and the motion was carried.[35]

The Bostonians were enraged by the action of the Court. Storming out of the meetinghouse, they swarmed in peevish indignation into the market place and neighboring lanes. Defeated and baffled at every turn, they continued to grope for some means of reprisal and self-justification. The suggestion that they should attempt yet another petition was eagerly seized upon by all.[36] William Aspinwall was delegated, or more probably, in view of his zeal and impetuousity, volunteered to draft a fresh appeal to the Court. In short time he penned a document which—after more cautious hands had rephrased some intemperate passages—seemed to most of the remonstrants a satisfactory expression of their displeasure.[37] The petitioners protested that Mr. Wheelwright had been quite sincere in his efforts to promote reconciliation on the Fast Day. They pointed out that the ensuing weeks had produced no material evidence that his sermon promoted sedition. With a notable absence of tact, they intimated that it may well have been Satan who stirred up the Court to attack the doctrine of free grace, even as he had aroused opposition to Paul and to Christ himself. The remonstrants further beseeched the Court not to meddle with the prophets of God, but sadly failed to provide any authoritative criteria for distinguishing true prophets from false.[38]

The revised petition and remonstrance—as they called it—was circulated among Mr. Wheelwright's sympathizers and subscribed by seventy-four persons. Most of these, of course, were Bostonians; but five of the petitioners were from troubled Salem and five from Roxbury, and there were two each from Ipswich and Charlestown and three from Newbury.[39] At a later date five of these signatories protested that they had not consented to the use of their names. Several others contended that they had signed only with the understanding that Mr. Cotton's approval would be obtained before the petition was submitted to the Court.[40] If such an assurance was offered, it was conveniently forgotten or ignored. The document was presented to the Court without further alteration, and, like

35. Winthrop, *Journal*, I, 212.
36. *Antinomianism*, 133.
37. *Ibid.*, 153-54.
38. *Ibid.*, 133 ff.
39. *Colony Records*, I, 211-12.
40. *Winthrop Papers*, III, 513-14; *Antinomianism*, 154. James Brown, John Clarke, Nicholas Parker, James Penniman, and Richard Wayte later denied having signed the remonstrance.

its predecessors, seems to have been rejected. But it was to be submitted again and its contents were to be employed as the means by which the dissenting faction was at last broken up and brought under control.

(iv)

May 17—the grassy plain of Newtown common shone green gold under the midday sun. Among the junipers and rocks of the north field runty cows shambled listlessly in search of spring's tender new clover and with placid and indifferent eye observed the strange invasion of their pastoral domain. At the foot of the common in the angle of forked paths a scattering of men had already begun to gather for the annual Court of Elections. Sprawled lazily in the shade of the great oak over by Charlestown path, or standing about in shirt-sleeved clusters, they muttered their grim opinions of the business before them. By twos and threes, others converged on the field from south and east, emerging through the palisade encompassing the town or coming along the forest road from Charlestown.[41]

Waiting in flushed and impatient comfort for the Court to convene, there was much to engross their attention. Doubtless significant nods and glances were cast often toward the Boston delegation: more trouble and obstruction was to be expected from that quarter. The colony was still agog with the affront the Bostonians had recently dealt to the Reverend Peter Bulkley of Concord. On the day of his ordination, as was customary, officials of church and state had been invited to pay their respects and take part in the installation ceremony. But those of Boston—Vane, Wheelwright, Cotton, and the two elders, Leverett and Oliver— had chosen to register their disapproval by remaining absent.[42]

At the moment, however, Indians challenged erronists for the center of attention. Once again the threat of Pequot hostilities had aroused fears in Connecticut. A month before, the Bay Colony had dispatched Captain Underhill with a force of twenty men to hold the fort at Saybrook—perhaps as much in fear of the designs of the Dutch as of the Indians. On April 18 an extraordinary session of the Court had been convened "for the speciall occasion of prosecuting the war against the Pecoits." The deputies had voted

41. Hutchinson, *History*, I, 54 n. See the excellent map of Newtown in 1637 in Morison, *Founding of Harvard College*, opposite 193.
42. Winthrop, *Journal*, I, 212 ff.

to levy a special tax of £600 and raise a military force of 160 men who were to leave for the wars promptly after the Court of Elections.[43]

One o'clock. Sun glinted on halberds and morions as the governor's guard emerged from the Newtown gate and swung smartly along the road to the common. The buzz of discussion was stilled; small knots of men disjoined, heaved themselves to their feet, brushing dirt and grass from their clothes; the clusters gravitated into a tight-churning throng which moved slowly toward the great oak where the Governor and his guard had come to a halt. Harry Vane stepped forward and called for order. Suddenly, a voice broke through from the midst of the crowd. He had at hand a petition from the Boston church, the speaker called out, which he would like the Court to receive and read. Murmurs and grumbles of dissent greeted this motion. Winthrop saw what was afoot and hastily interceded. The motion was out of order, he protested; this was a Court of Elections, and only after that business was done could petitions be considered. Winthrop had little doubt that after this election the Boston petition would receive the attention it deserved. Other voices rose in support of Winthrop and the debate crackled threateningly, but the Bostonians would not desist. Until the petition was read, Vane stormed above the hubbub, the Court would not proceed to elections. Tempers frayed and bitter words gave way to blows as angry zealots on both sides struck out for their opinions.[44] Through this muttering, jostling, fuming throng, John Wilson elbowed his way to the foot of the oak. Helpful hands lifted and shoved him to a secure position on the lowest limb, and there over the heads of the crowd, he bellowed for their attention. Look to your charter, he roared at them, and consider the present work of the day. The impatient, overheated crowd responded with noisy cheers and cries of "Election!" "Election!" [45] Mounting this tide of emotion at the full, Winthrop shouted to the crowd to divide into two groups, either for or against proceeding directly to election. The crowd stirred restlessly, then broke apart, leaving the Bostonians in a defiant minority, stubbornly refusing to accept even this dramatic judgment. All patience exhausted, Winthrop announced that if the Bostonians would not go to election at once, he and his side must proceed without them. Seeing the futility of

---

43. *Ibid.; Colony Records,* I, 192.
44. Winthrop, *Journal,* I, 215.
45. Hutchinson, *History,* I, 54, quoting a MS. life of Wilson since lost.

continued resistance, Governor Vane resumed his ill-fitting mantle of authority and one by one the Bostonians surrendered to harsh political reality.[46]

When the formalities of election were completed, it was evident that Mrs. Hutchinson's supporters had suffered a crushing political defeat. Governor Vane, William Coddington, and Richard Dummer of Newbury had all been swept from the exclusive circle of the magistracy. Once again Winthrop was elevated to the governor's chair, with Dudley as his deputy.[47] But even this was not received by Boston without a petulant rejoinder. When the election results were announced, Edward Hutchinson, the elder, and the three other Boston sergeants who were standing by Governor Vane as his honor guard lay down their halberds and withdrew from the field. This untimely defection left the new governor in a position of some embarrassment. The ordinary function of the governor's guard was to attend him on his trips to and from the meetinghouse in his own community and lend dignity to his other public appearances. Accordingly, it was necessary for the guard to be chosen from his own townsfolk, and by custom this distinction was bestowed on the sergeants of the local military company. Unfortunately, sergeants were in short supply, and at the moment all those of Boston were partial to the tenets of Mrs. Hutchinson and disinclined to lend pomp and circumstance to the comings and goings of her most dedicated opponent.[48]

But transports of zeal had not blinded the Bostonians to the astringent realities of political life. Anticipating a possible reversal at the polls, they had deliberately postponed the selection of their own deputies until after election in order to be better equipped to meet all contingencies. On Thursday morning, the day after election, by "publique notice" a general meeting was called. The assembled freemen then engaged to reaffirm their support of Mrs. Hutchinson in terms that would be unmistakable. Defying conservative opinion throughout the colony—and defying the Court that had just unseated Vane and Coddington—they chose as their representatives three of the most outspoken proponents of the Hutchinson doctrine, Henry Vane, William Coddington, and Atherton Hough.[49]

When the Court reconvened that afternoon, the element of defi-

46. Winthrop, *Journal*, I, 215.
47. *Colony Records*, I, 194 ff.
48. *Ibid.*, 142; Winthrop, *Journal*, I, 216.
49. "Boston Town Records, 1634-1660," 18.

ance in Boston's choice did not pass unobserved. But it was pointed out, perhaps by Winthrop himself, that the new deputies might not be entitled to assume seats in the Court because two of Boston's freemen had not been properly notified of the town election. The Court seized on this technicality as a means of invalidating what was indubitably a popular choice. Vane and his colleagues were once again unseated and, returning to Boston that evening, they undertook more scrupulous arrangements to legalize their status. A second town meeting was summoned, this time "by private and particular warning from house to house." [50] On Friday morning, May 19, the freemen of Boston gathered again in their meetinghouse and reaffirmed their former choice. Again Vane, Coddington, and Hough tramped back to Newtown with proper accreditation, and the Court had no choice but to accept them.

Meanwhile, the Court pressed ahead with the urgent business at hand. With "a solemn public invocation in the name of God," a lot was cast between two of the ministers to determine who should serve as chaplain on the Pequot expedition. Although the Divine was invoked, a malign fate intruded to throw the choice upon John Wilson—a catlike fate which sought to tease and tempt Wilson's enemies to strike out at him again and hasten their own destruction.[51]

John Wheelwright was haled before the Court to hear sentence delivered. Having now the power to crush him, the Court sought to display its moderation, or at least so Winthrop defined their motivation. According, sentence was deferred until the August session of the Court; in the interim Wheelwright might retract and reform his error. Wheelwright scorned to accept their clemency. If he were really guilty of sedition, he hotly challenged, they should put him to death. But if they intended to proceed in this case, he, for his part, meant to appeal to the King's Court. As for retraction, there was nothing he had said that he would now abjure. If Winthrop was disturbed by this threat of appeal to the King, he managed to conceal it. The Court saw the justice of its proceeding, he informed Wheelwright, and if it were to do it again would pronounce the same judgment.[52]

But renewed and refurbished authority did not lull the orthodox into unwariness. As the counterattack was pressed, word reached New England that the Bostonians were expecting the arrival of

50. *Ibid.; Colony Records,* I, 195.
51. *Colony Records,* I, 195; Winthrop, *Journal,* I, 218.
52. Winthrop, *Journal,* I, 217, 218.

reinforcements from England. According to rumor many parishioners of the notorious Roger Brierly of Lancashire were arranging to remove to the Bay Colony.[53] Although an ecclesiastical court had cleared Brierly of the charge of heresy some nine years past, the odor of his erstwhile "Grindletonian familism" still clung to him and his disciples.[54] The magistrates were for taking no chances; the new Zion must have the means of protecting itself against irregular opinions. The Court adopted an alien act, ordering that no newcomer should be allowed to purchase habitation or remain more than three weeks within any town without the express consent of one of the council or two of the other magistrates.[55] If a new wave of erronists could be kept from entering the colony, Court and church might manage to root out those already on hand.

Winthrop had managed this crucial session with great forcefulness and skill. Although the passage of the alien act had pressed the colony's right of self-preservation to an illiberal extreme, it was, he could rationalize, subject to expiration within a year. In the meanwhile it might serve to stabilize the situation while new offers of clemency and reconciliation were made to the dissenters. True, the orthodox doctrines left the Winthrop party relatively inflexible in their conciliatory gestures, but with persuasion and logic they might not need to remove the velvet glove.

No cheering crowds filled Boston's streets to greet the new governor on his return from Newtown. The doors remained shut, and the townsfolk turned away in scorn as Winthrop stalked down the dusty High Street toward his home, attended only by two of his own servants bearing halberds before him. Winthrop was hurt by this deliberate slight, but he bore the injury with aristocratic grace. On Sunday at the meetinghouse, the glacial disparagement continued. Vane and Coddington, long accustomed to sitting with Winthrop on the magistrate's seat, now ostentatiously quit their familiar places and crossed the hall to sit with the deacons. Although the meaning of this gesture did not escape Winthrop, his instinctive gentility overcame the feelings of resentment. He sent word that he would be pleased to have his old colleagues join him once again on the seat of honor. The offer was abruptly spurned.[56] The battle was at the full, and for the retreating belligerents, there was no place for the frivolous amenities of war.

53. *Ibid.*, 219.
54. Alexander Gordon in *DNB* s.v. "Brereley, or Brierley, Roger."
55. *Colony Records*, I, 196.
56. Winthrop, *Journal*, I, 219, 220.

XII

"Assembly of the Churches"

June–September 1637

(i)

IN THE shadow of defeat Boston's mood grew black and menacing.
Opposition to the new administration, passing the bounds of
contempt, bordered perilously on sedition. The Boston congregation now withdrew its support from the colonial struggle against
the hostile Pequot tribe. Because Pastor Wilson had been designated chaplain, the men of the church—through personal resentment, or in fear of imperiling their immortal souls, or perhaps a
little of both—flatly refused to join the military expedition into
Connecticut. Being less immediately sensitive to the spiritual needs
of the unregenerate, however, they did not scruple to draft instead
"one or two whom they cared not to be rid of, and but a few others,
and those of the most refuse sort." [1] In extenuation they could claim
that Winthrop himself had declared the state of emergency was
past. The main body of the Pequots having been destroyed, the
Governor had suggested that the levy of reinforcements could be
safely reduced. [2] Nonetheless, the Bostonians' relegation of fundamental responsibilities upon a group of second-class citizens came
ill from men who regarded themselves as the essential guardians
of the social welfare. Had the Indian peril been greater, Boston's
scruples might have endangered the existence of the entire colony.

An issue which rankled even more deeply than Wilson's appointment was the passage at the late Court of Elections of the alien

1. *Antinomianism*, 142.
2. Winthrop, *Journal*, I, 221.

law intended to exclude from the colony all those whose opinions did not meet the approval of the magistrates. It was generally recognized that this enactment had been designed to prevent the admission of friends of Wheelwright and Mrs. Hutchinson whose arrival was shortly expected. Just as anticipated, when Samuel Hutchinson and other friends and relatives from Lincolnshire reached Boston in early July, Governor Winthrop judged them unfit to remain permanently in the colony. But to allow them adequate trial, he permitted them to remain four months.[3] Winthrop's arbitrary decision enraged the Hutchinsonians afresh and occasioned another bitter exchange of speeches in the meetinghouse.

The Winthrop decision also produced an acrimonious debate between the Governor and Henry Vane. Winthrop, not unreasonably, suspected that the blunt terms of the enactment required further explication and defense. In what was apparently designed as a public declaration, he set forth the abstract right of any community to secure its own safety within bounds legally determined by consent of the freemen. He further defended this right in terms of the charter: "If we are bound to keepe off whatsoever appears to tend to our ruine or damage, then we may lawfully refuse to receive such whose dispositions suit not with ours, and whose society (we know) will be hurtfull to us, and therefore it is lawfull to take knowledge of all men before we receive them." [4]

A precise construction of the charter would possibly support such an interpretation, though it would hardly have won the approval of that "Carol Caesare" whose signature was so handsomely scrawled at the foot of the patent.[5] Curiously, the alien law was a departure from the Puritans' own principles regarding the treatment of persons of unsound opinion. It was their customary view that opinions differing from their own were to be expected in the natural course of events and might be safely tolerated as long as they were not openly declared or acted upon.[6] But in the present instance entry was denied to any whom the magistrates suspected might broach their opinions at some future time. "It is worse,"

3. *Ibid.*, 226.
4. *Winthrop Papers*, III, 423.
5. *Colony Records*, I, 17. The charter read in part: "That it shall and maie be lawfull to and for the cheife commaunders, governors, and officers of the said company . . . for their speciall defence and safety, to incounter, expulse, repell, and resist by force of armes . . . and by all fitting waies and meanes whatsoever, all such person and persons as shall at any tyme hereafter attempt or enterprise the destruccon, invasion, detriment, or annoyaunce to the said plantation or inhabitants."
6. See pp. 116-19.

Winthrop held, "to receive a man whom we must cast out againe, than to denye him admittance." [7] It was not to be expected that Winthrop should display any great respect for the principles of religious freedom, but he sadly neglected to prove that such arbitrary interference with personal liberty was in the present instance required.

If Winthrop erred in his failure to appreciate the principles of religious liberty, it is more surprising that Vane, in his reply to Winthrop, was equally negligent. He neither supported the general principles of freedom of conscience nor adopted the more conservative position that in the present situation a negative toleration might be consistent with the safety of the state. Indeed, quite the contrary, he vigorously contended that Wheelwright's doctrines alone were sound and true.[8] In this debate the future champion of religious liberty is nowhere apparent. But Vane found and exposed two serious defects in the enactment and in Winthrop's argument. The Order in Court, he pointed out, went a dangerous way toward the promotion of arbitrary government in its failure to stipulate precisely the grounds on which the magistrates might deny entry to prospective settlers. "The question is," Vane asserted, "whether the admitting or rejecting of persons should depend upon such unlimited and unsafe a rule, as the will and discretion of men." He also raised a timeless problem: Should men be denied admission to a community because of their opinions and their presumed intent? Vane assumed a liberal position for his day, "for men," he stated, "are not to keep off whatsoever appeares to tend to their ruine, but what really doth so." [9] His position seems less bold, however, and Winthrop's more dubious, when it is recalled that both men were discussing the disposition—not of aliens —but of fellow subjects of the British Crown.

Winthrop drafted a rebuttal to Vane's *Briefe Answer* but withheld it from public view, hoping that the forthcoming Synod might conclusively settle some of the disputed points.[10] He conceded a legal defect in the Order bestowing such broad discretionary authority on the magistrates. Time had not allowed the drafting of more particular instructions, he apologized, but Vane's charges he

7. *Winthrop Papers*, III, 424.
8. Henry Vane, "A Briefe Answer to a Certaine Declaration," *Hutchinson Papers*, ed. W. H. Whitmore and W. S. Appleton (Prince Society, *Publications*, 2 vols. [1865]), I, 91, 95.
9. *Ibid.*, 86, 87.
10. *Antinomianism*, 138.

held, were a slur against the good conscience of the magistrates in the performance of their duty. Returning to a defense of a policy of selectivity in the admission of settlers, Winthrop again appealed to the charter as authority for their exclusionary right: "Let the patent be perused, and there it will be found, that the incorporation is made to certaine persons by name, and unto such as they shall associate to themselves, and all this tract of land is granted to them and their associates." [11] Under the charter the grant was conveyed to the members of the Company, "their heires and assignes for ever, to their onlie proper and absolute use and behoofe for evermore." [12] Whether King Charles had anticipated that this clause should be so illiberally interpreted is a moot question. If such was their right, it should be remembered that the Puritans used it mainly to avert the institution of a rival religious establishment, a situation universally regarded as intolerable at that time.

Although the law in question obviously aimed to effect the exclusion of undesirable persons, it levied the fines and penalties solely on present inhabitants who harbored undesirables or conveyed property to them.[13] This was doubtless a shrewd legal device by which the Massachusetts authorities sought to ward off assault by the English courts. Winthrop, in his Reply, referred obliquely to the possibility that undesirable aliens might settle within uninhabited portions of the grant. But he withheld any encouragement on this point and deliberately clouded the issue by concluding, "That question may fall to be discussed upon some other occasion." [14]

(ii)

As June drew to an end a stifling heat wave closed down on the New England coast. Many newcomers, unaccustomed to the paralyzing extremities of New England weather, died of sunstroke while searching for homesites.[15] But the sun could not long have daunted Anne Hutchinson on her errands of mercy, and it is likely

11. *Winthrop Papers*, III, 469.
12. *Colony Records*, I, 6. J. G. Palfrey, although a rabid partisan and apologist of Puritan policy, not unreasonably, it seems to me, contends with reference to the charter rights of the Bay Company, "no principle of jurisprudence is better settled than that a grant is to be interpreted favorably to the grantees, inasmuch as the grantor, being able to protect himself, is to be presumed to have done so to the extent of his purpose." Palfrey, *History of New England* (Boston, 1858), I, 306.
13. *Colony Records*, I, 196.
14. *Winthrop Papers*, III, 468.
15. Winthrop, *Journal*, I, 223.

that she made her way to Wollaston in time to assist when her sister-in-law Mary Wheelwright gave birth to another daughter.[16]

John Winthrop, too, braved the oppressive heat, on a journey of state to Saugus, Salem, and Ipswich. In these remote outposts he was secretly gratified to receive the honors withheld by his own fellow townsmen. At each town a large and enthusiastic welcoming committee greeted him, and on his travels between towns, he was provided with an honor guard befitting the dignity of his office. But the heat of day became so intense that Winthrop was at last compelled to retreat homeward under the cover of darkness.[17]

On reaching Boston, he learned that a distinguished visitor had arrived during his absence. Lord Ley, a sober and unassuming youth of nineteen, son to the Earl of Marlborough, had crossed the Atlantic on a brief sightseeing trip. Upon disembarking, Ley had taken up residence at Samuel Cole's inn, next door to the Hutchinson house. Winthrop was shocked that a gentleman of such eminence should be quartered at the common inn and promptly paid him a visit, offering the hospitality of his home. The young lord graciously declined, however. He had found Mr. Cole's hostelry quite comfortable and well-ordered, and besides he preferred not to inconvenience anyone during his brief stay. This polite refusal was thoroughly consistent with Ley's modest carriage and may have been sincerely intended. But it is equally probable that Vane, still embroiled in controversy with Winthrop, had sought out his fellow aristocrat and, pouring forth his troubles, pressed Ley to take sides in the dispute. In any case, a few days later when Winthrop arranged a great dinner party in honor of Lord Ley, he was most ungently snubbed by both young peers. Vane, who had also been invited, tartly replied that his conscience would not allow him to attend. When dinner time arrived, the guest of honor and his new-found friend sailed across the Bay to Noodle's Island to dine in the more congenial company of the independent Mr. Maverick.[18]

Boston was a scene of picturesque confusion during the succeeding days. Captive Indian women and children were marched into town to await disposal to prospective owners; a deputation of Niantick braves came to powwow with the great white chief; Narragansett warriors came back from the war gruesomely bearing the

16. "Boston Births, Marriages and Deaths," 5.
17. Winthrop, *Journal*, I, 223.
18. *Ibid.*, 224, 225.

severed heads and hands of Pequot victims. In the midst of these grim reminders of the hostile frontier, Samuel Hutchinson and his friends arrived from England, to be met by Winthrop's refusal to let them remain. The controversy was inflamed to a new peak of bitterness. Charges and countercharges were angrily exchanged in the meetinghouse, and at this time Vane made his bitter reply to Winthrop's defense of the alien act.[19] During his brief sojourn Lord Ley had doubtless seen enough to persuade him that the frays and animosities of the New World were no improvement on those of the Old.

On Thursday morning, August 3, Henry Vane and Lord Ley took their departure from New England. Far out in the Bay, the ship which was to carry them home tugged restlessly at its anchor chain. For three days now the General Court had been in session, but those of Vane's adherents whose presence was not required at the meetinghouse gathered to see him off.[20] Bendall's Dock was thronged with friends and admirers waiting dejectedly to bid their champion farewell. Vane sought briefly to console them with a few parting words of hope. Then, after warm handshakes and good-byes all around, he and Ley clambered down into the boat which was to carry them to their ship. As the boat drew away from the dock, the men on shore raised their muskets and fired a series of shattering volleys, and the resounding echo was taken up by the boom of the cannon.[21] The boat dwindled to a black, bobbing speck on the wrinkled harbor and Henry Vane was gone.

At the meetinghouse a block away, the debate droned on. As the crash of muskets and cannon sounded through the open windows, John Winthrop, in his magisterial seat, perhaps cocked his head quizzically toward the sound, and, probing his beard with an errant finger, heaved—not too conspicuously—a sigh of profound relief. Who can say what thoughts coursed through his mind? During his fifty-odd years, John Winthrop had lived deeply and well. Tragedy had struck often at his door, and he was no stranger to hardship, but these he had borne with fortitude and composure. He was instinct with the order of life and enamored of its symmetry. Although his beliefs would not permit him to encourage "untruth," he was inclined by nature to be understanding of human foibles. To his mind Vane's instability was shifting sand on which

19. *Ibid.*, 225, 226, 229, 231.
20. *Colony Records*, I, 200 ff.
21. Winthrop, *Journal*, I, 229.

to rest a state and Vane's policies were a menace to public order and spiritual safety. Yet he could refer to Vane as "a wise and godly gentleman." [22] Throughout his journal one detects a note of sadness, rather than bitterness, in his comments on Vane. Eight years later he said of him that "both now and at other times he showed himself a true friend to New England, and a man of noble and generous mind." [23] But for the present it was well for New England that Vane should struggle to attain his manhood elsewhere.

No one need offer an apologia for Henry Vane. He has achieved his own lustrous chapter in the history of human liberty. The same qualities that he so disturbingly displayed in Massachusetts—the impulsiveness of spirit, the warmth of heart, the stubborn refusal to submit tamely to autocratic pretensions—all played their part in the creation of his final legacy. But these attributes are perhaps more appropriate to the needs of a settled state than to those of an unstable infant colony. In their efforts to adjust the delicate balance of freedom and security, both John Winthrop and Henry Vane may have erred, each according to his own predilections. But Winthrop saw more clearly than Vane that the present must be served before the future could be gained.[24]

(iii)

Two days after Vane's departure John Wilson returned to Boston. Summoned by Winthrop, he had relinquished his military post in Connecticut and, in the company of Thomas Hooker and Samuel Stone, ministers of Hartford, hastened northward to help arrange the forthcoming Synod.[25] With the orthodox party firmly secured in the seats of power, it was deemed essential to resolve the disputed points of theology beyond all cavil—to label heresy as such, and to reach an accommodation with Mr. Cotton. Only then, it was thought, could the civil authorities take appropriate measures to restore domestic harmony. But a synod under such conditions is at best the last desperate resort of perplexed theologians, as likely to create fresh schism as it is to produce agreement. Despite their presumed solidarity, the ranks of the canonical wing had more than once been divided and confused by Cotton's subtle logic. When

22. *Ibid.*, 201.
23. *Ibid.*, II, 256.
24. The best biographical study of Vane is Hosmer, *The Life of Young Sir Henry Vane.*
25. Winthrop, *Journal,* I, 229; *Winthrop Papers,* III, 483.

plans for the Synod were communicated to Mr. Hooker, he had expressed his apprehensions, but on quite another score. "My ground is this," he wrote. "They will be chief agents in the synod who are chief parties in the cause, and for them only who are prejudiced in the controversy, to pass sentence against cause or person, how improper! how unprofitable!" [26] But the mounting heat of controversy apparently melted away his scruples, and Hooker now came forth to play a central role in the assembly.

From all over the colony ministers converged on Boston and for a crowded three weeks busied themselves at private councils, fast days, and lectures. Meeting in closed session, they spread a drag-net to bring in all the errors which the Hutchinsonians held, or were presumed to hold, or might conceivably, by logical derivation, hold at some time in the future.[27]

Then Mr. Cotton was made the object of their scrutiny. His sermons were ransacked and his conference records dissected to lay bare any opinions that might prove erroneous. The result of their investigation was a fresh roster of questions—now reduced to five —pertaining to the conversion process. The ministers met privately with Cotton and, propounding their queries, demanded a prompt and explicit reply. Cotton obliged them with his promptness, but his equivocation on some points left much dissatisfaction in the minds of his interrogators. For the orthodox clergy, if the covenant had any meaning, it signified a willingness on man's part to believe in Christ's redemptive power *before* Christ would accept him in spiritual union. The regenerate process was not an abrupt seizure of the will, but was advanced by easy stages wherein the prospective believer might prepare himself and show his readiness to believe. Under great pressure Cotton clung tenaciously to his own views, seeking to express them in terms that might be consonant with theirs. A conjunction of nature and grace such as his colleagues implied was, to his mind, intolerable; but, nonetheless, the role and order of faith were not to be incautiously defined. He agreed that union with Christ could not be complete before or without faith on the part of the regenerate. Yet "in order of nature," he hastened to add, that union is complete "before our faith doth put forth it self to lay hold on him." This negated the very point they had sought to make. Cotton's examiners shifted their

26. Hutchinson, *History*, I, 60.
27. Winthrop, *Journal*, I, 230; Cotton, *Way of the Congregational Churches Cleared*, 41.

ground. Was Mr. Cotton of the opinion that faith was "an instru-
mentall cause in applying Christs righteousnesse to our Justification?" Again Cotton eluded them. Faith was indeed instrumental,
he concurred, in that it constitutes a fit disposition of the subject
to be justified. Like an urn that is emptied of its contents, it stands
clean and ready to be filled with oil. But, he concluded, an empty
urn, however clean, does not cause the pouring of the oil.[28]

Here was matter for dismay among Cotton's loving brethren.
Despite the humiliating cross-examination to which they had subjected him, despite the menacing tide of recent events, he had
clung stubbornly to his conviction that "man is as passive in his
Regeneration as in his first generation." [29] However subtly he might
arrange his metaphors, however gently assuage the voice of wrath,
his opinions still smacked of the Antinomian proposition that a
man "must see nothing in himselfe, have nothing, doe nothing,
onely he is to stand still and waite for Christ to doe all." [30]

But the clergy had extracted one concession from Cotton during
their conferences. Consternation spread through the meetinghouse
on Sunday, July 16, when Cotton blandly announced his complete
satisfaction that Pastor Wilson, in his speech to the Court of the
previous December, had not meant to impugn any doctrines
preached by Mr. Cotton or Mr. Wheelwright. Wilson had at last
been able to persuade them that when he had spoken he had referred to some three or four opinions "privately carried" in Boston
and other parts of the country.[31] The misunderstanding on both
sides was perhaps natural considering the transparent thinness into
which doctrine was being sliced these days. Cotton's announce-
ment raised some fears among his parishioners that their teacher
was preparing to beat a strategic retreat, but his clerical brethren
were by no means so sure of his intent. Nor, for that matter, was
Cotton.

(iv)

On Wednesday, August 30, the Synod began. Newtown parched
in midday heat as the solemn-faced little band of ministers and
magistrates made their way from the town landing up Water
Street. Passing the neat row of slate shingled cottages, they came
to the meetinghouse which stood on Spring Street, hard by the

28. Cotton, *Way of the Congregational Churches Cleared*, 41, 43.
29. Cotton, *Covenant of Grace*, 55.
30. *Antinomianism*, 74.
31. Winthrop, *Journal*, I, 230.

market place.[32] A rather substantial fleet of boats must have set forth up the Charles River from Boston that morning, for in addition to ministers and magistrates, there had also arrived a large deputation of Bostonians, most of whom could profess a somewhat more than academic interest in the forthcoming proceedings.

Visitors and Newtownians together jammed the little hall to capacity and waited in sweating impatience for the formalities to commence. The murmur of voices and the restless rustle of gowns suddenly faded and dissolved into a respectful hush as the "holy heavenly, ... and soul-ravishing" Mr. Shepard ascended the pulpit.[33] With eyes lifted heavenward, he intoned a prayer for divine guidance, larded with much discourse about the "unscriptural enthusiasms and revelations" that had long troubled the colony. When at last he came to an end, Mr. Wilson rose at his seat and appealed to the assembly; "You that are against these things, and that are for the Spirit and the word together, hold up your hands!"[34] A multitude of hands strained upward to proclaim their virtuous indignation. The ministers glowed confidently on this propitious display and commenced the proceedings in earnest. One of the elders mounted the pulpit and gravely recited a list of eighty-two erroneous opinions reputed to have been circulated abroad, and this was followed by a roster of unsafe and unwholesome expressions too carelessly spoken by some persons. Stunned by the enormity of such heterodoxies, awed listeners stole furtive glances about them to see what guilt-ridden or defiant faces might reveal ownership. What exercise is more gratifying to settled sanctity than the recitation of another's evil!

Most of the errors in question hinged on the basic Antinomian tenet that a person who has received immediate assurance from the Holy Spirit stands above the injunctions of Biblical law and does not require the evidences of sanctification or of good works to know that he is saved. Implicit in many of the errors was the assumption that zeal in the performance of duties or misgivings about one's good estate because of sins committed were sure signs that a person labored under a Covenant of Works. On these basic themes the learned theologians of the Bay had rung every conceivable change. The errors ranged in quality from the most grotesque

32. William Wood, *New England's Prospect* (London, 1635), 34; Winthrop, *Journal*, I, 232; Johnson, *Wonder Working Providence*, 171; Morison, *Founding of Harvard College*, map opposite 192.
33. Johnson, *Wonder Working Providence*, 252.
34. Mather, *Magnalia*, I, 282; Winthrop, *Journal*, I, 232.

extremes of Familism to subtle points of doctrine that hovered on the hairline border between orthodoxy and heterodoxy. As though fearful that some elusive heresy might slip through their fingers, individual errors were variously formulated, brought forth, and paraded in multifarious guises, and scanned from diverse angles. Indeed, as Wheelwright later observed, the clergy had so "lavishly tautologized" that it seemed they hoped to overwhelm the opposition by sheer weight of numbers.[35]

Too often, however, they had flatly labeled as errors certain tenets that would not bear a direct and unequivocal interpretation. Both Cotton and Wheelwright were several times caught on this hook. Error 21, for instance, struck obliquely at the complex problem of the order and nature of faith over which Cotton had labored during the pre-Synod conference. Error 64, "A man must take no notice for his sinne, nor of his repentance for his sinne," was an unfair thrust at Cotton's conviction that "Sometimes [God's sealed children] such as doe so fall [into sin] may yet reteyne or doubtless clayme unto Gods fatherly love." [36] Wheelwright also found several of the professed errors to be "neither true nor false," but apparently incorporated in the list merely to "fill up the number." Error 24, "that the whole letter of the scripture holds forth a covenant of works," was, he asserted, in one sense quite true. On the other hand, "in its Anagogue" wherein it intends Christ to be the author of sufficiency, "it pitches upon the Covenant of Grace." [37] He also found Error 33, "to act by virtue of . . . a command is legal," was at best a debatable proposition, to be examined more narrowly and answered more precisely than the orthodox brethren would allow.[38] Surely, he contended, "they act legally who think to do things in their own strength formally." [39] Most of the errors, however, were so extreme that both Cotton and Wheelwright could, in good faith, roundly disavow them.

With Mrs. Hutchinson, however, it was a different matter. Quite a few of these alleged errors could be safely laid at her door, and there were others that might be more cautiously ascribed to her. She would have promptly laid claim to Error 40; "There is a testi-

---

35. Wheelwright, *Writings*, 208.
36. *Antinomianism*, 102, 115; John Cotton to Samuel Stone, Mar. 1638, Cotton Papers, Boston Public Library. See also Cotton, *Covenant of Grace*, 125, 128, 130-31.
37. Wheelwright, *Writings*, 202, 207, 209.
38. *Antinomianism*, 105.
39. Wheelwright, *Writings*, 209.

mony of the Spirit, and voyce unto the Soule, meerely immediate, without any respect unto, or concurrence with the word"; and likewise to the closely allied Error 71, "The immediate revelation of my good estate, without any respect to the Scriptures, is as cleare to me, as the voyce of God from Heaven to Paul." [40] Already she had confounded the local clergy with her insistence that "no Minister can bee an instrument to convey more of Christ unto another, than hee by his own experience hath come unto." [41] Error 67, that "a man cannot evidence his justification by his sanctification," was one of the prime tenets of her doctrine. It also seems quite likely that she may have advocated Errors 18 and 23; "The Spirit doth worke in Hypocrites, by gifts and graces, but in Gods children immediately," and "We must not pray for gifts and graces, but onely for Christ." Related to those two was the problem of hypostatical union with Christ, as expressed in Error 7, "The new creature, or the new man mentioned in the Gospell, is not meant of grace, but of Christ." [42] Henry Vane had already admitted to a belief in such an intermingling of "personal proprieties" and it seems probable that Mrs. Hutchinson shared the same conviction.[43]

But among the welter of errors was a good deal of rank Familism, which Mrs. Hutchinson would have strenuously repudiated. Certainly, she would not have claimed that "to take delight in the holy service of God, is to go a whoring from God." [44] Nor would she have allowed that the example of Christ's life was "not a patterne according to which men ought to act." Although the problem of the perseverance of grace was central to her thought, Anne would have hesitated to defend Error 20, "That to call into question whether God be my deare Father, after or upon the commission of some hainous sinnes (as Murther, Incest, etc.,) doth prove a man to be in a Covenant of workes." [45] But, like Cotton, she would have found it difficult to abandon her conviction that once God's children had been sealed in His love, the seal could not be removed. Here, of course, was a crucial test of the validity of a subjective witness. In such circumstances Anne would have been compelled to endanger the whole framework of her doctrine by conceding that a believer so fallen had been deluded by a false wit-

40. *Antinomianism*, 108, 118.
41. Error 54, *ibid.*, 112.
42. *Ibid.*, 116, 100, 103, 97.
43. Winthrop, *Journal*, I, 196, 201.
44. Error 57, *Antinomianism*, 113.
45. Errors 6 and 20, *ibid.*, 96, 101.

ness, Satanically induced. And this would have been, essentially, to surrender the field to the legalists.

Although the clerical saturation policy may have unfairly imputed to Anne and her friends many errors that were not properly theirs, it cannot be denied that the net safely encompassed all the errors they had ventured. To top all, the concluding "error" was a shrewd precautionary device which aimed to stop the mouths of any who questioned the procedures of the present assembly: "A Minister must not pray or preach against any errour, unlesse he declare . . . the names of them that hold them." [46]

After this "litter of fourescore and eleven . . . brats [had been] hung up against the Sunne" that all might observe and stand amazed, the ministers turned to the task of arranging the procedures of their convocation.[47] Thomas Hooker of Hartford and Peter Bulkley of Concord—"than whome none could thunder louder"— were chosen moderators for the ensuing sessions.[48] The Synod declared itself intent on the confutation of errors rather than the censure of persons.[49] In order that the errors might be thoroughly aired, it was agreed that any person could dispute for or against any of the cited opinions without suspicion of holding that opinion unless he so declared himself.[50] One may wonder what innocent observer had the hardihood to risk possibility of suspicion. Errors may well have been the present business of the clergy, but few were naively unaware that erronists would in due course become the object of their scrutiny.

The next morning the disputation got under way in noisy earnest. As the debate advanced, Cotton grew disturbed at the frequency with which his own parishioners defended certain of the errors. "Brethren," he at last anxiously interposed, "if you be of that judgment which you plead for, all these Bastardly Opinions, which are justly offensive to the Churches, will be fathered upon *Boston*." [51] The perils of the disputational procedure had not escaped his observation: It was all too easy to confound a devil's advocate with the devil himself. One of the Boston delegates pointed out that his

46. *Ibid.*, 124.

47. *Ibid.*, 72.

48. Mather, *Magnalia*, I, 362; Winthrop, *Journal*, I, 232.

49. Mather, *Magnalia*, II, 512.

50. Johnson, *Wonder Working Providence*, 171. The Reverend Mr. Weld was more candid in describing the arrangement. "A place was appointed," he wrote, "for all the Opinionists to come in and take liberty of speech . . . as much as any of ourselves and as freely." *Antinomianism*, 86.

51. Cotton, *Way of the Congregational Churches Cleared*, 47.

party did not necessarily support the opinions in question, but on the other hand, neither could they flatly condemn them. These men were not of Cotton's flock for nothing. Who else could have taught them so well that theological problems are seldom unambiguous in their resolution?

Nor had the Bostonians overlooked the possibility of just such a blanket condemnation as Cotton had feared. The disputation and confutation of errors continued for a full week. During that time, the Boston delegates tried to guard themselves against the insinuation that they favored indiscriminately all the errors cited. Whenever the more radical doctrines were submitted for disputation, Coddington or one of his fellows rose to inquire who was charged with holding such an error. The moderators firmly replied that there was sufficient testimony to support the citation, but for the present it was not fit to name persons, because this assembly was concerned only with doctrines. The Bostonians were incensed at the use of a procedure that might broadly incriminate their party. They insisted that in fairness each shoe must be fitted individually to determine whether it really had an owner. The hall crackled with protests that witnesses be summoned to testify under oath. When at last even the thunder of Bulkley failed to quiet the remonstrants, Governor Winthrop rapped vigorously for order. If they would not forbear, he warned, "it would prove a civil disturbance, and then the magistrate must interpose." [52]

The magistrate had nothing to do with this assembly, one of the Bostonians angrily retorted. Winthrop eyed him coldly; if the speaker wished to make trial of the matter, he might well see it carried out. Disinclined to venture this possibility and enraged at the frustration of their efforts, several of the Bostonians stormed from the hall and did not return. Those who remained discreetly kept their silence.[53]

Cotton suffered no little embarrassment from this episode and considered the wisdom of promptly disengaging himself from complicity with the departed factionists. Confronting the assembly, he informed them that he "esteemed some of the Opinions, to bee blasphemous; some of them, hereticall; many of them, Erroneous; and almost all of them, incommodiously expressed." [54] However,

52. Winthrop, Journal, I, 232 ff.; Hutchinson, History, I, 61; Cotton, Way of the Congregational Churches Cleared, 47 ff.; Mather, Magnalia, II, 512-13.
53. Winthrop, Journal, I, 233.
54. Cotton, Way of the Congregational Churches Cleared, 48.

he took care to except certain opinions on which he had hitherto expressed his own indecision.

At week's end Mr. Hooker was finally able to pronounce the canonical obliteration of the whole chaotic array of errors and expressions. As the arraignment died away, one stupefied onlooker managed to gasp, "What shall be done with them?" Pastor Wilson —never one to shrink from the insuperable—disposed of the heap with one magnificent sweep of the Augean shovel; "Let them go to the devil of hell from whence they came." [55]

(v)

The exorcism of errors was child's play compared to what followed. The clergy turned now to Cotton and Wheelwright and for two weeks labored to devise a compromise formula which might restore those aberrant clerics to the ranks of theological respectability, thereby isolating the Hutchinson faction from clerical aid and comfort.

For a week or so the reverend gentlemen went about their assignment with systematic care. On the first forenoon they gathered and thoughtfully framed their arguments. They singled out for their purpose nine main points on which all the others seemed to hinge. After midday meal, when the Synod formally assembled, the nine points with their supporting arguments were read aloud to Cotton and Wheelwright. The next afternoon the two ministers offered their rebuttal, and on the day following the orthodox reply was presented.[56] By this means the nine points were reduced to five, which, though not identical, were similar to those Cotton had answered at the pre-Synod conference. The method was exhaustive but, straining to get at the heart of the matter, the participants found it exasperatingly slow and at last abandoned it in favor of spontaneous open debate.[57]

Inevitably they returned to the problem of the order and place of faith in the conversion process. One day, near the end of the Synod, Wheelwright was arguing for God's freedom to pour out saving grace on whomsoever He chose regardless of that person's spiritual condition. This was a key point in the debate, on which hinged the vital matters of God's freedom and man's responsibility.

55. Mather, *Magnalia*, I, 282.
56. *Antinomianism*, 86; Winthrop, *Journal*, I, 234; Mather, *Magnalia*, II, 515.
57. Winthrop, *Journal*, I, 234.

An incautious step in either direction might easily place one among the ranks of the heretics. Cotton had hitherto straddled the issue as circumstances seemed to require. In his debate with the Arminians of old Boston, he had held that "God doth sometime pour out the spirit of grace upon the most bloody, and most haynous, and most desperate, and most prophane, and most abominable sinners." [58] In the pre-Synod conference he had conceded that faith must be implanted before justification—but he had continued to insist that at the outset faith could play, at most, a passive role. Now, as he sat in the Newtown meetinghouse and listened to Pastor Wheelwright argue for God's unlimited freedom, Cotton weighed the delicate issue afresh. Bringing to his support the reasoning of his old predestinarian antagonist, Dr. Twisse, he ventured the proposition that "God may bee said to justifie me before the habit, or act of Faith, and the habit is the effect of my Justification." [59]

The ministers were stunned by this proposal. Their desperate efforts to rescue Cotton from the Hutchinsonian embrace had apparently failed. The next day was devoted wholly to debate on Cotton's proposal. With many tears and lamentations his brethren begged him to reconsider his untimely thesis. One account, which Cotton does not convincingly refute, claims that some of the ministers, casting aside patience and decorum, bitterly admonished him for his inconstancy and heterodoxy. [60] Evening brought adjournment with the problem as yet unresolved. That night must have been agonizingly sleepless for Cotton, his brain teeming with tortuous arguments and echoing with the pleas and rebukes of his fellow ministers.

When morning came and the assembly reconvened, Cotton gained the floor and to the immense relief of his colleagues returned to the more moderate position he had held before the Synod. The ministers "greedily and joyfully laid hold upon the reconciling offers of Mr. Cotton." After some further discussion it was agreed among them "that we are not united and married unto the Lord Jesus Christ without faith, giving an actual consent of the soul unto it: that God's effectual calling of the soul unto the Lord Jesus Christ, and the soul's apprehending by an act of faith the offered righteousness of the Lord Jesus Christ, is in order of nature before God's act of justification upon the soul." [61] This delicate distinction

58. Cotton, *Way of Life*, 109.
59. Cotton, *Way of the Congregational Churches Cleared*, 50.
60. *Ibid.*; Mather, *Magnalia*, II, 514; Baylie, *Dissuassive From the Errours*, 58.
61. Mather, *Magnalia*, II, 514.

Cotton further cut into a narrow scantling when he reiterated that "wee be not active in laying hold on Christ before hee hath given us his spirit." [62] Here was matter for subtle minds to ruminate.

With Cotton safely clutched from the burning, events drew rapidly to a head. The five points in question were whittled down to three, and to these Cotton guardedly offered his assent. Wheelwright, however, could not find it in his conscience to accept this summary agreement which may well have been as the ministers would have it. Cotton was far too important a figure for the ministers to alienate and the support of his prestige would much improve their position. Wheelwright, however, not only enjoyed less influence, but his familiarity with the Hutchinsonians was too close to allow a comfortable accommodation with the clerical party. Now that Vane had departed and Cotton had been won away, Wheelwright was isolated from all effective ecclesiastical or magisterial support and stood by himself, a marked man.

The three summary points united the ministers in agreement that there were no gracious conditions or qualifications in the soul before faith, on which the promise of grace was in any way contingent. But faith, they conceded, must not be regarded as a means by which man might actively lay hold on Christ before He had freely imparted His spirit.[63] The ministers also settled to their satisfaction the vexing problem of how far sanctification might serve to evidence justification. According to Winthrop's report, they agreed that "some saving sanctifications" were always "coexistent" and "concurrent" with the Witness of the Spirit. However, the concession was offered to Cotton that such sanctification was not always necessarily "coapparent." [64] Cotton reported the conclusion in terms rendering his sentiments more explicit: that a man may not "gather the first evidence or assurance of . . . his justification by his sanctification"—and then added "but he must first have seen Christ by faith." [65]

Cotton emerged almost unscathed from this trying ordeal. Although subjected to humiliating pressures he was, in the last analysis, obliged to do little more than restate his original position in less equivocal terms. His opponents, however, in their eagerness to separate Cotton from the Boston faction, appear to have gravitated toward placing less emphasis than formerly on the perform-

62. Cotton, *Gospel Conversion*, 40.
63. *Ibid.*, 1, 40.
64. Winthrop, *Journal*, I, 233.
65. Cotton, *Gospel Conversion*, 8, 23.

ance of works and duties. In actuality neither party had surrendered much, but each had been impelled to restore to conventional proportions an aspect of doctrine they had hitherto accentuated in order to serve their respective predilections and needs.[66]

After three exhausting weeks of debate, the Synod came to an end on September 22. Having dealt thus lengthily with the abstruse data of theology, they turned on the final day to matters of more tangible concern. It was resolved that henceforth private meetings such as Mrs. Hutchinson had sponsored were to be discouraged as "disorderly and without rule." A further restraint on the Hutchinsonians was obtained by forbidding church members to question ministers in such a way as to asperse the doctrines delivered in their sermons.[67]

As the assembly was about to break up, Governor Winthrop rose to make a proposal. Inasmuch as "matters had been carried on so peaceably, and concluded so comfortably in all love," he suggested that it might be fit to convoke such a council every year.[68] All but the most combative ministers present must have blanched at the prospect. Few among them could coolly contemplate an annual recurrence of the "jarring and dissonant opinions," the "ventilation and emptying of private passions," the "jealousies, and heates, and paroxysms of spirit" which they had thus long endured.[69] The proposal had its merits, they conceded, but for the moment they were not quite ready to commit themselves to such a regimen.

(vi)

Thomas Hooker had seen fit to pocket his scruples when he joined the Synod, perhaps in the hope that his presence might moderate the partisan animus of the Bay clergy. When he left Newtown, he was relieved that God's work had been done, but his mind was still much troubled about the outcome of this controversy. The spleen of Mrs. Hutchinson's antagonists had not escaped his observation, and he feared that in their determination to defend the scriptural way some innocent persons might suffer. Arriving at

66. See Miller, *The New England Mind: From Colony to Province*, 69-76, for a careful analysis of the manner in which the delicate equilibrium of the covenant theology was sustained.
67. Winthrop, *Journal*, I, 234.
68. *Ibid.*, 235.
69. Hutchinson, *History*, I, 61, quoting the description of an anonymous witness; Cotton, *Way of the Congregational Churches Cleared*, 63.

Hartford, he wrote to Winthrop, expressing his apprehensions. "Attend nothing for ground of determination," he advised, "but that which will cary an undeniable evidence to an impartiall judge." [70] This warning fell upon deaf ears. Winthrop was now steeled in his resolution that the colony must be rid of the troublers, and there was no place in his heart for impartiality.

"For execution," Hooker continued, "let it be so secret and sud-dayne that it cannot be prevented, so resolute and uncontrolable that it may tak off hope from the adversary that it can be resisted." [71] On this score Winthrop was more than receptive; indeed he had already begun to act. With the Hutchinson opinions under a clerical ban, the conventicles forbidden, and Pastor Wheelwright isolated from all effective support, Winthrop moved swiftly to bring about the end which the Synod had prepared.

Four days after the Synod ended, the General Court which was elected in May was hastily dissolved, and new elections were ordered. Having achieved the political rout of the Hutchinsonians at the Easter term, the magistrates had continued to convoke this same Court throughout the summer. Through a series of adjournments, Winthrop kept them in session as though he were counting on them to finish the task they had but started. Or perhaps he was fearful that a new election would upset the majority he had won. But nothing more happened. The Wheelwright case was put over from one meeting to the next without action. Possibly they were waiting to see what counsel the Synod might offer. Perhaps there was a minority of deputies who were reluctant to press for more punitive measures against the Hutchinsonians. At last the magistrates came to realize that a freshly chosen body might grapple more vigorously with the problem.[72]

In any case the Court that was elected in October was quite a different group from that which had been dissolved. Only seventeen members of the old Court were re-elected, and of the thirty-

70. Thomas Hooker to John Winthrop [ca. Oct. 1637], *Winthrop Papers*, III, 499.
71. *Ibid.*
72. The General Court met by law at least four times a year, by original design on the last Wednesday of Easter, Hilary, Trinity, and Michaelmas terms—that is, in May, August, October, and January. The deputies were to be elected before each court. The Easter Court (the Court of Elections) of 1637 first met on May 17. This Court was then adjourned to August first. It was adjourned again to September 14, and then finally adjourned to the twenty-sixth of September. At this last session the Court dissolved itself and ordered new elections, in effect intimating the quality and temper desired of its successors. *Colony Records*, I, 11, 118, 200, 202, 204. Max Farrand, ed., *The Book of General Lawes and Liberties, 1648* (Cambridge, Mass., 1929), 16.

two deputies in the new Court, fifteen were newcomers. In one respect the pattern of change is suggestive. The need for a change seems to have been felt only with respect to certain towns, while others were apparently regarded as safe. There was a complete turnover in the Roxbury, Hingham, Ipswich, and Weymouth delegations. Newtown and Charlestown each sent two new men of the three to which they were entitled. Salem elected one new deputy. The Bostonians substituted Coggeshall for Hough, to support the defensive efforts of Aspinwall and Coddington. But the other six towns introduced no change whatsoever in their delegations.[73]

The stage was now set and the actors prepared.

73. *Colony Records*, I, 194, 204, 205. See Appendix VI.

XIII

Winterset

October 17–November 7, 1637

(i)

WINTER struck New England with untimely fury. October had scarcely faded when a northeast storm lashed the coast.[1] The wind out of the Great Cove moaned around the eaves of the Hutchinson house, flinging snow against the leaded panes. Inside, the children pressed eager faces to the cold windows, sharing the excitement of all children at the first snowfall of winter with its promise of fun and frolic.

Their mother, busy at her household chores, shared none of their elation. The snow, coming too early, threatened a long, hard winter and the sense of foreboding that had troubled her these many days seemed heightened by the storm. Wherever her restless mind turned, there was only apprehension of the future or painful memories of the recent past. She tried to pull herself back to the comforting realities of pans and dishes, the small, familiar problems of food and family.

1. Winthrop, *Journal*, I, 238; Wheelwright, *Writings*, 226; Felt, *Ecclesiastical History of New England*, II, 101. The episode that follows is based on the credible portions of the narrative provided in Winthrop, *Journal*, I, 266-68. I have assumed the liberty of suggesting that on the day of the storm, two weeks later, Mrs. Hutchinson had not yet escaped recollection of the unhappy event. An imaginative and deeply sensitive woman, Anne could not fail to be emotionally moved by what she now observed. For weeks thereafter, she must have relived the dreadful scene in her imagination and brooded over the question of its providential meaning. Precisely how the episode may have influenced her later course of action, I would not venture to suggest. But like the rest of her life experience, it was absorbed into the totality of her being and must be assumed to have counted for something in organizing her succeeding attitudes and actions.

Now even the thought of family served only to remind her that Edward's young wife was due to give birth to her first child—Anne's first grandchild. Even at this moment, shut off by the storm, the labor might be starting and how would she get to them? Or how would they reach her for help? But even this anxiety was to be preferred to the agonies of imagination that had tortured her for the past two weeks. The event, so eagerly awaited for months, when she would hold her first grandchild, had become a matter of dread.

Anne no longer suffered these fears for herself, but she was burdened with stranger misgivings. As the wearying cycles of pregnancy and nursing drew to a close, she found herself in the grip of cruel discomfort. Numbing headaches and dizziness overcame her without apparent cause. Even in the cold of November, an unaccountable warmth suffused her body, then as suddenly gave way to shivering coldness. The most routine tasks of the day, the most innocent play of the children, made her cross and irritable. Black moods of depression swept over her and left her groping for comprehension—struggling anew for self-discovery.[2]

The crises of the past month had tried her sorely. The forthcoming meeting of the General Court summoned for extraordinary session a day or two hence presaged no good. There was no telling how this might touch her friends or even herself, and her mind should be clear and alert to meet whatever contingencies might be ahead. But so many painful thoughts disturbed her it was difficult to listen for a "still small voice" in the midst of such tempest.

The snow mounted against the shed and lined the side of Deacon Coggeshall's house, visible beyond the drifted kitchen window. Blown snow ghosted across back lots and up the hill to where Mr. Cotton's house huddled on the side of Trimountaine. Cotton was now separated from her by barriers more insuperable than drifted snow; since his acceptance of the Synodical conclusions and his joining in the attack on her meetings and teachings a great breach had existed between them. For a brief moment, two weeks before, they had bridged that gap when she turned to him in desperation. The circumstances leading to that visit still haunted her.

She had been called out to assist Goody Hawkins at the delivery of Mary Dyer's baby. Even as she hurried down the High Street to the little house by the cow pond on Mylne Road, she was filled with apprehension, knowing that Mary's term had not been ful-

2. See p. 248n.

filled. Once there she turned quickly to the task at hand, putting
the several neighbor women to various chores by tactful suggestion.
One could not work in a room cluttered with people. There were
meals to be prepared, small children to be cared for, and poor
William Dyer worriedly fretting and pacing in the foreroom. The
women, knowledgeable in the ways of childbearing, were aware
that this was not going well. Their fears were in the very air, so
that it was a relief to have them out of the room. This was not
going well at all. Mary was a strong woman with two healthy children, and a seven-month baby should be a light load to deliver.
But it went badly. Hours ago there had been life evident, delivery
had seemed imminent. Still Mary strained and gasped, the terrible
animal groans tearing through her clenched teeth. Goody Hawkins,
mumbling incoherently to herself, saw the problem. The child was
breached hip-wise and could in no way come out until it was
turned. Anne held Mary tightly in her strong arms, wrestling her
to stillness against the agony as Goody Hawkins turned the child.
There was a little lull, then it began all over again. Anne was oblivious to the sweat which soaked her from her own efforts and the
heat of the fire which must be kept burning in the closed room.
Mary still labored. Long since there had ceased to be any sign of
life from the creature within her. If it were God's will that the
child be lost, still they must labor on to save the mother. Again
Goody Hawkins tried to free the child. The last frightful scream
tore from Mary's throat and she fell back, mercifully unconscious.
It was for Anne and Goody Hawkins to see the hideous fruit of
Mary's labors. A creature so horrible in its malformation as to bear
only the slightest terrifying resemblance to mankind. Something
such as only a nightmare of hell could conceive. It was most mercifully dead.

There was no time to spend on it. One must press horror back
into the brain, sternly drag the reeling senses to attention, and administer to the exhausted Mary. Before the frightful evidence could
be concealed or a course of action decided on, the door opened,
and one of the women entered. Anne tried to block the woman's
view, but, quickly as she stepped to shield the scene, the horrified
gaze told her that enough had been noticed. With swift authority,
she persuaded the witness to keep silence. Meanwhile, she asked
herself, what course should they take? The law required that all
births be registered. The house was full of neighbors who were
sure to ask questions. She would have to tell Mary something—and

William. What was God's will? How could she speak of God's will to Mary when, in this desperate hour, her own faith was shaking? If one of His sealed children, such as Mary, could be so cruelly stricken what did it portend? Pain and sorrow and death—these could be borne as instruction. But for the very laws of nature to be overthrown, life and birth and creation itself to become instruments of punishment!

It was while the exhausted Mary slept that Anne slipped out of the house and made her way to Mr. Cotton's door. However betrayed she might feel at his renunciation of her cause, she knew that he could be trusted in a matter of such human anguish. Cloistered with him in the study, she gasped out the whole hideous story. Cotton was stunned, but strove to deliberate as coolly as his troubled spirit would allow. What if this had befallen his own sweet Sarah, he reflected. How would she feel, and he too—if the horrid tale were carelessly gossiped abroad? But, if it were God's will, the sentiments of man must not be permitted to intrude upon His inscrutable design. Yet had not God arranged that this horror should be concealed from the many women who had been working so near at hand? Perhaps it was His intent to edify only the unhappy parents and those who had chanced to be present. With these reflections he comfortingly assured Mrs. Hutchinson that it was best to inter the creature unseen and make no further mention of it.

For that brief time, all differences put aside, they had been united in doing God's work. Cotton's counsel had been some consolation and she had hastened to carry it out. The simple truth that the child was dead was sufficient for the sympathetic neighbors. Telling William the facts was more difficult, and breaking it to Mary by degrees was torture. She feared for her friend's health and sanity. For these two weeks the experience had haunted her, and not even her own desperate plight would serve to wipe it from her mind. What was God's purpose? If, as Cotton had said, this experience had been for the instruction of those who witnessed it, what did it mean? Why did not God speak to her? Or had he spoken? Was there some divine judgment against her in all this? It seemed to bode some great calamity. Pray God it touched not on Edward's child.

This fear she could tell no one. Bound to keep silence regarding the Dyers' ordeal, she could find no release. There was no voice to comfort her save God's.

(ii)

Over the snow to Newtown came the deputies and assistants of the Great and General Court of Massachusetts. There was an element of vindication in the prominence that Newtown had lately acquired at Boston's expense—or, at least, so Thomas Dudley may have felt. For almost a year it had been found expedient to hold the Court at Newtown, remote from the disturbing influence of Mr. Cotton's parishioners. The Synod had gathered there, and, even now, plans were afoot to seat the new college on the bank of the Charles. When the seat of government had first been moved to Boston, it had been over Dudley's protests; now he could gather some grim satisfaction in witnessing the discomfiture of those who had forced the decision against him.[3]

On Thursday, November 2, the members of the new Court took their places in the little meetinghouse on Spring Street. Bundled heavily in cloaks and great coats, they waited in frigid impatience for the session to commence. The Governor was announced. A hush settled over the hall as Winthrop, proudly flanked by two halberdiers, strode down the aisle to take his seat at the center of the magistrates' table.

The first business of the Court was the examination of members' credentials. One by one each name was offered and entered in the record without objection until the name of William Aspinwall was submitted. This was Aspinwall's second appearance as a deputy: his association with Mrs. Hutchinson was well known.

Was Mr. Aspinwall "fit to bee received as a member of the Court?" one of the magistrates coldly inquired.[4] Had he not been among those who subscribed to that seditious remonstrance "which was so much to the dishonour and contempt" of the Court?

The Bostonians were suddenly alert to the strategy of the opposition. Having gained a Court that would bend to its will, it was now intent on purging the refractory remnant. But before Aspinwall could protest that the petition, having been submitted to a previous Court, was hardly the proper concern of this present assembly, Winthrop intervened. Would Mr. Aspinwall, he probed, still maintain the principles advanced in that troublesome petition?

It was not in Aspinwall's nature to back down. His feelings were well known, he defiantly announced, nor would he now deny them.

3. Winthrop, *Journal*, I, 84 ff.
4. *Antinomianism*, 136.

Winthrop's tactic had succeeded. A motion was offered that the delegate from Boston was not fit to be a member of the Court and should be dismissed forthwith. A show of hands sufficed to manifest the pleasure of the deputies.

Appalled by this arbitrary dealing, John Coggeshall sprang to his feet. "Seeing [you have] put out Mr. Aspinwall [you had] best make one work of all," he stormed. "As for [myself], though [my] hand [was] not to the Petition, yet [I] did approve of it, and [my] hand was to a Protestation, which was to the same effect." [5]

Winthrop eyed him coolly. He had not anticipated such co-operation from the Bostonians. He would be more than pleased to accommodate Mr. Coggeshall: the good deacon's contempt of authority should certainly receive its due. Another motion; another show of hands, and Coggeshall too, was ejected from his seat. Raging down the aisle, he turned at the door and called out, "[I] pray that [your] eyes [may] be opened to see what [you do], for . . . [it is] the greatest stroke that was ever given to N[ew] E[ngland]." Winthrop scowled; to his ears the expostulation had sounded more menacing. He would deal again with Mr. Coggeshall.[6] He turned to Mr. Coddington, now the sole representative of Boston. Would Mr. Coddington kindly inform his constituents that they must now select two new deputies?

The examination having been concluded, Coddington gained the floor. On the instruction of the people of Boston, he wished to move that the censure against Mr. Wheelwright should be presently reversed. On the same authority he further requested that the alien law might be repealed.

The Court was quite ready to take notice of these proposals. Winthrop declared he had observed with great displeasure Mr. Wheelwright's contumacious behavior in maintaining his faction contrary to the will of the Synod. The Court therefore desired that Mr. Wheelwright be speedily summoned to attend the justice of this present session. As to the alien law, the Governor indicated that on the morrow he would be pleased to edify the assembly on the intent and scope of that much abused enactment.

Accordingly, on Friday morning, Winthrop brought with him the correspondence which he and Vane had exchanged on that subject the previous summer. All three papers were read aloud in their

5. *Ibid.*, 137, 138. Transposition from indirect to direct quotation in this chapter is indicated by the use of brackets.
6. *Ibid.*, 149.

exhausting entirety, at the end of which, Winthrop was gratified to record, "some that...had taken offence at the Law, did openly acknowledge themselves fully satisfied." [7]

(iii)

Boston was far from satisfied with the expulsion of her two chosen representatives. Buzzing indignantly over Winthrop's high-handed methods, the Bostonians assembled in town meeting to act on the Court's election warrant. This gratuitous insult would not be accepted. They resolved to return Aspinwall and Coggeshall to their rightful places and let Master Winthrop make of it what he would.

One timorous townsman appears to have slipped away from the meeting to inform Mr. Cotton of this perverse course of action. Fearing that such defiance might precipitate a dangerous crisis, Cotton hurried to the meeting hoping to make them reconsider. His arguments for selecting deputies more acceptable to the Court were weighed. Reluctantly, Coggeshall and Aspinwall were set aside and William Colburn and young John Oliver were chosen in their stead. [8]

Like their predecessors, and indeed like almost every other Bostonian eligible for the posts, both men were supporters of Mrs. Hutchinson. But by now there were few Bostonians, irrespective of their religious sentiments, who did not resent Winthrop's over-bearing manner. Colburn and Oliver prepared to leave for New-town, but meantime the day's business had proceeded without them.

Only Coddington represented Boston as Wheelwright faced the Court that Monday afternoon. His case had been deferred from month to month, Winthrop sternly reminded him, in hope that he might finally see the error of his ways. There could be no more delay: he must acknowledge his offense or abide the sentence of the Court. Wheelwright stood firm, denying that he was guilty of the crimes charged against him. He "had delivered nothing but the truth of Christ," he insisted. [9]

It lay not within their province to censure his doctrine, Winthrop rejoined, but they could not overlook its disturbing effect on

7. *Ibid.*, 138, 139. See Chapter XII, Section i.
8. *Antinomianism*, 140; "Boston Town Records, 1634-1660," 20.
9. *Antinomianism*, 140.

the community. Before Wheelwright had delivered his Fast Day Sermon, he went on, there had been "a peaceable and comely order in all affaires in the Churches, and civill state." Although this claim may have occasioned some raised eyebrows throughout the hall, its accuracy went unchallenged. Winthrop proceeded to lay at Wheelwright's door blame for all the dissensions that had lately troubled the colony as well as for some which would seem to have occurred before Wheelwright arrived. Boston's refusal to join the Pequot War, the various slights offered to Pastor Wilson and Winthrop himself, the many controversies in the town meeting and in other "neighbour meetings"; all were due to Wheelwright's speech. Though ministers and magistrates had sought by conference and writing to restore him to the paths of regularity and brotherhood, his proud spirit had obdurately refused to incline to their pleadings. Wheelwright remained unmoved: he would, "by the helpe of God, make good his doctrines, and free them from all the arguments which had beene brought against them." [10]

Since it had grown dark within the meetinghouse, the passing of sentence was put off until morning.

(iv)

On Tuesday morning the Court reconvened with a lengthy docket and but dim prospects of a decently early adjournment. Mr. Wheelwright was not in his place at the appointed hour, and his tardiness was noted as a further indication of his contempt for authority.[11]

But the two new Boston deputies were on hand to submit their credentials. Although Colburn's attachment to Mrs. Hutchinson was known, he was a respected citizen and a deacon of the church, and there was no sound reason for refusing him his seat. If he were not eligible, who among the Bostonians would be? Sergeant Oliver, however, though a "gracious" young man of "sweet disposition," had exposed the measure of his youthful indiscretion by placing his hand to the Wheelwright petition.[12]

The Court inquired whether he would acknowledge his error in joining that seditious enterprise. No, he would not, Sergeant Oliver asserted. So he too was dismissed and another election warrant issued to the town of Boston. This second affront they haughtily

10. *Ibid.*, 141, 143, 145.
11. *Ibid.*, 145.
12. Winthrop, *Journal*, II, 267.

ignored and, for the duration of the present Court, Boston was represented by but two deputies.[13]

The tardy Wheelwright now took his place before the bar. Could the defendant allege any reason why sentence should not now proceed against him, the Governor formally intoned. Wheelwright saw ample reason: the Court had not proved that he was guilty of either sedition or contempt, he flashed. As to the charge that he had libeled the ministers and magistrates as enemies of Christ, would the Court show him on what page or leaf of his sermon he had said so much.

Winthrop scowled at the defiant culprit, "He who designes a man by such circumstances, as doe note him out to common intendments, doth as much as if he named the party." As Wheelwright puzzled over this circumlocution, the Governor cited several instances to support his claim.[14]

Wheelwright remained unimpressed. The troubles of the civil state had been caused by the Lord Jesus Christ, he averred. Only by chance had he been called to deliver his sermon in the midst of these dissensions. Though usually susceptible to the argument of providential causation, Winthrop was presently indisposed to consider such a likelihood. Whatever the cause, it was evident that the man before them was "the instrument of [their] troubles." Until the relationship could be proven merely accidental, the blame for these troubles must lie on him alone, "for we know that Christ would not owne them, being out of his way."

Wearying at last of argument, the Court declared Wheelwright guilty for troubling the civil peace, for his corrupt and dangerous opinions, and for his contemptuous behavior toward the magistrates. Finding that they "could not continue together without the ruine of the whole," he was sentenced to be disfranchised and banished from the colony.[15]

Wheelwright was indignant. He would appeal his case to the King's justice, he stormed at his judges. "An appeale [does] not lie in this case," Winthrop coolly instructed him, "for the King having given us an authority by his graunt under his great Seale of *England* to heare and determine all causes without any reservation, we [are] not to admit of any such appeales . . . ; if an appeale should

13. *Antinomianism*, 140.
14. *Ibid.*, 145.
15. *Ibid.*, 146, 147.

lie in one case, it might be challenged in all, and then there would be no use of government amongst us." [16]

Wheelwright, apparently impressed by this dubiously exagger· ated claim, abandoned his attempted appeal. But still he refused to offer security for his quiet departure, so he was committed to the custody of the marshal to spend the night in solitary reflection. By morning he was sufficiently chastened to return to Court and provide the required assurance. The Court insisted that he should forbear preaching in the time before his departure. This, Wheelwright would by no means agree to. Winthrop shrugged his shoulders; there was little enough harm the man could do to them now. Wheelwright must leave the colony within two weeks, he was informed, or submit himself to the custody of one of the magistrates until such time as the Court should further dispose his case.[17]

Leaving Newtown and the Court behind him, Wheelwright made his way over snow and ice back to Wollaston to ready his departure. The first stage of his New World adventure had ended in disaster. He had left home and England in the belief that he might safely preach his convictions among sympathetic listeners. Instead he had been trapped as in a vise, his doctrines violently misunderstood and attacked on the one side and distorted beyond all recognition on the other. Despite his divine calling he could not put down the bitterness he felt against the clergy who had so cruelly abused him. Why could they not, for all their learning, see the fatal inconsistencies in their doctrine!

Nor was his sister Hutchinson entirely without blame for his present plight. A good woman, but rash and naive in matters of doctrine. Although she and her friends had noisily espoused the Covenant of Grace, it seemed to him "they took away the Grace of the Covenant." [18] Finding some likeness between his doctrines and

16. *Ibid.*, 147. This was perhaps a questionable claim. Although the Governor and Company could "and maie be capeable and enabled, as well to implead and to be impleaded, and to prosecute, demaund, and aunswere, and be aunsweared unto, in all and singuler suites, causes, quarrells, and acctions of what kinde or nature soever" and they had "full and absolute power and authoritie to correct, punishe, pardon, governe, and rule all such subjects ... that shall at any tyme hereafter inhabite within the precincts and partes of Newe England," this was to be done according to "lawes and ordinances ... not contrarie or repugnant to the lawes and statutes of this our realme of England." It was also with the understanding that all inhabitants "shall have and enjoy all liberties and immunities of free and naturall subjects within any of ... [the king's] dominions ... to all intents, construccions, and purposes whatsoever, as yf they and everie of them were borne within the realme of England." *Colony Records*, I, 10, 12, 16, 17.

17. *Antinomianism*, 148.

18. Cotton, *Way of the Congregational Churches Cleared*, 61.

their own, they had embraced him so closely that he could not disavow them without seeming to reject his own beliefs. And now he
had been dragged down to disaster with them. He did not know
what fate might befall them, but he was well content to let them
go their own way and disinclined to share their company.

But the past was past and he must now move on and start afresh.
Even to a man of his vigor and tenacity, the prospect of removing
—and at this season—was disheartening. The snow lay deep upon
the ground and the air was so cold, he recalled in a grim attempt at
humor, that "had he the very extracted spirits of sedition and contempt they would have been frozen up and indisposed for action." [19]

He could have turned south to Rhode Island whither Roger Williams had already ventured and where Mrs. Hutchinson and her
friends were soon to go. But instead, guided as always by his own
iron whim, he turned northward, across the icy Merrimac and into
the bleak, inhospitable foothills of New Hampshire.

(v)

No sooner had they dealt with Wheelwright—remanding him to
custody that Tuesday—than the Court summoned John Coggeshall.
Startled to hear his name called out, Coggeshall apprehensively
came forward and stood before the magistrates.

They had sent for him, Winthrop sternly explained, "partly by
occasion of his speeches and behaviour in this Court the other day,
and partly," he added darkly, "for some light miscarriages at other
times, and that they did looke at him as one that had a principall
hand in all our late disturbances of our publike peace." Mr. Coggeshall had confessed to signing the protestation, Winthrop went on,
so "we take you to be of the same minde with those who made the
Petition." [20]

But he was then a member of the Court, Coggeshall expostu-
lated, thinking to stand upon parliamentary liberty. He was not a
member of the Court, Winthrop rapped out, but was "standing
upon tryall whether to be allowed or rejected." Even had he been
then properly accredited, the Governor reminded him, it was "no
privilege of a member to reproach or affront the whole Court[;] it
is licentiousnesse, and not liberty, when a man may speake what

19. Wheelwright, *Writings*, 226.
20. *Antinomianism*, 148, 149.

he list." [21] Nor was this the only time Mr. Coggeshall had spoken menacingly to the Court, the indictment continued; at the last Court of Elections he had offered ill-tempered threats which had not been overlooked or forgotten.

Coggeshall became wary. These men would let nothing pass. He confessed that he had, perhaps, spoken too hastily on both occasions. But surely they had mistaken his words; he had meant no threat to the Court.

The Court refused to be put off by his explanations and motion was offered for his banishment. Coggeshall was stunned. What could they lay to his charge, he stammered; no more than difference of opinion. Would one among them cite a single example in Scripture where a man had been banished for his judgment?

If he had kept his judgment to himself, Winthrop replied, "so as the publike peace had not beene troubled or endangered by it," he would have been left to himself. "We doe not challenge power over mens consciences, but when seditious speeches and practises discover such a corrupt conscience, it is our duty to use authority to reforme both." [22]

The Court was divided on how to punish him. Many of them favored banishment; having rid themselves of Wheelwright the time seemed ripe to make a clean sweep. But others felt that Mr. Coggeshall's modest and submissive manner argued well for lenience. So his sentence was reduced to disfranchisement, with an admonition not "to occasion any disturbance of the publicke peace, either by speech or otherwise, upon paine of banishment." [23]

Now the Court called William Aspinwall. The Bostonian defiantly took his place before the magistrates; they would find that he was not so easily cowed as brother Coggeshall. The Court's time was short and valuable; Winthrop saw no need to waste it with a formal recitation of the charges. Aspinwall had heard all that was brought against Coggeshall, and the same was also charged against him. What said he to the indictment?

Aspinwall promptly owned to signing the petition, indeed "his heart was to it as well as his hand." That he had also written the petition he was not quite ready to boast, for all his blazing indignation. They had punished Mr. Wheelwright unjustly, he stormed on, for he had been only delivering "the truth of Christ." [24]

21. *Ibid.*, 149.
22. *Ibid.*, 149, 150.
23. *Ibid.*, 151; *Colony Records*, I, 207.
24. *Antinomianism*, 151.

As a member of the Court, Winthrop sharply reminded him, he had violated his oath by countenancing seditious persons and practices. He had but proffered a humble petition, Aspinwall countered heatedly, no more than Mephibosheth to David or Esther to Ahasuerus, and might not these be allowed? Winthrop brushed the precedent aside as irrelevant to his purpose.

But it is lawful for subjects to petition, Aspinwall insisted. This was no petition, Winthrop rapped out, but a seditious libel, which had offered a "peremptory Judgement" directly counter to the judgment of the Court. What was worse, they had employed language which might well incite the people's minds to violence.[25]

Faced with the passage of sentence Aspinwall demanded that Winthrop show him a rule in Scripture for banishment. Ishmael and Hagar were banished for disturbance, Winthrop shot back. "If a Father give a child a portion and sent him forth, [that is] not banishment," the prisoner demurred. Winthrop stood his ground, "The Scripture calls it a casting out, not a sending forth." Dudley grunted agreement; Mr. Aspinwall "is a childe worthy of such a portion."

Aspinwall's defiance had undone him. His judges had planned only to disfranchise him as they had done Coggeshall; it was now decided that his contemptuous behavior merited banishment as well.[26]

Winthrop leaned back wearily, his eyes vacantly fixed on the indignant prisoner's back as he retreated down the aisle. The hour at last had come. "All these . . . were but young branches, sprung out of an old root[.] The Court had now to do with the . . . breeder and nourisher of all these distempers." [27]

25. *Ibid.*, 152.
26. *Ibid.*, 153; *Colony Records*, I, 207.
27. *Antinomianism*, 157-58.

XIV

"Dux Foemina Facti"

November 7–8, 1637

(i)

THROUGH all the business of that Tuesday morning, Anne Hutchinson had sat for weary hours at the rear of the meetinghouse as, one by one, the Court condemned her friends.[1] Wheelwright banished, young Oliver discharged, Coggeshall disfranchised, Aspinwall banished. Calamity indeed! Whatever lingering hope she may have entertained that morning was by now thoroughly dispelled. These men were ruthlessly bent upon her destruction, and there seemed little she could do to avert their purpose.

Among the stern, unfriendly faces of the Court that she must face, who was there to befriend her? Mr. Coddington and William Colburn would surely do their best, but they were hopelessly outnumbered. Mr. Cotton, seated at the side of the hall with the ministers, had kept his own counsel. What of him? Despite his attack on her teachings, he was a man of compassionate and charitable nature.

Little of compassion or charity could be expected from the row of grim-faced judges facing her. Anne knew Winthrop's mind all too well and had long recognized in him her chief and most formidable opponent. Beside him sat Thomas Dudley, who in later years, lest any should mistake his mind, carried next to his heart a verse of his own composition:

> Let men of God in courts and churches watch
> O'er such as do a toleration hatch,
> Lest that ill egg bring forth a cockatrice
> To poison all with heresy and vice.[2]

1. Hutchinson, *History*, II, 366-67.
2. Mather, *Magnalia*, I, 122.

However hidden the verses, his sentiments were plain upon his face, as Anne could well discern.

She had no hope in the turbulent John Endicott, flamboyant mustache and goatee bristling with ill-concealed impatience. Richard Bellingham of "stern looke" and "melancholic disposition" was less likely to follow where Winthrop led, but his vast learning in English law had not been conspicuously exercised during the morning's proceedings and there was small likelihood of his sympathy in her cause.[3] Israel Stoughton, himself a stiff-necked dissenter on occasion, was disinclined to be Winthrop's tool, but his orthodoxy was unimpeachable. And so on down the table—Roger Harlakenden, a staunch friend of Thomas Shepard; Increase Nowell, head bowed over his record book; Simon Bradstreet, Dudley's son-in-law; John Humfry—she counted them off one by one.[4]

The recess for midday meal had been a welcome respite from the grim business of the morning, but hot food and a warm fireside had not thawed the hearts of the judges perceptibly. Nor had the meetinghouse grown any warmer during their absence, nor the benches any softer. The unrelieved bleakness and frigidity of the hall only served to accentuate the hostility of the men she was now to face.

Adding their chill to the general atmosphere, eight of the ministers were on hand, stiffly garbed in black gowns and Geneva bands, eagerly waiting to assist at the prosecution. Most of them were from the nearer towns, not inconveniently remote from their charges, but Hugh Peter had plowed through the snow all the way from Salem. He was not one to shrink from the Lord's battles. Wilson and Cotton had both come from Boston, the former to play a restrained role in the coming business, but nonetheless intent on witnessing the downfall of the subverter of his pastoral endeavors these past two years. Thomas Weld, one of Mrs. Hutchinson's most vindictive accusers, was on hand from Roxbury with his gentle colleague John Eliot, who, for all his mildness, was sternly opposed to the controverted doctrines. Watertown's George Phillips was present, and Zachariah Symmes from Charlestown, still burning with indignation at the embarrassment Anne had caused him during their transatlantic passage. Thomas Shepard, mild in his way as Eliot, but equally opposed to the new doctrines, observed with

3. Johnson, *Wonder Working Providence*, 97; Winthrop, *Journal*, I, 321, II, 46.
4. *Colony Records*, I, 205.

interest and concern the momentous proceedings that now took place within his own meetinghouse.

There was small reassurance afforded the woman who waited to be called as she took stock of the forces ranged against her. Yet "the fear of man is a snare," and, amid all the past and present troubles surrounding her, God had vouchsafed her one beam of light to shine through the darkness. Last week she saw young Edward's wife safely through her delivery of a daughter. The relief at having her fears concerning the child dispelled, the joy of holding this first perfect little grandchild, had done much to ease her heart. Happily she had heard the child baptized Elishua—"God is my salvation." [5]

As that monstrous birth had been a sign, so, too, was this a sign to weigh against it. If one was calamitous evil, surely so was the other a promise—"God is my salvation!"

She heard her name called and rose from her place. Neighbor Coggeshall, despite his own punishment, remained in the hall to interpose what strength he had. Judges and spectators alike watched as she moved from her place. "The fear of man is a snare"—"God is my salvation." Head erect she moved down the aisle to face her accusers.

(ii)

John Winthrop, from his seat at the center of the long table, surveyed the crowded hall. At last the hour had come when his defense of the faith and his concern for the commonweal must bring fruition.

Down the aisle came neighbor Hutchinson, a woman of proud bearing who had lived across the street from him these past three years. How unlike his gentle Margaret whose letter from "Sad Boston" written with "a tremblinge heart" had reached him. "Thear is a time to plant and a time to pul up that which is planted, which I could desyre mite not be yet, but the Lord knoweth what is best, and his wil be done." [6]

Even so. He must do the Lord's will. The business of the past days was but a preliminary. For they must be pulled up root and branch.

Winthrop stared penetratingly at the woman who now stood before him. "Mrs. Hutchinson," he began firmly, "you are called

5. "Boston Births, Baptisms, Marriages and Deaths," 5.
6. *Winthrop Papers*, III, 510.

here as one of those that have troubled the peace of the commonwealth and the churches here; you are known to be a woman that
hath had a great share in the promoting and divulging of those
opinions that are causes of this trouble." She had closely associated
with those already sentenced, he went on, had maintained disorderly conventicles both before and after the Synod had prescibed
them, and was reputed to "have spoken divers things . . . prejudicial to the honour of the churches and ministers."

"Therefore we have thought good to send for you to understand
how things are, that if you be in an erroneous way we may reduce
you that so you may become a profitable member here among us[.]
Otherwise, if you be obstinate in your course that then the court
may take such course that you may trouble us no further. . . . Therefore I would entreat you to express whether you do not assent and
hold in practice to those opinions and factions that have been han-
dled in court already, that is to say, whether you do not justify Mr.
Wheelwright's sermon and the petition."[7]

Mrs. Hutchinson was no Aspinwall to rise to the first bait offered
her. She heard Winthrop out, then replied coolly, "I am called here
to answer before you but I hear no things laid to my charge."

There can be few vexations equal to being asked for an explanation of what one conceives to have been already explained and this
could hardly have endeared her to Winthrop. He protested that he
had told her some charges and could tell more. She calmly challenged him to be specific, whereupon Winthrop harassedly singled
out the weakest of the charges: "you did harbor and countenance
those that are parties in this faction."

"That's [a] matter of conscience, Sir."

"Your conscience you must keep or it must be kept for you."
Winthrop found himself being drawn from the point and briskly
returned to it by insisting that in helping transgressors of the law
she shared their guilt.[8]

Sensing a weak spot, Anne probed. What law had they broken?

"Why, the Fifth Commandment," Winthrop stated, "which commands us to honour Father and Mother, which includes all in au-

---

7. Hutchinson, *History,* II, 366. There are two accounts of Mrs. Hutchinson's
trial, a stenographic transcript in the Appendix to Hutchinson's *History* and a narrative description in Winthrop's *The Short Story.* In the following chapter I have
relied primarily on the former, which seems to be more accurate and authentic.
Winthrop's description appears to be doctored for purposes of propagandistic effect
and clarity, but includes a couple of significant exchanges which were omitted from
the Hutchinson transcript.

8. Hutchinson, *History,* II, 366.

thority[.] But these seditious practices of theirs have cast reproach and dishonour upon the Fathers of the Commonwealth." [9]

It was plain in a moment that Mrs. Hutchinson was equally ready to argue the fine points of the Fifth Commandment and its applicability. In a characteristic turn of argument she suggested that parents who fail to honor the Lord as wisely as their children might be disobeyed with impunity. Winthrop, struggling to avoid this soggy ground, engaged to put her in her place. "We do not mean to discourse with those of your sex," he emphasized with some asperity, "but only this; you do adhere unto them and do endeavor to set forward this faction and so you do dishonour us." [10]

Mrs. Hutchinson refused to accede to this conclusion, and Winthrop could neither easily develop nor disavow it, so he decided on a fresh line of attack. "Why do you keep such meeting at your house as you do every week upon a set day?" Anne was growing more confident. This practice, she reminded him, had existed long before she arrived in Boston. She had taken up the practice partly to allay gossip that she was too proud and held such meetings unscriptural. After all, it was their own practice.

Winthrop, conceding that the practice, as normally observed, was lawful, insisted that her meetings were not. What about the presence of men? She denied that there were any, and for the moment Winthrop let it pass. By what warrant did she hold to such a course?

"I conceive there lyes a clear rule in Titus, that the elder women should instruct the younger." [11]

The verbal sparring continued. How did such a rule apply when she taught not only younger women but elder also, and men as well, and not privately, but publicly? "I teach not in a publick congregation," she insisted. Her meetings were private, held within her own home, and those who came were unsolicited. "The men of *Berea* are commended for examining *Pauls* doctrine; wee do no more but read the notes of our teachers Sermons, and then reason of them by searching the Scriptures." [12]

Unhappily she had stumbled onto the very path which Winthrop was most eager to explore. "You do not as the *Bereans* search the Scriptures for their *confirming* in the truths delivered, but you open your teachers points, and declare his meaning, and correct

9. *Antinomianism*, 165.
10. Hutchinson, *History*, II, 367.
11. *Ibid.*, 367, 368.
12. *Antinomianism*, 167.

wherein you think he hath failed . . . as if hee could not deliver his matter so clearly to the hearers capacity as your self." [13]

"Prove that!" she hotly challenged, "That anybody doth that." But she knew full well that this sally had touched her closely. Anne sagged under the strain. The stolid figures at the far side of the table blurred and swam dizzily in her view. Fatigue drew haggard lines in her face. Winthrop paused apprehensively in his examination, then ordered an attendant to bring forward a chair for the defendant. Once seated, Anne gathered her faculties and ventured fresh authority for her conduct. "*Aquila* and *Priscilla,* tooke upon them to instruct *Apollo* more perfectly, yet he was a man of good parts, but they being better instructed, might teach him." [14]

The ridiculous irrelevance of this provoked Winthrop to attack. "See how your argument stands," he scoffed. "*Priscilla,* with her husband, took *Apollo* home to instruct him privately, therefore Mistress Hutchinson without her husband may teach sixty or eighty."

The magistrates smiled wryly at the unhappy culprit, but Mrs. Hutchinson refused to be put off by Winthrop's heavy wit. "I call them not, but if they come to me, I may instruct them."

"Yet you show us not a rule," Winthrop pressed.

"I have given you two places of Scripture."

"But neither of them will sute your practice."

"Must I shew my name written therein?" she flared.[15]

She must certainly find a reasonable equivalent, Winthrop maintained, or else give over her practice. "Your course is not to be suffered," he declared. She had seduced honest persons from their work and families. All these present troubles had arisen from those who had frequented her meetings. "We see no rule of God for this," he rapped out. "We see not that any should have authority to set up any other exercises besides what authority hath already set up. . . . What hurt comes of this, you will be guilty of and we for suffering you. . . . We must therefore put it away from you or restrain you from maintaining this course."

"If you have a rule for it from God's word you may," she said obstinately.

Such temerity was insufferable! "We are *your* judges," Winthrop sternly reminded her, "not you *ours* and we must compel you to it!"

Her prompt compliance in agreeing that of course she must obey

13. *Ibid.,* 168. My italics.
14. *Ibid.,* 168.
15. *Ibid.,* 168-69.

their authority was so anticlimactic as to take the wind out of their sails momentarily. There seemed nothing more to say about the meetings, but the Court found itself the victim of its own momentum and continued the questioning although it was apparent that it was leading nowhere.

Dudley, who had learned with shocked surprise of the attendance of men and had tried to make something of this point, was the first to pull himself up to a fresh line of attack. They could quibble all day concerning the legality of the meetings. There were more damning matters than these.

"I would go a little higher with Mrs. Hutchinson," he began. She had been a cause of disturbance since her arrival—even before, on the trip over! Her strange opinions—of which Mr. Cotton had cleared himself—had so perverted the minds of susceptible people that they were a potent party endangering the constituted authority. And worst of all, she had traduced the ministers by saying that they "preached a covenant of works, and only Mr. Cotton a covenant of grace." Since it was so clear that Mrs. Hutchinson was the foundation of this building "we must take away the foundation." [16]

Anne employed her tactic of direct evasion. "I pray Sir prove it that I said they preached nothing but a covenant of works."

Dudley exploded. "*Nothing* but a covenant of works, why a Jesuit may preach truth sometimes!"

Whatever Dudley thought, Anne was sure that his accusations were based solely on hearsay. She insisted, "Did I ever say they preached a covenant of works then?"

"If they do not preach a covenant of grace clearly," Dudley hedged, "then they preach a covenant of works."

"No Sir," she parried triumphantly. "One may preach a covenant of grace more clearly than another so I said."

But Dudley was not to be put off so easily. What was her present position? "When ... [ministers] do preach a covenant of works do they preach truth?"

"Yes Sir, but when they preach a covenant of works for salvation, that is not truth."

"[But] when the ministers do preach a covenant of works, *do* they preach a way of salvation?" he prodded.

"I did not come hither to answer questions of that sort," Mrs. Hutchinson sidestepped.

As Winthrop remarked, it was evident that Mrs. Hutchinson

16. Hutchinson, *History*, II, 369, 370. My italics.

knew "when to speak and when to hold her tongue ... we desire her to tell her thoughts ... she desires to be pardoned." She might be too canny to be drawn into a public statement, but Dudley doggedly held to his allegation. She might deny as much as she wished. He would prove it.

"I will make it plain," Dudley insisted, "that you did say that the ministers did preach a covenant of works. . . . And that you said they were not able ministers of the new testament, but Mr. Cotton only!" [17]

Dudley's confident assertions gave Anne pause. She knew what she had spoken, and to whom. It was becoming plain that what she had considered a private, privileged statement must have been repeated, at least in part.

"If one shall come unto me in private, and desire me seriously to tell them what I thought of such an one, I must either speak false or true in my answer." Her eyes passed over the faces of the ministers searchingly.

Dudley, ignoring this byplay, plunged ahead. "Likewise I will prove this: that you said the gospel in the letter and words holds forth nothing but a covenant of works and that all that do not hold as you do are in a covenant of works."

Not only had the ministers broken their word to her, but they had garbled her statements. She hotly defended herself, "I deny this for if I should so say I should speak against my own judgement."

"It is one thing," she went on scornfully, "for me to come before a public magistracy and there to speak what they would have me speak and another when a man comes to me in a way of friendship privately. There is difference in that!" she blazed, with a glance of accusation at the ministers.[18]

"What if the matter be all one?" Winthrop inquired.

During all this interchange, the ministers had kept their silence. Knowing full well to what Dudley had referred, it was uncomfortably clear to them all, as well as to Anne, that one of them had violated the secrecy which had implicitly cloaked their conference with Mrs. Hutchinson. Dudley had not gotten his information from heaven. Although each, in his way, was eager to do the Lord's work and to help the Court, none could bring himself to betray a confidence without solid justification. But to Hugh Peter, simmering

17. *Ibid.*, 370, 371. My italics.
18. *Ibid.*, 371.

impatiently to get on with God's business, the solution was plain. If the Court would *command* them to speak, he suggested, they might overcome their reluctance.[19]

Winthrop had scarcely time to give him encouragement before Peter launched ahead. Assuring the Court that they desired not to be thought "informers against the gentlewoman, but as it may be serviceable for the country and our posterity" he divulged all that he knew. He recounted the circumstances of their meeting with Mrs. Hutchinson and specified that at that time she had said there was "a wide and broad difference between our brother Mr. Cotton and our selves. I desired to know the difference," Peter drove on, "She answered that he preaches the covenant of grace and you the covenant of works and that you are not able ministers of the new testament and know no more than the apostles did before the resurrection of Christ." [20]

Anne was incensed. If Mr. Wilson would produce his transcript of the meeting, her judges might see that the conversation was not precisely as Peter had reported. Wilson confessed that he no longer had the record of the meeting in his possession—nor had he set down therein all that was said on that day.

To clear all doubts Dudley requested the other ministers to rise and present their recollection. One by one, Weld, Phillips, Symmes, Shepard, and Eliot all attested to the authenticity of Peter's remarks. She had said that they were not able ministers of the new testament because they were not sealed.

Only Shepard saw fit to soften their damning testimony with an appeal to charity. "I desire to speak this word," he interposed. "It may be but a slip of her tongue, and I hope she will be sorry for it, and then we shall be glad." [21]

But not Dudley. He gloated over his coup. "I called these witnesses and you deny them. You see they have proved this and you deny this, but it is clear. . . . now there are two other things which you did affirm . . . that the scriptures in the letter held forth nothing but a covenant of works, and likewise that those that were under a covenant of works cannot be saved."

"Prove that I said so," Mrs. Hutchinson hotly demanded.

"Did you say so?" Winthrop challenged.

"No Sir it is your conclusion."

19. *Ibid.*
20. *Ibid.*, 371, 372.
21. *Ibid.*, 374.

Dudley reminded her that Mr. Ward had heard her make these statements. "He set it down under his hand and I can bring it forth when the court pleases. His name is subscribed to both these things, and upon my peril be it if I bring you in not the paper and bring the minister . . . to be deposed." [22]

"What say you to this?" Winthrop inquired.

Anne carefully searched her memory and recalled having cited Corinthians to Mr. Ward to prove that ministers of the letter did preach a covenant of works. When he had denied that there was any such Scripture, she had fetched the Bible and showed him the passage: "Who also hath made us able ministers of the New Testament; not of the letter but of the spirit: for the letter killeth but the spirit giveth life." [23] Mr. Ward had sought to assure her that this meant the letter of the law, but she insisted that it referred to the letter of the Gospel.

Winthrop nodded; he was all too familiar with her discourse on this subject.

Anne went on in her recollection. Mr. Ward had acknowledged that manifestation of the spirit was the best way to prove a good estate. But, he had asked her, will you not grant that which we hold forth to be a way wherein we may have hope. "No, truly," she had replied, "if that be a way it is a way to hell!" [24]

Unfortunately for the prosecution, it was becoming too dark within the meetinghouse to continue their inquiry. Mrs. Hutchinson had been dangerously exposed. To the minds of her judges some damning admissions had been made, not least of which was this last statement which Dudley had forced from her.

With some reluctance Winthrop called a temporary halt to the questioning. "Mrs. Hutchinson, the court you see hath laboured to bring you to acknowledge the error of your way that so you might be reduced, the time now grows late, we shall therefore give you a little more time to consider of it and therfore desire that you attend the court again in the morning." [25]

(iii)

Back in Boston that evening, Anne sat poring over the transcript of her December conference with the ministers. Her study con-

22. *Ibid.*, 375, 376.
23. II Corinthians 3:6.
24. Hutchinson, *History*, II, 376.
25. *Ibid.*

firmed her belief that there were discrepancies existing between that report and the account given by the ministers that afternoon. It seemed obvious that if these inconsistencies could be brought out in court, the credibility of the ministers' testimony would be seriously undermined. Although the logic of this course was nigh faultless, the means she unhappily chose to implement it could only further incite the court against her.

The following morning Winthrop summed up the case against her thus far. It had been established to the full satisfaction of the Court, he contended, that Mrs. Hutchinson had indeed claimed that most of the clergy were not able ministers, lacking the seal of the spirit, and that they did preach a covenant of works. Did anyone wish to speak further in this cause?

Mrs. Hutchinson addressed her judges. Having perused her notes of the conference, she had found things not to be as alleged. "The ministers," she went on, "come in their own cause. Now the Lord hath said that an oath is the end of all controversy; . . . therefore I desire they may speak upon oath." [26]

As the implications of her request gradually penetrated the minds of magistrates and ministers, it produced a furor in the courtroom. Mrs. Hutchinson had committed a tactical error that was to prove dangerously prejudicial to her cause. But, if she came to recognize the nature of her mistake, it did not alter her determination. To demand an oath where it was manifestly unnecessary seemed to Deputy Brown to be taking God's name in vain. "The ministers are so well known unto us," Endicott offered, "that we need not take an oath of them."

Israel Stoughton was less sure. He did not question the truthfulness of the ministers, he hastened to assure his colleagues, but still, he for one would hesitate to vote censure in the course of justice unless an oath were administered.

"An oath . . . is an end of all strife," Anne righteously maintained.

"A sign it is what respect she hath to their words," Endicott blustered. "You lifted up your eyes as if you took God to witness that you came to entrap none and yet you will have them swear." [27]

As the wrangling continued, the ministers hung back indecisively. Although eager to affirm the truth of their words, they were reluctant to adopt a course which might impugn their status. "I

26. *Ibid.*
27. *Ibid.*, 377, 378, 379.

know no reason of the oath," Shepard ventured tentatively, "but the importunity of this gentlewoman." Dudley sought to divert the argument. "Mark what a flourish Mrs. Hutchinson puts upon the business that she had witnesses to disprove what was said and here is no man to bear witness." Amidst the confusion she had promoted, Anne remained coolly sure of herself. "If you will not call them in that is nothing to me."

The prospect of other witnesses and differing testimony gave the ministers some delay. Mr. Eliot spoke for the group: "We desire to know of her and her witnesses what they deny and then we shall speak upon oath. I know nothing we have spoken of but we may swear to." "Ay, and more than we have spoken to," Symmes confidently snorted.[28]

Mr. Coggeshall rose to suggest that it might be of use for Cotton to confer privately with his brethren before they took an oath. Irritated and impatient at all this unnecessary delay, Endicott was gratified to find a target for his quivering temper. "I will tell you what I say," he barked at the hapless Coggeshall. "I think that this carriage of your's tends to further casting dirt upon the face of the judges!"

William Colburn ventured to suggest that Mr. Cotton might sit by the defendant. Winthrop found this a reasonable request and agreed. As Cotton moved to Anne's side, Endicott eyed him sourly: "This would cast some blame upon the ministers," he growled. "Well, but whatsoever he can or will say[,] we will believe the ministers."

"Let her witnesses be called," Dudley impatiently intruded.

"Who be they?" asked Winthrop.

"Mr. Leverett and our teacher and Mr. Coggeshall," Anne informed him.

"Mr. Coggeshall was not present," Winthrop protested.

Coggeshall rose in his place at the rear of the hall. "Yes but I was," he called out, "only I desired to be silent till I should be called."

"Will you Mr. Coggeshall say that she did not say so?"

"Yes I dare say that she did not say all that which they lay against her." [29]

Hugh Peter exploded with wrath. "How dare you look into the court to say such a word!"

28. *Ibid.*, 379.
29. *Ibid.*, 380.

Taken aback by the fury of his assault, Coggeshall paused to reflect. Yesterday he had but barely escaped disaster, and now again the pit loomed before him. "Mr. Peters takes it upon him to forbid me. I shall be silent." Having thus easily silenced Anne's first witness, the Court turned to the next. "Well, Mr. Leverett," Winthrop testily inquired, "What were the words? I pray speak."

As Leverett remembered it, Mrs. Hutchinson had said that the other ministers did not preach a Covenant of Grace so clearly as Cotton did, because they were in a state like that of the Apostles before they had received the Witness of the Spirit. This seemed safe enough; who could fairly label it flattery or insult?

Mr. Cotton was then asked to testify. "I did not think I should be called to bear witness in this cause," he apologized, "and therefore did not labour to call to remembrance what was done." He did recall that when they had pressed her to explain why she thought they did not preach so clearly as himself she had replied, "You preach of the seal of the spirit upon a work and he upon free grace without a work or without respect to a work." He had assured her at the time that this was a distinction which he would not have ventured himself.

"This was the sum of the difference, nor did it seem to be so ill taken as it is and our brethren did say also that they would not so easily believe reports as they had done. . . . And I must say," he concluded, "that I did not find her saying they were under a covenant of works, nor that she said they did preach a covenant of works." [30]

This testimony—surely as valid as theirs—was disturbing to the ministers. Hugh Peter strove to refresh Cotton's memory on essential points. "Do you not remember," he prompted, "that she said we were not sealed with the spirit of grace, therefore could not preach a covenant of grace[.] And she said further[,] you may do it in your judgement, but not in experience, but she spake plump that we were not sealed."

Yes, Cotton now recalled that she had claimed they were not sealed with the seal of the Spirit. There had been much confusion about the seals that day. "[But] that she said you could not preach a covenant of grace I do not remember such a thing," he firmly reiterated.

The Court was confounded by the contradictory claims of Cot-

30. *Ibid.*, 381, 382.

ton and his fellows. They hesitated momentarily over lesser matters, uncertain what course to follow. Dudley pressed Cotton again, as if finally to convince himself that what he had heard was actually so. "They affirm that Mrs. Hutchinson did say they were not able ministers of the new testament."

"I do not remember it," Cotton flatly stated.[31]

If they had mistaken him before there could now be no doubt in anyone's mind. It was Cotton's word against theirs and—irrespective of his doctrinal vagaries—his honor could not be questioned. To press the matter further on this ground would only serve to impugn all of the ministry. The prosecution appeared to have fallen apart at the seams. The course of justice—had justice been their concern—would now have been to release the defendant and dismiss the charges against her.

Then Mrs. Hutchinson spoke. Had she modestly kept silence, gratefully accepting a providential deliverance from catastrophe, her story might well have had a different ending.

"If you please to give me leave I shall give you the ground of what I know to be true." No one gave her leave. No one had asked her. Winthrop irritatedly gestured for her to be quiet.[32] Whatever the judgment on Mrs. Hutchinson, she was not a stupid woman. Her mental adroitness had been well demonstrated. She had displayed remarkable acuteness in defending herself. If escape were her first concern, she was already three-fourths out of a trap which had seemed shut. Had she suddenly lost all sense that she rushed thus blindly to her own destruction? Or was it rather a deliberate risk she was taking in order to find vindication? Or even an unheeding and exultant impulse to affirm her own being—to rise triumphantly from the ashes of humiliation and annihilate her persecutors with the terrible brilliance of her heavenly champion?

Ignoring Winthrop's sign she plunged ahead. "Being much troubled to see the falseness of the constitution of the churches of England," she told them, "I had like to have turned separatist; whereupon I kept a day of solemn humiliation and pondering of the thing[.] This scripture was brought unto me, 'He that denies Jesus Christ to be come in the flesh is antichrist.'" After she had long weighed the meaning of this Scripture without obtaining satisfaction, the Lord brought her another citation: "He that denies the testament denies the testator." From this she had concluded

31. *Ibid.*, 382, 383.
32. *Ibid.*, 383; *Antinomianism*, 172.

that those who did not preach the Covenant of Grace had the spirit of anti-Christ.

"And ever since, I bless the Lord, he hath let me see which was the clear ministry and which the wrong. Since that time I confess I have been more choice and he hath left me to distinguish between the voice of my beloved and voice of Moses, the voice of John Baptist and the voice of antichrist. . . . Now," she triumphantly concluded, "if you do condemn me for speaking what in my conscience I know to be truth[,] I must commit myself unto the Lord."

This excursus had touched on nothing that was not essentially familiar to her downcast judges and proved mildly diverting while they collected their scattered thoughts. Increase Nowell, who had been hitherto occupied with his record book, looked up to ask her casually, "How do you know that that was the spirit?"

"How did Abraham know that it was God that bid him offer his son, being a breach of the sixth commandment?" Anne had been invited around the dangerous corner that led to her downfall.

Dudley raised his eyebrows with renewed interest. "By an immediate voice," he tentatively offered.

"So to me by an immediate revelation!"

Dudley's eyes opened wide in astonishment. "How! by an immediate revelation!"

"By the voice of his own spirit to my soul!" Anne exulted.[33]

Scarcely did her judges hear the lengthy speech that followed. Nor had they need to. Mrs. Hutchinson had done their work for them. In the midst of their blindness she had painstakingly prepared a pitfall for herself and then obligingly walked into it. Why had they not thought of this? There had been repeated rumors of her revelations and yet they had not thought to charge her with them. God's continuing presence and His special providences, these were essential to their theology—but revelations? The age of miracles and revelations was long past, nor could their doctrine well bear the interposition of heavenly voices or inspiration from any source other than Scripture and clergy.

Mrs. Hutchinson flashed ahead with her story. She told how God had revealed to her that she must follow Mr. Cotton into the wilderness. He had warned her that she would meet with affliction. But He had assured her as He had saved Daniel out of the lion's den so would He also deliver her.

"Therefore I desire you to look at it," she warned, "for you

33. Hutchinson, *History*, II, 383-84.

see this scripture fulfilled this day[.] And therefore I desire you that you tender the Lord and the church and commonwealth to consider and look what you do. You have power over my body but the Lord Jesus hath power over my body and soul[.] And assure yourselves thus much, you do as much as in you lies to put the Lord Jesus Christ from you, and if you go on in this course you begin you will bring a curse upon you and your posterity[.] And the mouth of the Lord hath spoken it."

The judges were aghast. She had defied the Court and threatened the commonwealth with God's curse. Winthrop, incredulous, cautiously ventured the possibilities of this new situation. "Daniel was delivered by miracle[.] Do you think to be deliver'd so too?"

"I do here speak it before the court. I look that the Lord should deliver me by his providence."

A dangerous rip tide had now surged through the proceedings which threatened to sweep Anne Hutchinson to disaster. Threatened? Anne had plunged into the crest and exultantly soared with it. Less willingly, Cotton too, was almost caught up in the flood. Striving courageously to save his errant charge, he found himself dragged dangerously in until it was all Winthrop could do to pluck him loose from Mrs. Hutchinson and restore him to safety.

Endicott, prompted by some perverse design, maneuvered to pitch Cotton into the maelstrom. "She saith she now suffers and let us do what we will she shall be delivered by a miracle. . . . Now because her reverend teacher is here I should desire that he would please to speak freely whether he doth condescend to such speeches or revelations . . . and he will give a great deal of content." [34]

Cotton's courage was with him and he coolly brought his vast theological knowledge to bear on the distressing problem. He distinguished two forms of revelations, those without Scripture, which were fantastical and dangerous, and also "such as are breathed by the spirit of God and are never dispensed but in a word of God," which latter is generally dispensed in the ministry of the Word, or in the reading of the Word.

This definition satisfied Endicott. "Therefore I desire you to give your judgement of Mrs. Hutchinson," he prodded.

"I know not whether I do understand her," Cotton faltered, "but this I say, if she doth expect a deliverance in a way of providence —then I cannot deny it. . . . If it be by way of a miracle then I would suspect it."

34. *Ibid.*, 384, 386.

Dudley joined the cry, "Do you believe that her revelations are true?"

"That she may have some special providence of God to help her is a thing I cannot bear witness against."

Dudley was insistent. "Good Sir I do ask whether this revelation be of God or no." [35]

"I would know of her whether she expects to be delivered from that calamity by a miracle or a providence of God." Cotton turned to Anne in quiet desperation, hoping that she would know his mind and choose the course of safety.

Mrs. Hutchinson saw the nature of her peril and followed whither Cotton beckoned: "By a providence of God I say I expect to be delivered from some calamity that shall come to me."

Before she could explain away too many of her words, Winthrop hastily interceded. He knew a providence when he saw it and was not a man knowingly to slight divine signs and symbols. "The case is altered and will not stand with us now," he pronounced with abrupt finality. "I see a marvellous providence of God to bring things to this pass that they are. . . . Now the mercy of God by a providence hath answered our desires and made her to lay open her self . . . for this is the thing that hath been the root of all the mischief."

"We all consent with you," one of the magistrates agreed.

"Aye, it is the most desperate enthusiasm in the world," Winthrop continued, "for nothing but a word comes to her mind and then an application is made which is nothing to the purpose."

Still Endicott, terrier-like, harassed her teacher. "I speak in reference to Mr. Cotton," he leaned forward over the table, pointing menacingly. "I am tender of you Sir and there lies much upon you in this particular . . . therefore I beseech you that you'd be pleased to speak a word to that which Mrs. Hutchinson hath spoken of her revelations. . . . Whether you do witness for her or against her."

"This is what I said, Sir," Cotton wearily reiterated. "My answer is plain that if she doth look for deliverance from the hand of God by his providence, and the revelation be in a word or according to a word, that I cannot deny."

Endicott withdrew, "You give me satisfaction."

But not Dudley. "No, no," he growled, "he gives me none at all."

"But if it be in a way of a miracle or a revelation without the

35. *Ibid.*, 386-87.

word," Cotton went on, "that I do not assent to, but look at it as a delusion, and I think so doth she too as I understand her."

"Sir, you weary me and do not satisfy me," Dudley peevishly snarled.

Nowell was appalled, "I think it is a devilish delusion."

"Of all the revelations that ever I read of[,] I never read the like ground laid as is for this," Winthrop resumed incredulously. "The Enthusiasts and Anabaptists had never the like!" [36]

Cotton protested that their revelations broached new matters of faith and doctrine, but the time for theological niceties was past.

"So do these," Winthrop retorted, "and what may they breed more if they be let alone?"

"I never saw such revelations as these among the Anabaptists," Dudley claimed, "therefore am sorry that Mr. Cotton should stand to justify her."

"I can say the same, and this runs to enthusiasm," Peter attested. Like Dudley he had lived in the Lowlands and was presumed to speak with authority, and like Dudley, he professed dismay that Cotton should continue to offer Mrs. Hutchinson his support.

Things were going badly for Cotton, and it appeared that only a very special providence could save him from the fate marked out for Mrs. Hutchinson. Now the deputies joined the hue and cry. "It is a great burden to us," Mr. Collicut ventured, "that we differ from Mr. Cotton and that he should justify these revelations. I would intreat him to answer."

Winthrop had had enough. Were ever such hounds as these to go baying off on the wrong scent? "Mr. Cotton is not called to answer to any thing," Winthrop sharply called them off, "but we are to deal with the party here standing before us."

Cotton, at least, was safe, but his courage had not prevailed to save his parishioner. Now the pack closed relentlessly in on her. Winthrop was instructing the Court to consider sentence when suddenly Coddington interrupted. "I do think that you are going to censure, therefore I desire to speak a word." [37]

Winthrop nodded impatiently. "I pray you speak."

"There is one thing objected against the meetings. What if she designed to edify her own family in her own meetings, may none else be present?"

The astounding irrelevance of this query exasperated Winthrop.

36. *Ibid.*, 387-88.
37. *Ibid.*, 388-89.

"If you have nothing else to say but that, it is a pity, Mr. Coddington, that you should interrupt us in proceeding to censure!"

"I would say more Sir," Coddington moved boldly to his point. "Another thing you lay to her Charge is her speech to the elders. Now I do not see any clear witness against her, and you know it is a rule of the court that no man may be a judge and an accuser too." Quite ignoring this last cogent point, Winthrop brushed aside the need for witnesses. "Her own speeches have been ground enough for us to proceed upon."

"I beseech you do not speak so as to force things along," Coddington begged, "for I do not for my own part see any equity in the court in all your proceedings. Here is no law of God that she hath broken nor any law of the country that she hath broke, . . . therefore I pray consider what you do."

"Things thus spoken will stick," young Harlakenden interjected. Dudley seethed impatiently, "We shall all be sick with fasting." [38] But Coddington's appeal had effected doubts among the magistrates. Stoughton thought once again of the oath. "I shall desire that no offence be taken if I do not formally condemn her because she hath not been formally convicted as others are by witness upon oath."

"That is a scruple to me also," Coddington said. "Every man is partial in his own cause, and here is none that accuses her but the elders, and she spake nothing to them but in private." Winthrop turned to the elders. "In regard Mr. Stoughton is not satisfied, to the end all scruples may be removed we shall desire the elders to take their oaths."

The ministers conferred busily among themselves. There was much shaking of heads and some drew back, apparently reluctant to deliver themselves further of matters discussed in private. "Any two of you will serve," Winthrop urged impatiently, "—you, Mr. Weld, and Mr. Eliot." The two men stood and raised their right hands as Winthrop administered the oath. Hugh Peter, eager as always to be included, poked up his hand and chimed in the oath.

"What you do remember of her speak, pray, speak," Winthrop hurried them on. Eliot recalled that Mrs. Hutchinson had said they preached a Covenant of Works because as she explained it, "to put a work in point of evidence is a revealing upon a work."

"What say you, Mr. Weld?"

"I will speak to the things themselves—these two things I am

38. *Ibid.*, 389-90.

fully clear in—she . . . said this that I am fully sure of, that we were not able ministers of the new testament and that we were not clear in our experience because we were not sealed." [39]

Eliot further recalled that she had said they were not able ministers because they were like the Apostles before the Ascension. "This was I hope no disparagement to you," Coddington interjected in the bitter humor of defeat, "—methinks the comparison is very good."

Coddington's sallies were passed by as the Court went remorselessly to an end. Winthrop formally intoned the question: "If it be the mind of the court that Mrs. Hutchinson for these things that appear before us is unfit for our society, and if it be the mind of the court that she shall be banished out of our liberties and imprisoned till she be sent away, let them hold up their hands."

All but three of the deputies and magistrates so agreed.

"Those that are contrary minded, hold up yours."

Coddington and Colburn alone dissented.

Mr. Jennison stated that he could not vote either way and would explain if the Court should so desire. The Court did not desire, being interested only in the lonely figure standing before them.

"Mrs. Hutchinson," Winthrop addressed her, "the sentence of the court you hear is that you are banished from out of our jurisdiction as being a woman not fit for our society, and are to be imprisoned till the court shall send you away."

"I desire to know wherefore I am banished," Anne insisted.

"Say no more," Winthrop glared triumphantly, "the court knows wherefore and is satisfied." [40]

39. *Ibid.*, 390-91.
40. *Ibid.*, 391.

XV

"After Hagar and Ishmael"

November 15, 1637–March 7, 1637/8

WHEN Court had convened that past Monday, John Winthrop had foreseen a long and arduous week. "SWEET HEART," he wrote to Margaret, "I was unwillingly hindered from comminge to thee, nor am I like to see thee before the last daye of this weeke: therefore I shall want a band or 2 and cuffes. I pray thee also send me 6 or 7 leaues of Tobacco dried, and powdred. have care of thy selfe this colde weather." [1] So, handsomely furbished in fresh band and cuffs and fortified with a comforting pipe for after-hours, Winthrop had superintended the pulling up of John Wheelwright and John Coggeshall, of William Aspinwall and Anne Hutchinson.

Much remained to be done, but the deputies had been long from home, and their own affairs neglected. After the marshal had led Mrs. Hutchinson away, the Court recessed until Wednesday the fifteenth—a week hence.[2] Winthrop planned to return home on Saturday; until then the magistrates had ample opportunity to meet in private caucus to plan the bold coup that was to follow.

On November fifteenth the Court returned to Newtown and the wheels of justice were again set in motion. The two Boston sergeants, William Balston and the elder Edward Hutchinson, were promptly summoned to the bar. Charged with signing the Wheelwright petition, both men readily admitted as much and defended their behavior in vigorous terms. "If such a petition had been

1. *Winthrop Papers*, III, 507-8.
2. *Colony Records*, I, 207.

made in any other place in the world," Balston hotly contended, "there would have been no fault found with it." [3]

Both men were disfranchised and "for that they were known to bee very busie persons," suffered the additional penalty of heavy fines. Told that he must pay £40, Hutchinson scornfully turned his back on his judges. "If [you take] away my estate," he muttered, "[you] must keep [my] wife and children." For this contempt he was hustled off to prison, there to spend the night in frigid rumination on the error of his ways.[4]

For three days the Court concentrated its energies on the chastisement of the more troublesome factionists. Thomas Marshall, the ferryman, was brought before them, and William Dinely, the barber-surgeon, who—one observer claimed—"so soon as they were set down in his chair, he would commonly be cutting of their hair and the truth together." [5] William Dyer, the milliner, and Richard Gridley, the brickmaker, were also summoned. All of them, though deferentially attentive to the strictures of the Court, clung firmly to their convictions. So they too were disfranchised.[6]

Then came Captain Underhill; swashbuckler, braggart, libertine, lecher, and liar—the full scope of his sins as yet undreamed of—the dashing captain was requested to acknowledge his fault in signing the petition. Underhill would by no means own up to the error. As a man of the sword, he blustered, he was entitled to speak freely to his employers. Had not Joab spoken roughly to King David? he instanced.

This precedent Winthrop pronounced irrelevant. "The Captaine was but a private man, and had no calling to deale in the affaires of the Court." Underhill protested that while serving in Holland he had often spoken as firmly to the Count of Nassau without suffering reproach. Winthrop's sympathy went silently forth to the worthy Count, but he was indisposed to emulate his forbearance. "Wee are not to look at what some do tolerate," he sharply replied, "but what is lawfull!" [7] At last, wearying of the captain's disputatious temper, the Court disfranchised him and dismissed him from his office.[8]

3. *Antinomianism*, 154-55.
4. *Ibid.*, 155; *Colony Records*, I, 207. Transposition from indirect to direct quotation is indicated by the use of brackets.
5. Johnson, *Wonder Working Providence*, 192.
6. *Colony Records*, I, 208.
7. *Antinomianism*, 181, 182.
8. *Colony Records*, I, 208.

The vigorous display of authority in the Newtown meetinghouse created alarm and division among the factionists. Mrs. Hutchinson's Charlestown disciples, now bereft of their leader, agreed to throw themselves on the mercy of the Court before the dragnet should encompass them. On Friday, ten Charlestownians stood before the magistrates and appealed for clemency, offering to retract their signatures from the petition. George Bunker and James Brown had failed to join their fellow townsmen, but a week later Brown indignantly denied that he had ever seen the pernicious document.[9] The Charlestown penitents were generously forgiven their fault. Then the Court hurriedly recessed for the weekend, as though fearful that others might similarly circumvent punishment.[10]

Winthrop now moved with the utmost vigilance against the remaining schismatics. On Monday morning it was ordered that all the powder and ammunition belonging to the colony should be removed from Boston and stored at Newtown and Charlestown. Then, claiming "just cause of suspicion that they, as others in Germany in former times, may, upon some revelation, make some suddaine irruption upon those that differ from them in judgement," the Court resolved to disarm all those who had signed the petition.[11]

Perhaps Winthrop recalled Hooker's counsel: "For execution let it be so secret and suddayne that it cannot be prevented." [12] That day or the next an agent of the Court armed with a lengthy schedule of names marched down the High Street of Boston. From time to time, checking his list, he stopped before a house to rap imperatively at the door. When the door swung open and the family head appeared, a court order was produced and read aloud to him. Within these ten days the householder must deliver to Mr. Keayne's house "all such guns, pistols, swords, powder, shot, & match as they shalbee owners of, or have in their custody, vpon paine of ten pound for every default to bee made therof." [13] However, it was added, if the defendant would attend on the Court and "acknowledge [his] sinn in subscribing to the seditious libell," he might be exempted from the penalty of the present order.

And so, from door to door down the High Street to Gunnison's, Coddington's, Balston's, Hutchinson's, and up the side lanes to

9. *Winthrop Papers*, III, 515.
10. *Colony Records*, I, 209.
11. *Ibid.*, 209, 211.
12. *Winthrop Papers*, III, 499.
13. *Colony Records*, I, 211.

Dyer's, Gridley's, and Eliot's, and about the town to some fifty other homes. And so too, in Roxbury, Salem, Ipswich, Newbury, and Charlestown, the constables went their appointed rounds. Altogether seventy-five men received the warning: fifty-eight from Boston, five each from Salem and Roxbury, three from Newbury, and two each from Ipswich and Charlestown.[14]

The court order shocked and dismayed the Hutchinsonians, but it sufficed to break the ranks of the movement. Within a day or so, singly or in small groups, thirty men appeared before Winthrop and shamefacedly begged that their names be stricken from the petition. Elder Thomas Oliver and his son, young Sergeant John, now bowed to the weight of authority. William Dinely and Samuel Cole, the innkeeper, acknowledged their error, and, in great agony of mind, Anne's own son-in-law, Thomas Savage, came forward to confess the sinfulness of his course. Still another five men came to Newtown in indignant pique to vow that their names had been added to the petition without their knowledge or consent.[15]

But the rest grimly refused to recant, despite the hardships that must attend their course. For those in the outlying communities, it meant defenselessness against Indian attack. For all it meant the loss of means to protect their livestock against predators or to supplement their larders against a long harsh winter. But, most deeply, it wounded their self-esteem. Underhill and Morris, Spencer and Sanford, Balston and Hutchinson, and a number of others were military officers, proud of their positions and taking keen satisfaction in their skill with weapons. To be ordered to submit themselves personally at the door of a junior officer and surrender their arms was deeply humiliating. They protested and grumbled and delayed, "but, at last, when they saw no remedy they obeyed." [16]

(ii)

The trials which now ended remain a dismal page in the history of Massachusetts. All but the most rabid apologists agree that a shocking miscarriage of justice was enacted on Anne Hutchinson and her colleagues. "Trials they were not," a modern observer sums up the majority opinion, "but relentless inquisitions used by the

14. *Ibid.*, 211-12.
15. *Winthrop Papers*, III, 513-15.
16. Winthrop, *Journal*, I, 241; *Antinomianism*, 185 *n*.

government for the purpose of crushing the opposition." [17] The proceedings of the Court, it is held, were but a legal farce, deliberately contrived on trumped-up grounds to rid the colony of persons who could not be expelled by legitimate means, a mere front to make their vindictive bigotry appear legally respectable.

It is undeniable that in the course of the several trials grave legal errors were committed, even according to the crude judicial standards of that day and place. But these are not precisely the errors ascribed by modern commentators, who are too often prone to examine the proceedings from the viewpoint of twentieth-century justice. An examination, first of the charges preferred against the several defendants, and second, of the trial procedures employed, may serve to place the episode in a more usefully revealing perspective.

In March 1637, John Wheelwright was charged with the crimes of sedition and contempt and found guilty by the General Court sitting in judicial session. Sedition involves words or conduct that aim to excite discontent against the government. To quote the definition of Zechariah Chafee, Jr.:

The term sedition has come to be applied to practices which tend to disturb internal public tranquility by deed, word or writing but which do not amount to treason and are not accompanied by or conducive to open violence. . . . The English courts have recognized as misdemeanors at common law seditious words, seditious libels and seditious conspiracies. The use of the adjective signifies that the practices are accompanied by a seditious intent, the legal definition of which has changed, however, with the development of toleration and political rights.[18]

During the sixteenth and seventeenth centuries, British laws of sedition were evolving in response to the enhanced needs of an insecure dynasty and an emergent nation-state in a hostile world. Given the prevailing conception of church-state uniformity; in a situation where dynastic claims were intimately bound up with the religious establishment, sedition laws necessarily bore some concern for the security of the state church.

17. Herbert L. Osgood, *The American Colonies in the Seventeenth Century* (New York, 1904), I, 189. See also James Truslow Adams, *The Founding of New England* (Boston, 1921), 210, and Charles McLean Andrews, *The Colonial Period of American History* (New Haven, 1934), I, 485.

18. Zechariah Chafee, Jr., "Sedition," *Encyclopedia of the Social Sciences* (New York, 1934), XIII, 636. See also Chafee, "History of the Law of Sedition," *Free Speech in the United States* (Cambridge, Mass., 1948), 497-516.

In the Wheelwright case the General Court of Massachusetts, sitting as a bench without jury, was obliged to examine the problem both as a matter of law and as a matter of fact. That is, it had to decide, as a question of law, whether Wheelwright's words in his Fast Day Sermon were actually of a seditious nature, likely to incite discontent against the government. It was also their responsibility to ascertain whether he had actually spoken the words attributed to him and whether these words meant what the prosecution alleged they meant, which were matters of fact.

Under the circumstances these were painfully difficult problems and perhaps all too arbitrarily settled by the Court. In another society, or under more normal and peaceable conditions in Massachusetts, Wheelwright's sermon might have seemed at best a flamboyant but innocuous theological exercise. However, it must be remembered that his words were spoken in a community where scriptural typology and analogy were matters of fundamental concern and at a time when the public peace was unsettled and all minds were divided over precisely those issues on which he now chose to speak. To the Puritan mind the meaning of Wheelwright's words was fairly evident, and Wheelwright was himself sufficiently cognizant of the circumstances to realize what meaning could be attached to his words. True, he did not understand the Covenant of Grace in precisely the same sense as did his listeners, but since he failed to make that distinction clear, they were free to interpret his words according to their own light.

Winthrop's wise observation that "every truth is not seasonable at all times" [19] brings to mind Justice Holmes's remarks in the Schenck case:

We admit that in many places and in ordinary times the defendants in saying all that was said . . . would have been within their constitutional rights. But the character of every act depends upon the circumstances in which it is done. . . . The question in every case is whether the words used are used in such circumstances and are of such a nature as to create a clear and present danger that they will bring about the substantive evils that Congress has a right to prevent. It is a question of proximity and degree.[20]

Certainly the General Court had the right and obligation to prevent a schism in the established, state-supported church. At this

19. *Antinomianism*, 210.
20. *Schenck v. United States*, 249 U.S. 47 (1919).

time very few nations were prepared to disavow that obligation. The question would seem to be whether Wheelwright's words were of such a nature as to create a clear and present danger of producing such a schism.

Within the intellectual and legal framework of English, Puritan Massachusetts, Wheelwright's words might readily have been judged seditious. That he spoke these words intentionally was irrefutable and, indeed, self-admitted. That he spoke them with seditious intent and that these words meant precisely what the state alleged they meant were, perhaps, more disputable matters. In later years it would have been necessary to establish, in fact, that seditious words were spoken or written with the deliberate intent of arousing dissatisfaction with the government and disturbing the public peace. In the seventeenth century it was enough that such words should have the capacity to produce these ends, whether or not so calculated.[21]

But certainly Master Wheelwright spoke with the intent of effecting some change in the minds of his hearers, or, more precisely, of confirming the wisdom of a change of mind hitherto effected. Wheelwright also knew that the change advocated was offensive to the ministry and magistracy of the colony because they regarded their authority as resting on a contrary assumption. Given these considerations, Wheelwright's choice of words and even his manner and tone of voice were unfortunate, to say the least, and might well be construed as seditious in intent as well as capacity.

All too soon events were to bear out the apprehensions of Wheelwright's judges. Mrs. Hutchinson's disciples came to look upon Wheelwright as a champion of their radical opinions, and he neglected to discourage this view. In consequence, their succeeding course of action came to hinge closely on him. After he was indicted for his Fast Day Sermon, they were prompted, in defense of him and in defense of the principles presented in his sermon, to adopt an even more menacing attitude toward the authorities. At the May Court of Elections, their disorderly behavior constituted a rout; however unsuccessfully, they had sought by violent means to impede the lawful processes of government. The defection of the governor's guard and the refusal to join the Pequot expedition savored dangerously of mutiny. There were, of course, other factors underlying their behavior, but Wheelwright, as a teacher and as a symbol, was so deeply implicated in the conduct of the move-

21. Chafee, "Sedition," *Ency. of Soc. Sciences,* XIII, 636.

ment that for the moment his influence was very nearly paramount.

The case of Mrs. Hutchinson's followers was more readily determinable. Aspinwall, Balston, Dinely, Dyer, Underhill, Marshall, Gridley, and Edward Hutchinson were specifically charged with joining in "a seditious libell," for so the petition and remonstrance was regarded and termed.[22] This was no legal trumpery; the offense was well established in English law of the sixteenth and seventeenth centuries. Seditious libels, that is, libels against magistrates or other authorities of government or established church, were looked upon as a serious threat to the security of the state. "Let all men," it was said in the Star Chamber, "take heed how they complayne in wordes against any magistrate, for they are Gods."[23] Any words which traduced a magistrate were regarded as a seditious libel, irrespective of their pertinence to the official functions of that dignitary and irrespective of the truth or falsity of such claims. Indeed the possibility that the libelous words might be true would tend to make them more likely to produce a breach of the peace. The most casual and careless expostulations in criticism of authority were indictable as seditious libels. All such libels were regarded as "a scandal of government," and the great Justice Coke himself had announced that "a libel is a breach of the peace and is not to be suffered but punished. This is as poison in the commonwealth."[24]

As Holdsworth points out, the construction of a libel will depend largely on the prevailing relationship between rulers and subjects. In a society where the ruler is regarded as superior to his subjects and is presumed by the nature of his position to be wise and good, "it must necessarily follow that it is wrong to censure him openly ... even if he is mistaken, his mistakes should be pointed out with the utmost respect and ... whether mistaken or not, no censure should be cast upon him likely, or designed to diminish his authority."[25]

Down to the beginning of the eighteenth century, the essence of a libel was the intentional publication of a document that bore "the seditious or defamatory meaning alleged by the prosecution." Malice was implied as a necessary ingredient of the crime, and even in a later and much more liberal age, it was regarded as immaterial whether or not the defendant intended the words to be

22. *Colony Records*, I, 207.
23. William Searle Holdsworth, *A History of English Law* (Boston, 1926), V, 208.
24. *Ibid.*, V, 210, 211; VIII, 339.
25. *Ibid.*, VIII, 338.

defamatory.[26] The question was not what the defendant intended the words to mean, but rather, what reasonable men, knowing the circumstances under which the words were published, would understand to be their meaning.[27] A seditious libel at this time was, in effect, any statement that the government saw fit to regard as critical of its purposes or operation or of its personnel even in their most unofficial capacities. As late as 1704 it was still held that any criticism of the government amounts to a seditious libel.[28]

In the present instance the members of the Hutchinson faction had submitted to the Court a "petition and remonstrance" wherein they criticized and beseeched the reversal of a judicial decision of that body. Although much of Aspinwall's insolent language had been pared away, there remained the incautious insinuation that the Court in making its decision may have been the victim of Satanical guidance.[29] For all its garb of righteous humility, the petition could be readily construed as a seditious libel within the broad terms currently allowable. All that was necessary was for the Court to establish that the defendants had joined in subscribing the document, and this they freely admitted.

Mrs. Hutchinson's case was more complex because more was charged against her, but essentially the charges added up to the same fault—a seditious libel, but, in this instance, directed more particularly against the ministers. Winthrop put the indictment in scriptural terms: Mrs. Hutchinson had broken the Fifth Commandment by dishonoring the Fathers of the Commonwealth. Although her meetings were condemned and her opinions were cited as being at the root of all their recent troubles, the charge most closely developed was her disparagement of the ministers: "You have spoken divers things . . . very prejudicial to the honor of the churches and ministers thereof." [30] In the long run the Court was prepared to rest its case upon this item, and it was with respect to this that witnesses were summoned to testify against her.

The problem confronting the Court was twofold: to determine whether the defendant's words were defamatory, and to ascertain whether they had been sufficiently public in their pronunciation to constitute a libel. On both counts the prosecution's case was somewhat insecure. It was common knowledge that Mrs. Hutchin-

26. *Ibid.*, VIII, 345, 373.
27. "Libel," *Encyclopaedia Britannica*, XIII, 996.
28. Holdsworth, *History of English Law*, VI, 266.
29. *Antinomianism*, 134-35.
30. Hutchinson, *History*, I, 366.

son had spoken disparagingly of the ministers to her disciples. But this "knowledge" rested solely on hearsay, for it had been thus far impossible to produce two sound witnesses to testify to its truth.[31] The prosecution was thus compelled to rest its entire case on the exchange that had taken place at Mr. Cotton's house in the previous December. The ministers, who now solemnly testified that she had uttered precisely those defamatory words alleged against her, were themselves the complainants and obviously partial in the cause. The case for the prosecution was seriously weakened when two trustworthy eyewitnesses for the defense testified that she had not spoken as alleged.

As to the publicity given her remarks, having been elicited under a pledge, or at least a presumption, of confidence, they could hardly be described as public property. But at this time the publication of a libel or slander to a third person was not necessary to constitute the crime. This had been established in the case of De Libellis Famosis in 1606.[32] More pertinent was the problem of whether Mrs. Hutchinson's statements were indeed privileged. During this period the law as to privilege was vague, and the distinction between absolute and qualified privilege had not yet been established. Practically all such cases turned upon documents or statements made in the course of judicial proceedings.[33] At a later time, if malice could be proven, the defense of privilege was not allowed.[34] There was little doubt in the minds of the present complainants or the prosecution as to the malice of Mrs. Hutchinson's remarks, but in this instance the whole question of privilege was peremptorily brushed aside in the interest of seeing the Lord's work done. Public or private, the question resolved itself to whether or not she had said precisely those defamatory words ascribed to her, and this the Court could not easily settle.

Fortuitously the judges were delivered from their quandary by an estoppel. By divulging her revelations in the presence of the Court, the defendant created so conclusive a presumption of guilt that no further evidence was deemed admissible or necessary.[35] Not only were such revelations an item of heresy, which was, of course, a matter for the church to deal with, but the content of her locutions, now freely proclaimed before the Court, conven-

31. Cotton, *Way of the Congregational Churches Cleared,* 52, 57, 58.
32. Theodore F. T. Pucknett, "Libel and Slander," *Ency. of Soc. Sciences,* IX, 431.
33. Holdsworth, *History of English Law,* VIII, 376.
34. Pucknett, "Libel and Slander," *Ency. of Soc. Sciences,* IX, 431, 432.
35. Holdsworth, *History of English Law,* IX, 146.

iently constituted a seditious libel wherein she did impugn and threaten the whole state.[36]

Had the judges seen fit they might also have applied English statutes which declared the delivery of false and fantastical prophecies to be a misdemeanor.[37] But they had enough to serve their present purposes and were well content.

(iii)

In the past criticism has been directed chiefly against the procedures employed in the several trials. It is protested that the Court failed to observe the most fundamental procedural safeguards thus far attained in English law. In cases of such heavy consequence, critics contend, the defendants were entitled to trial by jury. The Court has been further criticized for having denied the defendants the advice of counsel and for failure to present a specific indictment. In Mrs. Hutchinson's case, they are charged with having bullied the defendant and harassed the witnesses. It is asserted that, except in two instances, evidence was not given on oath and that much of the evidence was mere hearsay.[38]

To the modern mind the conduct of these trials is shocking. But it should be remembered that in many respects the procedures employed by the Court were no different than those which currently obtained in English courts. Procedures were then in a state of developmental flux, and there were few fixed rules to govern the precise conduct of trials.[39] Although the defendant was presumed to be innocent until proven otherwise, in both the Star Chamber and the common-law courts procedure was regulated to favor the interest and security of the state. The prisoner was kept ignorant of the details of the case against him and was denied a copy of the indictment, thus rendering him incapable of preparing an adequate defense. The prisoner was also denied the aid of counsel during the trial and so was obliged to conduct his own defense as

36. As recently as 1917 in the United States "a woman was convicted for saying in conversation, 'I wish Wilson was in hell, and if I had the power I would put him there.' This was held to be a threat to kill the president, because, as the Court reasoned, he could not be in hell unless he were dead." *U.S.* v. *Clark*, 250 Fed. 499, cited by Chafee, "Sedition," *Ency. of Soc. Sciences*, XIII, 638.

37. Holdsworth, *History of English Law*, IV, 511. Such prophecies were presumed to be aimed at stirring up rebellion.

38. See Osgood, *American Colonies*, I, 189.

39. Holdsworth, *History of English Law*, IX, 180, 195, 223. See also George Lee Haskins, *Law and Authority in Early Massachusetts* (New York, 1960), 49-50.

best he could. There were no clear rules governing the examination of defendants or witnesses. Judges as well as prosecuting counsel closely questioned the defendant, and this questioning was often of a bullying, rough-and-tumble nature. The defendant was compelled to answer all queries directed to him and enjoyed no immunity against self-incrimination.[40]

Only two witnesses were required to testify on oath as to the truth of the charges against the defendant, and hearsay evidence was generally admissible. Until well into the seventeenth century, the defendant was denied the right to produce witnesses in his own behalf. When that right was finally conceded, defense witnesses were not allowed to testify under oath, thus effectually invalidating any testimony they might offer counter to the sworn statements of prosecution witnesses. Not only the defendants, but defense witnesses as well, were sorely pressed by the prosecution and judges and compelled to answer even those questions which might incriminate them.[41]

So it would appear that in many respects, the Winthrop Court did not differ greatly from those in England. In New England as well as Old, defendants and witnesses alike were harassed and pressed to incriminate themselves. Mr. Coggeshall, witnessing for Mrs. Hutchinson, was rudely treated and abruptly cut off, but it should be kept in mind that he was, by his own admission, an accomplice in these misdemeanors. As Holdsworth observes, "the evidence of accomplices was not only suspected, but was even regarded as especially cogent." [42] Winthrop, however reluctantly, did finally satisfy the technical requirement that two witnesses must testify on oath, but at that juncture their testimony was surely supererogatory. And so on down the list, the New England magistrates acted according to the pattern with which they were familiar.

A more serious charge against the Massachusetts Court relates to their failure to grant the right of trial by jury in a case or cases of such consequence. However, there are two separate grounds on which such an exception might have been based. The act of the General Court of May 14, 1636, stipulated that "noe tryall shall passe vpon any, for life or banishment, but by a jury soe summoned or by the General Courte." [43] The fact that these were state trials of the highest significance may have impelled the magistrates to

40. Holdsworth, *History of English Law*, IX, 223, 229, 195, 181, 199.
41. *Ibid.*, 203, 204, 195, 199.
42. *Ibid.*, 223.
43. *Colony Records*, I, 118.

adopt the latter course. In so doing, they did not lack for legitimate precedent. In the case *De Libellis Famosis* (1606), Justice Coke had affirmed that seditious libels could be punished either by indictment at common law or by proceedings in the Star Chamber.[44] However, in the common-law courts defamation was almost exclusively examined as a civil rather than a criminal offense. This neglect of the criminal aspects of defamation created a large gap in the criminal law—a gap which was filled, "and on the whole, adequately filled, by the Star Chamber." [45] By default the trial of seditious libels fell within the exclusive jurisdiction of a prerogative court which sat in judgment without a jury. It is ironical that Mrs. Hutchinson's judges were friends and allies of that party in England which was so vigorously combatting the prerogative courts —but in this instance it would seem to be a matter of whose prerogative was being gored.

But all this diversity of judicial primitivisms and irregularities were inconsequential by contrast with that flaw which overthrew any semblance of justice the proceedings might have offered. That Governor Winthrop and his fellow magistrates should act as both judges and prosecutors was a shocking miscarriage of justice. That they should have done so without a jury to examine and amend their conclusions is doubly shocking. Even the Star Chamber maintained a formal distinction between judges and prosecutors, however often the judges may have confused their roles.

If the Massachusetts Court saw fit to sit as a bench without jury —as the best precedent seemed to allow—certainly Winthrop should have disqualified himself as partisan in the cause. Endicott and Dudley might graciously have done so as well. There were other men in the Court, most notably Bellingham and Stoughton, who were equally well qualified to sit as judges, and conspicuously less prejudiced against the defendants. Winthrop might then have appointed a special prosecutor in the case. The fact is the Governor and Company of Massachusetts Bay had a substantial case against Anne Hutchinson and her friends, but by a fundamental flaw in their procedure, they created what even a seventeenth-century lawyer must have regarded as a mistrial.

The Court had, however irregularly, accomplished its end. The Hutchinson faction had been broken up, the remonstrants disarmed, the ringleaders disfranchised or banished. The magistrates, having

44. Holdsworth, *History of English Law*, VIII, 339.
45. *Ibid.*, V, 207.

acted swiftly and ruthlessly, now determined to prevent any recurrence of the dangers so narrowly averted. Their own body of law was as yet sketchy and formative. From one session to the next, new laws were added as the need became apparent. They knew themselves subject to fundamental English law. More importantly, they held themselves subject to the law of God. Presumably the magistrates were conversant with the legal framework within which they operated. Certainly Winthrop was. If they inwardly questioned the possibility of mistrial, no matter: the law of God had been upheld. But to doubly secure this victory it was held necessary to make the will of the Court thoroughly explicit. No sooner had the last of the offenders been disposed of than the General Court drafted and passed its own law of seditious libel. However belatedly, the purport of the preceding trials was made clear to all observers, and any future remonstrance effectively stifled:

This Courte, being sensible of the great disorders growing in this commonwelth through the contempts which have of late bene put vpon the civill authority, & intending to provide remedy for the same in time, doth order and decree, that whosoever shall hereafter openly or willingly defame any court of iustice, or the sentences and proceedings of the same, or any of the magistrats or other iudges of any such court, in respect of any act or sentence therin passed, & being thereof lawfully convict in any Generall Court, or Court of Assistants, shalbee punished for the same by fine, imprisonment, or disfranchizement, or banishment, as the quality and measure of the offence shall deserve.[46]

(iv)

However fearful the deputies, there was little sentiment among the Bostonians to take up arms against the established authorities —nor was there a John of Leyden at hand to urge them on. The Hutchinsonians were, nonetheless, incensed by the proceedings of the Court, finding it especially intolerable that one of their own brethren should have led the pack. The new law of seditious libel had placed Winthrop and his colleagues comfortably beyond the reach of criticism or chastisement by private persons. But they saw that while Winthrop was yet a fellow in church covenant with them, he did not stand above the admonition of the church.

46. *Colony Records*, I, 212-13.

Determined to express their resentment, several of the congregation consulted with Cotton and Wilson, urging them to admonish Winthrop in the name of the church. Wilson was by no means disposed to reprimand the Governor for pursuing a course with which he was wholeheartedly in accord. Whatever Cotton's feelings may have been, he saw fit to reject the scheme.

Seeing the possibility of greater troubles, one or both of the ministers informed the Governor of the plan that was afoot. Winthrop grasped the meaning of the situation and vigorously seized the initiative himself. After the sermon that Sunday, he rose from his seat and, looking squarely into the hostile faces of his brethren, bluntly informed them that the church had no authority "to inquire into the justice and proceedings of the Court." [47] Both in rule and practice Christ had disclaimed such power, he reminded them. As a private person, Winthrop conceded, a magistrate was, like any other man, accountable to the church for his private failings. But the church must not presume to call a magistrate to account for his official acts, however unjust they might seem.

For himself, Winthrop insisted, he had always sought to follow the dictates of his judgment and conscience in providing for the public good. He would offer but one ground for his judgment in the present case: "Those brethren," he believed, "were so divided from the rest of the country in their judgement and practice, as it could not stand with the public peace, that they should continue among us. So, by the example of Lot in Abraham's family, and after Hagar and Ishmael, [I] saw they must be sent away." [48]

Winthrop's speech to the Boston congregation was a significant and useful step in defining the complex relations of church and state in Massachusetts. Although the magistrates often leaned heavily upon the advice of the ministers, it was by now well established that such counsel should be provided only when the Court so requested. Similarly, although the ministers could assume the freedom of their pulpits to influence and advise the freemen on political matters, the freemen had on occasion seen fit to disregard that counsel. Now Winthrop laid it down that the churches could not curtail or inhibit political authority on what purported to be religious grounds. In an essay drafted at this time, he developed his reasoning further on the problem. If the church had "power to Call any Civill Magistrate, to give Account of his Juditiall proceed-

---

47. Winthrop, *Journal*, I, 256.
48. *Ibid.*, 257. Transposed to direct quotation.

ing in any Court of Civill Justice . . . the Church should become the supreame Court in the Jurisdiction, and capable of all Appeales." [49] This would bestow upon the church a power that it lacked the means to employ properly, "for the Churche cannot call in forrein witnesses: nor examine witnesses vpon Oath, nor require the view of the Records of the Court: all which may be needfull for findinge out the trueth in many Cases." [50]

He might have also argued that the threat of admonition could operate as a veto power on the legislative activities of the Court. At present the freemen of each town could govern themselves in their own town meetings and, by the election of deputies, had a proportional voice in the government of the commonwealth. If that same group of freemen, in their authority as a church, were able to admonish deputies and magistrates for their official behavior on professedly religious grounds, the legislators would be deprived of freedom to translate the popular will and the commonweal into public policy according to the dictates of their judgment and conscience.

(v)

The winter taxed Boston cruelly. Woodpiles shrank at an alarming rate and the frozen Bay took its toll of those who dared to venture forth to replenish their fuel supply. Shivering beside cautiously banked fires, the Bostonians were tempted to the desperate extremity of abandoning homes and town for warmer refuge on the mainland.[51]

Mrs. Hutchinson, however, was more warmly sheltered in the Roxbury home of Mr. Joseph Weld. By the order of the Court, she had been placed in the custody of Pastor Weld's brother until the coming of spring would allow her to depart the colony. During this confinement none but ministers and members of her own family were permitted to visit her. By this means, it was hoped, she might cease troubling the colony, until they could at last be rid of her.[52]

But Massachusetts had not heard the last of Mrs. Hutchinson. Despite her imprisonment her doctrines continued to multiply and spread. In her enforced idleness, she had ample opportunity to

49. *Winthrop Papers*, III, 505.
50. *Ibid.*, 505.
51. *Ibid.*, IV, 9; Winthrop, *Journal*, I, 258.
52. *Colony Records*, I, 207.

explore the remote and fascinating recesses of her doctrine and to cogitate on the wonders she found there. By some means, these, or closely related tenets, were conveyed to Boston. She may have recounted her discoveries to William and Edward on their occasional visits, and by them the new notions were relayed to Boston. Or the new doctrines may have burst spontaneously from the minds of disciples frigidly pent in defeat and discomfort. One way or another, doctrines that had hitherto been cautiously examined by way of inquiry now began to raise their heads as matters of positive conviction. The icy air of Boston was warmly agitated by new tenets about revelations, the mortality of souls before union, and the resurrection of the body.[53]

Once again magistrates and ministers gathered to deal with this fresh array of "foul errors." They were dissected in meetings and denounced in sermons.[54] But the authorities were unduly alarmed, for the great majority of Bostonians were now thoroughly subdued. The power of the state had prompted some to reconsider their opinions more precisely. Others had been troubled by the extremism of Mrs. Hutchinson's address to the Court, or by the doctrines her friends had lately expressed. It had seemed before that Mrs. Hutchinson had but spoken Mr. Cotton's thoughts, perhaps more clearly and straightforwardly than he was wont to do. Now it was apparent that it was not Mr. Cotton's thought but her own that she had disseminated.

In Roxbury Weld and Eliot moved to cut off the contagion before it reinfected their bailiwick. The obdurate remnant of Hutchinsonians were lectured, cajoled, and admonished. At long last, when no other means had prevailed, three of them—Henry Bull, Philip Sherman, and Thomas Wilson—were cast out of the church.[55]

These were painful times for John Cotton, and history has not judged him kindly for the path he walked. "The ignominious page in an otherwise worthy life," one historian asserts. "He made haste to walk in a Covenant of Works—and the walk was a very dirty one." [56] It is assumed that Cotton, browbeaten by ministers and magistrates, and fearful for the security of his position, now sur-

53. Winthrop, *Journal*, I, 259; *Antinomianism*, 183.
54. Winthrop, *Journal*, I, 259.
55. "Roxbury Land and Church Records," Boston Registry Dept., *Records Relating to the Early History of Boston* (Record Commissioners of the City of Boston, *Sixth Report* [Boston, 1884]), 78, 79, 91; Winthrop, *Journal*, I, 258; *Antinomianism*, 187.
56. Charles Francis Adams, Jr., *Three Episodes in Massachusetts History* (Boston, 1896), I, 515.

rendered his principles in order that he might walk safely with "natures lower than his own." [57]

There is no doubt that Cotton's colleagues bore heavily upon him, and it would be simple and dramatically convenient to suppose that this pressure forced Cotton to recant his beliefs and turn vehemently upon his erstwhile friends. But this is not only inconsistent with Cotton's character, it is inconsistent with the facts.

Cotton, it is true, was a peaceable and mild-natured man, but he did not lack the courage of his convictions. Those convictions, admittedly, were so complex and ambivalent that it required much of his energy and acumen to sustain the delicate equipoise which was their very life and essence. Indeed it was the ambivalence of his views that had led him into all this difficulty. Cotton's naturally sweet and charitable disposition, alloyed with a degree of naïveté about the motives and attitudes of others, had led him to accept the Hutchinsonian claims that they believed precisely as he did. Up through the final hour of Mrs. Hutchinson's trial, he had continued to defend the ambiguity of her perceptions and to insist on the possibility that his colleagues had misinterpreted her meaning. He seems to have had a greater tolerance than his clerical colleagues for the layman's fumbling endeavors with theological vocabulary; a greater willingness to assume that a sound meaning might be faultily expressed. He acceded in the conclusions of the Synod because these had condemned, not his essential doctrines, nor, so far as he could then determine, those of Mrs. Hutchinson, but rather those heterodox opinions which might be incautiously drawn from his doctrines and hers. He agreed to the Synodical ban on Mrs. Hutchinson's meetings because it was by then apparent, even to him, that amateur theologians might all too easily go astray while exploring the intricate byways of doctrine.

Once Mrs. Hutchinson's trial was past, and she had openly spoken her mind, all those desperate and radical conclusions he had long hoped to avert now raised their heads. Cotton was, rightly or wrongly, persuaded that his parishioners had gulled him, that they had used him as their dupe and "stalking horse." [58] It seemed to him that they had masqueraded as his particular disciples only to give their teachings respectability. Now he, who had so narrowly escaped the fate of the hare, cast his lot with the hounds, and appeared to be foremost in the chase. Bewailing his credulity,

57. Adams, Founding of New England, 173.
58. Winthrop, Journal, I, 259.

he endeavored publicly and privately to track down the new-sprung errors and restore the erronists to the path of orthodoxy.[59]

But Cotton's zeal did not lead him to the house of legalism, nor yet prompt him to abandon those fine-spun conceptions that had begotten Mrs. Hutchinson's errors. The opportunity soon arose to express his thinking on this point. With the approach of spring, it was rumored that the magistrates proposed to enforce the alien law against "some godly passengers" who shared Cotton's views on the "Doctrine of Union, and the evidencing of Union." Cotton was much disturbed. If such a policy were carried out, he complained, "wee should receive no more Members into our Church, but such as must professe themselves of a contrary judgment to what I be-leeved to bee a Truth." [60]

Rather than "breed any further offensive agitation," Cotton re-solved to leave Massachusetts and take up residence with those now settled at New Haven. This hardly supports any view of his being cowed into an abandonment of his convictions. His forth-right proposal to remove was most unwelcome to the magistrates; they realized that his departure would tarnish the reputation of the colony and might dangerously impugn their motives in dealing with the Hutchinsonians.

Winthrop eagerly assured Cotton that there had been a misun-derstanding. The newcomers were suspect on grounds quite other than those that Cotton shared with them. The magistrates, while conceding that they could not fully agree with Mr. Cotton's views on union and evidence, "did not look at them to be of such funda-mental concernment either to civil or church peace as needed to occasion any disturbance in heart (much lesse in place) amongst godly brethren." [61]

So Cotton, with his principles intact, was persuaded to remain in Boston, but not without suffering some suspicion as to the sound-ness of his doctrine. "As concerning any tenet wherein he may seem singular," one of his colleagues pointed out with guarded charity, "remember he was a man, and therefore to be heard and read with judgement, and haply sometimes with favor." [62]

Cotton's dilemma was not unlike that of Wheelwright; the essen-tial difference between the two men lay not in their doctrines but in

59. *Antinomianism*, 183.
60. Cotton, *Way of the Congregational Churches Cleared*, 53.
61. *Ibid.*, 54; John Cotton, "*A Reply to Mr. Williams his Examination*," Narra-gansett Club, *Publications*, 1st Ser., 2 (1867), 81.
62. Norton, *Memoir of John Cotton*, 76.

their personalities. Where Wheelwright was contentious and outspoken, Cotton was mild and tractable. Neither was tempted to follow the way of the Hutchinsonians; they were both too precise and circumspect in their theology for such extremism. Nor could they turn back to the stern empiricism of their colleagues. But it was in Wheelwright's nature to separate from those who had disdained and abused him; it was in Cotton's nature to make his peace on terms that did not compromise his essential principles.

There can be little doubt that gentle Cotton suffered great agony of mind when at last impelled to turn upon his errant parishioners. He had long undergone much discomfiture and humiliation in their defense. The conviction that he had been betrayed was painful to consider. But in his denunciations, he was, perhaps, as unjust to his erstwhile disciples as later critics have been toward him. It seems unlikely that Mrs. Hutchinson and her friends would deliberately use Cotton as a Trojan horse to dissemble their beliefs. More probably they had accepted his doctrines in good faith, but unskilled in theological niceties and stirred to excess by the uncharitable example of their legalist opponents, had gradually tipped the delicate balance and deposited Cotton's Covenant of Grace into the pit of heterodoxy. Cotton had long foreseen such a possibility and should have guarded more carefully against it. Had he done so, this crisis might never have arisen.

(vi)

"We were in a heate, and Chafed, and were all of vs to blame. In our strife, we had forgotten wee were brethren." [63] Recalling the conciliatory words, Coddington strove to remember who had said them: Bellingham, perhaps, or Keayne, or Leverett? No matter, it was true enough. How could men of good will have come to such a pass? It seemed so senseless. Yet how long could one go on constantly fearful, caught in contention, hostility, and suspicion?

From his snug, brick house on the High Street, the world outside seemed cold and hostile. Across the road at Bendall's Dock, vessels swayed at their moorings, creaking under the load of ice that coated bulwarks and rigging. The harbor beyond was clogged by jagged, tide-washed floes which smashed and piled at the shoreline.

William Coddington looked at the men gathered about him:

63. *Winthrop Papers*, IV, 278.

brother Coggeshall, Will and Ned Hutchinson, Will Colburn, Sam Wilbore. How, out of his own uncertainty, could he advise them? In the face of such a difficult decision, he could almost envy Will Hutchinson, who had no choice to make. He must leave within two months. But for the rest of them, there was a problem to be faced. Although formal charges had not yet been preferred, Coddington was full aware that the magistrates had now marked him for their quarry. Mr. Winthrop's letter had made their intent unmistakable.

The injustice of the recent trials had enraged William Coddington. Not one to bluster and storm, the provocation was at last so great that he could no longer restrain his indignation. "I do not see any equity . . . in all your proceedings," he had protested.[64] The trials over, he and Coggeshall and Colburn with some few others had drafted a fresh remonstrance against the actions of the Court. It had taken Winthrop an unconscionable time "to reade it advisedly," but at last he had done so, and, as they might have expected, proceeded to lecture them in schoolmasterish fashion on "some miscarriages therein." [65]

"You have broke the bounds of your calling," he had written, "that you did publish such a writinge. . . . You goe about, to overthrow the foundations of our Com[mon]w[ealth] and the peace thereof . . . against the rule of the Ap[ost]le, who requires every soule to be subiect to the higher powers and every Ch[ristia]n man, to studye to be quiet, and to meddle with his own business."

"I earnestly desire you," Winthrop went on, "to consider seriously of these things: and if it pl[ease] the Lo[rd] to open your eyes, to see your failings, it wilbe much ioy to me, and (I doubt not but) the C[our]t wilbe very redy to pass them by, and accept of your submission." [66]

A far cry from the not so distant past when Coddington and Winthrop had sat together at Court and church in all brotherly affection—when, indeed, Master Winthrop had more than eagerly besought him to marry into his own family.[67] But that was the past, and if he were to gain any peace of mind, he must put it behind him and think constructively of the future. What future could lie before him in Boston, bereft of his magisterial office, under sentence of the Court, and suffering contumely for his beliefs?

He turned to Coggeshall; what could he propose? Deacon Cogge-

64. Hutchinson, *History*, II, 389.
65. *Winthrop Papers*, IV, 8.
66. *Ibid.*, 9.
67. *Ibid.*, III, 22, 34.

shall saw the future quite clearly. Why should not the two of them,
Coddington and he, and some few others—Coggeshall looked in-
quiringly into the faces of his companions—"remoue, for their peace
and settelement?" [68] Boston was not the whole of the western
world, nor yet was Massachusetts. A rich and pleasant land lay
beyond them. To the south, near Mr. Williams, was ample room for
another plantation.

Coddington was interested but unsure. How could they remove
without offense to the Court or their brethren of the church? As
a deacon of the church, Coggeshall reminded them, he could procure a meeting of the congregation and seek their approval and a
friendly dismission.

Accordingly, a "solomon meeting" was arranged and the matter
put forward for discussion. The congregation seemed amenable to
the proposal, but Mr. Cotton being out of town, his counsel was
lacking. When he returned, they met again and "with the generall
advice and consent of all" Coddington and his little company
"were commended to the grace of God in Christ Jesus." [69]

Coddington, meanwhile, undertook the more delicate task of
requesting the magistrates to allow them to depart in peace rather
than abide the overhanging sentence of the Court. Alone he went
to Winthrop's house to thrash the matter out with him. The Governor welcomed him and seemed for a while the Winthrop of old.
He proved surprisingly sympathetic to their design. He had had
enough of this business already. Some few others were yet to be
dealt with for their miscarriages, but these men were his brethren.
It might be best for all, he professed, if they removed themselves
for a season to escape the censure of the Court. [70] But, Winthrop
ventured hopefully, it would please him much if Mr. Coddington
would not depart. He was sure that he could help Coddington
make his peace with the Court. [71] Coddington shook his head sadly:
No, he could no longer go on living in strife with those whom he
respected. [72] Winthrop reluctantly agreed; he would write forthwith to obtain the assent of his fellow magistrates. Dudley gruffly
consented to their proposal, with the churlish proviso that they

68. *Ibid.*, IV, 245.
69. *Ibid.*, 245.
70. *Ibid.*, 246.
71. Entry of September 26, 1639, First Church of Boston, Records and Baptisms, 1630-1687 (Mass. Hist. Soc.).
72. *Winthrop Papers*, IV, 246.

"departe out of this Patent within a moneth from hence follow-ing." [73]

This was on the nineteenth of February. Thus assured, Cogge-shall and Aspinwall wrote hurriedly to Roger Williams, inquiring about the availability of the lands near him.[74] Gradually the little company was enlarged. Will Hutchinson's brother and son-in-law threw in their lot with the rest, John Porter and his son-in-law Philip Sherman, both of Roxbury, joined the group. The servant lad Henry Bull decided to go along. And a couple of promising newcomers, Dr. John Clarke, a man learned in medicine and the-ology, and one Randall Holden asked to be included.

On March 7, 1638, nineteen men gathered in the spacious fore-room of William Coddington's house and joined in civil compact:

We whose names are underwritten do here solemnly in the pres-ence of Jehovah incorporate ourselves into a Bodie Politick and as he shall help, will submit our persons, lives and estates unto our Lord Jesus Christ, the King of Kings and Lord of Lords and to all those perfect and most absolute lawes of his given us in his holy word of truth, to be guided and judged thereby.[75]

They chose from among them William Coddington to be their judge, unto whom they did "convenant to yield all due honour according to the lawes of God." [76] And so, "after Hagar and Ish-mael," they were sent away and wandered in the wilderness.

And the Angel of God called unto Hagar: "Arise, lift up the lad, and hold him in thine hand, for I will make him a great nation." [77]

73. *Ibid.*, 14.
74. *Ibid.*, 17.
75. *Records of the Colony of Rhode Island and Providence Plantations in New England* (Providence, 1856), I, 52. The nineteen men were: William Coddington, John Clarke, William Hutchinson, John Coggeshall, William Aspinwall, Samuel Wilbore, John Porter, John Sanford, Edward Hutchinson, Jr., William Freeborn, Philip Sherman, John Walker, William Dyer, Richard Carder, William Balston, Edward Hutchinson, Sr., Henry Bull, Randall Holden, and Thomas Savage.
76. *Ibid.*
77. Genesis 21:18.

XVI

"Withdraw Yourself as a Leper"

March 12–28, 1638

(i)

WHEN THE Court reassembled at Newtown on Monday, March 12, there were still many loose ends to be caught up or cut away. The deputies promptly issued the formal license that was to speed William Coddington and his associates on their way. Gratuitously, they added several persons to the group, among them a few of Roger Williams's disciples, of whom they were anxious to be rid.[1]

Having dispatched that business with such forthright economy of energy, they then summoned four of the military officers to give satisfaction for their expressions of sympathy toward "the familistical persons and opinions." [2] Ensign Jennison's reasons for refusing to vote for Mrs. Hutchinson's banishment were now made clear. It appeared that Edward Gibbon and Robert Harding of Boston were similarly infected, as was Thomas Cakebread of Charlestown.[3] Indeed, it must have seemed to the Court that the military suffered an extraordinary susceptibility to the heretical opinions, although the more observant may have noted that the mercantile affiliations of these four gentlemen perhaps weighed more heavily in the formation of their views. Three of the merchant-militiamen relented and provided the required satisfaction. But Robert Harding, whose strongminded, voluble wife remained one of Mrs. Hutchinson's warmest supporters, had his case put over till the next Court.[4]

1. *Colony Records,* I, 223.
2. Winthrop, *Journal,* I, 262.
3. *Ibid.,* 224, 225, 226.
4. Entry of September 1, 1639, First Church of Boston, Records and Baptisms, 1630-1687, Mass. Hist. Soc.

Jane Hawkins, having been, of late, too much in the public eye, was called and forbidden "to question matters of religion." The magistrates further instructed her "not to meddle in surgery, or phisick, drinks, plaisters, or oyles," thus cutting off her livelihood. Happily for Jane, the magistrates had not yet heard of those potions of mandrake oil which she was wont to administer to importunate brides.[5]

Most importantly the Court engaged to amend the faulty condition of their laws that had so often required the application of ex post facto remedies. Possibly the recent judicial miscarriages bore heavily on their collective conscience, but more probably they sought to gain as much independence of English laws and precedents as they might. Because the want of written laws had put the Court "into many doubts and much trouble in many perticuler cases," the towns were instructed to "collect the heads of such necessary and fundamentall lawes as may bee sutable to the times and places whear God by his providence hath cast us." This done, a committee of ministers and magistrates would then undertake to provide "a compendious abrigment of the same." [6]

When Thursday came, the Court excused. Governor Winthrop and Mr. Bellingham to return to Boston on urgent business. "The Elders of Boston had declared their readinesse to deale with Mrs. Hutchinson in a Church way." [7]

(ii)

During the dreary winter of her imprisonment in Mr. Weld's Roxbury home, Anne Hutchinson had ample time to pursue her scriptural studies. For four long months all the normal activities of her busy life were suspended. In addition to an enforced idleness, broken by few diversions, was the knowledge that the lives of others went on without her. Her distress over the outcome of the trial was not mitigated by the physical symptoms that plagued her. Climacteric bore heavily on her body, exacerbating the emotional strain. Left to herself for long hours, she sank into a morbid and neurotic pondering of death. Her scriptural searchings became preoccupied with the meaning of resurrection and immortality; yet the words of Scripture were bafflingly imprecise. On every page she

5. *Colony Records*, I, 224; Winthrop, *Journal*, I, 268.
6. *Colony Records*, I, 222.
7. Winthrop, *Journal*, I, 260-61; *Antinomianism*, 217.

stumbled on anomalies and met with perplexing allusions that brought her no closer to the reassurance she sought. In this dark hour a cruel irony led her to that compendium of disillusion, the Book of Ecclesiastes. The gloomy Koheleth was a poor comforter. "I said in mine heart concerning the estate of the sons of men," she read, "that God might manifest them, and they might see that they themselves are beasts. For that which befalleth beasts; even one thing befalleth them; as the one dieth, so dieth the others; yea, they all have but one breath. . . . All go unto one place; all are of the dust, and all turn to dust again. Who knoweth the spirit of men that goeth upward?" [8]

It would have been better for Anne had she ended her search with the first chapter; "In much wisdom is much grief: and he that increaseth knowledge increaseth sorrow." But the enigmas of death and eternity drew her on. How did this relate to the doctrine of union and salvation as she had learned it? What of Corinthians? "So also in the resurrection of the dead," she read, "it is sown in corruption; it is raised in incorruption. . . . It is sown a natural body; it is raised a spiritual body. There is a natural body, and there is a spiritual body." [9] Might these passages, taken together, mean that the soul with which we were born is mortal and that only the spirit infused into us on regeneration is truly immortal? Then, indeed, there could be no gifts and graces in us—no, nor life itself, but *all* must be in Christ Jesus. "I live, yet not I, but Christ lives in me." [10]

On and on she plodded. Surely somewhere these bewildering paths must converge. God, in his infinite wisdom, must have intended that they all say and mean the same thing, that they all lead to the one point toward which she must strive.

She shared these questionings with her visitors—with William and Edward who, while sympathetic listeners, could offer no solution—or with the more learned Mr. Weld and Mr. Eliot, whose proximity made them frequent visitors, and Mr. Shepard, who made the long trip from Newtown several times. The ministers assured her they did not come to entrap her, but sought to know her mind and set her aright. Thus encouraged, she sat hour after hour pouring out her anguished doubts to the men who displayed such great concern for her perplexities.[11]

When March arrived, the ministers of Boston announced their

8. *Antinomianism,* 287, 323; Eccles. 3:18-21.
9. *Antinomianism,* 287; Eccles. 1:18; I Cor. 15:42-44.
10. *Antinomianism,* 328; Gal. 2:30.
11. *Antinomianism,* 289-90.

readiness to deal with Mrs. Hutchinson "in a Church way." Shepard
and Eliot professed they could submit abundant evidence of her
heresies. They offered to collate and classify into a formal ecclesiastical indictment the numerous errors they had heard from her
own lips during these past weeks. This done, Mrs. Hutchinson was
summoned from Roxbury to stand before the church of Boston.[12]

(iii)

The lecture was appointed for ten o'clock on Thursday morning,
two hours earlier than usual in anticipation of a grueling session. At
the end of a hard, dull winter Boston was suddenly taut with excitement. Well before the designated hour, the meetinghouse was
packed with townsfolk and curious outlanders.[13]

The sermon over, Mrs. Hutchinson was admitted to the meetinghouse. Pale and drawn from her long confinement and continuing
illness, she walked unsteadily down the aisle. The congregation
watched her in hushed, expectant concern. There were few among
them whose emotions were not in dazed conflict. The ministers—
all now on hand to defend the pristine integrity of their doctrine
—knew exactly how they felt about the troublesome woman before
them. Over the months their indignation had mounted to such a
pitch of concentrated hatred that it was unlikely that any of them
could now sort out and weigh the element of personal vindictive-
ness underlying their animosity. Except for Cotton, of course, and
who could tell what emotions now warred in his heart. Torn between charity for man and love for God—between genuine affection
for his pupil on the one hand, hurt pride and an urge for self-
justification on the other—he struggled desperately to play the role
that was expected of him.

And so, too, with the congregation—Anne's neighbors and friends
who had cherished her warmth and guidance during these past
years. Some had come to fear that she had willfully deceived them,
but they were still too close to her to entertain that calculated aver-
sion in which the ministers now luxuriated. Others were less sure,
not knowing, in all this, who was right and who was wrong, and
guiltily fearful lest they had abandoned Anne only to secure their
own safety and quiet. There were few on hand who fully agreed
with her. William and his friends were absent, having gone south-

12. *Ibid.*, 218; Winthrop, *Journal*, I, 260.
13. *Antinomianism*, 218.

ward to consult with Roger Williams about a new place of settlement. It was "a good providence of God," Winthrop held, that took them away so that the church might not be diverted from its firm purpose.[14] Of her immediate family, only young Edward and Thomas Savage with their wives were now present.

Mr. Oliver rose to explain Anne's late arrival; "not out of any Contempt or Neglect to the Ordinance, but . . . she is so weake that she conceaves herselfe not fitt nor able to have bine hear soe longe togeather." [15] Winthrop sniffed skeptically: "pretending bodily infirmity," was his impression.[16]

Thomas Leverett, as ruling elder, was charged with the management of the examination. He called Mrs. Hutchinson forth and read off the numerous errors charged against her by the ministers of Newtown and Roxbury. Anne was incensed that Weld, Eliot, and Shepard, contrary to their professions of good faith, had so betrayed the privacy of their conversations. This time she resolved that the procedures should be set aright at the outset.

"By what Rule of the Word," she inquired, "[should] these Elders . . . come to me in private to desire Satisfaction in some poynts, and doe professe in the sight of God that they did not come to Intrap or insnare me, and now . . . would come to bringe it publicly into the Church before they had privately dealt with me?" [17]

Mr. Shepard was testily defensive. "I desire to ask this . . . of Mrs. Hutchinson: whether she accuse any of us, or no, of such a Breach of Rule?"

Anne hastily assured him that she did not; she had only asked a question. Shepard offered to refresh her memory. On the occasion of his last visit, he had borne witness against her erroneous opinions and had then dealt roundly with her. But, Anne protested, she had merely put these views forward by way of inquiry; they were not her opinions.

"I would have this Congregation know," Shepard pronounced, "that the vilest Errors that was ever brought into the Church was brought in by way of Questions." [18]

Her point of privilege swept aside, Anne was told to answer the objections brought against her. The examination which followed was a dismaying horror: for nine hours the interrogation and dis-

14. Winthrop, *Journal*, I, 264.
15. *Antinomianism*, 286.
16. *Ibid.*, 218.
17. *Ibid.*, 288-89.
18. *Ibid.*, 289-90.

putation wore on, plunging farther and farther into the murky depths of scriptural dialectic. Text was matched for text; for every citation offered another was produced to qualify or contradict it. Her black-capped judges—rigidly sure of themselves, stonily incapable of suffering her doubts or deviation—labored strenuously to defend the precarious structure of their faith. The unhappy victim, distraught and bewildered, knowing far too much for her own peace of mind, yet knew not a fraction enough to resolve her perplexity. On and on she led them through a trackless mire of text without end or beginning.

Of all the articles offered against her, only four were touched upon that day, and all of these treated of resurrection and immortality. The initial exchange between Anne and her teacher amply suggests the continuing tenor of the debate.

"Your first opinion layd to your charge," Cotton led off, "is *That the souls of all Men by nature are mortall and die* like Beastes, and for that you alledge Eccl[esiastes] 3:18-21." [19]

Ecclesiastes had indeed been baffling to Mrs. Hutchinson. "I desire that place might be answered," she pleaded, "the Spirit that God gives returns."

"That place speaketh that the spirit ascends upwards, soe Eccles. 12:7," Cotton assured her. "Mans spirit doth not returne to Dust as mans body doth but to God. The soul of man is immortall." [20]

But Anne had other texts which did not jibe with this. "Every man consists of Soul and Body," she dilated. "Now *Adam dies not except his soul and Body dye,* and in Heb: 4, the word is lively in Operation, and devides between *soule* and Spirit. So," she concluded, "the Spirit *that God gives man, returnes to God indeed.* . . . And That is the spirit Eccles[iastes] speakes of, and not of the Soule."

The ministers stared at her in speechless incredulity. The astonished Cotton hastened to correct her. "If you hould that Adams Soule and body dyes and was not redeemed or restored by Ch[rist] Je[sus], it will overthrough our Redemption . . . Eccles. proveth that the soule is the Gift of God and that it hath no Relation to such fadinge and destroyinge matter as his Body was made of. . . . Thear is a soule that is immortal Mat[thew] 10:28, and our nature shall goe into heaven but not our corrupt Nature." [21]

19. *Ibid.*, 290.
20. *Ibid.*, 290-91.
21. *Ibid.*, 291-92.

"Than you have both a Soule and a Spirit that shall be saved," Anne offered in dismay. "I desire you to answer that in 1 Thess[alonians] 5:23, Your [w]hole *Spirit Soule and Body,* and that in Psalms he hath redeemed his soul from hell?"

"Sister," Cotton implored, "doe not shut your Eyes agaynst the Truth. All thease places prove that the soule is Immortall."

If, instead of quoting Scripture, Anne had challenged her judges to define body, soul, spirit, and resurrection in terms of Mary Dyer's monstrous birth, how clear would their answers have been? For here indeed had been a creature, which had had life, a body which had been "sown." But a soul? And a body which would be resurrected? What confutation of doctrine lay here, and why should she not doubt?

But at no time did she particularize her doubts in terms of her human experience. The scriptural quotations flew back and forth like shuttlecocks. Her doubts seemed to be hardening into conviction. *The Spirit is immortall indeed, but prove that the Soule is:* for that place in Mathew which you bringe of Casting the soul into hell, is ment of the Spirit."

"Thease are principles of christian Fayth," Cotton despairingly insisted. "The Spirit is sometimes put for the Contience [conscience], and for the Giftes of the Spirit that fitts the soule for Gods Service."

Anne was unconvinced. "The ho[ly] Ghost makes this Distinction between the soule and Body and not I."

So the disputation moved, in maddening, ever-narrowing circles. At last Mr. Davenport intervened. Briefly and simply he stated the point that Cotton and Wilson had labored over for the past hour. *A soule may be Immortall and not miserable.* Now the Curse is this, that Misery is annexed to Immortalitie." [22]

Mrs. Hutchinson leaned forward. This seemed somewhat to the point. Mr. Davenport continued, "Immortalitie was a Gift to the Spirit in thear very Beinge: the *soule cannot have Imortalitie in itself but from God from whom it hath its beinge.*" This delicate distinction brought immediate response from Anne. Her confusion had been in the varying uses of the word "soul" to indicate either *esse* or *animus* according to the context. For some reason Davenport seemed to have clarified the whole problem—for the moment.

"*I thanke the Lord I have light,* and see more Light by a greate deale by Mr. Damphords opening of it."

22. *Ibid.,* 292, 297.

Winthrop wondered. It seemed to him that "shee was convinced before, but she could not give the honour of it to her owne Pastor or teacher, ... whom she had so much slighted." [23]

But Anne, certain they would all now understand one another, reaffirmed her comprehension, "Soe thear was *my Mistake. I tooke* [the word] *soule* [to mean] *Life.*" [24]

Was she now ready to concede her error on these points, it was asked.

"I doe not acknowledge it to be an Error," she affirmed, "but a Mistake. I *doe acknowledge my Expression to be Ironious [erroneous], but my Judgment was not Ironious [erroneous],* for I held befor as you did but could not express it soe."

It was hardly surprising that she "could not express it soe"—but her reasoning thus far failed to suggest that her judgment was at one with her inquisitors, nor did that which followed give them any greater cause for self-congratulation on this score.

The discussion turned to resurrection. Anne directed their attention to the fifteenth chapter of I Corinthians, "for I doe quest[ion] whether the same Body that dies, shall rise agayne." Then were there deaths and bodies and spirits assayed in bewildering multiplicity? Out of this occult gallimaufry, Mr. Bulkley plucked an inference "of the earth, earthy," which brought the debate crashingly down to a level of human comprehension.

"I desire to know of Mrs. Hutchinson," he barked, "whether you do hold that foule, groce, filthye and abbominable Opinion held by Familists, *of the Communitie of Woemen?*"

This gave them pause. Here was indeed matter for rumination. But Anne brushed it distastefully aside. "I hould it not."

The idea intrigued Mr. Davenport: "Mr. Buckley's quest[ion] ... is a right principle, for if the Resurrection be past than Marriage is past: ... *than if thear be any Union betwene man and woman, it is not by Marriage but in a Way of Communitie.*"

"If any such practice or conclusion be drawn from it, than I must leave it, *for I abhor that Practice,*" Anne protested.[25]

Davenport gave up and turned back to the hypostatic congestion Anne had propounded. "*You tell us of a new Body, and of 2 bodies, that is three,*" he added up. "*Now which of these Bodies do you hould shall rise agayne?*"

23. *Ibid.*, 297, 222-23.
24. *Ibid.*, 298.
25. *Ibid.*, 299-302.

Eliot became uneasy about the effect on the laity of such discussion. "We thinke it is very dangerous to dispute this Question soe longe in this Congregation." [26]

But still Mrs. Hutchinson pursued the point until at last Davenport impatiently broke in. "Thease are Opinions that cannot be borne. Thay shake the very foundation of our fayth and tends to the Overthrough of all Religion. Thay are not slight [but] matters of greate Wayte and Consequence." [27]

It had grown dark within the meetinghouse. Though only four questions had been touched on, the disputants were weary from talk that always came back to where it had started. Wilson seized on the interruption to bring matters resolutely to a head. "If the Church be satisfied with the Arguments propounded," he announced to the congregation, "that they are convinced in thear judgments that thease are Errors, *let them expres it by thear usuall sign of houldinge up thear Hands.*"

Edward Hutchinson interceded. Would the elders advise him whether he might assent when it was plain that his mother was not yet convinced one way or the other.

"You are not to be led by naturall affection," Mr. Davenport instructed him. "The Quest[ion] was not whether the Arguments were waytie enough to convince your Mother, but whether you have Light enough to satisfie your Contience [conscience] that they are Errors."

Wilson again put the question: "*If the church . . . conceave we ought to proceed to Admonition,* we will take thear Silence for Consent: *if any be otherwise minded, thay may express themselves.*" [28]

In the face of that silent crowd and the menacing elders, it took great courage to speak. Now Thomas Savage rose and redeemed his earlier recantation. "I am not yet satisfied," he announced. There was no rule in Scripture for the admonition of a member who had only sought light on matters uncertain to her. "*I cannot consent that the church should proceed yet to admonish her for this.*"

Lieutenant Gibbon was emboldened by this protest to suggest that the church might delay until God should bring Mrs. Hutchinson to see her error. This request seemed not unreasonable. Mrs.

26. *Ibid.*, 303.
27. *Ibid.*, 304.
28. *Ibid.*, 304-5, 306.

Hutchinson had raised these issues, not in dogmatic certitude, but by way of doubt and inquiry. But the ministers saw better than the laymen that Christian eschatology could not bear this line of reconstructive scrutiny. As Eliot had quite properly suggested, protraction of the debate could only serve to confuse the hearers.

The ministers may have also observed—though this seems less likely—that the structure of Mrs. Hutchinson's doubt was scarcely conducive to an orthodox resolution. She had raised questions which, though unresolved in her own mind, could eventually unsettle her belief in the orthodox eschatology. That these new notions corresponded to her own preconceptions on union and grace would only make their hold on her the stronger. But even more significantly, she had developed a strong emotional resistance to the tutelage of the Massachusetts clergy. She had established herself as their peer in the eyes of the community and by so doing had created a self-image that she could not easily surrender. Had Anne been a weaker woman, she might have been impelled, by fears for her own safety, to break down and recant. She came very near to doing just that. But in the last analysis she could not concede that she was really and wholly wrong and that the ministers were unimpeachably right. This inability to unlearn the questions she had asked was to prove her undoing.

The ministers had been confounded by the objections of her sons and Lieutenant Gibbon. If the church were to act on this matter, it must do so of one accord and that now seemed impossible. They were rescued from their quandary by the priggish perspicacity of young John Oliver. Recantation had not soured in *his* bosom! Inasmuch as the church must speak with one voice, was it not meet, he suggested, "to lay thease two Bretheren under an Admonition with thear mother?"

This ingenious expedient for the attainment of unanimity met Mr. Wilson's hearty approval. "I think you speake very well!" he applauded, "it is very meete!"

Once again the question was propounded. Lieutenant Gibbon heard and understood and "the whole Church by thear Silence, Consented to the Motion." [29]

"As one whose Wordes . . . may be of more Respect, and sinke deeper," Mr. Cotton was requested to deliver the admonition. He was left to decide, "as God should incline his hart," whether the sons should be admonished as well. Divine or other, some force

29. *Ibid.*, 306, 310.

brusquely inclined him that way, for he launched immediately into a slashing assault on the misguided loyalty which had prompted those young men like "*vipers, to eate through the very bowells of* ... [*their*] *Mother.*" [30] In the cause of God, he instructed, they must disavow both mother and father. And the "Fathers of the Commonwealth?" Anne may well have bitterly reflected.

Turning to the women of the congregation, Cotton counseled them to cherish whatever good they may have gained from Mrs. Hutchinson, "but," he warned sharply, "if you have drunke in with this good any Evell or Poyson, make speed to vomit it up agayne and to repent of it and to take [care] you doe not harden her in her Way by pittyinge of her."

Cotton then faced the exhausted woman who stood before him. It was to this point that the events of recent years had ineluctably led. Now these two sensitive and dedicated individuals who had journeyed so long in seeming harmony found themselves in fateful opposition. "And now, Sister," he quietly commenced, "let me address myselfe to you. The Lord put fitt Words into my Mouth, and carry them home to your Soule." He had not forgotten nor undervalued her usefulness in the community. "I would speake it to Gods Glory [that] you have bine an Instrument of doing some good amongst us. . . . he hath given you a sharp apprehension, a ready utterance and abilitie to exprese yourselfe in the Cause of God." [31] But her unsound tenets outweighed all the good she had done. She had endangered the spiritual welfare of the community and led many weak souls astray with her teachings. Especially did he fear the consequences of her recent reflections on resurrection.

"You cannot Evade the Argument . . . that filthie Sinne of the *Communitie of Woemen;* and all promiscuous and filthie cominge togeather of men and Woemen without Distinction or Relation of Marriage, will necessarily follow. . . . Though I have not herd, nayther do I thinke you have bine unfaythfull to your Husband in his Marriage Covenant, *yet that will follow upon it.*"

Although this was a gratuitous deduction, Cotton saw, as a layman could not, the precarious balance in which the doctrinal structure was poised. "*Nay though you should not hould thease Things positively,* yet if you doe but make a Question of them, and propound them as a doubt for satisfaction, yet others that hear of it will conclude them positively.

30. *Ibid.*, 310, 312.
31. *Ibid.*, 313.

"*Therefor*," he solemnly intoned, "*I doe Admonish you, and alsoe charge you in the name of Ch[rist] Je[sus], in whose place I stand* ... that you would sadly consider the just hand of God agaynst you, *the great hurt you have done to the Churches, the great Dishonour you have brought to Je[sus] Ch[rist],* and the Evell that you have done to many a poore soule." [32]

Anne strove weakly to defend herself. Midway in the admonition she had interrupted Cotton. "All that I would say is this," she ventured, "that *I did not hould any of thease Thinges before my Imprisonment.*" [33]

Shepard was shocked by this assertion and eyed her indignantly. When Cotton had come to an end, he sprang to his feet to protest "that she shuld thus Impudently affirme soe horrible an Untruth and falsehood, in the midst of such a solemn Ordinance." [34] She had herself said, he reminded her, that had he spoken to her before her restraint, she could have told him many other things.

But it was now eight o'clock and cold and dark within the meetinghouse, so this accusation was passed over in silence. Mrs. Hutchinson was instructed to return on the next lecture day, and the congregation rose stiffly from their hard benches and made their way out into the night. Although many professed to observe "the special presence of God's spirit," some may have searched earnestly and found it not.[35]

(iv)

On Thursday, the twenty-second of March, Mrs. Hutchinson was again summoned to the meetinghouse. With the Court's permission, she had spent the intervening week at Mr. Cotton's home. Perhaps Cotton had arranged this sojourn in the hope of restoring his errant pupil. Conditions seemed ripe for such a recovery. Her views, however irregular, apparently had not crystallized, and could yet be rectified, he may have thought. Also, Mr. Davenport was then residing with Cotton, and perhaps he could sway her mind. All week long these reverend gentlemen labored with their charge, and at last were prepared to announce their victory over the forces of evil. Anne had seen the error of her course, and under

32. *Ibid.*, 314, 315.
33. *Ibid.*, 314.
34. *Ibid.*, 317.
35. Winthrop, *Journal*, I, 261.

their supervision she had written out a formal recantation of all the unsound opinions that were objected against her.[36]

Now, in the meetinghouse, Anne rose and in a subdued voice, read her recantation to the congregation. To most of those present, it must have seemed that the ministers had at last gained all they sought. To make this proud, strong-minded woman submit to the bitter humiliation of a public confession was surely the most that any inquisitor could decently request. But Mr. Wilson was not yet through. He had not forgotten Anne's final words at the last session, and he undertook to make her answer for them now. She had professed that she held none of these errors before her imprisonment. Mr. Shepard, however, had alleged the contrary. What might she say to that?

Anne humbly confessed that she had spoken many things "rashly and unadvisedly" at her civil trial, but she had not then been prompted by these new errors. "If Mr. Shepard doth conceave that I had any of these Thinges in my Minde, than he is deceaved." She spoke so weakly that Cotton was obliged to repeat the substance of her statement to the congregation.[37]

But Shepard did not need to hear a second time. It was an aspersion on his veracity which he felt no need to tolerate. "If this day whan Mrs. Hutchinson should take Shame and Confusion to herselfe for her groce and damnable Errors, she shall cast Shame upon others and say thay are mistaken, and to turne of[f] many of those groce Errors with soe slight an Answer as *your Mistake*, I fear it doth not stand with true Repentance."

As Shepard resumed his seat, quivering with ill-suppressed rage, Mr. Eliot rose to recall that Mrs. Hutchinson had made similar claims to him. Cotton, too, reflected uneasily. "Sister," he said, turning to her, "Was thear not a Time, whan once you did hould that thear was *no distinct graces inherent in us, but all was in Ch[rist] Je[sus]*?" [38]

"*I did mistake the word Inherent*," Anne confessed.

"She did not only deny the word inherent," Shepard snapped, "but denied the very Thinge itselfe."

Anne was distraught in the face of this renewed assault, and sought desperately to justify herself. "*I confes my Expressione was that way, but never my Judgment.*"

36. *Colony Records*, I, 225; *Antinomianism*, 225.
37. *Antinomianism*, 321.
38. *Ibid.*, 322-23.

Cotton strove to set the issues straight: "Thear are 2 thinges to be clerd, 1. what you doe now hould, 2[nd]ly what you did hould?"

Anne clung to her position. "My Judgment is not altered though my Expression alters."

"I fear thease are no new Thinges," Mr. Symmes querulously protested, "but she hath ayntientlye [anciently] held them." [39]

Now Mr. Dudley joined the fray. He was here only as a visitor, but one who entertained more than a casual curiosity about the present case. "Mrs. Hutchinsons Repentance is only for Opinions held since her Imprisonment," he caustically observed. "I think her Repentance will be worse than her Errors . . . and for her forme of Recantation," with an ominous sidelong glance at Cotton, "whether she had any helpe in it I know not and will not now Inquire to, but sure *her Repentance is not in her Countenance.*"

Dudley's brusque intrusion was a clarion call to general on-slaught. All restraint and charity was thrown to the winds as the clacking tongues flailed her from every quarter. Anne sat speech-lessly aghast at their vituperation.

Now could Wilson vent his full spleen for the humiliation he had suffered at her hands: "[The root of] your errors . . . is the *slightinge of Gods faythfull Ministers and contemninge and cryinge down them as Nobodies.*"

"I believe, that she hath vilde [vile] Thoughts of us," Hugh Peter stormed, "and thinkes us to be nothinge but a company of Jewes." [40]

"You have not only to deale with a Woman this day . . . that never had any trew Grace in her hart. . . . Yea, this day she hath shewed herselfe to be a Notorius Imposter!"—this from the "sweet . . . soul-ravishing" Shepard.[41]

Now Wilson saw the way and the light. "I cannot but reverence and adore the wise hand of God. . . in leavinge *our sister to pride and Lyinge.*"

"Yes," Eliot joined, "it is a wonderfull Wisdom of God . . . to let her fall into such Lies, as she hath done this day."

"Consider how we cane . . . longer suffer her," Wilson breathlessly resumed, "to goe on still in seducinge to seduce, and in deacevinge to deaceve, and in lyinge to lye!" [42]

Cotton too saw the light and perceived how he might be spared from delivering the final blow. "The matter is now translated, the

39. *Ibid.*, 323, 324.
40. *Ibid.*, 324, 326, 323.
41. *Ibid.*, 329.
42. *Ibid.*, 331, 332.

last day she was delt with in poynt of Doctrine, now she is delt with in poynt of practise, and soe," he breathed with relief, "it belongs to the Pastors Office to instruct and . . . correct in Righteousness. . . . I thinke we are bound upon this Ground to remove her from us . . . seeinge she doth prevaricate in her Words."

The ministers had moved with appalling swiftness toward excommunication and now some of the congregation sought to stay them.

"How [may] the Church . . . proceed to *Excommunication*," one member interceded, "whan the Scripture saythe he that confesseth and forsaketh sine shall have Mercy?" Another begged that she have time to consider. "In Distraction . . . she cannot recollect her Thoughts." [43]

But the clergy would not be stayed. The victim had delivered herself up into their hands and they now saw the way to be rid of her.

"This is not for poynt of Doctrine, wherin we must suffer her with patience," Cotton informed the congregation, "but we now deal with her in poynt of fact or practice, as the makinge and houldinge of a Lye."

"Not to *drop* a Lye," Shepard spat, "but to *make* a Lye and *mayntayne* a Lye . . . in the sight of God."

Mr. Leverett reminded them that the Scripture called for a second admonition before proceeding to excommunication. Dudley brushed this objection peremptorily aside: "I would answer this to Mr. Leverett . . . Mrs. Hutchinson hath bine delt [with] and admonished, not once, or twice nor thrice, but many Times, by privat Bretheren and by Elders . . . and by her owne Church." [44]

Wilson addressed the congregation: "The Church consentinge to it we will proced to excommunication." He paused. There was no sound nor movement as all waited hopefully or fearfully. Wilson turned to Mrs. Hutchinson.

"Forasmuch as you, Mrs. Hutchinson, have highly transgressed and offended . . . and *troubled the Church with your Errors* and have drawen away many a poor soule, and have *upheld your Revelations;* and forasmuch as *you have made a Lye.* . . . Therefor in the name of our Lord Je[sus] Ch[rist] . . . *I doe cast you out* and . . . *deliver you up to Sathan* . . . and account you from this time forth to be a Hethen and a Publican . . . *I command you* in the name of

43. *Ibid.*, 332-33, 334.
44. *Ibid.*, 335. My italics.

Ch[rist] Je[sus] and of this Church *as a Leper to withdraw your selfe out of the Congregation.*"[45]

Anne Hutchinson, having heard the words, sat momentarily listening to the silence as they died away. She had tried conflict, argument, persuasion. When all else had failed, she had tried to bend the pride of her spirit in humility. But she had not found it in her to quench that final spark of pride and self-esteem. Clearly, now it was God's will that, in spite of all, she must go forth! The blow had struck, and she still lived and breathed. In the silence she could hear the cords of her bondage snap and fall away. There was nothing left to fear that man could do to her.[46] She turned to face the congregation and, with head erect, walked down the aisle.

They sat and watched her pass. Saint? Devil? Prophetess? Or merely a stubborn woman? As she advanced, Mary Dyer, her comely face aglow with love and loyalty, rose from her seat, and slipping her arm in Anne's walked with her.[47] A man standing by the door broke the silence as the women passed, "The Lord sanctifie this unto you."

"The Lord judgeth not as man judgeth," Anne calmly answered. "Better to be cast out of the Church than to deny Christ."[48]

She stepped out into the pale sunlight of early spring. The warm smell of thawing earth mingled with the salt air of the harbor. She breathed deeply of the free air.

(v)

On March 28, 1638, Anne Hutchinson turned toward the new home her husband was making in Rhode Island. But even there she could not elude the fascinated gaze of those who had so recently been plucked from her spell. Shortly before Anne's departure, word of Mary Dyer's monstrous birth had leaked out and was fastened on as a sign of heavenly displeasure with the erronists. Now it was Anne's turn to suffer the same obloquy. After rejoining her husband she became pregnant of a "menopausal baby" which promptly aborted into a hydatidiform mole. The mole or mass, following the typical pattern for such growths, developed rapidly and was expelled with great difficulty and loss of blood in July or

45. *Ibid.*, 336.
46. Winthrop, *Journal*, I, 264.
47. *Ibid.*, 268.
48. *Antinomianism*, 228.

early August.[49] Reports of this doleful event were pored over by the clergy and magistrates of Massachusetts and solemnly pronounced a conclusive evidence of providential justice, confirming the wisdom of their own course.

Despite this abuse and occasional efforts made by her prosecutors to communicate their continuing displeasure, Mrs. Hutchinson found freedom for a few years to teach her vaguely mystical doctrines. But, though there was none to restrain her, there were many to disagree, and before long the little settlement in Narragansett Bay was the scene of fresh theological conflict. In 1642, when her devoted William died, Anne took her six youngest children and moved to a lonely spot on Long Island Sound within Dutch territory. This was to be her last home. She was now alone with only her children about her and but two neighbors for miles around. For ten years she had been moving steadily toward this final isolation. Gregarious and affectionate though she was, her efforts to gain social approval seem destined to promote controversy and alienation. Time and again she had withdrawn from settled communities when she could not find peaceful acceptance of her views. From Alford to Boston to Rhode Island she had at last come to the lonely concord of silence at "Anne's Hoeck" on Pelham Bay. There, in the late summer of 1643, she and five of her children were ruthlessly tomahawked by a band of Indians vengefully intent on clearing all white settlers from their hunting ground.

So Anne Hutchinson's tortuous path came to an end, but where she had been, there remained signs of her passing.

49. A minute description of Mrs. Hutchinson's delivery written by Dr. John Clarke, the attending physician, indicates that she had expelled an hydatidiform mole. (Dr. Clarke's description is reprinted in Appendix VII.) This information, weighed in conjunction with other available details of her medical history, suggests that Mrs. Hutchinson's behavior during this crucial period can be explained largely in terms of menopausal symptoms. For a diagnosis along these lines by Paul A. Younge, M.D., Assistant Clinical Professor, Department of Gynecology, Harvard Medical School and Associate Chief Surgeon, Free Hospital for Women, Brookline, Massachusetts, see Appendix VII; the possibility that this might be the correct diagnosis was first suggested to me by Dr. Robert Freeman of Highland Park, New Jersey. Some months after this chapter was written I received additional confirmation in all particulars from an article on "New England's First Recorded Hydatidiform Mole" in The New England Journal of Medicine, 260 (1959), 544-45, written by Margaret V. Richardson, Senior Research Assistant, Department of Pathology, Harvard Medical School, and Arthur T. Hertig, M.D., Shattuck Professor of Pathological Anatomy and Head, Department of Pathology, Harvard Medical School.

XVII

"Vile Sectaries"

The Social Pattern of Religious Protest

(i)

THE notion that an historical event may be, to paraphrase Emerson, "the lengthened shadow of a man" has long since been abandoned as a workable hypothesis by historians if, indeed, it was ever seriously accepted by them. But some historical subjects continue to be treated substantially as though this concept remained relevant. One such event is the so-called Antinomian Controversy in the Massachusetts Bay Colony.

In an episode of this nature it is perhaps inevitable that interest should focus primarily on the dynamic personality of the leader. Certainly, Mrs. Hutchinson's complex personality and doctrines demand the closest attention. But such concentration does little to explain the totality of the event and may obscure much of its essential meaning. Most studies of the Antinomian Controversy make no effort to discuss the nature of Mrs. Hutchinson's following beyond the simple assumption that it comprised almost all the members of the Boston congregation plus a few people from neighboring towns. Their backgrounds and stations in life are not analyzed, the degrees of their enthusiasm or complicity are not examined, and their motivations are left unexplored.

Why should recondite doctrines, so widely at variance with accepted Puritan beliefs, have suddenly achieved such immoderate popularity? If, as Winthrop claims, few understood the issues involved, is it unreasonable to suppose that there may have been other, nonreligious motives, for supporting the insurgent move-

249

ment? Why did not the Hutchinsonian tenets, which met with such acclaim in Boston, spread with equal effect into other parts of the colony where conditions were presumably similar? Were there reasons other than religious that led the outlying settlements to take so vigorous a stand against the Antinomian dissenters?

This is not to suggest that Mrs. Hutchinson's disciples were prompted to support her solely or even primarily in expectation of fulfilling their own private and ulterior motives. But with very rare exceptions, individuals who become involved in social movements do so because the ideology and goals of that movement support their own personal or social values. For better or worse, the tools of motivational research were not on hand in 1636, and it is now obviously impossible to state precisely what factors, subjective or external, prompted Mrs. Hutchinson's followers to extend their allegiance. Nor is it possible to determine in every instance the identity of all of her followers. But there is, nonetheless, sufficient data to identify most of her supporters and provide a general understanding of the kind of people they were, their needs and interests, and the degrees of their enthusiasm for Mrs. Hutchinson's cause, all of which may suggest some of their motivations.

(ii)

If ever there were a society, large or small, that uniformly fulfilled the needs of its members, it is not a matter of current record.[1] At all times and in all places, there are isolated individuals who, for widely varied reasons, chafe under the controls of their society. Usually these are regarded as cranks and are tolerated or curbed according to the degree of their dissent and the flexibility of the society. But most societies also undergo periods of widespread unrest in which individual manifestations of dissatisfaction coalesce into a more or less systematic collective endeavor to introduce appropriate changes in thought, behavior, or social relationships. The present problem is chiefly to determine why such social unrest should occur.

Essential in the cohesion of any society are the cultural norms that have proved functional and are generally accepted and trans-

1. The substance of the section which follows is drawn primarily from Hadley Cantril, *The Psychology of Social Movements* (New York, 1941), Part I; C. Wendell King, *Social Movements in the United States* (New York, 1956), *passim;* and Norman F. Washburne, *Interpreting Social Change in America* (New York, 1954), chap. 3.

mitted from generation to generation. In due course, some of these norms are rendered more explicit and provided sanctions through institutionalization. Others continue to be enforced through the exertion of more informal social pressures. The consistency of the normative pattern and the degree of its acceptance depend largely upon the complexity and scope of the society. Primitive and folk cultures enjoy normative patterns that are consistent and whole, almost universally accepted, and subject only to the most imperceptibly gradual change. "For most questions there are unequivocal answers, and the cultural universals, the norms and values to which most adults in the society subscribe, are many and powerful." [2]

In more complex and heterogeneous societies, there are fewer universal values on which everyone will agree. Such a society is comprised of a multiplicity of competing or uneasily reconciled interest groups and subcultures. Many of the values and ideals that an individual derives from the subgroup or groups of which he is a member may well be disparaged or opposed by other subgroups. Many of the universal norms that all groups accept may be so general and inexact as to be subject to the most equivocal interpretation and may conceivably conflict with other equally ambiguous norms. But ordinarily the various subgroups with their specialized needs and values are reconciled to each other in a more or less stable equilibrium that is sustained by acceptance of the universal norms of the whole society.

Certain conditions within a society appear to be commonly associated with expressions of social discontent, and at least two of them are characteristic of complex societies. First, cultural confusion, a widespread lack of agreement on standards and the interpretation of standards within a community, may be highly conducive to general unrest. When the cultural norms are weak or ambiguous, when certain norms have become dysfunctional without being abandoned, or when new and strange conditions have emerged for which there are as yet no adequately defined norms, there is large scope for individual dissatisfaction and frustration. Individuals may often find themselves faced by problems which offer "alternative solutions with undefined or ill-defined consequences." [3]

Social heterogeneity is a second factor underlying social discon-

2. King, *Social Movements,* 14.
3. *Ibid.*

tent. Many of the cultural ambiguities and contradictions just noted may have their inception in the internal divisions of the society. When differing groups entertain competitive needs and interests, each group is predisposed to interpret the dominant norms according to its own standards. Conflicting interpretation of norms and clashes of interest will inevitably produce conflicts for power in order that group interests may prevail. The more numerous and varied the subgroups, the more thinly the universals are spread and the more ambiguously they are stated in hope of embracing all and antagonizing none.

Third, there is the vital factor of individual discontents. It is essential to the psychological security of a human being that the framework of events and relations in which he is implicated should have meaning for him; in the final analysis, it should have such meaning as will confirm the individual's sense of his own worth—an estimate, which is, of course, largely derived from the value system of his particular society. The weak and diffuse cultural integration of complex societies creates a situation in which large numbers of people have only a confused understanding of their roles and goals and relationships, and inadequate data for solving some of the problems which confront them. Such weak cultural integration can impinge upon the individual in a variety of ways. Often the values that a man has gained from his own subgroup may be disparaged or opposed by members of other subgroups. Or it may be that the individual feels his status in the society is inadequately recognized by other individuals or subgroups.

Whatever their origins, the individual's frustrations will induce in him a strong desire for meaning, for a consistent and congenial interpretation of the situations he encounters—consistent, that is, from the point of view of his own needs. Under such conditions the individual is more than ordinarily susceptible to suggestion and becomes grist for the mill of the appropriate social reformer. Individuals do not often support social movements for altruistic or intellectual reasons alone; they are generally "seeking answers they do not have, reassurance that the answers they have are right or ways of implementing the answers of whose rightness they are convinced." [4] The degree of their receptivity will depend on the extent to which they lack an adequate frame of reference and the particular circumstances that intensify their desire for meaning. More often than not, they will fail to recognize the real reasons

4. *Ibid.,* 17.

for their disaffection, and so will be the more inclined to support a social movement which provides a congenial answer to their dilemma. A social movement whose leaders hope to attract any considerable following must take care, in the definition of ideology and goals, not to violate those aspects of the total cultural framework that prospective supporters may regard as friendly or neutral to their interests.

The participants in a social movement may be viewed from various sociological perspectives. They may, for example, be seen as aligned along an "acceptance-rejection spectrum" indicating the degree of their sympathy and involvement in the movement. Each individual's position can then be examined in terms of a multiplicity of alienative or adaptive factors; for example, hardships suffered, or advantages enjoyed, personality organization which inhibits or enhances social adaptation, and the lack or presence of roots in the society.

It is also possible to examine the participants in terms of their orientation toward the proclaimed objectives of the movement. Most people who join social movements are "goal-oriented"; that is, they assume that the values of the movement coincide with their own and that they will benefit from the changes which the movement seeks to effect. Of course, even the goal-oriented may be widely dispersed along the "acceptance-rejection spectrum"; some may be fanatical in their dedication and others may entertain very strong reservations. Distinguished from the "goal-oriented" are those whom we may term "utilitarian." Their motivation is largely opportunistic in that they seek immediate benefits which are not related to the professed goals of the movement but which are implicitly attainable through the movement's operations. A third and much smaller group is "altruistic" in its motivation. They are idealistically dedicated to the attainment of the movement's goals but are not prompted to participate by the same personal needs as goal oriented members and seek no material rewards for themselves.

Social movements tend to expand as a rolling snowball gathers progressively larger increments of snow with each revolution. Numbers speak loudly to those on the fringe and often arouse an almost indefinable urge to go along with the crowd. A going and growing concern is a great needler of inertia and a potent persuader of the uncertain. Doubtless many people were swept up in the tide of the Antinomian movement simply because that was the prevailing opinion.

One additional consideration must be advanced in any discussion of the Antinomian Controversy. The seventeenth century was peculiarly a "religious age." Religion had long been that cultural trait to which European civilization was most deeply committed. It was the matrix in which all other cultural values were cast, the mold which gave them form and coherence. At this juncture the commitment to religion was doubly intense because the religious interpretation of life's problems was being challenged by rival, secular modes of understanding. The Protestant Reformation had been, in an important sense, a reaction against the secularizing influence of the Renaissance, and the Puritan movement was, itself, a desperate rearguard action in defense of the threatened ideal. But the struggle was becoming increasingly confused, since the "progressive" secularizing forces often defined their objectives in religious terms, while the "conservative" religious forces were quite unconsciously encouraging secular values and objectives.

The value system of those Englishmen who had come to America in the 1630's was constructed on a religious base. Their religious views provided an explanation and a rule for all aspects of life; their personal and social goals and behavior were defined in religious terms. Indeed, so intimate and organic was the relationship between the secular and religious aspects of life that a duality was not conceded. Their secular needs and interests were, of course, no less real and pressing than our own, but they were viewed as aspects of a totality that was explicable only in theological terms. For the Puritan the term "nonreligious" was meaningless. Consequently, any social movement directed at alteration of the prevailing normative pattern would impinge directly upon the theological assumptions which gave that pattern its form and meaning. Indeed, such a movement must be concerned basically with the religious tenets that supported the norms in question. The problem of women's dress, prices, the King's ensign, and the suffrage were all explored as religious problems and resolved in religious terms. So too with the Hutchinsonians. Their movement was essentially religious and directed toward the modification of certain theological tenets. Although this preoccupation with religious symbols should not obscure the underlying secular dimension of their concern, it should be remembered that the religious dimension was substantive and controlling.

The insurrectionary bent of the Hutchinsonians derived in no small measure from the inherent Jacobinism of Protestant theology.

When Luther had effectively repudiated the Papal claim to a monopoly over the channels of divine grace, he had made it impossible for any other church to set up the same claim and sustain it for any length of time. Thereafter, scarcely was a denomination freshly established before a process of amoebic replication brought forth another to challenge the pretensions of the parent body. Though good Protestants had tried to constrain this revolutionary dynamic, Protestantism proved irrepressibly particularistic and anti-authoritarian. This propensity had not originated with Luther: he had inhaled it in the very air he breathed. The emergent democracy of preceding centuries had communicated itself to the Protestant pioneers who, in their need, had adopted the sentiment and clothed it in moral and intellectual respectability. Great was their dismay to see it so soon turned against themselves.

For a century all Europe had been convulsed in little revolts and large, each occasioned by an inextricable complex of religious and secular grievances. Now the fever was upon England: scratch an Englishman in these days, and you might well find a revolutionary. A goodly number of insurgents had already made their way to New England's shore, some to protect the revolution they had already wrought, others bearing the seed of revolt yet to come. Small wonder then that John Winthrop's revolt against Pope Laud should be so promptly translated into Roger Williams's and Anne Hutchinson's revolt against Pope Winthrop.

(iii)

In 1636 and 1637 the population structure of the Bay Colony was strikingly homogeneous in several respects. There were no racial distinctions whatsoever; at this early period the whole population was of English stock. Regional differentiation—that is, with respect to their origins—was relatively slight. There is evidence that the great bulk of the population was drawn from east-central and southeast England.[5] The counties of Suffolk, Essex, Norfolk, and London, in that order, appear to have contributed the greatest numbers. The population structure of Boston seems to have followed the same pattern, except that relatively few people from Norfolk settled in the town, and a much higher percentage of Lincolnshiremen and Londoners settled there than elsewhere. One list

5. Charles Edward Banks, *Topographical Dictionary of English Emigrants to New England, 1620-1650* (Philadelphia, 1937), map opposite xiii.

indicates that over a third of all the Londoners and nearly half of all the Lincolnshiremen took up residence in Boston, the remainder being distributed more thinly throughout the other towns. Members of both these regional groups played a significant part in the Antinomian Controversy.

No one could protest that the normative pattern of the Bay Colony was weak, vague, or ambiguous. The behavioral norms of the community were essentially those of southeastern England, but refined and narrowed according to the more rigorous Puritan standards. Standards of behavior were comprehensive, precisely stated, strenuously observed, and supported with firm sanctions, both civil and religious. They may have been widely disliked, but they were generally respected. Although there were doubtless many minor infractions of discipline and violations of the more petty aspects of the Puritan code, the record of the General Court reveals no extraordinary amount of criminal activity nor serious disturbance of the public order prior to 1637. This was, on the whole, an orderly and law-abiding community, even according to its own narrowly prescriptive definition.

However, despite this apparent homogeneity there were significant distinctions within the colony which divided privileged from unprivileged elements, leaving sore spots capable of eruption under adequate provocation. A major point of distinction pertains to church membership and enfranchisement. The total population of the colony in 1637 and 1638 was approximately eight thousand,[6] about one fifth of whom, or 1,600, were adult males.[7] Of this body of 1,600, it is known for a certainty that 830—almost exactly half— had received the franchise by the end of 1637. Although only adult male church members could be enfranchised, not all of those eligible had become so. In Boston, for example, only 123 out of the 171 eligibles had chosen to adopt the privilege.[8] If the Boston figures are at all representative for the rest of the colony—that is, if about 50 out of every 171 adult male church members neglected to adopt the franchise—then for those 831 freemen, there must have been approximately 1,100 adult male church members out of a total adult male population of about 1,600.

6. Greene and Harrington, *American Population Before 1790*, 13.
7. Constantine Panunzio, *Major Social Institutions* (New York, 1947), 87. Table No. 21, based on eighteenth-century genealogical charts, indicates that before 1700 the average number of children per wife in America was 7.37.
8. *Colony Records*, I, 366-73; First Church of Boston, Records and Baptisms, 1630-1687, Mass. Hist. Soc.

Another divisive factor involved the relationship of late arrivals with the remainder of the population. Newcomers often discovered that the best land in settled areas had been pre-empted by their predecessors, and often they disagreed with some particulars or with the whole system of government and religion. Such a division could apply without reference to social status and could affect Saints and unregenerate alike.

It has already been noted that there was considerable area for disagreement between economic groups. At the time of the Hutchinson insurgency conflict seemed most acute, not between rich and poor, but between two fairly affluent groups, the agricultural yeomen and gentry on one hand, and the tradesmen and craftsmen on the other.

From the very outset these distinctions and other less general divisions within the colony had been susceptible to exploitation by disaffected groups or individuals, and now, in fresh combination of descending importance, they were operative in the Antinomian Controversy.

(iv)

Although the Hutchinsonian movement was inaugurated by a woman and its earliest and most enthusiastic supporters were the housewives of Boston, the nature of the available statistical data makes it necessary to examine the structure of the movement primarily in terms of the men who participated. For the most part, only the activities of men were a matter of public record in colonial Massachusetts. Of their womenfolk less is known except with reference to church membership, marriage, childbirth, and crime, all of which were assiduously recorded. There are, however, some assumptions that may be safely made. It can be assumed, for example, that the social and economic condition and attitudes of the women were virtually identical with those of their husbands. Also, inasmuch as the proselytizing activities of the women were largely responsible for arousing masculine interest, it can be assumed that in most instances there existed a similarity of family sentiment toward Mrs. Hutchinson and her doctrines.

One hundred eighty-seven males can be positively identified as having participated in some degree in the Hutchinson movement. Some of them were quite zealous in their attachment, some less deeply committed, and still others appear to have become involved almost by chance or for reasons less closely related to the stated aims of the movement. For the purposes of this study these 187 men can be divided into three categories: (1) the core group, (2) the support group, and (3) the peripheral group. The core group was comprised of those who were most closely affiliated with Mrs. Hutchinson and who chose or were compelled to join her in her banishment. The support group was made up of those who were also warm adherents of Mrs. Hutchinson but who, at the hour of crisis, decided to withdraw their allegiance and remain in Massachusetts. The members of the peripheral group were those who seem to have had only a casual and brief association with Mrs. Hutchinson, but who left the colony with her.[9]

(a) The Core Group

The core group is made up of thirty-eight men who seem to have been most outspoken in their support of Mrs. Hutchinson and most continuously loyal to her. Twenty-nine signed the petition championing John Wheelwright, and the remainder manifested their allegiance to the cause in other conspicuous ways. But their special distinction lies in their refusal to recant when pressure was placed upon them, choosing instead to leave the colony with Mrs. Hutchinson or Mr. Wheelwright.

Some of the most useful and distinguished men in the colony were included in this core group, most notably Coddington, Coggeshall, Dummer, Hutchinson, Brenton, and Vane. Fifteen of the group were entitled to apply the term Master before their names, and two of them were of the peerage.

Although the group is small, the regional origins of its members are revealing in some particulars. The county providing the largest representation was Lincolnshire, and not surprisingly, of the nine men from that county, five bore the name of Hutchinson; two others, Thomas and William Wardall, had been neighbors of the Hutchinsons at Alford. Also from Lincolnshire were William Coddington of Boston and John Wheelwright of Bilsby.

9. In the following sections footnotes will generally be introduced only to support direct quotations. In Appendices I-VI, the reader will find statistical tables illustrating the analysis provided here and lists of data on which the statistical tables are based. A series of separate bibliographies provides source references for every individual considered in these tables.

A number of men who were loosely associated with the movement, particularly in the exodus to Rhode Island, have been excluded from consideration because they could not be more closely identified nor characterized in any way. Because of inadequate data it is possible that a few men have been incorrectly classified or omitted. But most of those who were significantly involved are considered here, and certainly enough of them to provide a valid study.

An examination of the other categories seems to reinforce the impression that family relationships and regional proximity played a substantial role in attracting people into the movement. There were, in all categories, twenty-six Lincolnshiremen involved in the movement, the largest single regional element, although Lincolnshiremen constituted only the tenth largest group in the colony and the fourth largest group in Boston. Only five of Cotton's old parishioners seem to have been implicated in the movement as a whole. Most of the remaining Lincolnshiremen appear to have been related to the Hutchinsons or Wheelwright through family ties or proximity or both.

The second largest element in the core group is comprised of Londoners, eight in all, presumably because there happened to be more Londoners in Boston than in any other single town. More than a third of those in the colony were located in Boston, perhaps feeling themselves ill-qualified for a rural existence.

The members of the core group were, on the whole, early arrivals and well established in the colony before the controversy broke out. Twenty-three of them had arrived before 1634, when Mrs. Hutchinson appeared on the scene; twelve had come over in the Winthrop Fleet of 1630. Fourteen of them had arrived in the succeeding years of 1634 and 1635, and one—John Wheelwright—had arrived in 1636. Most of the men in the core group had put down roots and presumably had a considerable psychological investment in the community. The fact that at least thirty of them were married men with families would seem to make their investment even greater.

Inasmuch as the movement centered in Boston, it is not surprising that twenty-six of the core group members had their homes in that town. Six resided in Roxbury, which was near enough to be readily infected, and three came from remote Newbury where Richard Dummer and his wife seem to have evangelized when they left Roxbury. The remainder were scattered, one each from Wollaston, Ipswich, and Salem.

Thirty-five members of the core group were church members, most of them having attained that status at a fairly early date. Thirty-two were freemen, and in most instances they had been enfranchised before the end of 1634.

It is somewhat more difficult to establish precisely the vocations of these men. Of the core group the occupations of seven remain uncertain. But it seems significant that nineteen of them—exactly half—were merchants, skilled craftsmen, or professional men. Only four seem to have had farming as their primary occupation, and even these are so labeled only because they had extensive land-holdings and apparently had no other occupation. The remainder are scattered among vocations ranging from one "gentleman," pre-sumably without private employment (Henry Vane), to two un-skilled servants and one common laborer.

The economic condition of members of the core group is even more difficult to determine satisfactorily, but there are some clues to the degrees of their prosperity. Twelve of the men were among "the richer inhabitants" who were asked to contribute funds for the support of the Boston school; William Coddington was one of the richest men in the colony, and Richard Dummer and John Spencer of Newbury were also of considerable affluence. Spencer was one of the stockholders of the Bay Company, and Dummer had a suffi-cient competency to allow him to write off a hundred pound note which he held of John Winthrop. At the opposite extreme, there were three or four, servants and the like, who may be described as poor. The balance, as nearly as can be judged from their occu-pations, landholdings, and position in the colony, appear to have been men of moderate circumstances.

Most noteworthy in the composition of the core group is the number of men who held public office at either the colony or town-ship level. Eighteen were elected or appointed to some public position, and most of them held several offices. Sixteen of the core group held more than twenty-three different positions in the col-ony government. One—Henry Vane—was Governor, two—Codding-ton and Dummer—had served as both treasurer of the colony and assistant in the General Court. Eight had been elected deputies to the Court. The other five had held a diversity of lesser offices, nine being selectmen. At the township level twelve men held twelve different offices, nine of them being selectmen. Of this group of twelve only two had not also held some office in the colo-nial government.

On the other hand nine or ten members of the core group seem to have been men without any particular status or prestige in their respective communities. A very few were apparently wastrels or eccentrics, but most of them were ordinary citizens. Having com-mitted themselves as fully as their more distinguished colleagues in Mrs. Hutchinson's favor, they are necessarily categorized with them. Their presence gives the core group flavor, if not consistency.

One further distinction might be made among the members of the core group. When it came time for them to abandon their homes and go elsewhere, seven men elected to follow Pastor Wheelwright northward to New Hampshire. The choice suggests a difference in the degree of their disaffection. Not only was Wheelwright ultimately to prove less radical than Mrs. Hutchinson in his definition of the Covenant of Grace, but five of the men who joined him received formal dismission from the church of Boston. This indicated that they were regarded as being in good spiritual standing and were thus authorized to join another church or, if need be, to organize their own. It is also noteworthy that this small group included none of Mrs. Hutchinson's most active supporters, nor did it include any of the more eminent and affluent participants in the movement.

What do the figures suggest about the possible attitudes and motivations that led these men to become so deeply implicated in an heretical and seditious movement? Here is a group most of whom arrived early and were well established in the community. The majority had joined the church and become enfranchised at a relatively early date. A third of them were "rich men," according to contemporary definition, and half of them, being tradesmen or craftsmen, shared a common economic viewpoint. Most of the group were neighbors in Boston, and many had been neighbors or acquaintances in the Old World. For many of these men adaptive pressures were so numerous and compelling that it must have required very powerful alienative factors to prompt such a serious commitment. The members of the core group not only openly avouched their support for the movement, but they chose to abandon home and position rather than recant their views.

For that minority within the core group whose social and economic status was slight or ambiguous, the movement and its doctrines may have offered an outlet for the expression of latent hostilities against the society. Or it may have helped to confirm the individual's own self-evaluation, and to offer psychological compensation for an inferior status in the community. Biographical particulars of several of the men in this subgroup are suggestive. Four of them went on to embrace illuminist doctrines more extreme than those of Mrs. Hutchinson. Richard Carder, Robert Potter, and William Wardall became disciples of the notorious and troublesome Samuel Gorton, founder of a sect whose immoderate views and deportment displayed radically alienative tendencies.

Henry Bull, a young servant who was described as "weak and affectionate," adopted the Quaker faith, which, for that time, suggests that his general psychological organization was perhaps less intellectualized and inhibited than was common among other church members of the Bay Colony. Also, at that stage of its development, Quakerism propounded an interpretation of the cosmos and of society that was highly congenial to the emotional needs of the "disinherited."

How closely Richard Hawkins shared the illuministic tenets of his eccentric wife, Jane, or how favorably he looked upon her quackery is not known, but his loyalty suggests a readiness to resist those hostile forces that had marked her a witch. Of Philip Sherman's personality we know only that he was an "honest" man "of melancholy temper." Whatever disaffection prompted his melancholia, it presumably found some release when his father-in-law, John Porter, introduced him to the teachings of Anne Hutchinson. Sherman espoused her doctrines so enthusiastically that he was soon excommunicated—a fate that befell only a handful of the most zealous Hutchinsonians. The only other members of the core group who were excommunicated were Robert Potter and Henry Bull, both mentioned above, and Anne Hutchinson herself.

The rebellion of the "have nots" is a fairly comprehensible phenomenon, and there is little doubt that Mrs. Hutchinson's doctrines offered the members of this element improved status in a limiting social framework. That more of the "disinherited" were not deeply implicated in the movement may be partially explained in that this was essentially an intra-church doctrinal conflict, and most of the "have nots" were outside the ranks of the church. The rebellion of the "haves" prompts more difficult questions about motives. In this connection several axioms about religious movements may be profitably considered. It is a sociological commonplace that religious differences reflect and define differences in social conduct, and it is also well established that a "newly created religion is specifically alienated from and usually opposed to the social order within which it emerges." [10] However, a new religion will usually assume form within the essential ideological framework of the society, rearranging or augmenting that framework only enough to allow the exercise of values and norms that were hitherto disparaged or forbidden.

10. Robin Williams, *American Society, A Sociological Interpretation* (New York, 1955), 310.

There were vibrant socio-economic overtones in the religious convictions of the "haves" in the Hutchinsonian core group. One of the major conflicts in the colony at this time was between mercantile and agricultural elements over the problem of economic regulation.[11] A majority of the population, engaged primarily in agricultural pursuits, had sought means to control an inflationary spiral that seemed to be pressed upward by labor costs and imported commodity prices. The gentry and yeomanry who dominated the General Court, moved by an organic social philosophy and a substantial body of English legislative precedent, had experimented with various regulatory measures, none of which proved successful. In their endeavors these men had enjoyed the unequivocal support of the clergy who insisted on an organic social ethic as an intrinsic part of the Puritan moral code and demanded strict compliance in evidence of a regenerate state. This policy placed the merchants and the craftsmen of the colony, particularly those of Boston, in an awkward position. Most of them were church members and were resentful when their professions of faith were called into question because they entertained an economic code held objectionable by the rest of the colony. If they were to maintain their spiritual status without abandoning their social and economic values, it was necessary to reinterpret the doctrine of assurance in such a way as to circumvent the orthodox insistence on a narrowly construed organic philosophy. Mrs. Hutchinson filled their need by reasserting the primacy of the Covenant of Grace, the essential Witness of the Spirit. True assurance of grace, she had insisted, is essentially a mystical experience which precedes and precludes any consideration of moral effort on the part of the believer. Although neither she nor her companions were prepared to abandon the basic moral pattern of the community, this altered perspective allowed greater latitude within which to define what was morally sound and what was not. It permitted them to rest confident in their regeneration despite all contrary claims based on empirical data.

Unfortunately this hypothesis cannot be tested by a quantitative comparison of the Hutchinsonians with the whole Massachusetts population. In 1637 the population of the colony was growing at an explosive rate, and there were scores, if not hundreds, of people in the colony of whom little or nothing is known. However, it does seem feasible to test the hypothesis with a statistical analysis of

11. See Chap. VIII.

the Boston population.[12] It was in Boston, of course, that the movement had its center and from which it drew its strongest support. Although the population of Boston was by no means static at that time, the available records are so detailed that, with respect to certain revealing characteristics, the structure of almost the entire adult male population can be defined.

It is not the purpose of this analysis to reach conclusions about religious schisms or nonconformity in general. Rather, it is intended to expose to as many tests as possible the hypothesis offered above: i.e., there was a relationship between the economic and religious views of the Bostonians implicated in the Hutchinson movement, and Mrs. Hutchinson's doctrines were most attractive to those persons whose economic interests were frustrated by the organic morality of the orthodox clergy and gentry. This hypothesis will be tested by noting the extent to which the logical implications of the hypothesis are consistent with observable quantitative relationships.[13]

For the purposes of this analysis five questions were asked concerning each individual: (1) was he a church member, (2) was he enfranchised, (3) did he hold public office and if so of what degree, (4) what was his occupation, and (5) what was his economic condition? To the first three questions definite "yes" or "no" answers could be provided for all the respondents. In answer to the fourth question, the occupations of 186 men were firmly established and those of 177 were not.[14] However, the available evidence strongly indicates that most of the "unknowns" were husbandmen, general handymen, laborers, servants, or others who could profess

12. The statistical analysis offered here was made under the indispensable guidance of Harry C. Bredemeier, Professor of Sociology, Douglass College, Rutgers. See also Patricia Kendall and Paul Lazarsfeld, "Problems of Survey Analysis," in Robert K. Merton and Paul Lazarsfeld, eds., *Continuities in Social Research* (Glencoe, 1950). The data on which these statistics are based may be found in Appendices II-IV.

13. The study of relationships through statistical analysis necessarily involves serious limitations. Relatively few factors can be controlled and, as Paul Lazarsfeld observes, when "we can only control factors after the fact ... our findings are always open to doubt." (Merton and Lazarsfeld, *Continuities in Social Research*, 139.) Furthermore, it is often necessary to base important cross tabulations on relatively few cases, and in secondary analysis the more refined cross tabulations become the more seriously one is limited by vanishing cases. With these qualifications in mind, we may guard against inferring too much from the following analysis and realize that new data might materially alter our conclusions.

14. The slight discrepancy between these figures and those in Table IV can be explained by the fact that three persons (one from each group) there identified as residents of Wollaston are treated in the Boston records as citizens of Boston and are so regarded in the present analysis.

no specific craft or trade. Information relating to the last question was even more scanty, but where it exists it is strong and explicit. The Boston records provide a roster of those men who were regarded as the "richer inhabitants." [15] The names of some few others who were recipients of unusually large land grants have been added to this list. At the opposite end of the economic scale the records list a considerable number of the "poorer sort of the inhabitants." [16] This list has been supplemented by the names of known servants and laborers who would obviously share the same economic condition. Of that large group of men whose economic status is unknown, two or three may have been fairly affluent but the vast majority were doubtless of a middle economic class or poor.

The question of the social status of Mrs. Hutchinson's supporters may be considered first. One possible index of position in the status hierarchy of Boston may be constructed on the basis of three characteristics: church membership, freemanship, and secular officeholding. These three characteristics form a scale, in the sense that being a church member is the most widely possessed attribute of status (182 men), and tends to be a prerequisite for being a freeman, which is the next most widely held attribute (161 men). Freemanship, in turn, lends to be a prerequisite for the highest position in the hierarchy, officeholding (61 men).

As may be seen from Table I, there are eight logically possible combinations of these attributes, but only four of them contain a significant concentration of persons—viz., combinations 1, 5, 7, 8.

TABLE I

STATUS HIERARCHY

Rank	Office-Holder	Freeman	Church Member	Number of Persons
1.	+	+	+	54
2.	+	+	−	0
3.	+	−	+	2
4.	+	−	−	5
5.	−	+	+	104
6.	−	+	−	3
7.	−	−	+	22
8.	−	−	−	172

15. "Boston Town Records, 1634-1660," 160.
16. *Ibid.*, 6, 22-26.

Table II presents these four combinations, classified by their relationship to the Hutchinson movement.

TABLE II

BOSTON STATUS HIERARCHY

in terms of

OFFICEHOLDING, CHURCH MEMBERSHIP, AND FREEMANSHIP

	Hutchinson Supporters				Non-Supporters	Total Population
	Core Group	Support Group	Peripheral Group	All Groups		
No. 1 Officeholders, Freemen, and Church members	12	17	5	34	20	54
No. 5 Freemen and Church members	11	18	2	31	73	104
No. 7 Church members	2	..	1	3	19	22
No. 8 Residue	1	4	24	29	143	172

It therefore appears that the majority of Mrs. Hutchinson's supporters were drawn from the upper status group in terms of the secular hierarchy. That is, 66 per cent of them are officeholders and/or freemen in comparison to the 35 per cent of non-supporters who enjoyed a similar status. Furthermore, 80 per cent of the core group is drawn from this same element and 46 per cent of the core group is to be found in the very highest rank of the status scale provided.

Not only is it true that Mrs. Hutchinson's Boston supporters were mostly well-established people, but it would also seem that the more firmly established an individual was, the greater was the likelihood of his being one of Mrs. Hutchinson's supporters. Sixty-two per cent of the highest rank cited on the chart were her followers, as were 29 per cent of the non-officeholding enfranchised church members. However, only 13 per cent of the unenfranchised church members and 16 per cent of the unregenerate Bostonians were impelled to offer active support.

TABLE III

PARTICIPATION OF RICH AND OFFICEHOLDERS
IN THE HUTCHINSON MOVEMENT

	Total Population		"Rich"		Officeholders	
	Supporters	Non-Supporters	Supporters	Non-Supporters	Supporters	Non-Supporters
Churched	70 (39%)	111 (61%)	33 (69%)	15 (31%)	36 (65%)	20 (35%)
Un-churched	29 (16%)	151 (84%)	1 (50%)	1 (50%)	0 (0%)	5 (100%)

Application of a different perspective tends to confirm the impression that a remarkably high percentage of persons occupying a high secular status were disposed to follow Mrs. Hutchinson. Table III indicates that, while only 39 per cent of the church members elected to support her openly, 69 per cent of the *"rich"* church members did so, and 65 per cent of the *secular officeholding* church members did so. Combining both secular factors (wealth and officeholding) reveals (Table IV) that 73 per cent of the "rich" officeholders were supporters, as compared to 52 per cent of the "non-rich" officeholders.

TABLE IV

PARTICIPATION OF RICH OFFICEHOLDER

in the

HUTCHINSON MOVEMENT

	Supporters	Non-Supporters
Rich Officeholders	24 (73%)	9 (27%)
Non-rich Officeholders	11 (52%)	10 (48%)

In the description of the core and support groups it has been suggested that Mrs. Hutchinson's relatively permissive doctrines might prove most attractive to persons whose nonreligious roles

gave them interests that would be frustrated by the organic morality of Puritanism. It seemed especially probable that under the prevailing conditions merchants and craftsmen who were also church
members may have suffered role conflicts that would predispose
them toward Mrs. Hutchinson's views. Consistent with this hypothesis, Table V indicates that those who were merchants and
craftsmen were more than twice as likely to join Mrs. Hutchinson
as those who were not (45 per cent as opposed to 19 per cent).

TABLE V

PARTICIPATION OF MERCHANTS AND CRAFTSMEN
IN THE HUTCHINSON MOVEMENT

	Total Population		"Rich"		Non-"Rich"	
	Supporters	Non-Supporters	Supporters	Non-Supporters	Supporters	Non-Supporters
Merchants and Craftsmen	54 (45%)	67 (55%)	22 (81%)	5 (19%)	32 (34%)	62 (66%)
Others and Unknown	45 (19%)	195 (81%)	9 (43%)	12 (57%)	36 (16%)	183 (84%)

Note further in this connection that if the merchants and craftsmen were successful in their secular roles—i.e., if they were "rich"—
they were even more likely to support Mrs. Hutchinson: 81 per cent
were supporters. Of those who had not attained this order of success, however, only 34 per cent were supporters. In other words,
these entrepreneurial roles seem to have made their incumbents
susceptible to Mrs. Hutchinson's kind of appeal, and the more in-
tensively they pursued the demands of the roles, the more susceptible they seem to have become.

True, the Antinomian Controversy was essentially concerned
with theological matters. But for the Puritan, doctrinal debate was
not an intellectual game; it was the definitive mode of compre-
hending the concrete data of human existence. Indeed, the substance of his doctrine was, to him, more concrete and meaningful
than the particulars of his life. He turned as promptly and unre-
servedly to the covenant theology for a resolution of his dilemmas
as contemporary man turns to the general dicta of Marx and Freud.
But because the Puritan examined his economic problems in the-

ological terms is not to say that he had no economic problems, or that his motivations were not in considerable part economic. It would be a rash commentator, however, who would claim to know where religious motivation left off and economic began.

There were, of course, other factors—personality traits and psychological quirks, most of them now concealed—that propelled some of these men along their errant course. It is difficult, if not impossible, to establish the extent to which genuine mysticism (whatever that may be) prevailed among Mrs. Hutchinson's adherents. In an ideological relationship such as that of the Hutchinsonians, there is no necessary similarity between the psychological motives or the intellectual processes that prompt the leader to articulate ideas, on the one hand, and the characteristics of his audience that lead them to respond favorably on the other. Certainly, the personalities of most of Anne's adherents were distinctly unlike that of their troubled mentor. However, there were some among her disciples whose basic psychological organization was apparently analagous to hers in certain respects and, like hers, was distinctly out of place in that cultural setting. A few were impelled by the peculiar intensity of their emotional needs to pursue their mystical bent into an even more rarefied atmosphere than Mrs. Hutchinson had attained.

One of Mrs. Hutchinson's most enthusiastic disciples was Henry Vane, a brilliant man despite his youthful instability, tolerant of all sects and guided always by his warm sympathy. Vane's mystical propensity increased rather than waned after he left Boston, and in later years he showed a strong predilection for the Quakers. However, he chose not to affiliate himself permanently with any single party. Exposed to the mystical writings of Jakob Boehme, his religious thought became so obscure and confused that one uncharitable observer was prompted to remark that "few could understand him [and] some thought he could not understand himself." [17]

After settling in Newport, Nicholas Easton, whom Winthrop had described as "a man very bold, though ignorant," undertook to preach a doctrine quite like Mrs. Hutchinson's.[18] The pith of his teaching was that man has no power nor will in himself, so that in all he does God acts directly on and through him. William Cod-

17. Richard Baxter, *Autobiography of Richard Baxter, Being the Reliquiae Baxterianae*, ed. J. M. Lloyd Thomas (London, 1931), 73.
18. Winthrop, *Journal*, II, 41.

dington and John Coggeshall, leaders in the Hutchinson movement, embraced Easton's views, to the dismay of more conservative
folk in the Newport settlement. When the first Quaker mission-
aries reached Rhode Island in 1656, Easton and Coddington were
among the earliest to adopt the new faith, and they were soon
joined by William Freeborn, another member of the core group.
Coggeshall had died before the Quaker incursion, but his son
Joshua, who had been fifteen during the Antinomian crisis, soon
became a zealous Quaker.

Mary Dyer had also found emotional solace in the mystical beliefs propounded by Mrs. Hutchinson, and it seems quite natural
that she too should turn to the Quaker faith. While in Boston both
William and Mary Dyer had been so "notoriously infected" with
Mrs. Hutchinson's doctrines that they were regarded as equally
"censorious and troublesome." [19] But in Rhode Island William's
ardor seems to have cooled and there is no evidence to suggest that
he followed his wife into the Quaker fold. Mary, on the other hand,
became one of the most ardent and fearless proselytizers of the
"inner light." Pursuing her missionary efforts with an almost psy-
chotic zeal, she was twice imprisoned and at last achieved a tragic
martyrdom high on the gallows of Boston.

Another "irregular" was William Aspinwall, a restless, compulsive individual whom even his friends had been obliged to caution
against the use of intemperate speech. Discontented among the
heretics of Rhode Island, he returned to Boston for another try at
respectable orthodoxy. Again finding himself in difficulty with the
authorities, he departed for England where he became a dedicated
Fifth Monarchy man and between 1653 and 1655 penned four
books warning mankind of the imminent millennium.

There were some few whose acceptance of mysticism verged on
the pathological; this might be ventured of Mary Dyer, for one;
of Samuel Gorton, the self-appointed "professor of the mysteries
of Christ"; [20] or of the old midwife, Jane Hawkins, whose eccen-
tricity had aroused suspicions of witchcraft. Some few, like the
rakish Captain John Underhill, probably professed mystical and
Antinomian beliefs only to mask their own flagrant immorality.
Underhill claimed to have received the Witness when he indulged
in "moderate use of the creature called tobacco"—a habit which

19. *Ibid.*, I, 266.
20. Gorton has been somewhat tentatively located in the peripheral group below;
he was a latecomer, but nonetheless an enthusiastic champion of Mrs. Hutchinson's
views, until such time as his own ripened.

the Puritans did well to frown upon if it stimulated such fantasies as these. Suspected of incontinence with a neighbor's wife, the bluff soldier was haled to the bar to explain his conduct. The episode bore Chaucerian overtones, which are sharpened by the credulous sobriety of Winthrop's account. "The matter was," the solemn-faced Governor wrote, "that the woman being young and beautiful, and withal of a jovial spirit and behaviour, he did daily frequent her house, and was divers times found there alone with her, the door being locked on the inside. He confessed it was ill, because it had an appearance of evil in it; but his excuse was, that the woman was in great trouble of mind, and sore temptations, and that he resorted to her to comfort her; and that when the door was found locked upon them, they were in private prayer together. But this practice was clearly condemned also by the elders, affirming that it had not been of good report for any of them to have done the like, and they ought, in such a case, to have called in some brother or sister, and not to have locked the door." [21] A volume of psychoanalytic jottings could scarcely reveal more about Underhill's motivations and character—nor about Winthrop's "sense of humor."

The great majority of Hutchinsonians, however, were practical, hardheaded Puritans, temperamentally indisposed to the extremes of mysticism, and gave intellectual credence to Mrs. Hutchinson's doctrines without being overborne by their emotional connotations. At no time during the course of the struggle was there any indication of the violent hysteria that so commonly accompanies religious movements of this sort. Some religious enthusiasm and a good deal of bitterness and contention made their appearance, but the movement never degenerated into the extremes of primitive revivalism. As individuals, the Puritans were predominantly of a rational-dogmatic type, governed by strong inhibitory controls, and inclined to subordinate their feelings and imaginations to rational considerations. On two later occasions—the witch scare and the Great Awakening—these inhibitory restraints were overwhelmed by a great wave of terror that drove a few descendants of the Puritans to primitive emotional excesses. Almost all of Mrs. Hutchinson's adherents, however, while thoroughly sympathetic to her teachings, continued to exercise a critical judgment that restrained them from following the immoderate course their enemies feared they would take.

21. Winthrop, *Journal*, I, 276 ff.

(b) *The Support Group*

The support group was comprised of fifty-nine men, a third again larger than the core group. In structure and attitudes this component seems to have been very similar to the core group in many fundamental respects. All but six members of this group had signed the Wheelwright petition, and the exceptions expressed their advocacy of Mrs. Hutchinson's cause in various other ways. But one essential factor distinguishes the support group from the core group. When the final hour of decision arrived, these men recanted their views and decided to remain in the colony. Four men who do not satisfy this essential criterion are included in this category because they seem to have been closer to Mrs. Hutchinson's cause than those of the peripheral group, but perhaps not so close as those of the core group. These are Dr. John Clarke and Samuel Hutchinson, who, although loyal supporters of Mrs. Hutchinson, arrived too late to take an active part in the controversy; and Stephen Greensmith and Thomas Wilson, who expressed their strong support but do not seem to have been at the center of the movement. None of these four men signed the petition, but all of them left the colony. Although their inclusion may weaken the consistency of this group, it seemed inappropriate to place them elsewhere.

Again the regional origins of this category are suggestive in that the largest element—eight men—came from Lincolnshire. Two of this Lincolnshire group were Mrs. Hutchinson's neighbors from Alford; four were Boston parishioners of Mr. Cotton; and two were from Donington, a few miles south of Boston. Six had come from Suffolk, five from Essex, and four from London. The rest were widely scattered in their regional origins.

The great majority, thirty-nine in all, were currently residents of Boston, but eleven were from Charlestown, four from Salem, and one from Wollaston. One seems to have come from Plymouth, but he may well, in the interim, have resettled within the Bay Company's limits.

About two-thirds of this group were early arrivals in the colony, a proportion approximately the same as that of the core group. Forty-one came to the colony before 1634, twenty-one of this number having arrived with the Winthrop fleet, and three having come even earlier with Endicott. Sixteen more arrived from 1634 through

1636, and two, the aforementioned Clarke and Hutchinson, appeared on the scene in 1637.

Fifty-one of the group were church members and at least twenty-seven joined before 1634. Forty-nine of them were freemen, and twenty-five were enfranchised by the end of 1634. In this group there is conspicuously less officeholding at the colony level, but somewhat more at the local level. Thirteen men held office in the government of the Massachusetts Bay Company, but most of the offices were of much less importance than those filled by the core group: one assistant, six deputies, and six lesser posts. At the township level five were selectmen, and twenty were minor functionaries of various descriptions. Of these lesser posts it might be observed that they lacked prestige, and it was often necessary to appoint men to them against their will; but nonetheless, the townsfolk insisted that these frequently irksome jobs should be assumed by responsible individuals. In the support group there was not only less officeholding and fewer important officials, but there was far less plural officeholding than was the case in the core group.

The occupational pattern of the support group is markedly similar to that of the core group. Thirty of these men were engaged in pursuits in which the regulation of prices and wages would seem to affect them closely. There were four professionals, four merchants, fifteen skilled craftsmen, and eight were involved in some form of public service, such as innkeeper, sawyer, or miller. Incidentally, it is interesting to note that in all three groups, there were at least fifteen men who were somehow engaged in the cloth trades as mercers, drapers, clothiers, or tailors. In the support group, eleven were probably primarily farmers, to judge from their holdings and the absence of any other identification.

Nineteen members of the support group would appear to have been men of some affluence in their respective communities. Fourteen of them were among the "richer inhabitants" who had been asked to contribute to the support of the Boston school.[22] Six, most of them from other towns, had landholdings extensive enough to suggest that they might properly be regarded in this category.[23] Although it is very difficult to determine exactly, this group seems to have proportionately fewer members who can be described as

22. Bendall, Biggs, Bosworth, Button, Cole, Eliot, Gridley, Hudson, Leverett, T. Marshall, Odlin, Oliver, Rainsford, and Salter.
23. Bunker, W. Denison, Frothingham, Hough, E. Mellows, and Scruggs.

poor. However, the group includes seven servants as against the two in the core group.

What, in summation, are the general characteristics of this levy? They are, for the most part, like their fellows in the core group, early arrivals, churched and enfranchised at a relatively early date. A great majority are tradesmen or craftsmen and most of them seem to be either fairly affluent or in moderately comfortable circumstances. In these respects their orientation might be presumed to be similar to that of the core group members. As with the core group, it would appear that one aspect of their motivation to support Mrs. Hutchinson was a revolt against a theological emphasis on "works" that required acquiescence in an organic theory of commonwealth as defined by a magistracy comprised primarily of landed gentry. The social values and economic norms they regarded as essential to their way of life were disparaged and threatened by authorities of church and state. Mrs. Hutchinson offered an attractive creed which encompassed the aspersed values, or at least did not offer them violence.

The interesting question about this group is why its members did not follow through with their commitment. What circumstances allowed them to reconcile and adapt themselves to a presumably hostile environment? Why were they less alienated than their fellows in the core group, with whom they had so much in common?

Many of the answers to these questions lie in the realm of individual psychological differences. The marks of alienation are not always perceptible over a space of three hundred years. It is known that none of this group was seized by the pietistic enthusiasm which betokened the alienation of so many in the core group. Only Dr. John Clarke, who was soon to become the Baptist leader in Rhode Island, even approximated this type of orientation. The remainder managed to readjust themselves to the demands of Puritan orthodoxy.

One consideration may prove suggestive, though it is based upon too little data for a conclusive interpretation. The support group assumes the same general economic and social lineaments as the core group, but a more precise scrutiny of some details indicates that the social status and economic standing of core group members is generally a cut higher than that of support group members. The differences in officeholding have already been observed. Furthermore, although the core group contained fifteen men who were entitled to term themselves "Master," in the support group there are only five who are invariably so-called, and three others to whom the term is irregularly applied. Half as many—in a group which is one-third larger.

If the contributions to charity of the "richer inhabitants" of Boston properly indicate their relative economic standings, here is another point of distinction. There were twelve members of the core group who contributed to the school fund and fourteen contributors from the much larger support group. Among them the twelve core group members donated £15 19s.—that is, practically sixteen pounds—as compared to the £4 9s. 4d. provided by the fourteen support group members. Here it may be fairly protested that Henry Vane's £10 donation creates a radical and deceptive imbalance. But even if Vane's contribution is discounted, there remain eleven men offering substantially six pounds as against the four and a half pound donation of the larger group. Although more men of the support group contributed to the fund, in almost every instance their donations were substantially smaller than those of the core group members.

From these and similar considerations, it would appear that, generally speaking, the social and economic status of support group members, although favorable and promising, was less secure than that of the core group members. Many of the core group had, in effect, "arrived"; their assets were sufficiently large and viable to allow removal without disastrous losses. Support group members, on the other hand, seem to have been on the way up. Their more modest holdings may have rendered them less mobile, more committed to the environment in which they were currently involved, more inclined to cling tenaciously to what they had. Although less prominent, less successful, and less highly placed than the leading members of the core group, they were among the upcoming men of their communities—but at a stage in their careers when radical change may have seemed undesirable.

It might also be cautiously ventured that those psychological traits that helped core group members to the attainment of economic and social success probably prompted them to react more vigorously against the hostile environment and venture a further risk by leaving the colony and starting afresh.

When the members of the support group realized that the specific ideological goals of the Hutchinsonian movement did not lie within their means, that these goals were presumably irreconcilable with and unattainable within the limits of their given environment, they chose to abandon these goals and readapt themselves to the environment. For them, presumably, that environment posed less hostility than for the men of the core group.

(c) *The Peripheral Group*

At the periphery of the Hutchinson movement were ninety men who do not seem to have played any central role nor evinced any strong commitment toward Mrs. Hutchinson's doctrines. Some were only casually or perhaps even mistakenly implicated; some were involved through family relations; and a good many appear to have followed the movement with the utilitarian aim of attaining unrelated ends of their own. Only five of these names appeared on the Wheelwright petition, and all five men categorically denied that they had signed it themselves or allowed the use of their signatures.[24] Of the ninety members of the peripheral group, seventy-nine—all but eleven—left the colony with Wheelwright or Hutchinson.

In most respects the structure of this group is radically different from that of the other two groups. The most marked similarity appears in their regional origins. The largest single regional component was, as before, from Lincolnshire—a group of ten men with their families. The second largest group was comprised of seven men from Hampshire.

The members of the peripheral group were, on the whole, late arrivals, only nineteen of them having come to the colony before 1634. Thirty-two had arrived between 1634 and 1636, and thirty-nine had appeared as late as 1637 and 1638. Of this last detachment some could scarcely have been able to unpack their trunks before they moved on to another settlement. Although thirty-one can be identified as residents of Boston, the great majority were scattered widely throughout the colony. Only fifteen of the whole group were church members, and of that number no more than thirteen were freemen of the Company. Four of them had held office at the colonial level, three were deputies, and eight held office at the township level.

The occupational pattern, where it can be traced, is not unlike that of the other groups. Unfortunately, almost half the men had so recently arrived or were so inconspicuous or loosely affiliated

24. These men are included on the assumption that they must somehow have expressed sympathy or interest in the Hutchinson cause to have prompted the remonstrants to include their names out of the many dozens that might have been chosen.

that their vocational pursuits remain unknown. Of the remainder two were professionals (a clergyman and a schoolmaster), one was a merchant, fourteen were craftsmen, and three were engaged in some form of public service occupation. Eight seem to have been farmers, and seventeen were servants. Of the whole group only seven appear to have been men of any considerable affluence.

What can be said of the orientation and motivations of this group? On the whole it would seem to be more confused and inconsistent than the preceding groups. Most of its members were latecomers who were without status, prestige, or substantial property holdings in the community. They are neither so deeply implicated in the life and operation of the community as to engender that intense alienation which was observed in the core group, nor are they sufficiently rooted to allow the adaptation which characterized the core group. Indeed, although there were many and varied causative agencies at work within this group, the most common factor among them would seem to be their position on the periphery of the community. Lacking deep roots and loyalties, they seem to have been caught up in the centrifugal force of the Hutchinson movement. Many of them apparently had little to gain by staying where they were and less to lose by going elsewhere; they were apparently content to drift wherever they were carried, and to share the rewards as well as the hazards of the more dedicated members.

Undoubtedly, religious considerations played a role in the conduct of some of these people. A few who had arrived in the summer of 1637 were suspected of sharing Mrs. Hutchinson's opinions and denied the right of permanent residence in the colony. There were doubtless others who might be accounted Puritans or were amenable to Puritan discipline, but who were now alienated by the dogmatic authoritarianism of the Puritan leaders. Some few, like Townsend Bishop or the Reverend Robert Lenthall, seem to have assimilated Mrs. Hutchinson's teachings almost as an afterthought, as the controversy waned and was dying away. Ten men of the peripheral category, though not closely associated with Mrs. Hutchinson, entertained a similar psychological orientation toward the more emotional forms of religious experience. Three of them became Quakers in due course, four adopted the radical doctrines of Samuel Gorton, and three followed Dr. John Clarke into the Baptist fold.

For most of the members of this group, religious considerations probably played a secondary role in prompting their adherence; for others it may have played no part at all. Family and community ties seem to have drawn many people into the peripheral group. It has been noted that ten of these men were from Lincolnshire and seven from Hampshire. Of the Lincolnshire men, nine had come from the small complex of parishes about Alford and five of this contingent—Lawson, Rishworth, Storre, Wentworth, and Leavitt—were related to the Hutchinsons or Wheelwright or both. The Hampshire delegation seems to have been closely linked to the fortunes of Richard Dummer. Several men left Hampshire with his family and they later traveled together to Rhode Island where they were specifically registered as "Mr. Dummer's party." [25] There is even evidence to suggest a liaison of some sort between the Lincolnshire and Hampshire groups. Although they had left Hampshire with the Dummer group, Edmund Littlefield and his family apparently came originally from the Alford community. Confronted with a choice of destinations and companions on leaving Massachusetts, they cast their lot with their old acquaintances from Wheelwright's parish. Family relations would also appear to have been a decisive factor when Dr. John Clarke's two brothers and his brother-in-law followed him into Rhode Island.

A different kind of relationship served to convey a good many servants into the outskirts of the Hutchinson movement. Of the seventeen enumerated among the ranks of the peripheral group, at least six can be identified as the servants of Coddington, Coggeshall, Freeborn, and the elder Edward Hutchinson. These men and other indentured servants, whose masters cannot be identified,

---

25. *Rhode Island Colonial Records*, I, 59. A fascinating and perplexing footnote relates to Dummer's association with the "Plough Company" or "Company of Husbandmen." In July of 1631 Winthrop made the following cryptic entry in his journal: "A small ship of sixty tons arrived at Natascott, Mr. Graves, Master. She brought ten passengers from London. They came with a patent to Sagadahoc, but not liking the place they came hither.... These were the Company called the Husbandmen, and their ship called the Plough. Most of them proved *familists* and vanished away." In 1630 the "Company of Husbandmen" obtained a patent from Gorges and proposed to settle in Maine. They acquired the ministerial services of Stephen Bachellor, a vigorously eccentric non-conformist clergyman of Newton Stacy, Hants, and he apparently drew in his kinsman, Richard Dummer. When the company disbanded, a few settled down in Massachusetts and the remainder moved elsewhere. The curious fact is that, though Winthrop claimed they were familists, none of the group except Dummer was in any way affiliated with the Hutchinson movement. Even Bachellor, though he remained a thorn in the side of Puritan orthodoxy, failed to evince any interest in Mrs. Hutchinson's tenets. V. C. Sanborn, "Stephen Bachiler and the Plough Company," Maine Historical Society, *Collections*, 3d Ser., 2 (1906), 342-69; Banks, *Planters of the Commonwealth*, 94; *Colony Records*, 92, 125, 132, 143; Winthrop, *Journal*, I, 81, 169, 88.

may have been dedicated to Mrs. Hutchinson's doctrines, but it seems more likely, since they have no record of religious activity, that being indentured, they were drawn thither willy-nilly, and were largely indifferent to their whereabouts as long as they might live comfortably. Indeed, the Rhode Island atmosphere was to prove highly congenial to servants of Hutchinsonian predilections. Many of them prospered in due course, one of them to become governor of the colony and another to gain an appointment to Governor Andros's Council.

The Hutchinson movement, like most such enterprises, suffered the usual quota of waifs, strays, and rascals, men of rude manners, and cruder morals. At least six men in the peripheral group showed some capacity for disturbing the peace and achieved a dubious immortality on court records for idleness, drunkenness, burglary, fornication, and related forms of disorderly conduct. Mrs. Hutchinson's doctrines may have seemed a useful justification for their knavery, but it seems more likely that they simply regarded Rhode Island as a safer place for their disportment.

In summation, it appears that the members of the peripheral group were, for the most part, less specifically goal-oriented than those in the other groups. Unsettled and rootless, frustrated in the attainment of various individual needs, they were suggestible to an interpretation of the situation that would sustain their own self-evaluation. But most of them probably found adequate vindication of their own worth in an uncritical acceptance of the condemnatory stereotypes in which the opposition was portrayed, rather than through adherence to the positive doctrinal ideals of the movement. Participation in a concerted attack on the official custodians of sanctity and on those "hypocrites" who labored under a Covenant of Works would release feelings of hostility, and help support the emotional conviction that even those who did not pursue the disciplinary rigors of Puritan orthodoxy might be of worth.

It might be argued that the peripheral group actually seems less marginal than the support group because the former had offered the ultimate token of allegiance by leaving the colony with Mrs. Hutchinson. However, the preponderant evidence suggests that for most of the peripherals departure was not unduly oppressive. For the core and support groups there was a serious tension between centripetal and centrifugal forces which was with difficulty resolved one way or the other. For most of the peripherals there was no such tension.

The vital distinction between the core and support groups on the one hand and the peripherals on the other lies not in their behavior at the moment of resolution but in their attitudes and actions prior to that time. Core and support group members actively announced their dissent from the prevailing norms of the community and challenged the legitimacy of those norms. The peripherals offered no such challenge. Core and support group members engaged in a strenuous effort to change the norms of the community and to introduce norms they regarded as morally legitimate. Peripherals found it expedient simply to escape the norms then existing. Recognizing the consequences that their behavior could elicit, core and support group members did not hesitate to act and speak in accord with their values and sentiments. There is no evidence to suggest that more than a small fraction of the peripheral group was motivated by principle and even they took no part in the struggle preceding their departure.[26]

(v)

Any association of human beings requires leadership and organization to fulfill its purposes in an efficient and orderly manner. This is especially true of social movements that aim to alter a status quo hallowed by tradition and fortified by inertia. Strictly speaking, the Antinomian dissent was not a social movement at all, though the term has been somewhat loosely applied on the preceding pages for purposes of convenience and simplicity. The Hutchinson coterie, lacking the explicit formal goals, the centralized leadership, and the coherent organization that characterizes a social movement might be more precisely termed an ideological schism, a social protest, or perhaps an incipient embryonic social movement. The components of discontent were present in abundance, but the means for attaining satisfaction eluded them. The goals of the Hutchinson group were vague and ill-defined, its leadership diffuse and uncertain, its relations disorderly and incoherent.

For all their noisy endeavor the Hutchinsonians never reached the point of actually attempting to achieve specific and definable goals—to have a doctrine officially revised, a basic law changed, a text rewritten. Their chief object was to realize the ascendancy in the Boston church of the tenets of John Cotton as they were ex-

26. See Robert Merton, *Social Theory and Social Structure*, rev. ed. (Glencoe, 1957), 360.

pounded by Anne Hutchinson. They sought to attain this end, not by formal definition and official pronouncement, but rather by elevating John Wheelwright to the Boston pulpit where he might offset the influence of Pastor Wilson. When this stratagem failed, they strove to undermine Wilson's authority by publicly embarrassing and insulting him. As the controversy boiled over, the Hutchinsonians were impelled to defensive measures: to petition the General Court to free Wheelwright of the charge of sedition which they correctly construed as an attack on their own principles; then to obtain reversal of the alien law aimed at the exclusion of prospective adherents to their cause. All of these were instrumental objectives except the first, and that, in the context of Puritan theology as expounded in Massachusetts, was so ambiguous as to defy precise definition. It had become progressively apparent that Master Cotton's teachings meant many things to many men.

The center of the Antinomian Controversy was, of course, Anne Hutchinson herself. Some conjecture concerning her personality has already been advanced, but quite apart from such speculation, it is not difficult to understand why the people of Boston were drawn to her side in such numbers. Her warmth and compassion would have gained her friends in any circumstances. Her dynamic insistence on softening the aseptic perfectionism of the Puritan creed was calculated to draw even wider attention.

For many of Mrs. Hutchinson's disciples, there was doubtless an element of what Max Weber has termed the "charismatic" in her leadership. Weber depicts the charismatic leader as one who commands the allegiance of his followers, not because of the prescriptive sanctities of custom or law, but due to the compelling qualities of his own personality. His disciples regard him as infallible, omniscient, and incorruptible. They assume that he has the capacity to solve complex and ambiguous social problems, not through resort to traditional values nor through application of rational and legally defined means, but as one endowed with essentially suprahuman powers. They believe that he can, by some indeterminate means, find a solution that has eluded more conventional men and measures.[27] The concept of the charismatic leader is, of course, an ideal typical construct. Charismatic qualities are not simply the special property of certain leaders, but are part of a complex emo-

27. Max Weber, *Essays in Sociology*, trans. H. H. Gerth and C. Wright Mills (New York, 1946), 78-79, 245 ff.; James C. Davies, "Charisma in the 1952 Campaign," *American Political Science Review*, 48 (1954), 1083-1102.

tional relationship between leaders and followers. Charismatic leadership is capable of realization only in the degree to which a considerable number of people are so wrought by crisis and anxiety as to be predisposed toward that kind of leadership as a desirable form of problem solution.

Mrs. Hutchinson was strongly inclined to visualize her own role in essentially these terms. Indeed, her problem solving technique, through divine illumination, would seem to approximate the ideal charismatic form. In addition, her dynamic personality and her facility with words and ideas made her a fearless and accomplished agitator. Skillfully seizing on ambiguous aspects of the cultural pattern, she defined her goals and described her adversaries in emotionally charged terms providing concrete objects on which her followers' diffused hostilities could concentrate.

Much of the comment about Mrs. Hutchinson suggests that some of the men and probably more of the women in her following were inclined to accept a charismatic image of their leader. But it seems likely that the normative pattern and institutional structure of the society were not favorable to a generalized charismatic interaction. Indeed, this may have been one of the major shortcomings of the movement. As a woman in a seventeenth-century Puritan society, Mrs. Hutchinson, for all the luster and prestige she might acquire, lacked the status to control effectively the velocity and direction of the movement. The strong local traditions circumscribing feminine activity would make it difficult for many men—even those within her own movement, as later events were to prove—to defer to her judgment in all respects. Furthermore, when Mrs. Hutchinson's doctrines became the subject of political controversy and the movement was obliged as a matter of self-defense to adopt the essential features of a political party, Mrs. Hutchinson was ineligible to perform important functions of leadership in the political arena. In her default political leadership seems to have been taken over by Vane, Coddington, Coggeshall, and Aspinwall.

This assumption of responsibility by men who were already located in positions of appropriate authority would appear to be as close as the movement ever came to an organizational hierarchy while it was in Boston. There is no evidence to suggest that Mrs. Hutchinson possessed any marked organizational talent. Indeed, her behavior and attitudes while in Rhode Island indicate that she lacked the most rudimentary comprehension of the necessity of

distributing responsibility within an organizational framework.[28]
Nor do her political agents in the Bay Colony seem to have displayed
the skills essential to the success of a movement of this type. Vane
was continuously inept in the performance of his functions and
his juvenile deportment must have won the movement more enemies than friends. Of the other men, Coddington and Coggeshall
were loyal lieutenants, of more stable temperament and greater
political sophistication; but there is nothing in the record to suggest that they possessed the powers of persuasion or the political
dexterity that might have secured any degree of popular or legislative support for the movement. Nor is there any evidence to
indicate that their responsibilities were meaningfully distributed
or their functions efficiently coordinated.

There does not appear to have been any formal organization to
disseminate Mrs. Hutchinson's tenets or to enforce their acceptance as the official doctrine of the Boston church. Twice a week
Mrs. Hutchinson's house was open to those who chose to hear her
lectures. She contended that no solicitation of particular individuals was attempted and that all who came were welcome. Her
most regular listeners were presumably those of the core and support groups who had gone on record in defense of the principles
espoused by her and Wheelwright. Most were Boston people,
church members, and of her social class, thus most likely to be
exposed to social interaction with her and with each other. This
relationship allowed ample opportunity for the informal circulation
of Mrs. Hutchinson's ideas throughout a community in which theology was a chief intellectual preoccupation. The fact of economic
differentiation may have reduced opportunities for the non-Hutch-
insonians to be exposed to her ideas; there was, perhaps, less social
interaction between shopkeepers and agriculturists than the shopkeepers enjoyed among themselves. But in a community as small
and tightly knit as Boston, this distinction could hardly have been
a substantial barrier to the communication of ideas. However, it
may have played some part in inhibiting sympathetic response to
those ideas.

The transmission of the Hutchinsonian tenets to the peripheral
element took place during the final stages of the controversy when
these teachings were a matter of common gossip and the subject
of strenuous proselytization by earlier adherents. The peripherals
being mostly newcomers without a strong commitment to the com-

28. Winthrop, *Journal*, II, 39.

munity were more or less free to extend their loyalty or not as they saw fit.

Organization for the enforcement of the Hutchinson ideals appears to have been equally haphazard and spontaneous. According to contemporary reports, the crucial decision to petition against the Wheelwright indictment was made on the spur of the moment though in time cooler heads counseled to refine Aspinwall's bitter protestations. The decision to attempt the elevation of Wheelwright to the Boston pulpit was doubtless more carefully prearranged, but there is no evidence to indicate that any formal organization or procedure was adopted to procure this end. The Boston town meeting proved a convenient vehicle for some of the decision-making of the Hutchinson coterie, though whether there was any formal caucus to direct debate and voting is not known. On the whole it is almost impossible to determine when the Hutchinson program was governed by preconcerted policy and when it was simply a reflection of the personal viewpoint of individual members. The evidence suggests that much of the time it was the latter.

(vi)

There is a convenient stereotype in the portfolio of the social and religious historian that defines pietistic movements as deriving their chief support from the "disinherited"; from the lowly, the humble, and the semi-literate. However pertinent the formula may have been elsewhere, it cannot be so loosely applied to the Antinomian movement. Although some of the "disinherited" were among Mrs. Hutchinson's disciples, the backbone and sinew of the movement was drawn from an altogether dissimilar social element. They were men (and women) of some affluence, eminence, and prestige in the community, people of education and gentle breeding who were not normally given to emotional excess.

They were also, to judge by the concentration and ordering of the group, persons who were the victims—or regarded themselves as victims—of conditions not widely experienced outside of Boston. Part of the problem is to determine what these conditions were. All Massachusetts, Saints and unregenerate alike, was hedged around by the barbed web of Puritan theology and discipline but all Massachusetts did not rise up against it in 1637. Although the unregenerate had sufficient cause to resent the elect, and the poor felt cause to resent the rich, neither the unregenerate nor the poor committed themselves in any great numbers to the principles and objects of the Hutchinson movement. Those members of the Boston and neighboring churches who responded to Mrs. Hutchinson's message were, on the whole, no more nor less profoundly religious than their colleagues from the countryside who failed to be attracted. Nor were most of them, in their cultural backgrounds or psychological make-up, more precisely oriented toward the acceptance of mystical doctrines. For all the diversity of motivation that prompted participation in the movement, it would seem that Mrs. Hutchinson's closest supporters were the victims of specific secular anxieties of a kind that would make them especially susceptible to her peculiar teachings. It is understandable, given their cultural conditioning, that the Hutchinsonians should examine their secular concerns in religious terms. To them the problem was a religious one, but to the historian their religious and secular motivations appear to have been so closely intermingled as to be practically indistinguishable.

XVIII

Epilogue:
Zion Preserved

(i)

SOON after Anne Hutchinson, "the breeder and nourisher of all these distempers," [1] had been sentenced to banishment from the colony, Governor Winthrop produced a pamphlet to defend the action of his administration. His presentation was obviously biased and his attacks on the unfortunate Mrs. Hutchinson were violent in the extreme. But he saw then, as he had seen throughout the controversy, the perilous metaphysical implications of the Antinomian doctrine, and the way in which it threatened the continued existence of the social structure which he and his fellows had so painstakingly wrought out of the wilderness. "She walked by such a rule," he wrote, "as cannot stand with the peace of any State; for such bottomlesse revelations... if they be allowed in one thing, must be admitted a rule in all things; for they being above reason and Scripture, they are not subject to controll." [2]

Stripped of its theological allusions, Winthrop's declaration might serve equally well as an indictment of the subjectivistic principles of a Hume or Rousseau. Mrs. Hutchinson's expulsion from Massachusetts Bay was not narrowly based on religious principle alone. Her prosecutors claimed that she represented an anarchistic subjectivism which was inherently fatal to social cohesion. The doctrines she expounded elevated the individual conscience above all external authority and exempted the believer from any considerations of conduct. It was feared that the propagation of these doctrines might well destroy all moral values and subvert the power of properly constituted authority.

1. *Antinomianism*, 157-58.
2. *Ibid.*, 177.

Antinomianism, however ominous it may have appeared, was simply a theological idea, and did not necessarily entail any kind of unsocial behavior. Practically considered, an Antinomian conviction, however intensely held, would be quite innocuous and perhaps even constructively beneficial, in any person who had successfully internalized the cultural values of his milieu. Certainly with Mrs. Hutchinson and her colleagues the deeply implanted inhibitions of Puritan morality precluded the grosser behavioral possibilities of the Antinomian position. But nonetheless their language lent itself to misconstruction. The question remained whether any denomination could safely presuppose sufficient normative internalization on the part of their communicants. Indeed, the main developmental line of Christianity had been founded on just this point; that there are qualities in every man which render him constitutionally incapable of social adjustment without divine intervention and ecclesiastical guidance. The Puritans remained sufficiently hard-headed and pragmatic in their view to demand a sight of the empirical proof. They feared Antinomianism because it seemed to promote a "monistic egotism," which dissolved all those psychological distinctions man had invented to "check, circumscribe and surpass himself." [3]

Much like ourselves, John Winthrop and his colleagues were buffeted about by the contrary winds of a chaotic century—a century which was painfully undergoing a revolutionary shift in values. For ages unity had been an established and accepted fact. As late as 1630 the medieval heritage of a coherent and comprehensible universe was still generally assumed as the working basis of all organic social relationships. But the seventeenth century was born shrouded with misgivings. Though unity was the plan, diversity was the omnipresent and confusing reality. Aggressive national states had sprung up, wielding an irresponsible power which mocked the comforting postulates of cosmic order. Churches had split and multiplied with the bewildering rapidity of amoebae. Violent economic pressures had wrenched men free from the rigid degrees of social status which they had long endured and placed them on a contractual basis which was at once more flexible and more confusing. The "new philosophy calls all in doubt," John Donne lamented. The stability of the earth had given way to a mad whirl about the sun. Chaos had dissolved degree in the universe and in society. Puny men had o'erleaped their prescribed stations and

3. Huehns, *Antinomianism in English History*, 15.

claimed a singularity which bore no coherent relation to their fellow creatures.

> 'Tis all in pieces, all coheerence gone;
> All just supply and all relation.
> Prince, Subject, Father, Sonne are things forgot,
> For every man alone thinks he has got
> To be a Phoenix, and that then can bee
> None of that kinde of which he is, but hee.[4]

The organic and uniformitarian concepts which had governed society for centuries were being swept aside by atomistic pressures implicit in the new philosophy, science, and economics. The last feeble sparks of medieval thought were being snuffed out by the onrush of an age of individualism and democracy.

Mrs. Hutchinson, like Hampden, Lilburne, Winstanley, and many more, heralded the arrival of that new man who was to be so startlingly delineated by Rousseau a century later; an uncommon man who struggled to break down the restrictive barriers of an organic society, who demanded full freedom to assert his talents and idiosyncrasies—if need be at the expense of his fellow men—who sought to prove that there was "none of that kinde of which he is, but hee."

The Puritans had dallied with this way of life. They had indulged in contractualism and pushed individualism to its uttermost within the limits of traditional concepts. But at the hour of crisis, fearful of what it might cost to relinquish their hold on the past, they sternly rejected that future which Mrs. Hutchinson had held out to them.

The bitter struggle had been carried to a decisive conclusion and the victory had gone to a conservative element which was determined that the orthodox dogmas should be indisputably established as the intellectual focus of the community. Of the several issues at variance, it was now safely resolved that the churches of the commonwealth were to be responsible bodies, committed to the fulfillment of a broadly social function, rather than a purely evangelical service; that the Saints were under obligation to submit their private considerations to higher sanctions of a public nature, and to subject their spiritual ecstasies to the most searching intellectual examination and rigorous moral confirmation. The concepts of freedom of expression and untrammeled choice of religious

4. John Donne, *Poems*, ed. Herbert Grierson (Oxford, 1912), 237 ff.

belief, which had never been seriously entertained in Massachusetts, were now definitely placed behind them, and the commonwealth entered upon an era in which the established church was the sole repository of religious truth, with full scope to determine who had erred against that truth in matters of doctrine and morals.

The Antinomians had struck a heavy blow—if not for freedom of thought, certainly for that heterogeneity which leads to freedom of thought—but, in so doing, they had aroused a fresh and inordinate dread of heterodoxy. The Puritans refused to accept the warning implicit in the event, but rather, rallied to the defense of bastions already crumbling with age.

APPENDICES

APPENDICES

Appendix I

STATISTICAL TABLES
ON THE HUTCHINSONIAN MOVEMENT

TABLE I
REGIONAL ORIGINS

County of Origin	Banks's Topographical Listing			Hutchinsonian Movement			
	Total to N. E.	Total to Mass.	Total to Boston	Core Group	Support Group	Peripheral Group	All Groups
Bedfordshire	53	44	2	..	2	3	5
Berkshire	32	32	9	..	1	..	1
Buckinghamshire	78	60	7	..	..	1	1
Cambridgeshire	29	17	..	..	..	2	2
Chester	13	6	..	..	..	..	..
Cornwall	15	6	1	..	..	..	..
Cumberland	1	..	..	..	..	..	..
Derbyshire	24	10	4	..	1	..	1
Devonshire	175	73	7	..	..	..	..
Dorsetshire	128	102	8	..	2	..	2
Durham	3	1	..	..	..	..	..
Essex	266	200	32	5	5	4	14
Gloucestershire	75	42	11	..	3	..	3
Hampshire	73	61	5	2	..	7	9
Herefordshire	7	3	..	..	..	..	..
Hertfordshire	108	72	6	1	3	2	6
Huntingdon	8	5	3	1	..	1	2
Kent	197	110	7	..	1	2	3
Lancashire	43	32	7	1	..	..	1
Leicestershire	44	26	3	..	1	1	2
Lincolnshire	76	70	30	9	8	10	27
London	203	133	50	8	4	2	14
Middlesex	79	50	11	1	..	1	2
Norfolk	168	148	8	..	1	1	2
Northamptonshire	71	58	20	..	2	..	2
Northumberland	19	18	1	..	..	..	..
Nottinghamshire	29	15	2	..	..	..	..
Oxfordshire	27	22	..	..	..	1	1
Rutland	9	4	3	..	..	..	..
Shropshire	153	110	11	..	..	4	4
Somersetshire	14	10	3	..	..	..	..
Staffordshire	14	6	1	..	..	..	..
Suffolk	298	273	39	2	6	4	12
Surrey	55	24	9	1	3	2	6
Sussex	32	15	..	..	..	..	..
Warwickshire	61	31	10	1	..	1	2
Wiltshire	107	75	7	..	..	1	1
Worcestershire	17	3	1	..	..	..	..
Yorkshire	81	56	10	..	2	..	2
Unknown				6	14	39	59
TOTALS				38	59	90	187

Banks lists adult males who came to New England between 1620 and 1650. The list is, of course, far from complete and is used here only to suggest relative trends. It should be observed that by far the greatest number of those he lists arrived between 1630 and 1638.

TABLE II
COMPARATIVE TABLE OF REGIONAL ORIGINS

	Banks's Topographical Listing			Hutchinson Movement			
	To N. E.	*To Mass.*	*To Boston*	*Core Group*	*Support Group*	*Peripheral Group*	*All Groups*
1	Suffolk 298	Suffolk 273	London 50	Lincoln 9	Lincoln 8	Lincoln 10	Lincoln 27
2	Essex 266	Essex 200	Suffolk 38	London 8	Suffolk 6	Hampshire 7	London 14
3	London 203	Norfolk 148	Essex 32	Essex 5	Essex 5	Essex 4	Essex 14
4	Kent 197	London 133	Lincoln 30	Suffolk 2	London 4	Suffolk 4	Suffolk 12
5	Devonshire 175	Kent 110	Northants 20	Hampshire 2	Herts 3	Somerset 4	Hampshire 9

TABLE III

TIME OF ARRIVAL

Date of Arrival	Core Group	Support Group	Peripheral Group	All Groups
1628	..	3	..	3
1629	..	..	1	1
1630	12	21	5	38
1631	..	1	..	1
1632	2	1	1	4
1633	4	3	3	10
Before 1633	3	5	4	12
Before 1634	2	7	5	14
Total Arrivals 1628 through 1633	23	41	19	83
1634	7	1	2	10
1635	3	7	17	27
1636	1	..	2	3
Before 1635	..	3	7	10
Before 1636	4	5	4	13
Total Arrivals 1634 through 1636	15	16	32	63
1637	..	2	10	12
1638	..	..	6	6
Before 1637	..	..	4	4
Before 1638	..	..	19	19
Total Arrivals 1637 and 1638	..	2	39	41
TOTALS	38	59	90	187

TABLE IV
PLACE OF RESIDENCE

Residence	Core Group	Support Group	Peripheral Group	All Groups
Boston	26	39	31	96
Cambridge	..	..	..	..
Charlestown	..	11	4	15
Dorchester	..	..	2	2
Gloucester	..	..	..	..
Hingham	..	..	1	1
Ipswich	1	..	6	7
Newbury	3	..	2	5
Plymouth	..	1	4	5
Roxbury	6	3	1	10
Salem	1	4	4	9
Sandwich	..	..	1	1
Saugus	..	..	..	..
Watertown	..	..	4	4
Wollaston	1	1	4	6
Weymouth	..	..	7	7
Transient	..	..	8	8
Unknown	..	..	11	11
TOTALS	**38**	**58**	**90**	**187**

TABLE V
CHURCH MEMBERSHIP

Year Churched	Core Group	Support Group	Peripheral Group	All Groups
1628	..	1	..	1
1629	..	..	..	..
1630	7	13	2	22
1631	..	1	..	1
1632	2	2	..	4
*1633	9	10	1	22
*1634	7	6	5	18
1635	3	7	2	12
1636	4	4	1	9
No Date	3	7	4	14
Total Members	35	51	15	101
Not Members or Uncertain	3	8	75	86
TOTALS	**38**	**59**	**90**	**187**

*Years of "Cotton conversions."

Table VI
FREEMEN

Date of Enfranchisement	All Freemen	Core Group	Support Group	Peripheral Group	All Groups
1631	136	5	5	2	12
1632	52	4	2	..	6
1633	46	3	6	2	11
1634	232	12	12	..	24
1635	135	3	6	4	13
1636	138	3	13	5	21
1637	102	2	5	..	7
Total free	831	32	49	13	94
Not free	..	6	10	77	93
TOTALS	..	38	59	90	187

Table VII
OCCUPATIONAL CATEGORIES

Occupation	Core Group	Support Group	Peripheral Group	All Groups
Professions	2	3	2	7
Merchants	9	4	1	14
Craftsmen	8	15	15	38
Services	1	8	3	12
Maritime	1	1	5	7
Husbandry	4	11	8	23
Military	2	..	..	2
Servant (Skilled)	..	4	6	10
Servant (Unskilled)	2	3	11	16
Gentleman	1	..	..	1
Laborer	1	..	..	1
Unknown	7	10	39	56
TOTALS	38	59	90	187

TABLE VIII
OFFICEHOLDING

Office	Core Group	Support Group	Peripheral Group	All Groups
Mass. Bay Company				
Governor	1	..	..	1
Treasurer	2	..	..	2
Assistant	2	1	..	3
Deputy	8	7	3	18
Magistrate	2	..	..	2
Other	8	6	1	15
Total Company Officers	23	14	4	41
Towns				
Selectmen	9	5	2	16
Other	3	20	6	29
TOTALS	35	39	12	86

Key to Tables in Appendices II-IV

Age   —as of 1637

Property   —R = of the "richer sort"
          P = of the "poorer sort"

Complicity—Pet. = name appeared on the Wheelwright
          petition of March, 1637.

Removal   —Perm. = Did not return to Massachusetts
          Temp. = Soon returned to Massachusetts

Key to References in Appendices II-IV

[For complete citations, see the Bibliography.]

Aspinwall	"Aspinwall Notarial Records"
Austin	John Osborne Austin, *Genealogical Dictionary of Rhode Island*
Boston Ch	Records of the First Church of Boston (unpaged manuscript)
Boston Rec	"Boston Town Records, 1634-1660"
Banks PC	Charles Edward Banks, *Planters of the Commonwealth*
Banks TD	Charles Edward Banks, *Topographical Dictionary of English Emigrants*
Chastn Rec	"Charlestown Land Records, 1634-1802"
Exeter	Charles H. Bell, *History of the Town of Exeter*
Lechford	Thomas Lechford's *Notebook*
Mass Rec	*Records of the Governor and Company of the Massachusetts Bay*, Volume I
NEHGR	*New England Historical and Genealogical Register*
NYGBR	*New York Genealogical and Biographical Record*
Pope	Charles Henry Pope, *Pioneers of Massachusetts*
Possessions	"Boston Book of Possessions"
RI Rec	*Records of the Colony of Rhode Island and Providence Plantations*, Volume I
Roxbury Ch	"Roxbury Church Records"
Roxbury Land	"Roxbury Land Records"
Salem	James D. Phillips, *Salem in the Seventeenth Century*
Savage	James Savage, *Genealogical Dictionary of the First Settlers of New England*
Suffolk	*Suffolk Deeds*, Liber I
WJ	John Winthrop, *Journal*
WP	*Winthrop Papers*
WWP	Edward Johnson, *Wonder Working Providence*

Bibliographical References to Appendix II

Alford, William:
Pope, 13; Salem, 136; Mass Rec, 212; WP, 3, 163; Aspinwall, 411

Aspinwall, William:
Pope, 22; Banks TD, 58; WJ, I, 52, 239, II, 56, 164; WP, IV, 17; Possessions, 30, 33; Boston Rec, 12, 20, 29; Suffolk, 16; Aspinwall, I-X; Mass Rec, 77, 113, 119, 123, 159, 180, 189, 196, 201, 204, 205, 207, 338, 367; Boston Ch; NEHGR, XLVII, 39; RI Rec, 52

Balston, William:
Mass Rec, 81, 120, 199, 207, 208, 212, 223, 228, 238, 245, 366; Pope, 30; Banks PC, 59; Banks TD, 37; Austin, 16; RI Rec, 52; Boston Rec, 10, 16, 20, 30, 31, 35, 38

Brenton, William:
Pope, 66; RI Rec, 358; Boston Rec, 15, 14, 18, 29; Banks TD, 110; Banks PC, 61; Austin, 252; Aspinwall, 13, 18; Lechford, 93; Mass Rec, 369; Boston Ch

Bulgar, Richard:
Mass Rec, 153, 212, 244, 366; Pope, 77; Banks PC, 62; RI Rec, 282; Austin, 30; Aspinwall, 21; Boston Rec, 23; Lechford, 107, 282; Exeter, 21, 436; Boston Ch

Bull, Henry:
Roxbury Ch, 81; WP, II, 377; Mass Rec, 106, 212, 373; Pope, 77; Banks TD, 168; RI Rec, 52, 87; Austin, 264

Carder, Richard:
Mass Rec, 212, 223; Pope, 88; Roxbury Ch, 80; RI Rec, 52; Austin, 270; Boston Rec, 41, 49; Lechford, 228

Coddington, William:
Mass Rec, 69, 70, 95, 105, 118, 129, 145, 174, 182, 204, 205, 223, 372; WP, III, 22, 34, 119, 217, IV, 23, 161, 215, 278, 393; Pope, 107; Banks PC, 65; Banks TD, 94; Boston Rec, 8, 18, 20; Lechford, 62, 67; RI Rec, 52; Austin, 276; Suffolk, 15, 26; Boston Ch

Coggeshall, John:
Roxbury Ch, 75; NEHGR, XCIX, 315, C, 14; LXXIII, 24, 30; Pope, 108; Banks TD, 47; Austin, 49; RI Rec, 52; WJ, 239; Boston Rec, 8, 20, 27, 30, 31; Lechford, 69; Mass Rec, 104, 112, 113, 116, 119, 120, 125, 135, 136, 142, 144, 145, 174, 175, 178, 180, 185, 191, 198, 205, 207, 212, 223, 377; Boston Ch

Compton, John:
Exeter, 21, 436; Mass Rec, 212, 223; Pope, 113; WP, IV, 353; Aspinwall, 15; Boston Rec, 94, 96; Possessions, 27

Dummer, Richard:
Roxbury Ch, 74, 77; Suffolk, 13; Pope, 146; Banks TD, 60; WP, IV, 114; WJ, II, 4; WP, III, 67, 69, 101, 169, 103; Mass Rec, 112, 114, 125, 141, 145, 147, 150, 151, 152, 156, 164, 167, 171, 173, 174, 175, 176, 177, 184, 191, 196, 204, 212, 258, 290, 297, 301, 315, 328, 339, 345, 367

Dyer, William:
Boston Ch; Mass Rec, 208, 211, 371; Pope, 148; Banks TD, 103; RI Rec, 52; Austin, 290; WJ, I, 266; Boston Rec, 29; Lechford, 69

Easton, Nicholas:
WJ, II, 41; Mass Rec, 125, 135, 175, 212, 223, 231, 370; Pope, 149; Banks TD, 61; RI Rec, 58, 87; Austin, 292; Chastn Rec, 73

Elkins, Henry:
Mass Rec, 211, 370; Pope, 154; Boston Rec, 25; Boston Ch; Exeter, 21

Foster, William:
Mass Rec, 212, 238, 266; Pope, 173; Lechford, 101, 135; Savage, II, 191; Austin, 80; Aspinwall, 229, 267, 351; RI Rec, 90, 92, 93, 100

Freeborn, William:
Mass Rec, 212, 223, 369; Pope, 175; RI Rec, 52; Austin, 296

Grosse, Isaac:
Mass Rec, 212; Pope, 202; Possessions, 22; Boston Rec, 15, 26; WP, III, 513; Exeter, 21; Boston Ch

Harding, Robert:
Lechford, 78, 207, 330; Mass Rec, 78, 113, 120, 191, 203, 212, 226, 262, 366; Pope, 210, 212; Banks TD, 40; WP, IV, 112; Aspinwall, 11, 12; Boston Rec, 8, 20, 28, 30, 41, 43, 44; Boston Ch; Suffolk, 320

Hawkins, Richard:
Mass Rec, 224, 329; Pope, 222; Banks TD, 73; RI Rec, 72; WJ, II, 8, I, 266, 268; Aspinwall, 259

Hutchinson, Edward, Sr.:
Mass Rec, 207, 212, 223, 245, 368; Pope, 249; Banks TD, 93; Boston Rec, 38, 40; Lechford, 69; RI Rec, 52; Boston Ch; NYGBR, XLV, 23

Hutchinson, Edward, Jr.:
Mass Rec, 207, 212, 223, 245, 368; Pope, 249; Banks TD, 93; Boston Rec, 38, 40; Boston Ch; Lechford, 69; RI Rec, 52; NYGBR, XLV, 23

Hutchinson, Francis:
Mass Rec, 336, 340, 344, 370; Pope, 250; NYGBR, XLV, 23; Lechford, 435

Hutchinson, Richard:
Mass Rec, 212, 370; Pope, 250; NYGBR, XLV, 3; Lechford, 156, 186

Hutchinson, William:
Boston Rec, 7, 8, 14, 19, 20, 30; Suffolk, 22, 23; Lechford, 69, 101, 156, 317, 385; Mass Rec, 145, 149, 153, 156, 164, 174, 177, 178, 181, 185, 211, 370; Pope, 250; RI Rec, 52; Banks TD, 93; NYGBR, XLV, 23; Boston Ch

Morris, Richard:

> Boston Ch; Lechford, 92, 223; WJ, I, 122; WP, IV, 29, V, 165; Mass Rec, 103, 110, 112, 119, 124, 130, 135, 164, 165, 181, 212, 237, 366; Pope, 320; Banks PC, 82; Banks TD, 108; Exeter, 21, 436; RI Rec, 77, 110, 121

Porter, John:

> Mass Rec, 212, 223, 368; Roxbury Ch, 78, 79; Banks PC, 87; Banks TD, 46; Pope, 369; Austin, 155; RI Rec, 52

Potter, Robert:

> Roxbury Ch, 80, 187; Austin, 156; Mass Rec, 212, 369; RI Rec, 70, 91, 111, 123

Sanford, John:

> Boston Ch; NEHGR, CIII, 208; Mass Rec, 107, 120, 125, 142, 179, 183, 206, 211, 367; Pope, 400; Banks PC, 9; Austin, 171; RI Rec, 52; Boston Rec, 20, 27, 29; WP, III, 2, 3, 4, 108, 133, 138

Savage, Thomas:

> Mass Rec, 212, 372; Pope, 401; NEHGR, CXVII, 198; Banks TD, 69; Possessions, 8, 19; Boston Rec, 15, 43, 44, 51, 53, 58, 69; Suffolk, 53; Lechford, 16, 69, 137, 157, 189, 206, 207, 208; WP, III, 515; RI Rec, 52; Boston Ch

Sherman, Philip:

> Mass Rec, 212, 223, 368; Pope, 413; Banks TD, 48; Austin, 178; RI Rec, 52; Roxbury Ch, 78, 79; Boston Rec, 19; Suffolk, 44

Spencer, John:

> Mass Rec, 135, 145, 149, 156, 164, 167, 174, 175, 178, 185, 191, 195, 212, 369; Pope, 427; Banks TD, 168; NEHGR, XLIV, 390, LV, 110; WP, IV, 99

Underhill, John:

> Mass Rec, 75, 76, 99, 103, 112, 116, 120, 124, 129, 158, 160, 187, 191, 200, 208, 211, 237, 251, 301, 329, 335, 366; Boston Ch; Pope, 467; Banks TD, 175; Banks PC, 94; Boston Rec, 26, 39; Lechford, 408

Vane, Henry:

> Mass Rec, 168, 174, 176, 177, 184, 191, 193, 194, 200, 371; Boston Rec, 19, 27; Boston Ch; Hosmer, *Henry Vane*, chap. 1

Walker, John:

> Mass Rec, 212, 368; Pope, 478; Banks PC, 95; Austin, 214; RI Rec, 52; Roxbury Ch, 78, 80

Wardall, Thomas:

> Mass Rec, 212, 370; Pope, 479; Banks TD, 93; Boston Rec, 25; WP, III, 513; Exeter, 21, 436; Boston Ch

Wardall, William:

> Mass Rec, 212; Pope, 479; Banks TD, 93; RI Rec, 77, 131; Exeter, 21; Possessions, 9; Boston Rec, 15, 32; WP, III, 513; Boston Ch

Wheelwright, John:

> Mass Rec, 189, 196, 200, 205, 207, 211; Pope, 491; Banks TD, 95; Boston Rec, 15, 46; WP, III, 45, 46; Exeter, 21, 436

Wilbore, Samuel:

> Mass Rec, 144, 203, 211, 223, 368; Pope, 282, 497; Banks PC, 97; RI Rec, 52, 110; Austin, 227; WP, IV, 121; Boston Ch; Boston Rec, 19, 21, 34

APPENDIX II—PERSONNEL IN THE CORE GROUP

Name	Age	Place of Origin	Time of Arrival	Residence	Churched	Freeman	Vocation	Office (Colony)	Office (Local)	Property	Married	Complicity	Change of Religion	Disposition of Case	Removal
Alford, William (Mr.)		London	1634	Salem	....	....	Skinner		Yes		Yes	Pet.		Disarmed	Portsmth Temp.
Aspinwall, William (Mr.)		Lancaster	1630	Boston	1630	1632	Notary Surveyor	Deputy	Selectman	R	Yes	Pet.	Fifth Monarchy	Disarmed Disfranchised Banished	Portsmth Temp.
Balston, William		London	1630	Boston	1630	1631	Innkeeper	Jury Ensign	Selectman	R	Yes	Pet.		Disarmed Disfranchised Banished	Portsmth Perm.
Brenton, William (Mr.)		Middlesex	1630	Boston	1633	1634	Merchant	Deputy	Selectman	R	Yes			Disarmed Disfranchised Banished	Portsmth Perm.
Bulgar, Richard	29	London	1630	Boston	1634	1631	Bricklayer			R	Yes	Pet.		Disarmed	Exeter Temp.
Bull, Henry	27	London	1635	Roxbury	1636	1637	Servant			P	Yes	Pet.	Quaker	Disarmed Disfranchised Excommunicated	Portsmth Perm.
Carder, Richard			bef. 1636	Boston	1636	1637				P		Pet.	Gorton	Disarmed	Portsmth Perm.
Coddington, William (Mr.)	39	Lincoln	1630	Boston	1630	1636	Merchant	Treas. Asst. Deputy	Selectman	R	Yes		Quaker	Disarmed Banished	Portsmth Perm.
Coggeshall, John (Mr.)	46	Essex	1632	Boston	1632	1632	Silk Mercer	Deputy	Selectman	R	Yes		Easton	Disarmed Disfranchised Banished	Portsmth Perm.
Compton, John	30's		bef. 1634	Boston	n.d.	1634	Laborer				Yes	Pet.		Disarmed	Exeter Temp.

Name	Age	Origin		Town			Occupation	Office	R	Yes	Pet.	Religion	Action	Place
Dummer, Richard (Mr.)	39	Hampshire	1632	Newbury	1632	1632	Farmer ?	Treas. Asst. Magist.	R	Yes	Pet.		Disarmed	Portsmth Temp.
Dyer, William (Mr.)		London	bef. 1635	Boston	1635	1636	Milliner			Yes	Pet.	Wife a Quaker	Disarmed / Disfranchised	Portsmth Perm.
Easton, Nicholas (Mr.)		Hampshire	1634	Newbury	n.d.	1634	Tanner	Committee		Yes	Pet.	Indep. Preacher / Quaker	Disarmed / Banished	Portsmth Perm.
Elkins, Henry			bef. 1634	Boston	1634	1635	Tailor			Yes	Pet.		Disarmed / Dismissed	Exeter Perm.
Foster, William (Mr.)	20's	Suffolk	1634	Ipswich	....	....	Ship-master		R		Pet.		Disarmed	Portsmth Perm.
Freeborn, William	43	Suffolk	1634	Boston	n.d.	1634				Yes	Pet.	Quaker	Disarmed / Banished	Portsmth Perm.
Grosse, Isaac	ca. 50		bef. 1636	Boston	1636	....	Brewer			Yes	Pet.		Disarmed / Wife admonished by church	Exeter Temp.
Harding, Robert (Mr.)	30's	Essex	1630	Boston	1630	1631	Mercer	Ensign / Selectman	R	Yes	Pet.		Acknowledged error	Portsmth Temp.
Hawkins, Richard	ca. 50	Huntingdon	bef. 1636	Boston	....	....				Yes		Wife Familist	Jane Hawkins banished	Portsmth Perm.
Hutchinson, Edward, Sr.	35	Lincoln	1633	Boston	1633	1633		Serg't / Assessor	R	Yes	Pet.		Disarmed / Disfranchised	Portsmth Perm.
Hutchinson, Edward, Jr.	24	Lincoln	1633	Boston	1634	1634	Mercer			Yes			Banished	Portsmth Perm.
Hutchinson, Francis	17	Lincoln	1634	Boston	1634	1634							Banished in 1641	Portsmth Perm.

Name	Age	Place of Origin	Time of Arrival	Residence	Churched	Freeman	Vocation	Office Colony	Office Local	Property	Married	Complicity	Change of Religion	Disposition of Case	Removal
Hutchinson, Richard	22	Lincoln	1634	Boston	1634	1634	Linen-draper					Pet.		Disarmed	London Perm.
Hutchinson, William (Mr.)	46	Lincoln	1634	Boston	1634	1634	Mercer	Magist. Deputy	Select-man	R	Yes	Pet.		Wife banished; Excommunicated	Portsmth Perm.
Morris, Richard	ca. 45	London	1630	Roxbury	1630	1631	Military	Deputy Lieut.			Yes	Pet.		Disarmed; Dismissed	Exeter Perm.
Porter, John	ca. 27	Essex	1630	Roxbury	1633	1633	Farmer ?				Yes	Pet.		Disarmed; Banished	Portsmth Perm.
Potter, Robert			1630	Roxbury	1634	1634	Farmer						Gorton-ist	Banished; Excommunicated	Portsmth Perm.
Sanford, John (Mr.)	ca. 30	Essex	1630	Boston	1630	1632	Merchant	Can-noneer	Select-man	R	Yes	Pet.		Disarmed	Portsmth Perm.
Savage, Thomas	30	Herts	1635	Boston	1635	1636	Tailor	Cap-tain		R	Yes	Pet.		Disarmed; Acknowledged error	Portsmth Temp.
Sherman, Philip	27	Essex	1633	Roxbury	1633	1634					Yes	Pet.		Disarmed; Excommunicated; Banished	Portsmth Perm.
Spencer, John (Mr.)		Surrey	1633	Newbury	1633	1634	Farmer ?	Deputy Magist.	Capt.	R		Pet.		Disarmed; Discharged as Captain	Portsmth Perm.
Underhill, John (Mr.)	40	Warwick	1630	Boston	1630	1631	Military expert	Deputy Capt.	Select-man		Yes	Pet.		Disarmed; Banished	Dover Perm.

Name	Age	Eng. Origin	Emig.	Mass. Town			Gentleman	Governor/ Deputy	R		"Vanist"		England
Vane, Henry (Mr.)	25	London	1635	Boston	1635	1635	Gentleman	Governor Deputy					England Perm.
Walker, John			bef. 1633	Roxbury	1633	1635			Yes	Pet.		Disarmed	Portsmth Perm.
Wardall, Thomas		Lincoln	bef. 1633	Boston	1633	1634	Shoemaker		Yes	Pet.		Disarmed / Acknowledged error / Dismissed	Exeter Temp.
Wardall, William		Lincoln	bef. 1633	Boston	1633	....	Servant		Yes	Pet.	Gorton-ist	Disarmed / Acknowledged error / Dismissed	Exeter / Portsmth Perm.
Wheelwright John (Mr.)	45	Lincoln	1636	Boston Wollast	1636	n.d.	Clergyman		Yes			Disfranchised / Banished	Exeter Temp.
Wilbore, Samuel		London	1630	Boston	1633	1633	Merchant	Jury / Assessor	Yes	Pet.		Disarmed / Banished / Recanted—'39	Portsmth Temp.

Bibliographical References to Appendix III

Baker, William:
Mass Rec, 223, 369; Pope, 24; Chastn Rec, 47; *History of Malden*, 66

Bates, Edward:
Mass Rec, 211, 255, 260, 263, 288, 294, 301, 329, 336, 343, 372; Pope, 37; Boston Rec, 18, 28; Boston Ch

Bendall, Edward:
Mass Rec, 165, 176, 181, 211, 339, 369; Pope, 45; Banks PC, 60; Lechford, 69, 72, 228, 235, 295; Possessions, 21; Boston Rec, 21, 25; Boston Ch

Biggs, John:
Mass Rec, 103, 211, 368; Pope, 49; Banks PC, 60; Possessions, 14; Boston Rec, 22; Boston Ch; WP, III, 108, 115

Bosworth, Zaccheus:
Mass Rec, 211, 372; Pope, 59; Banks PC, 61; Suffolk, 92; Boston Ch; WP, III, 513

Bunker, George:
Mass Rec, 212, 229, 240, 370; Pope, 79; Banks TD, 1; Chastn Rec, 28; *History of Malden*, 66

Burden, George:
Mass Rec, 212, 373; Pope, 79; Banks TD, 56; Possessions, 17; Boston Rec, 32, 33, 34, 44, 53; Suffolk, 18, 154, 206; Boston Ch

Button, John:
Mass Rec, 211, 283, 300, 312, 369; Pope, 85; Possessions, 18; Boston Ch; Boston Rec, 54, 58, 59; WP, III, 242

Carrington, Edward:
Mass Rec, 182, 209, 371; Pope, 89; Chastn Rec, 53, 73; *History of Malden*, 66

Clarke, John (Dr.):
Mass Rec, 212; RI Rec, 52; Austin, 45; WP, III, 385; "Ill Newes From New England," 23, 24

Cole, Samuel:
Mass Rec, 155, 159, 198, 199, 208, 211, 226, 228, 244, 245, 279; Banks PC, 66; Pope, 110; Aspinwall, 2, 90; Possessions, 9; Boston Rec, 12, 29, 38; Lechford, 51, 175, 291; Boston Ch

Comins, William:
Mass Rec, 212; Pope, 125

Cooke, Richard:
Mass Rec, 211, 369, 370; Pope, 115; Possessions, 29; Suffolk, 102; Lechford, 91; Boston Ch

Davy, John:
Mass Rec, 212, 372; Pope, 132; Possessions, 19; WP, III, 218, 229, 513; Boston Ch

Denison, Edward:
Mass Rec, 212; Banks TD, 71; Roxbury Land, 20; Roxbury Ch, 86, 171, 190; Suffolk, 155

Denison, William:
Mass Rec, 112, 113, 122, 135, 143, 212, 266, 367; Pope, 137; Banks TD, 71; Roxbury Land, 4, 5; Roxbury Ch, 73, 172, 175

Dinely, William:
Mass Rec, 208, 211, 218, 373; Pope, 139; Banks TD, 94; Boston Rec, 24; Lechford, 11, 19; WWP, 192; Boston Ch

Eliot, Jacob:
Mass Rec, 212, 295, 342, 367; Pope, 153; Banks TD, 50; Possessions, 34; Boston Rec, 19, 20; WP, III, 514; Boston Ch

Ewar, Thomas:
Mass Rec, 209, 220, 230, 233, 248, 371; Pope, 159; Banks TD, 83; WJ, I, 228; Chastn Rec, 29, 30, 73; *History of Malden*, 67; Lechford, 35

Fairbank, Richard:
Mass Rec, 211, 221, 281, 369; Pope, 160; Possessions, 23; Boston Rec, 10, 19, 25; Boston Ch; WP, III, 513

Faunce, Mathias:
Mass Rec, 155, 211; Banks TD, 52

Flint, Henry:
Mass Rec, 289, 372; Mather, *Magnalia*, I, 443; Boston Ch; NEHGR, LV, 313

Frothingham, William:
Mass Rec, 209, 367; Pope, 177; Banks TD, 187; Chastn Rec, 26, 27, 73; *History of Malden*, 66

Greensmith, Stephen:
Mass Rec, 189, 196, 200, 245; Pope, 200; WP, IV, 275; Aspinwall, 314, 418; Lechford, 223; WP, III, 46; Boston Rec, 12

Gridley, Richard:
Mass Rec, 207, 211, 259, 368; Pope, 200; Banks TD, 154; Possessions, 33, 37; Lechford, 210; WP, III, 513; Boston Rec

Gunnison, Hugh:
Mass Rec, 211, 372; Pope, 204; Aspinwall, 5, 18; Possessions, 17; Boston Rec, 15; Boston Ch; Suffolk, 136; WP, III, 513

Hough, Atherton:
Mass Rec, 145, 150, 151, 155, 156, 162, 164, 171, 173, 194, 204, 220, 227, 230, 235, 250, 300, 308, 331, 368; Pope, 241; Banks TD, 94; WJ, I, 106; Possessions, 2; Boston Rec, 7, 18, 21; Boston Ch

Hubbard, Benjamin:
Mass Rec, 209, 245, 345, 369; Pope, 245; Chastn Rec, 55, 73; *History of Malden*, 66; WP, III, 509, V, 9

Hudson, Ralph:
Mass Rec, 212, 372; Boston Ch; Boston Rec, 3, 8; Lechford, 70; WP, III, 515; Banks TD, 187

Hull, Robert:
Mass Rec, 212, 373; Pope, 247; Possessions, 36; Boston Rec, 47; Boston Ch; WP, III, 513; Banks TD, 91

Hutchinson, Samuel:
Mass Rec, 207, 338; Pope, 250; Banks TD, 93; Suffolk, 53; Lechford, 137, 141, 186

Johnson, James:
Mass Rec, 212, 372; Pope, 260; Banks TD, 126; Possessions, 7; Boston Rec, 24, 38; Boston Ch; WP, III, 513

Jyans, Matthew:
Mass Rec, 211; Banks PC, 76; Pope, 252; Possessions, 38; Boston Rec, 22; Boston Ch

King, William:
Mass Rec, 212, 372; Pope, 271; Salem, 136; Banks TD, 37

Larnet, William:
Mass Rec, 208, 369; Pope, 281; Banks TD, 167; Banks PC, 79; Chastn Rec, 25; *History of Malden*, 66

Leverett, Thomas:
Mass Rec, 300, 368; Boston Ch; WJ, I, 110; Possessions, 4; Boston Rec, 8, 20, 25, 30, 36; Lechford, 69; NEHGR, IV, 121; Banks TD, 93; Pope, 284

Litherland, William:
Mass Rec, 211; Pope, 282; Banks PC, 79; Banks TD, 45; Possessions, 38; Boston Rec, 46; Boston Ch; Austin, 126

Marshall, Thomas:
Mass Rec, 207, 211, 370; Pope, 301; Banks TD, 93; Possessions, 9; Boston Rec, 27; Boston Ch

Matson, Thomas:
Mass Rec, 212, 368; Pope, 306; Banks PC, 80; Banks TD, 105; Boston Rec, 27, 28, 40; Lechford, 273; Boston Ch; WP, III, 513

Mellows, Edward:
Mass Rec, 209, 259, 368; Pope, 310; Banks TD, 2; Chastn Rec, 56; *History of Malden*, 66; Lechford, 410

Mellows, Oliver:
Mass Rec, 211, 369; Pope, 310; Banks TD, 94; Boston Rec, 21, 32; Boston Ch

Moulton, Robert:
Mass Rec, 54, 114, 117, 120, 124, 145, 149, 191, 366; Pope, 322; Banks TD, 169; Salem, 122, 361; Suffolk, 4

Mousall, Ralph:
Mass Rec, 173, 209, 221, 236, 366; Pope, 322; Banks PC, 82; Chastn Rec, 24; *History of Malden*, 66

Odlin, John:
Mass Rec, 212, 368; Pope, 334; Banks PC, 58; Possessions, 35; Boston Rec, 28, 36, 53; Boston Ch; WP, III, 514

Oliver, John:
Mass Rec, 120, 177, 206, 211, 220, 221, 224, 227, 228, 231, 238, 254, 368; Pope, 335; Banks TD, 56; Possessions, 9; WP, III, 515; WJ, II, 267; Boston Ch; Boston Rec, 14, 15, 20, 21, 29; Lechford, 62, 290; WP, III, 513

Oliver, Thomas:
Mass Rec, 211, 290, 342, 367; Pope, 335; Banks TD, 56; WJ, I, 97; Boston Ch; Boston Rec, 8, 20, 27, 30; Suffolk, 113

Pell, William:
Mass Rec, 212, 370; Pope, 352; Possessions, 27; Boston Ch; Boston Rec, 25; Lechford, 19; WP, III, 515

Rainsford, Edward:
Mass Rec, 211, 312, 373; Pope, 377; Banks PC, 88; Possessions, 34; Boston Ch; WP, III, 514

Rice, Robert:
Mass Rec, 212; Pope, 383; Possessions, 70; WP, III, 513; Boston Ch

Richardson, Ezekiel:
Mass Rec, 104, 156, 203, 209, 295, 366; Pope, 384; Banks PC, 89; Chastn Rec, 3, 73; *History of Malden,* 66

Salter, William:
Mass Rec, 212, 372; Pope, 397; Banks TD, 159; Possessions, 34; Boston Ch; Boston Rec, 23; Lechford, 4

Scruggs, Thomas:
Mass Rec, 164, 175, 178, 185, 212, 308, 371; Pope, 405; Banks TD, 123; Salem, 351, 361; WP, III, 484; Essex Institute, *Hist. Colls.,* IX, 14

Sherman, Samuel:
Mass Rec, 212, 315, 317, 377; Pope, 413; Boston Rec, 53; Suffolk, 44

Sprague, Richard:
Mass Rec, 209, 366; Pope, 428; Banks TD, 35; Chastn Rec, 33, 34, 73; Lechford, 301; *History of Malden,* 66, 69

Townsend, William:
Mass Rec, 212, 372; Pope, 459; Banks TD, 151; Possessions, 31; Boston Rec, 24; Boston Ch; Lechford, 210; WP, III, 513

Wayte, Gamaliel:
Mass Rec, 212, 370; Pope, 473; Possessions, 37; Boston Rec, 30

Wheeler, Thomas:
Mass Rec, 212, 373; Pope, 490; Banks TD, 6; WP, IV, 124; Possessions, 35; Boston Rec, 33; Boston Ch

Wilson, Thomas:
Mass Rec, 368; Pope, 504; Banks TD, 95; Roxbury Ch, 79; 187; Exeter, 17

Wilson, William:
Mass Rec, 212, 339, 372; Pope, 505; Banks TD, 95; Possessions, 13; Boston Ch; Boston Rec, 24

APPENDIX III—PERSONNEL IN THE SUPPORT GROUP

Name	Age	Place of Origin	Time of Arrival	Residence	Churched	Freeman	Vocation	Office Colony	Office Local	Property	Married	Complicity	Change of Religion	Disposition of Case	Removal
Baker, William	38		bef. 1633	Charlestown	1633	1634	Husbandry				Yes	Pet.		Acknowledged error	
Bates, Edward	36		bef. 1633	Boston	1633	1637	Servant					Pet.		Disarmed	
Bendall, Edward		Surrey	1630	Boston	1630	1634	Dockman		Constable	R	Yes	Pet.		Disarmed	
Biggs, John		Suffolk	1630	Boston	1630	1633				R	Yes	Pet.		Acknowledged error	
Bosworth, Zaccheus		Northants	1630	Boston	1630	1636				R	Yes	Pet.		Disarmed Acknowledged error	
Bunker, George		Bedford	bef. 1634	Charlestown	n.d.	1635	Husbandry		Constable	R	Yes	Pet.		Disarmed	
Burden, George	26	Gloucester	1635	Boston	1636	1637	Shoemaker		Constable		Yes	Pet.		Disarmed Acknowledged error	
Button, John	43		bef. 1633	Boston	1633	1634	Miller	Juryman	Fence Overseer	R	Yes	Pet.		Disarmed Acknowledged error	
Carrington, Edward	24		1632	Charlestown	n.d.	1636	Turner				Yes	Pet.		Acknowledged error	Portsmth Perm.
Clarke, John (Dr.)	28	Suffolk	1637	Boston	....	....	Physician				Yes		Baptist	Acknowledged error	
Cole, Samuel (Mr.)	30's	Essex	1630	Boston	1630	....	Innholder Confectioner			R	Yes	Pet.		Disarmed Acknowledged error	

312

Name	Age	Origin	Immigr.	Town	Date	Date	Occupation	Office	R	Signed	Pet.	Disposition	Subseq. residence
Comins, William (Mr.)			bef. 1636	Salem	.....					Yes	Pet.	Disarmed	
Cooke, Richard	37		bef. 1634	Boston	1634	1634	Tailor			Yes	Pet.	Disarmed; Acknowledged error	
Davy, John	33		1635	Boston	1635	1636	Joiner	Constable			Pet.	Disarmed	
Denison, Edward	21	Herts	1630	Roxbury	.....	.....		Deputy		Yes	Pet.	Disarmed	
Denison, William (Mr.)	ca. 45	Herts	1630	Roxbury	1631	1632	Merchant	Constable	R		Pet.	Disarmed	
Dinely, William	ca. 30	Lincoln	bef. 1635	Boston	1635	1637	Barber-surgeon			Yes	Pet.	Disarmed; Disfranchised; Acknowledged error	
Eliot, Jacob	31	Essex	1630	Boston	1630	1631		Committee man	R	Yes	Pet.	Disarmed; Acknowledged error	
Ewar, Thomas	42	Kent	1635	Charlestown	1635	1635	Tailor	Selectman		Yes	Pet.	Acknowledged error	
Fairbank, Richard	20–30		bef. 1633	Boston	1633	1634	Shopkeeper	Constable; Foldkeeper		Yes	Pet.	Disarmed; Acknowledged error	
Faunce, Matthias		Essex ?	1623?	Plymouth?	.....	.....					Pet.	Acknowledged error	
Flint, Henry (Mr.)		Derby	bef. 1636	Boston; Wollaston	n.d.	1636	Clergyman				Pet.	Acknowledged error	
Frothingham, William	25–35	Yorkshire	1630	Charlestown	1630	1631	Husbandry		R	Yes	Pet.	Acknowledged error	
Greensmith, Stephen (Mr.)			bef. 1636	Boston	.....	.....	Merchant					Acknowledged error; Fined; Committed	New Hampshire

APPENDIX III—PERSONNEL IN THE SUPPORT GROUP—Continued

Name	Age	Place of Origin	Time of Arrival	Residence	Churched	Freeman	Vocation	Office		Property	Married	Complicity	Change of Religion	Disposition of Case	Removal
								Colony	Local						
Gridley, Richard	36	Suffolk	1631	Boston	n.d.	1634	Brick-maker Bricklayer		Fence Over-seer	R	Yes	Pet.		Disarmed Disfranchised Acknowledged error	
Gunnison, Hugh			bef. 1635	Boston	1635	1636	Servant Vintner				Yes	Pet.		Disarmed Acknowledged error	
Hough, Atherton (Mr.)	ca. 40	Lincoln	1633	Boston	1633	1633	Gentleman	Ass't Deputy		R	Yes			Court rejects as Deputy	
Hubbard, Benjamin			bef. 1634	Charles-town	1633	1634	Surveyor				Yes	Pet.		Acknowledged error	
Hudson, Ralph	44	York-shire	1635	Boston	1635	1636	Draper	Jury-man			Yes	Pet.		Acknowledged error	
Hull, Robert		Leicester	1635	Boston	1636	1636	Black-smith		Con-stable		Yes	Pet.		Acknowledged error	
Hutchinson, Samuel	47	Lincoln	1637	Boston	....	....								Denied resi-dence	Portsmth
Johnson, James		Northants	bef. 1636	Boston	1636	1636	Leather-dresser Glover	Cap-tain of foot com-pany			Yes	Pet.		Disarmed Acknowledged error	Exeter
Jyans, Matthew	20-30	Essex	1630	Boston	1634	1636	Servant				Yes	Pet.		Disarmed	
King, William	42	Dorset	1634	Salem	n.d.	1636	Farmer ?	Com-mittee man	Town Officer		Yes	Pet.		Disarmed	
Larnet, William		Surrey	1630	Charles-town	1632	1634					Yes	Pet.		Acknowledged error	

Name	Age	Origin		Town			Occupation	Office	R		Pet.	Action
Leveret, Thomas	ca. 50											
Litherland, William	29	London	1630	Boston	1633	1635	Servant			Yes	Pet.	Disarmed
Marshall, Thomas	ca. 40	Lincoln	bef. 1634	Boston	1634	1635	Carpenter Ferryman	Fence Over-seer	R	Yes	Pet.	Disarmed Disfranchised
Matson, Thomas	20-30	London	1630	Boston	1630	1633	Gunsmith	Fence Over-seer		Yes	Pet.	Disarmed Acknowledged error
Mellows, Edward		Bedford	1630	Charles-town	1633	1633	Farmer	Sgt.	R	Yes	Pet.	Acknowledged error
Mellows, Oliver		Lincoln	bef. 1633	Boston	1634	1633		Fence Over-seer		Yes	Pet.	Disarmed
Moulton, Robert		Surrey	1628	Salem	n.d.	1631	Ship-wright	Deputy Select-man			Pet.	Disarmed
Mousall, Ralph	41	London	1630	Charles-town	n.d.	n.d.	Carpenter	Deputy Town Officer		Yes	Pet.	Dismissed from Court Acknowledged error
Odlin, John	34	London	1630	Boston	1630	1634	Cutler	Fence Over-seer	R	Yes	Pet.	Dismissed Disarmed Acknowledged error
Oliver, John	22	Glouces-ter	1630	Boston	1632	1634	Surveyor	Deputy Sgt.		Yes	Pet.	Disarmed Dismissed Acknowledged error
Oliver, Thomas (Mr.)	69	Glouces-ter	1630	Boston	1630	1632	Surgeon	Select-man	R	Yes	Pet.	Disarmed
Pell, William	20-30		bef. 1634	Boston	1634	1635	Tallow chandler			Yes	Pet.	Disarmed Acknowledged error

APPENDIX III—PERSONNEL IN THE SUPPORT GROUP—Continued

Name	Age	Place of Origin	Time of Arrival	Residence	Churched	Freeman	Vocation	Office Colony	Office Local	Property	Married	Complicity	Change of Religion	Disposition of Case	Removal
Rainsford, Edward	26		1630	Boston	1630	1637	Cooper			R	Yes	Pet.		Disarmed; Acknowledged error	
Rice, Robert		Suffolk	1630	Boston	1630	1634						Pet.		Disarmed; Acknowledged error	
Richardson, Ezekiel		Herts	1630	Charlestown	1630	1631	Farmer ?	Deputy	Constable			Pet.		Acknowledged error	
Salter, William	45	Suffolk	bef. 1635	Boston	1635	1636	Fisherman		Fence Overseer		Yes	Pet.		Disarmed	
Scruggs, Thomas		Norfolk	1628	Salem	1628	1635		Deputy	Selectman		Yes	Pet.		Disarmed	
Sherman, Samuel	20–30	Essex	bef. 1636	Boston	....	....	Farmer ?				Yes	Pet.		Disarmed	
Sprague, Richard	32	Dorset	1628	Charlestown	1630	1631		Lieut.	Town Officer			Pet.		Acknowledged error	
Townsend, William	36	Suffolk	bef. 1634	Boston	1634	1636	Servant; Baker				Yes	Pet.		Disarmed; Acknowledged error	
Wayte, Gamaliel	39	Berkshire	1630	Boston	....	....	Servant				Yes	Pet.		Disarmed	
Wheeler, Thomas	33	Berkshire	1635	Boston	1636	1637	Servant				Yes	Pet.		Disarmed	
Wilson, Thomas		Lincoln	1633	Roxbury	1633	1634	Tailor; Miller				Yes			Excommunicated	Exeter
Wilson, William		Lincoln	1635	Boston	1635	1636	Joiner				Yes	Pet.		Disarmed	

316

Bibliographical References to Appendix IV

Adams, Nathaniel:
Pope, 10; Weymouth Vital Records; RI Rec, 92

Albro, John:
Austin, 234; RI Rec, 72, 127; Banks TD, 165

Allen, George, Jr.:
Pope, 13; Banks TD, 144; Suffolk, 17; Lechford, 392; RI Rec, 92

Allen, Ralph:
Pope, 13; Mass Rec, 267; RI Rec, 92

Allen, Samuel:
Mass Rec, 370; RI Rec, 92; Pope, 13; Boston Rec, 49; Suffolk, 9

Awarde, Richard:
Pope, 223; RI Rec, 70, 91, 100; Boston Rec, 31

Baker, William:
Austin, 10; Mass Rec, 209; RI Rec, 59, 91, 92; Watertown Records, 4, 8

Barlow, George:
Exeter, 21; Mass Rec

Bates, George:
Mass Rec, 372; Pope, 38; Possessions, 18; Boston Ch; Boston Rec, 25; Exeter, 21

Bennett, Robert:
Austin, 18; RI Rec, 300

Bishop, Townsend:
Mass Rec, 164, 174, 175, 178, 180, 205, 288, 371; Salem, 114; WP, IV, 72

Blackwell, Jeremiah:
Exeter, 21; Lechford, 387; Banks PC, 173

Briggs, John:
Austin, 25; RI Rec, 70, 75, 77; Banks PC, 177

Brown, James:
Mass Rec, 78, 154, 212, 312, 368; Pope, 72; Suffolk, 16; Chastn Rec, 73; WP, III, 515

Brown, Nicholas:
Austin, 28; Aspinwall, 47, 266; RI Rec, 70, 73, 79, 91

Bullock, Erasmus:
Boston Rec, 21; RI Rec, 70, 91

Burden, Richard:
Austin, 28; Banks TD, 80; RI Rec, 55, 64, 79, 91

Burrows, John:
Austin, 41; Banks TD, 123; Banks PC, 182; Mass Rec, 241

Carr, Robert:
Austin, 39; RI Rec, 67, 91, 111

Clarke, Jeremy:
Austin, 44; RI Rec, 63, 87, 91; Aspinwall, 234; Banks TD, 79

Clarke, John:
Pope, 94; Banks TD, 105; WP, III, 140, 177, 196, 514

Clarke, Joseph:
RI Rec, 67, 91, 95; Austin, 47; Banks TD, 163

Clarke, Thomas:
Austin, 47; Banks TD, 163

Colburn, William:
Mass Rec, 50, 95, 107, 135, 139, 144, 145, 148, 156, 185, 191, 205, 209, 219, 238, 254, 342, 366; Pope, 109; Banks TD, 46; Banks, *Winthrop Fleet*, 65; Possessions, 33; WJ, I, 14, 53; WP, III, 21; Boston Ch; Boston Rec, 20, 26, 30

Colcord, Edward:
Exeter, 21; Lechford, 223

Cole, William:
Exeter, 21; Boston Rec, 15; Banks TD, 20

Cornell, Thomas:
Austin, 54; Mass Rec, 238, 247; RI Rec, 75, 76, 84; Suffolk, 26; Pope, 118

Cramme, John:
Boston Rec, 23; Exeter, 21; Banks TD, 95

Davis, James:
RI Rec, 70, 91; WP, IV, 259; Mass Rec, I, 296; Boston Rec, 25

Davis, Nicholas:
Banks TD, 112; Banks PC, 140; Austin, 63; RI Rec, 91

Dummer, Stephen:
Banks PC, 200; RI Rec, 59; Pope, 146; Suffolk, 79; Aspinwall, 59

Dummer, Thomas:
Banks PC, 200; RI Rec, 59; Pope, 146

Durdall, Hugh:
Banks PC, 200; Pope, 137; RI Rec 48, 92; Lechford, 390; WP, IV, 215

Field, Robert:
Banks TD, 60; Banks PC, 138; RI Rec, 59, 92, 95

Fish, Gabriel:
Pope, 166; WJ, I, 329; Possessions, 6; Lechford, 141; Banks TD, 97; Exeter, 21

Gilham, Robert:
Boston Rec, 19; RI Rec, 91

Gorton, Samuel:
Austin, 302; Pope, 194; Banks TD, 99; WP, IV, 455; NEHGR, IV, 201;
DNB, VIII, 251; The New Schaff-Herzog Encyclopedia, V, 25

Gould, Jeremy:
Banks TD, 67; Suffolk, 15, 16; Lechford, 573; RI Rec, 92, 108, 110;
Austin, 304; Banks PC, 201

Hawkins, Job:
Banks PC, 144; Banks TD, 162; Austin, 65; RI Rec, 71

Hazard, Thomas:
RI Rec, 87, 91, 99, 100; Austin, 320; Mass Rec, 372; Boston Ch

Helme, Christopher:
Banks TD, 169; RI Rec, 136, 210; Exeter, 21; Austin, 322; Suffolk, 106

Hunt, Enoch:
RI Rec, 91; Mass Rec, II; Weymouth Vital Records, I, 5; Banks TD, 9

Jeffrey, Robert:
RI Rec, 59, 90, 100, 111; Banks PC 157; WP, V, 118; Austin, 330

Johnson, John:
Mass Rec, 223; Pope, 260; WP, III, 433; RI Rec, 91

Lawson, Christopher:
Exeter, 21; Banks TD, 57; Suffolk, 54, 58, 61, 68, 94; Possessions, 112

Lawton, George:
Banks TD, 1; RI Rec, 70, 91, 210; Austin, 121

Layton, John:
RI Rec, 92; Austin, 122

Leavitt, Thomas:
Exeter, 21; Col. Soc. of Mass., *Publications*, I, 275

Lenthall, Robert:
RI Rec, 104, 110, 119; Banks TD, 167; Pope, 284; Mass Rec, 254;
WJ, I, 292 ff, II, 41

Leverett, John:
Boston Rec, 42; Possessions, 20; Banks TD, 94; Banks PC, 106; Boston
Ch; Pope, 284

Littlefield, Edmund:
Exeter, 21; Banks PC, 200; Banks TD, 63

Littlefield, Francis:
Exeter, 21; Banks PC, 200; Banks TD, 63

Maccumore, John:
RI Rec, 92; Pope, 296

Makepeace, Thomas:
Pope, 298; Possessions, 13; Boston Rec, 19, 39; Suffolk, 105; Lechford,
412; Banks TD, 126, 174

Marshall, Christopher:
Exeter, 21; Boston Ch; Pope, 310

Marshall, John:
RI Rec, 66, 91; Possessions, 36; Boston Rec, 48

Maxson, Richard:
Austin, 342; RI Rec, 66, 70, 91; Boston Ch

Montague, Griffin:
Exeter, 21; Mass Rec, 144, 164

Mott, Adam:
Banks PC, 168; Austin, 344; RI Rec, 59, 63, 91, 110; Mass Rec, 241, 371; Roxbury Ch, 80; Aspinwall, 239; Banks TD, 12

Mott, Adam, Jr.:
RI Rec, 200; Banks PC, 168

Needham, Nicholas:
Pope, 325; Boston Rec, 15; Exeter, 21

Needham, William:
Pope, 325; Boston Rec, 41, 51; RI Rec, 91

Parker, George:
Austin, 143; Pope, 343; Banks PC, 157; RI Rec, 60, 85, 91, 111

Parker, Nicholas:
Pope, 344; Roxbury Ch, 78; Possessions, 28; Lechford, 228; WP, III, 514; Mass Rec, 368

Peckham, John:
Banks TD, 85; Austin, 147; RI Rec, 92, 111

Penniman, James:
Mass Rec, 212, 218, 291, 367; Pope, 353; Banks TD, 72; Banks PC, 79; Boston Ch; Boston Rec, 18, 36; WP, III, 514

Pettie, Thomas:
Pope, 356; Boston Rec, 21; Exeter, 21

Poole, Edward:
Banks PC, 127; RI Rec, 91; Weymouth Vital Records, I, 15; Aspinwall, 12; Lechford, 391

Pormont, Philemon:
Mass Rec, 370; Pope, 368; Banks TD, 95; Aspinwall, 9; Boston Ch; Boston Rec, 25

Quick, William:
RI Rec, 91; Suffolk, 50; Lechford, 158; Chastn Rec, 62; *History of Malden*, 66; Mass Rec, 284; Suffolk, 16, 50; WP, III, 320, 430, 434, IV, 128; Pope, 377

Randoll, Robert:
Mass Rec, 223, 310, 314; Pope, 378

Reade, Robert:
Pope, 380; Boston Rec, 23; Exeter, 21

Rishworth, Edward:
Exeter, 21; Suffolk, 87; Lechford, 141; Banks TD, 93

Rogers, James:
Austin, 368; RI Rec, 92, 108, 110

Salter, Sampson:
  Austin, 170; RI Rec, 92; Banks PC, 138; WP, IV, 323; Banks TD, 134;
  Pope, 397

Savorie, Thomas:
  Banks TD, 178; Banks PC, 110; Mass Rec, 248, 297; RI Rec, 92; WP, IV,
  215; Pope, 401

Searle, Richard:
  Pope, 406; Austin, 174; RI Rec, 91

Shotten, Sampson:
  Austin, 180; Boston Rec, 15; Lechford, 16; RI Rec, 70, 91, 119, 123,
  130; Banks TD, 90

Stafford, Thomas:
  Banks TD, 176; Austin, 384; RI Rec, 92, 302

Stannyon, Anthony:
  Exeter, 21; Boston Rec, 32; Lechford, 428

Storre, Augustine:
  Exeter, 21; Col. Soc. of Mass., *Publications*, I, 275

Thornton, John:
  Austin, 199; RI Rec, 301

Vaughan, John:
  Pope, 470; Austin, 400; Mass Rec, 112, 244, 284; RI Rec, 60, 92, 301;
  Watertown Records, 4

Waite, Thomas:
  Austin, 404; RI Rec, 72, 111; Banks TD, 53; NEHGR, XXXII, 188

Wayte, Richard:
  Mass Rec, 212; Pope, 473; Possessions, 36; Boston Rec, 30; Boston Ch;
  Suffolk, 317; Lechford, 19, 150, 223; WP, III, 514

Wenbourne, William:
  Pope, 505; Exeter, 21; "Boston Births, Baptisms, Marriages, Deaths," 6

Wentworth, William:
  Exeter, 21; Banks TD, 93

Weston, Francis:
  Mass Rec, 113, 114, 117, 155, 223, 233, 369; Austin, 220; Pope, 487;
  Salem, 349; Banks PC, 84; RI Rec, 15, 130

Williamson, Michael:
  Pope, 501; RI Rec, 92, 111; Banks PC, 141; Lechford, 206

APPENDIX IV—PERSONNEL IN THE PERIPHERAL GROUP

Name	Age	Place of Origin	Time of Arrival	Residence	Churched	Freeman	Vocation	Office Colony	Office Local	Property	Married	Complicity	Change of Religion	Disposition of Case	Removal
Adams, Nathaniel	36		bef. 1638	Wey-mouth	...	...	Dish turner		Town Officer		Yes				Newport Temp.
Albro, John	20	Suffolk	1634	Boston	...	...	Servant								Portsmth Perm.
Allen, George, Jr.	28	Somerset	1635	Wey-mouth	...	...	Boatman								Newport Temp.
Allen, Ralph		Somerset	1635	Wey-mouth	...	...									Newport Temp.
Allen, Samuel		Essex	bef. 1635	Wollas-ton	n.d.	1635	Sawyer				Yes				Newport Temp.
Awarde, Richard		Bedford	1629	Boston	...	...					Yes				Portsmth Perm.
Baker, William			bef. 1636	Water-town	...	...									Portsmth Perm.
Barlow, George			bef. 1637	Sand-wich?	...	...			Con-stable		Yes				Exeter
Bates, George			1635	Boston	1635	1636	Thatcher				Yes			Dismissed	Exeter Temp.
Bennett, Robert			bef. 1638		...	...	Servant				Yes				Newport Perm.
Bishop, Townsend (Mr.)			bef. 1635	Salem	n.d.	1635		Deputy	Select man	R	Yes			Examined by clergy	
Blackwell, Jeremiah	20	Lincoln	1635		...	...									Exeter Temp.
Briggs, John	28		1635	Water-town	...	...	Servant								Portsmth Perm.

Name	Age	County	Date	Town	1634	1636	Occupation	Office	R	Yes	Pet.	Religion	Action	Destination
Brown, James			1630	Charlestown	…	…				Yes			Denied signing	Portsmth Perm.
Brown, Nicholas			bef. 1638		…	…				Yes				Portsmth Perm.
Bullock, Erasmus			1632	Boston	…	…	Servant							Portsmth Temp.
Burden, Richard	36		bef. 1638	Newbury	…	…	Servant			Yes				Portsmth Perm.
Burrows, John	41	Norfolk	1637	Salem	…	…	Cooper					Quaker		
Carr, Robert	23		1635		…	…	Tailor					heretical tendencies	Charged by Court to keep silence	Portsmth Perm.
Clarke, Jeremy		Kent	bef. 1638	Watertown?	…	…		Constable		Yes		Quaker		Portsmth Perm.
Clarke, John		Suffolk	1630	Ipswich	…	…	Farmer ?				Pet.		Disarmed / Denied signing	Portsmth Perm.
Clarke, Joseph	19	Suffolk	1637	Boston	…	…								Portsmth Perm.
Clarke, Thomas	32	Suffolk	1637	Boston	…	…				Yes		Baptist		Portsmth Perm.
Colburn, William		Essex	1630	Boston	1630	1631		Deputy Selectman	R	Yes				
Colcord, Edward	22		bef. 1637	Salem	…	…								Dover Perm.
Cole, William	56	Somerset	bef. 1636	Boston	…	…	Carpenter			Yes				Exeter Perm.
Cornell, Thomas		Herts	bef. 1638	Boston	…	…	Innkeeper		R	Yes		Quaker		Portsmth Perm.
Cramme, John		Lincoln	bef. 1635	Boston	…	…	Farmer ?			Yes				Exeter Perm.

Name	Age	Place of Origin	Time of Arrival	Residence	Churched	Freeman	Vocation	Office		Property	Married	Completely	Change of Religion	Disposition of Case	Removal
								Colony	Local						
Davis, James			bef. 1638		……	……	Servant				Yes				Portsmth Perm.
Davis, Nicholas	42	Middlesex	1635	Charlestown	……	……	Tailor								Newport Temp.
Dummer, Stephen	37	Hants	1638	Transient	……	……	Farmer ?			R					Portsmth Temp.
Dummer, Thomas	18	Hants	1638	Transient	……	……									Portsmth Temp.
Durdall, Hugh	ca. 20	Hants	1638	Transient	……	……	Servant								Portsmth Temp.
Field, Robert		Hants	1635	Boston	……	……					Yes				Portsmth Perm.
Fish, Gabriel		Lincoln	bef. 1638		……	……	Fisherman								Exeter Temp.
Gilham, Robert			bef. 1637	Boston	……	……	Mariner								Portsmth Perm.
Gorton, Samuel	45	London	1636	Plymouth	……	……	Clothier				Yes		Gorton-ist		Portsmth Perm.
Gould, Jeremy (Mr.)		Herts	bef. 1637	Weymouth	……	……					Yes				Portsmth Perm.
Hawkins, Job	17	Huntington	1635	Ipswich	……	……	Servant								Portsmth Temp.
Hazard, Thomas	27		1635	Boston	1636	1636	Ship Carpenter								Portsmth Perm.
Helme, Christopher		Surrey	1637		……	……					Yes		Gorton-ist		Exeter, R.I.

Name	Age	Origin	Date	Residence			Occupation		Freeman	Status	Destination
Hunt, Enoch		Bucks	bef. 1638	Weymouth	....	....	Blacksmith		Yes		Newport Temp.
Jeffrey, Robert	37		1635	Charlestown	....	....			Yes	Banished	Portsmth Perm.
Johnson, John			bef. 1638	Wollaston	....	....	Coddington's Servant				Newport Perm.
Lawson, Christopher	21	Lincoln	1637	Boston	....	....	Cooper		Yes		Exeter Temp.
Lawton, George	ca. 20	Bedford	bef. 1638	Boston	....	....					Portsmth Perm.
Layton, John			bef. 1638	Ipswich	....	....					Newport Temp.
Leavitt, Thomas		Lincoln	1637	Transient	n.d.	....					Exeter
Lenthall, Robert (Mr.)	21	Surrey	bef. 1638	Weymouth	....	....	Clergyman		Yes		Portsmth Perm.
Leverett, John		Lincoln	1633	Boston	....	....			Yes		
Littlefield, Edmund	18	Hants	1638	Transient	....	....					Exeter Perm.
Littlefield, Francis		Hants	1638	Transient	....	....					Exeter Temp.
Macumore, John	20-30		bef. 1638	Plymouth	....	....	Carpenter	R			Newport Temp.
Makepeace, Thomas (Mr.)	45	Northants	bef. 1635	Dorchester	1635	1634	Gentleman farmer		Yes	Dismissed	Exeter
Marshall, Christopher			bef. 1634	Boston	....	....			Yes		Portsmth Temp.
Marshall, John			bef. 1638	Boston	....	....	Servant		Yes		
Maxson, Richard			bef. 1634	Boston	....	1634	Servant Blacksmith		Yes		Portsmth Perm.

APPENDIX IV–PERSONNEL IN THE PERIPHERAL GROUP–*Continued*

Name	Age	Place of Origin	Time of Arrival	Residence	Churched	Freeman	Vocation	Office		Property	Married	Complicity	Change of Religion	Disposition of Case	Removal
								Colony	Local						
Montague, Griffin			bef. 1635	Boston	...	...	Carpenter				Yes				Exeter / Perm.
Mott, Adam	41	Cambridge	1635	Hingham	1635	1636	Tailor				Yes				Portsmth / Perm.
Mott, Adam, Jr.	18	Hants	1638	Roxbury	...	...	Servant								Portsmth
Mott, John	ca. 20	Cambridge	1635	Newbury	...	...	Tailor								Portsmth
Needham, Nicholas			1636	Boston	...	...									Exeter / Perm.
Needham, William	20-30		bef. 1638	Boston	...	...									Newport / Temp.
Parker, George	26		1635		...	...	Carpenter				Yes				Portsmth / Perm.
Parker, Nicholas (Mr.)	ca. 30		1633	Roxbury	1633	1633	Farmer ?					Pet.		Disarmed / Denied signing	
Peckham, John	ca. 20	Kent	bef. 1638		...	...							Baptist		Newport / Perm.
Penniman, James	20-30	Essex	1630	Boston	1630	1631		Ap-praiser	Fence Overseer	R		Pet.		Disarmed / Denied signing	
Pettie, Thomas			1633	Boston	...	...	Servant								Exeter / Perm.
Poole, Edward	28	Somerset	1634	Weymouth	...	...	Servant / Sawyer				Yes				Newport / Temp.

326

Name	Age	Origin	Date	Place	1634	1635	Occupation		Sect	Dismissed	Destination
Pormont, Philemon	39	Lincoln	bef. 1634	Boston	....	....	School-master				Exeter Temp.
Quick, William			bef. 1636	Charles-town	....	....	Ship-master	Yes			Newport Perm.
Randoll, Robert			bef. 1638	Wollas-ton	....	....	Codding-ton's servant			Cited to appear before Court	
Reade, Robert			bef. 1634	Boston	....	....	Leather sealer	Yes			Exeter
Rishworth, Edward	20	Lincoln	1637	Tran-sient	....	....		Yes			Exeter Perm.
Rogers, James		London	1623	Plym-outh	....	....	Miller				Portsmth
Salter, Sampson		Oxford	1635		....	....					Newport
Savorie, Thomas		Wilt-shire	1633	Ipswich	....	....	Fisherman	Yes			Newport
Searle, Richard			bef. 1637	Dor-chester	....	....	Servant				Newport Temp.
Shotten, Sampson	32	Leicester	bef. 1636	Wollas-ton	....	....			Gorton-ist		Portsmth Perm.
Stafford, Thomas	26	Warwick	1626	Plym-outh	....	....		Yes			Newport Perm.
Stannyon, Anthony			1635	Boston	....	....	Glover	Yes			Exeter Temp.
Storre, Augustine	ca. 40	Lincoln	1637	Tran-sient	....	....					Exeter Perm.
Thornton, John	ca. 20		bef. 1638	Boston	....	....		Yes	Baptist		Portsmth Perm.
Vaughan, John	20–30		bef. 1633	Water-town	....	....		Yes			Newport Perm.
Waite, Thomas		Essex	bef. 1635	Ipswich	....	....		Yes			Portsmth Perm.

APPENDIX IV–PERSONNEL IN THE PERIPHERAL GROUP–*Continued*

Name	Age	Place of Origin	Time of Arrival	Residence	Churched	Freeman	Vocation	Office Colony	Office Local	Property	Married	Complicity	Change of Religion	Disposition of Case	Removal
Wayte, Richard	37		bef. 1634	Boston	1634	1636	Tailor		Sgt.		Yes	Pet.		Disarmed Denied sign-ing	
Wenbourne, William			bef. 1635	Boston	....	....	Farmer ?				Yes				Exeter Temp.
Wentworth, William	21	Lincoln	1637	Tran-sient	....	....									Exeter Perm.
Weston, Francis			1630	Salem	n.d.	1633		Deputy	Con-stable		Yes		Baptist Gorton-ist	Banished	Provi-dence
Williamson, Michael	32	Bedford	1635	Ipswich	....	....	Servant Locksmith				Yes				Portsmth

328

Appendix V

ADULT MALE POPULATION OF BOSTON, CIRCA 1637

Bibliographical Note

The data on which these tables were based were drawn from the following volumes:

Records of the First Church of Boston

Boston Town Records, 1634-1660

C. E. Banks, *Planters of the Commonwealth*

Records of the Governor and Company of the Massachusetts Bay,
Volume I

Boston Book of Possessions

C. H. Pope, *Pioneers of Massachusetts*

Boston Births, Baptisms, Marriages and Deaths, 1630-1699

APPENDIX V–ADULT MALE POPULATION OF BOSTON, CIRCA 1637

Name	Wife	Place of Origin	Time of Arrival	Churched	Enfranchised	Occupation	Office		Property	Complicity
							Colony	Local		
Abell, Robert		Leicester	1630	....	....				P	
Albro, John			1634	....	....					
Alcock, Thomas	Yes	Suffolk	1630	1630	1635	Servant			P	
Arnold, John			....	....	....	Plasterer				
Arat, John			....	....	....	Servant to Wm. Brenton				
Aspinwall, William	Elizabeth	Lancaster	1630	1630	1632	Clothier	Deputy	Selectman	R	Core
Atkinson, Theodorus	M. sister of Mrs. Matson		....	1634	....	Hatter–Servant to J. Newgate				
Audley, John (Odley, Odlin)	Margaret	London	1630	1630	1634	Armorer-Cutler		Fence Overseer	R	Supp.
Awarde, Richard	Yes	Bedford	1629	....	....				P	Peri.
Awkley, Miles	Mary		....	....	....					
Baker, Alexander	Elizabeth		....	....	....					
Baker, Francis			1635	....	1634					
Baker, John	Charity		1630	1630	1634	Tailor				
Balston, William	Elizabeth	London	1630	1630	1631	Innkeeper	Ensign Juryman	Selectman Assessor	R	Core
Bates, Edward	Elizabeth		bef. 1633	1633	1637	Servant to Thomas Leverett				Supp.
Bates, George	Anne		1635	1636	1636	Thatcher		Fence Overseer	P	Peri.
Beamsley, William	Anne		....	1635	1636	Laborer			P	
Beck, Alexander	Mary		....	1634	1634	Laborer-Servant to Wm. Colburn			P	
Belcher, Edward	Christian		1630	1630	1631	Servant to Wm. Brenton		Fence Overseer		
Belcher, Gregory	Yes		....	....	....					
Bell, Thomas			....	....	1636					
Bellingham, Richard	Elizabeth	Lincoln	....	1634	1636		Assistant, Deputy, Gov.	Selectman	R	

Name	Wife	Origin	1630	1630	1634	Occupation	Deputy	Constable	R/P	Category
Bendall, Edward	Anne	Surrey				Dockman / Merchant				
Bibbles, John	Sybil								R	Supp.
Biggs, John	Mary	Suffolk	1630 / d.1638	1630	1633				R	Supp.
Bill, John			bef. 1634							
Bishop, Nathaniel	Alice									
Blackburn, Walter										
Blackstone, William			1623		1631					
Blanchard, Joseph			d. 1637							
Blott, Robert										
Blott, Thomas										
Boswell, John		London	1630		1636					
Bosworth, Zaccheus	Anne	Northants	1630	1630	1636	Servant to Wm. Colburn			R	Supp.
Bourne, Jarrett	Mary			1634	1635			Jailer	P	
Bowen, Griffin	Margaret									
Brackett, Richard	Alice	Suffolk	1630	1630	1636					
Brand, Benjamin			1630							
Brenton, Richard										
Brenton, William	Dorothy	Middlesex	1633	1633	1634	Merchant	Deputy	Selectman / Assessor	R	Core
Brown, Edward				1634					P	
Browne, James			1630	1630	1633				P	
Browne, William	Thomasine ?			1634		Servant to John Winthrop				
Buckley, Edward	Sister of J. Underhill	London	1630	1635	1631	Brickmaker				Core
Bulgar, Richard				1634		Bricklayer				Peri.
Bullock, Erasmus			1632			Servant				Supp.
Burchall, Henry			1635			Tanner				
Burden, George	Anne	Gloucester	1635	1637	1637	Shoemaker				
Burden, Richard							Juryman			
Burnell, William	Mary		1630			Blacksmith				
Busecot, Peter										

APPENDIX V–ADULT MALE POPULATION OF BOSTON, CIRCA 1637–Continued

Name	Wife	Place of Origin	Time of Arrival	Churched	Enfranchised	Occupation	Office		Property	Complicity
							Colony	Local		
Bushnall, Francis	Anne		1635	....	....	Leatherdresser			P	
Buttalph, Thomas			1635	....	....	Glover				
Button, John	Grace		....	1633	1634	Miller	Juryman	Fence Overseer	R	Supp.
Button, Mathias	Lettyse		bef. 1633	....	....					
Carder, Richard	Mary		bef. 1636	1637	1637	Sawyer				Core
Chafey, Matthew			....	1636	1637	Ship Carpenter			P	
Chapell, Nathaniel			....	1634	....	Servant to Atherton Hough				
Cheeseborough, William	Anne	Lincoln	1630	1630	1631					
Church, Richard		Suffolk	1630	....	....					
Clark, John		Suffolk	1630	1630	1632					
Clarke, John, Dr.	Elizabeth	Suffolk	1637	....	....	Physician				Supp.
Clarke, Joseph		Suffolk	1637	....	....					Peri.
Clarke, Thomas	Jane	Suffolk	1637	....	....					Peri.
Clement, Augustine	Elizabeth	Berkshire	1635	....	1636	Painter				
Coddington, William	Mary	Lincoln	1630	1630	1636	Merchant	Assistant Treasurer	Selectman	R	Core
Coggan, John	Anne		....	....	1633	Shopkeeper		Selectman Constable	R	
Coggeshall, John	Marie	Essex	1632	1634	1632	Merchant	Deputy	Selectman	R	Core
Colburn, William	Margery	Essex	1630	1630	1631		Deputy	Assessor	R	Core
Colby, Anthony (Chaulby, Charelby)	Yes		1630	1630	1634			Assessor Prizer		Peri.

Name	Wife	English Origin				Occupation	Office	Status	Category
Cole, Clement		Suffolk	1635	....	....	Servant	Assessor	P	
Cole, John			1630	1630	....	Confectioner			
Cole, Samuel	Anne	Essex	1630	....	....	Innkeeper			Supp.
Cole, William	Eunice	Somerset	bef. 1636	....	....	Carpenter		R	Peri.
Compton, John	Susan ?		bef. 1634	n.d.	1634	Laborer		P	Core
Cooke, Richard	Elizabeth		bef. 1634	1634	1635	Tailor		R	Supp.
Cornell, Thomas	Rebecca	Herts	bef. 1638	....	....	Innkeeper			Peri.
Cotton, John	Sarah	Lincoln	1633	1633	1634	Clergyman		R	
Courser, William	Joan		....	1635	1636	Shoemaker		P	Peri.
Cowlishaw, William	Anne	Nottingham	....	1633	1633	Victualler ?			
Crabtree, John	Alice	Lincoln	bef. 1635	....	....	Joiner			
Cramme, John	Esther		1630	....	....	Farmer ?			
Cranwell, John		Suffolk	....	1630	1633				
Critchley, Richard	Alice Dinely in 1639		bef. 1635	....	1630	Blacksmith			
Cullimore, Isaac			....	....	....	Carpenter-Servant to A. Mellows			
Davisse, James	Joanna		....	1634	1635	Seaman			
Davisse, William	Mary		....	....	....	Locksmith			
Davy, John			1635	1636	1636	Gunsmith		P	Supp.
Denning, William (Dinny, Dennyn)			....	1634	1637	Joiner			
Dennis, Edward	Sarah		....	1636	1637	Servant to William Brenton		P	Supp.
Dillingham, John	Sarah	Leicester	1630	1630	1631	Servant to Wm. Hutchinson	Juryman	P	
Dinely, William	Alice	Lincoln	bef. 1635	1635	1637	Barber-surgeon		P	Supp.
Dinsdale, William			....	....	....				

APPENDIX V—ADULT MALE POPULATION OF BOSTON, CIRCA 1637—Continued

Name	Wife	Place of Origin	Time of Arrival	Churched	Enfranchised	Occupation	Office Colony	Office Local	Property	Complicity
Dorryfall, Barnaby			1630	1630	1636	Servant to George Burden			P	
Dowse, Francis			....	....	....					
Dyer, William	Mary	London	bef. 1635	1635	1636	Milliner				Core
East, Francis	Mary	Lincoln	1630	1630	1637	Carpenter				
Easton, Nathaniel (Heaton)	Elizabeth	Lincoln	1634	1634	1638	Mercer				
Edmunds, John	Mary	Essex	1630	1630	1630	Schoolmaster				
Eliot, Francis		Essex	....	....	....					
Eliot, Jacob	Margery		1630	1630	1634	Tailor	Committee	Selectman	R	Supp.
Elkins, Henry			bef. 1634	1634	1635				P	Core
Evered als Webb, John		Wiltshire	1635	....	....					
Evered als Webb, Stephen		Wiltshire	1635	....	....					
Everill, James	Elizabeth		....	1634	1634	Leatherdresser		Fence Overseer		
Faber, Joseph			1635	....	....	Shoemaker				
Fairbank, Richard	Elizabeth		bef. 1633	1633	1634	Cooper		Hogreeve Foldkeeper		Supp.
Fairweather, Thomas	Mary		1630	1630	1634	Shopkeeper		Fence Overseer		
Field, Robert	Deborah	Hampshire	1635	....	....					
Fitch, James	Abigail		1635	1635	....	Tailor			P	Peri.
Fitch, Richard			....	....	....				P	
Flacke, Cotton			....	1634	1634					
Fletcher, Edward			....	....	....					
Flint, Henry			....	....	....	Laborer				
Flint, Thomas		Derby	....	1635	1636	Clergyman				Supp.

Name	Wife	Origin	Date 1	Date 2	Date 3	Occupation	Captain	Office	R/P	Category
oster, Thomas		Suffolk	1684	....	....					Core
Foxcroft, George	Anne		....	....	....					
Foxhalls, John	Yes		1632	....	1632					
Foxwell, Richard	Alice		1630	....	1630	Tailor				
Franklin, William	Mary	London	n.d.	1630	1634	Blacksmith				
Freeborn, William	Susan		1630	1630	1632					
French, Thomas	Amy	Suffolk	1630	1630	1633					
Gage, John	Christovell	Suffolk	bef. 1634	1634	1634	Fisherman				
Gallop, John			bef. 1634	1634	....					
Gayle, John			1623	1630	1630	Servant to John Button				
Gibbons, Edward	Margaret		bef. 1634	1634	1635	Ship carpenter	Captain			Peri.
Gillam, Benjamin	Anne		bef. 1634	....	....					
Gillam, Robert (Gillham)		London	bef. 1637	....	....	Mariner				
Glover, John			....	....	....					
Glover, Ralph			1630	1630	1630					
Goordley, John			....	....	1634	Tailor				
Gosnall, Henry	Mary		1630	1630	....	Servant to R. Tuttle				
Gray, Henry	Frances		1635	....	1634					
Greene, Samuel (Gryne, Grane, Greames)			bef. 1634	1634	....					
Greensmith, Stephen			bef. 1636	....	....	Merchant				
Gridley, Richard	Grace	Suffolk	1633	Yes	1636	Brickmaker Bricklayer		Overseer of Fences	R	Supp.
Griggs, George	Alice	Bucks	1635	....	1636	Carpenter		Overseer of Fences / Assessor / Highway Surveyor	P R	Core
Grosse, Isaac	Anne		bef. 1636	1636	....	Brewer				
Grubb, Thomas	Anne		1630	1630	1634	Leatherdresser				
Gunnison, Hugh	Elizabeth		bef. 1635	1635	1636	Vintner-Servant to Bellingham				Supp.

APPENDIX V–ADULT MALE POPULATION OF BOSTON, CIRCA 1637–Continued

Name	Wife	Place of Origin	Time of Arrival	Churched	Enfranchised	Occupation	Office Colony	Office Local	Property	Complicity
Hansett, John (Hanchett)	Elizabeth		...	1634	1637	Servant to John Wilson			P	
Harding, Robert	Phillipa	Essex	1630	1630	1631	Merchant		Selectman	R	Core
Hardwood, George (Harwood)	Jane		1636	...	1638	Carpenter				
Harker, Anthony	Yes		...	1633	1636	Servant to T. Leverett			P	
Hawkins, James			bef. 1636	...	...					
Hawkins, Richard	Jane	Huntington		...	...					Core
Hawkins, Thomas	Hannah		1635	...	...	Baker ?				
Hayward, Samuel			1635 ?	...	...	Carpenter				
Hazard, Thomas	Martha	Lincoln	bef. 1634	1636	1636	Ship carpenter				Peri.
Hibbens, William	Anne									
Hill, Valentine	Frances			1636	...	Mercer				
Hitchen, Edward				1634	1634	Tailor				
Hogge, Richard	Joan			...	...					
Hollard, Angel	Catherine	Dorset	1635	...	1635					
Hollidge, Richard	Anne					Laborer				
Hopkinson, Michael						Servant to J. Eliot				
Hord, John	Mary		...			Tailor-Servant To Wm. Hutchinson			P	
Houchin, Jeremy				...	...		Deputy			
Hough, Atherton	Elizabeth	Lincoln		1633	1633		Assistant		R	Supp.
Houlton, Robert	Anne					Slater			P	
Howard, Samuel			1635 ?	1634	1634					
Howlett, Thomas		Suffolk	1630	1630	1634	Tailor				

336

Name	Wife	Origin				Occupation	Office	Office		
Hudson, Ralph	Mary Thwing	Yorkshire	….	1636	1636	Woolen draper	Water bailiff, Fence Overseer, Goat reeve	Constable	R	Supp.
Hudson, William	Susan	Kent	1630	1630	1630					
Hudson, William, Jr.		Kent	1630	….	….					Supp.
Hull, Richard	Elizabeth	Leicester	….	…1636	1634	Carpenter				
Hull, Robert			….	1636	1637	Chandler				
Hunne, George	Anne		….	1636	….	Blacksmith				
Hutchinson, Edmund	Sarah	Lincoln	1633	1633	….	Tanner				Core
Hutchinson, Edward, Sr.	Katherine	Lincoln	1633	1634	1634	Merchant	Sergeant	Assessor	R	Core
Hutchinson, Edward, Jr.		Lincoln	1634	1634	1634					Core
Hutchinson, Francis		Lincoln	1634	1634	1635	Merchant				Core
Hutchinson, Richard	Yes	Lincoln	1637	1634	1635	Merchant				
Hutchinson, Samuel	Anne	Lincoln	1634	….	….					Supp.
Hutchinson, William	Joan	Lincoln	1634	1634	1635	Merchant	Deputy Magistrate	Selectman, Prizer	R	Core
Inge, Maudit (Ingles, English)	Susan		….	….	….	Fuller-Servant to J. Parker				
Jacklinge, Edmund	Martha		….	1634	1635	Glazier				
Jackson, Edmund	Abigail		….	1635	1636	Shoemaker			P	
Jackson, John			….	….	….	Carpenter				
Jarvis, John	Margaret	Northants	1630	1636	1636	Leatherdresser, Glover				
Johnson, James			….	1636	1636		Captain			
Johnson, Peter (the Dutchman)	Joan		ca. 1630 1636	….	….					
Joyes, Thomas	Sarah		….	….	….	Carpenter				
Judkins, Job			….	….	….					

APPENDIX V—ADULT MALE POPULATION OF BOSTON, CIRCA 1637—Continued

Name	Wife	Place of Origin	Time of Arrival	Churched	Enfranchised	Occupation	Office		Property	Complicity
							Colony	Local		
Jyans, Matthias (Ijons, Irons, Ians, Ines)	Anne	Essex	1630	1634	1636	Servant to Colburn			P	Supp.
Keayne, Robert	Anne	Suffolk	1635	1636	1636	Merchant		Selectman	R	
Kendrick, John	Anne		....			Laborer				
Kidby, Lewis	Yes		1630	....	....	Laborer-Farmer				
Kinsley, Stephen		Lincoln	1636	....	....	Cooper				
Lawson, Christopher	Elizabeth		1637	....	....					Peri.
Lawton, George	Elizabeth	Bedford	bef. 1637	....	....					Peri.
Legar, Jacob	Elizabeth	Lincoln	1633	....	....					
Leverett, John	Hannah	Lincoln	1633	1633	....					Peri.
Leverett, Thomas	Anne		1633	1635	1634				R	Supp.
Leveridge, William			1630	1633	....	Clergyman				
Litherland, William	Margaret	London		....	1635	Carpenter				Supp.
Love, John (Lowe)	Jane		1636	....	....	Wheelwright				
Lugg, John			....	....	....					
Lyle, Francis (Loyall)	Alice		....	....	....	Barber				
Lynne, Henry	Sarah		....	1634	....					
Magson, Richard (Mason)	Yes		....	....	....	Blacksmith				Peri.
Mansfield, John			1635	....	1635	Servant to J. Everill				
Marshall, Christopher	Yes			1634	....		Ensign			Peri.
Marshall, Francis			1635	....	....					
Marshall, John	Sarah		....	....	....	Servant to Ed. Hutchinson				

Name	Wife	Origin				Occupation		Office		
Marshall, Thomas	Alice		....	1634	1635	Cordwainer		Overseer of Fences	R	Supp.
Martyn, John	Anne	Lincoln	1635	....	....	Ferryman				
Mason, Ralph	Katherine	Southwark	ca. 1635	....	....	Ship carpenter				
Mathews, Marmaduke			1630	....	....	Carpenter				
Matson, Thomas	Amy	London	1630	1634	1634	Gunsmith		Overseer of Fences		Supp.
Mattock, James			1637	....	1633	Cooper				
Maude, Daniel			1635	....	1632	Schoolmaster				
Maverick, Elias			....	....	1633	Clergyman				
Maverick, Samuel			....	....	1637					
Mawer, William	Katherine		....	1633	1636	Servant to Quincy				
Meakins, Thomas			....	....	....	Servant to Quincy				
Meakins, Thomas, Jr.	Elizabeth		....	1633	....	Husbandman				
Mears, Robert	Elizabeth	Lincoln	1635	n.d.	1633			Overseer of Fences		Supp.
Mellows, Oliver			....	1634	....	Ship carpenter				
Merry, Walter	Rebecca		....	1634	1633					
Millard, Thomas			1630	1630	1632	Carpenter				
Milles, John	Susan	Suffolk	1630	....	....					
Montague, Griffin	Margaret	Nottingham	1630	....	....					
Morris, Thomas	Sarah	Essex	....	....	....	Brickmaker ?				
Mount, Thomas	Dorothy		1635	1636	1636	Cooper				
Mylam, John	Christian		1636	....	....					
Needham, Nicholas	Anne		1635	1636	1636	Cooper			P	Peri.
Needham, William			1636	....	....	Salter				Peri.
Negus, Benjamin			....	....	....					
Negus, Jonathan			....	1634	1634					
Newcombe, Francis	Rachel		....	1636	....					
Newgate, John	Hannah		....	1634	1635	Hatter	Deputy	Highway Surveyor		
Oakes, Richard			....	....	....		Deputy	Selectman	R	
Oliver, John	Elizabeth	Gloucester	1630	1630	1634	Surveyor ?		Sergeant		Supp.

APPENDIX V–ADULT MALE POPULATION OF BOSTON, CIRCA 1637—Continued

Name	Wife	Place of Origin	Time of Arrival	Churched	Enfran- chised	Occupation	Office		Property	Complicity
							Colony	Local		
Oliver, Thomas	Anne	Gloucester	1630	1630	1632	Surgeon		Selectman	R	Supp.
Ormesby, Edward			 1635	....	....					
Orris, George			1630	1630	1631					
Palgrave, Richard	Anne		1630	1630	1631					
Palmer, John			....	....	....					
Parker, John	Jane		....	....	....	Carpenter				
Parker, Nicholas	Anne		....	....	1633					
Parker, Richard	Anne		....	....	....	Merchant				
Parker, Robert	Anne		....	1634	1634	Servant to Wm. Aspinwall				
Paynter, Thomas	Katherine		....	1630	....					
Pease, ...	Luce		....	....	....					
Pease, Henry	Susan		1630	1630	1634	Joiner-Servant to J. Winthrop				
Pelham, William	Alice		....	....	....				P	Supp.
Pell, William	Elizabeth		....	1634	1635	Tallow chandler			R	
Pemberton, John			....	ca. 1632	1634					
Penne, James	Katherine	Essex	1630	1630	1630 ?			Selectman	R	Peri.
Penniman, James	Lydia Eliot		1630	1630	1631			Appraiser Fence O'seer	R	
Pepys, Richard	Mary	Essex	1634	....	....					
Perkins, John	Judith	Warwick	1630	1630	1630					
Perry, Arthur	Elizabeth		bef. 1635	....	....	Tailor		Town Drummer		
Perry, Isaac			1630	1630	1632					
Pettie, Thomas	Christian		1633	....	....	Servant				
Phipenny, David	Sarah		....	....	1635					
Pierce, William	Bridget		1630	1630	1634	Shipmaster		Selectman	R	Peri.
Place, Peter			1635	....	....					
Pond, John		Suffolk	1630	....	....					
Pope, Ephraim			....	....	....					

340

Pormont, Philemon	Susan	Lincoln	....	1634	1635	Schoolmaster		P	Peri.
Porter, Abel	Judith	Northants	1633	1633	1634	Servant	Assessor	R	Supp.
Quincy, Edmund	Elizabeth		1630	1630	1637	Merchant-Cooper		P	Peri.
Rainsford, Edward			....	....	....	Servant to Mr. Coddington			
Randoll, Robert			....	....	....	Plasterer			
Rawlings, Richard			....	....	....	Leather sealer			
Reade, Robert	Hannah		bef. 1635	....	....			P	Peri.
Reade, William	Mabel		1630	?	1635				
Reading, Joseph			1630	1630	1634				
Reading, Myles			1630	1630	1634				
Reynolds, Robert	Mary	Suffolk	1630	1634	1634	Shoemaker		P	Supp.
Rice, Robert (Royce)	Elizabeth	Suffolk	1630	1630	1634				
Route, Ralph	Mary		1635	....	....	Laborer			
Ruggle, George	Elizabeth		....	1633	....				
Ruggle, Jeffrey	Margaret	Suffolk	1630	....	....				
Ruggles, John	Frances	Suffolk	1630	1630	1632	Fisherman ?			
Salter, William	Mary	Suffolk	....	1635	1636	Shoemaker ?	Overseer of Fences	R	Supp.
Sandys, Henry	Sybil	Essex	....	1638	1632	Merchant	Selectman	R	Core
Sanford, John	Bridget		1630	1630		Merchant	Cannoneer		
Saunders, Martin	Rachel		....	....	....				
Saunders, Sylvester			....	....	....				
Savage, Thomas	Faith	Herts	1635	1636	....	Bookbinder		R	Core
Saywell, Robert	Susan		....	....	....	Tailor			
Scott, Richard	Katherine		....	1634	1636	Shoemaker			
Scott, Robert	Elizabeth		....	1633	1636	Servant to John Sanford			
Scottow, Joshua			bef. 1634	....	....			P	
Scottow, Thomas			bef. 1634	....	....			P	
Sellen, Thomas			....	....	....				

APPENDIX V–ADULT MALE POPULATION OF BOSTON, CIRCA 1637–Continued

Name	Wife	Place of Origin	Time of Arrival	Churched	Enfranchised	Occupation	Colony	Local	Property	Complicity
Sellick, David	Susanna		1637							
Sharpe, Robert	Anne	Essex	1630							
Shelley, Robert			1632							
Sherman, Richard	Elizabeth	Essex				Servant to J. Coggeshall				Supp.
Sherman, Samuel	Grace		bef. 1636			Farmer ?				Peri.
Shotten, Sampson	Alice	Leicester								
Sinnot, Walter						Fisherman				
Smyth, John						Tailor				
Snow, Thomas	Mileah					Servant to Wm. Brenton				
Sprague, Ralph	Joan		1631	1631	1631	Husbandman		Sergeant		
Spurre, John	Elizabeth		1637 ?							
Stanley, (Spoor) Christopher	Susanna	London	1635			Tailor				
Stannyon, Anthony	Mary		1635			Glover				
Stevens, Henry	Alice		1637							
Stevenson, John										
Stickney, William			bef. 1635							
Stidson, William	Elizabeth									
Swanne, Richard	Yes									
Tallmadge, William	Yes	Hampshire	1630	1630	1634	Husbandman			R	
Tapping, Richard	Judith			1633	1633				R	
Taylor, John	Yes	Suffolk	1630		1631					
Tern, Miles	Sarah		ca. 1637			Leather dresser				
Thornton, John	Sarah					Servant to Mr. Coggeshall				Peri.

342

Name	Wife	Origin				Occupation	Office	Town Office		Status
Thwing, Benjamin		London	....	....	....					
Tilley, Nathaniel		London	:1635	....	....					
Tilley, William			1635	....	....					
Titus, Robert			bef. 1635	1634	1636				P	Supp.
Townsend, William	Hannah	Suffolk	....	1634	1636	Baker				
Truesdale, Richard	Penne		....	1634	1635	Servant to Cotton Butcher			P	
Turner, Richard			1630	1630	....					
Turner, Robert	Penelope		1630	1633	1633	Servant to Edward Bendall				
Tuttle, Richard	Anne	Northants	1635	1635	1635	Husbandman		Selectman	R	Core
Tuttle, William	Elizabeth		....	....	....	Merchant				
Tyng, William	Elizabeth		....	....	....		Deputy	Selectman		
Underhill, John	Helena	Warwick	1630	1630	1631	Professional Soldier	Captain			Core
Vane, Henry	Yes	London	1635	1635	1636	Gentleman	Governor		R	Core
Walker, John	Anne		....	1633	1634					
Walker, Richard	Sarah		....	....	1633					
Walker, Robert		Lancashire	1630	1630	1635	Linen webster			P	Core
Ward, Benjamin			....	1635	....				P	
Wardall, Thomas	Elizabeth	Lincoln	1634	1634	1635	Shoemaker			P	Core
Wardall, William	Alice	Lincoln	....	1634	....	Servant to Quincy				
Waterbury, William	Alice	Berkshire	1630	1630	1630					
Wayte, Gamaliel	Grace		1630	1633	1635	Servant to Ed. Hutchinson		Sergeant		Supp.
Wayte, Richard	Elizabeth	Berkshire	bef. 1635	1634	1637	Tailor				Peri.
Webb, Henry	Dosabell		....	....	....	Mercer				
Webb, John			....	1634	1636					
Wen, William	Elizabeth		bef. 1635	....	....					
Wenbourne, William	Elizabeth		bef. 1635	....	....					Peri.
Wheeler, Thomas	Rebecca	Berkshire	1635	1636	1637	Tailor		Assessor		Supp.
Wheelwright, John	Mary	Lincoln	1636	1636	n.d.	Clergyman				Core
Wilbore, Samuel	Anne	London	1630	1633	1633	Merchant				Core

APPENDIX V–ADULT MALE POPULATION OF BOSTON, CIRCA 1637–Continued

Name	Wife	Place of Origin	Time of Arrival	Churched	Enfranchised	Occupation	Office		Property	Complicity
							Colony	Local		
Wilkes, Samuel			bef. 1634	....	....				R	
Wilkes, William	Joan		1633	....	....					
Willey, Allen	Alice		1634	1634	....	Husbandman		Overseer of Fences		
Williams, Nathaniel	Mary		....	....	....					
Willis, John	Jane		1630	1630	....					
Willys, Nicholas	Anne		1634	Yes	1634	Mercer		Constable	R	
Wilson, Jacob			1630	1630	1632	Sawyer				
Wilson, John	Elizabeth	Lincoln	1635	1635	1636	Clergyman			R	
Wilson, William	Patience		....	1635	1636	Joiner			P	Supp.
Winchester, Alexander	Yes		....	....	....	Servant to Vane				
Wing, Robert	Judith	Suffolk	1634	1630	1629	Husbandman				
Winthrop, John	Margaret	Suffolk	1630	1635	1636		Governor	Selectman	R	
Winthrop, Steven		Suffolk	1630	....	....	Soapboiler				
Woodward, George			....	....	....					
Woodward, John			bef. 1633	....	....					
Woodward, Nathaniel			bef. 1633	1633	1637	Servant to Coddington			P	
Woodward, Robert			bef. 1633	....	....					
Wright, Richard	Margaret	Middlesex	1630	1630	1634				R	
Wright, Robert		London	1630	....	....					

Appendix VI

COMPOSITION OF THE GENERAL COURTS OF
MAY AND NOVEMBER 1637

Town	May Court	November Court
Boston	*Coddington Hough Vane (#*Aspinwall)	Coddington **Coggeshall Aspinwall
Charlestown	*Sedgewick Mousall Lynn	Sedgewick **Palmer **Sprague
Concord	*Willard	Willard
Dorchester	*Collicott *Glover Minot (#*Duncan)	Collicott Glover Duncan
Hingham	Eames Andrews	**Underwood **Ward
Ipswich	Appleton Medcalfe	**Denison **Bartholomew
Lynn	*Tomlyns *Howe	Tomlyns Howe
Medford	*Mayhew	Mayhew
Newtown	*Cooke Spencer Danforth	Cooke **Jackson **White
Newbury	*Woodbridge *Woodman	Woodbridge Woodman
Roxbury	Johnson I. Heath W. Heath	**Park **Weld **Alcocke
Salem	Trask (#*Hawthorne) Davenport *Batter	Hawthorne **Bishop Batter
Watertown	*Jennison *Brown	Jennison Brown
Weymouth	Smyth Upham	**Adams **Bridge?

*Re-elected to Court of November 1637
**Newly elected to Court of November 1637
#Replaced original incumbent at September session of Court

345

Appendix VII

A DIAGNOSIS OF MRS. HUTCHINSON'S BEHAVIOR IN TERMS OF MENOPAUSAL SYMPTOMS

Dr. John Clarke's description in 1638 of Mrs. Hutchinson's delivery indicates that she had expelled an hydatidiform mole. Weighing this information, which is printed below, in conjunction with other available details of her medical history, Dr. Paul A. Younge of the Harvard Medical School has given a diagnosis which differs considerably from that conventionally accepted. Mrs. Hutchinson was not pregnant at the time of her trial in November, 1637, nor did she become pregnant for at least five months thereafter. At this time and during the ensuing winter months, she displayed the symptoms of the initial phase of menopause. A climacteric, attended by anemia and general anxiety, and exacerbated by the emotional shock she had undergone, would induce amenorrhea which would in turn lead her to suspect that she was again pregnant. In the following April, however, after rejoining her husband, she did become pregnant of the "menopausal baby" which aborted into an hydatidiform mole.

Mrs. Hutchinson's behavior during this crucial period can be explained largely in terms of menopausal symptoms. She was now forty-six years old and passing the limit of her reproductive activity. Women in this stage of life are especially susceptible to uterine growths of this nature. For twenty-five years Mrs. Hutchinson had undergone a continuous cycle of pregnancies, deliveries, and lactations, while simultaneously bearing the heavy cares of rearing a large family. A woman suffering the anemia attendant on such an obstetrical history, subjected at a critical physiological period to extreme mental stress would almost certainly experience severe menopausal symptoms including neurotic manifestations. Under these conditions such aspects of the delusional system which Mrs. Hutchinson may hitherto have entertained inwardly could have been forced into open expression.

For additional details, see 248n above and the following: William

Boyd, *A Textbook of Pathology* (Philadelphia, 1943), 663-66, 674-76; E. C. Hamblen, *Endocrinology of Women* (Springfield, [Illinois], 1945), 529; "Gynaecology" and "Menopause," *Encyclopaedia Britannica* (Chicago, 1942), XI, 37; XV, 251; Oscar Kaplan, ed., *Mental Disorders in Later Life* (Palo Alto, 1945), 45.

DR. JOHN CLARKE'S DESCRIPTION OF MRS. HUTCHINSON'S HYDATIDIFORM MOLE [1]

"Mrs. Hutchinson, being removed to the Isle of Aquiday, in the Naraganset Bay, after her time was fulfilled, that she expected deliverance of a child, was delivered of a monstrous birth, which ... [Mr. Cotton] declared to be twenty-seven lumps of man's seed without any alteration or mixture of anything from the woman. Hereupon the Governor wrote to Mr. Clarke, a physician and a preacher to those of the island ... who returned this answer ... Mrs. Hutchinson, six weeks before her delivery, perceived her body to be greatly distempered, and her spirits failing, and in that regard doubtful of her life. She sent to me and not long after (in immoderato fluore uterino) it was brought to light and I was called to see it, where I beheld first unwashed (and afterwards in warm water) several lumps, every one of them greatly confused, and if you consider each of them according to the representation of the whole, they were altogether without form; but if they were considered in respect of the parts of each lump of flesh, then there was a representation of innumerable distinct bodies in the form of a globe, not much unlike the swims of some fish, so confusedly knit together, by so many several strings (which I conceived were the beginning of veins and nerves), so that it was impossible to number the small round pieces in every lump, much less to discern from whence every string did stretch its original, they were so snarled one within another. The small globes I likewise opened, and perceived the matter of them (setting aside the membrane in which it was involved), to be partly wind and partly water. Of those several lumps there were about twenty-six, according to the relation of those who more narrowly searched into the number of them. I took notice of six or seven of some bigness; the rest were small; but all, as I have declared, except one or two, which differed much from the rest both in matter and form, and the whole was like the [lobe] of the liver, being similar and everywhere like itself. When I had opened it the matter seem to be hard congealed.

The lumps were twenty-six or twenty-seven, distinct and not joined together; there came no secundine after them; six of them were as great

1. John Winthrop, *History of New England*, ed. James Savage (Boston, 1825), I, 271-73.

as his fist, and one as great as two fists; the rest each less than the other, and the smallest about the bigness of the top of his thumb. The globes were round things included in the lumps, about the smallness of a small Indian bean, and like the pearl in a man's eye. The two lumps which differed from the rest were like liver or congealed blood, and had no small globes in them as the rest had."

BIBLIOGRAPHY

I. PRIMARY SOURCES

A. Manuscripts

Cotton Papers, Boston Public Library.

First Church of Boston, Records and Baptisms, 1630-1687, Library of the Massachusetts Historical Society, Boston.

B. Printed Materials

Adams, Charles Francis, ed., *Antinomianism in the Colony of Massachusetts Bay, 1636-1638* (Boston, 1894).

Aquinas, Saint Thomas, *Selected Writings*, ed. M. C. D'Arcy (New York, 1939).

Aristotle, *De Anima*, trans. W. D. Ross (New York, 1942).

Augustine, Saint, *The City of God*, ed. Ernest Barker (New York, 1931).

————, *Confessions*, trans. J. G. Pilkington (New York, 1943).

Baxter, Richard, *Autobiography of Richard Baxter, being The Reliquiae Baxterianae*, ed. J. M. Lloyd Thomas (London, 1931).

Baylie, Robert, *A Dissuasive From the Errours of the Time* (London, 1645).

Boston Registry Department, *Records Relating to the Early History of Boston*, 39 vols. (Record Commissioners of the City of Boston [Boston, 1876-1909]):

"Aspinwall Notarial Records, 1644-51," *Thirty-Second Report* (1903).

"The Book of Possessions," *Second Report* (1902).

"Boston Births, Baptisms, Marriages and Deaths," *Ninth Report* (1883).

"Charlestown Land Records, 1638-1802," *Third Report* (1883).

"Dorchester Births, Marriages and Deaths to the End of 1825," *Twenty-First Report* (1891).

Boston Registry Department (*Cont.*)
    "Miscellaneous Papers," *Tenth Report* (1886).
    "Roxbury Land and Church Records," *Sixth Report* (1884).
    "Records of the Town of Boston, 1634-1660," *Second Report* (1902).

Bradshaw, William, *English Puritanism, Containing the Main Opinions of the Rigidest Sort of those that are Called Puritans in the Realm of England* (London, 1641).

Braintree, Massachusetts, *Records of the Town of Braintree, Massachusetts, 1640-1793*, ed. Samuel Bates (Randolph, Mass., 1886).

Browne, Robert, *A Treatise of Reformation Without Tarying for Anie* (Middleburg, Holland, 1582).

Bruce, John, *et al.*, eds., *Calendar of State Papers, Domestic Series, of the Reign of Charles I*, 23 vols. (London, 1857-97).

Bulkley, Peter, *The Gospel Covenant or the Covenant of Grace Opened* (London, 1646).

Calvin, John, *Institutes of the Christian Religion*, trans. Henry Beveridge, 5 vols. (Edinburgh, 1845).

————, *Ioannis Calvini Opera quae supersunt omnia*, 59 vols. (Brunsvigae, 1863-1900).

Cambridge, Massachusetts, *The Records of the Town of Cambridge, 1630-1703* (Cambridge, Mass., 1901).

Cobbett, Thomas, *The Civil Magistrates Power in Matters of Religion Modestly Debated, Impartially Stated According to the Bounds and Grounds of Scripture* (London, 1653).

Cotton, John, *A Briefe Exposition with Practical Observations upon the Whole Book of Ecclesiastes* (Edinburgh, 1868).

————, "An Abstract of the Lawes of New England," in Peter Force, ed., *Tracts and Other Papers Relating Principally to the Colonies in North America*, 3 vols. (Washington, 1836-46, reprinted New York, 1947), III, No. 9.

————, "A Letter of Mr. John Cottons, Teacher of the Church in Boston, in New England, to Mr. Williams, a Preacher there," Narragansett Club, *Publications*, 1st Ser., 1 (1866), 295-311.

————, "A Reply to Mr. Williams His Examination; and A Answer of the Letters sent to him by John Cotton," Narragansett Club, *Publications*, 1st Ser., 2 (1867), 9-237.

————, *Christ the Fountain of Life* (London, 1651).

————, "Gods Promise to His Plantations," *Old South Leaflets*, No. 53 (Boston [1896]).

————, *Gospel Conversion* (London, 1646).

Cotton, John, "John Cotton's Will," *New England Historical and Genealogical Register*, 5 (1851), 240-41.

———, *Severall Questions of Serious and Necessary Consequence Propounded by the Teaching Elders* (London, 1647).

———, *Sixteene Questions of Serious and Necessary Consequence propounded unto Mr. John Cotton of Boston in New England Together with his answers to each question* (London, 1644).

———, *Spiritual Milk for American Babes Drawn out of the Breasts of Both Testaments for their Souls Nourishment* (Boston, n.d.)

———, *The Bloody Testament Washed and Made White in the Bloud of the Lambe* (London, 1647).

———, *The Controversie Concerning Liberty of Conscience in Matters of Religion* (London, 1649).

———, *The Covenant of Gods Free Grace Most Sweetly Unfolded* (London, 1645).

———, *The Keyes of the Kingdom of Heaven, and the Power thereof, according to the Word of God* (Boston, 1852).

———, *The New Covenant, or a Treatise unfolding the order and manner of the giving and receiving of the Covenant of Grace to the Elect* (London, 1654).

———, *The Way of the Congregational Churches Cleared* (London, 1648).

———, *The Way of Life* (London, 1641).

Davenport, John, *A Discourse About Civil Government in a New Plantation whose Design is Religion* (Cambridge, Mass., 1663).

Dexter, Franklin B., ed., "A Report of the Trial of Mrs. Anne Hutchinson Before the Church in Boston, 1638," Massachusetts Historical Society, *Proceedings*, 2d Ser., 4 (1889), 159-91.

Donne, John, *Poems*, ed. Herbert Grierson (Oxford, 1912).

Edwards, Thomas, *Gangraena*, 3 pts. (London, 1646).

Farrand, Max, ed., *The Book of General Lawes and Liberties, 1648* (Cambridge, Mass., 1929).

Fitch, James, *The First Principles of the Doctrine of Christ* (Boston, 1679).

Groome, Samuel, "A Glasse for the People of New England," *Magazine of History*, 37, No. 3, Extra No. 147 (Tarrytown, 1929), 129-53.

Holy Bible, Authorized King James Version.

Hooker, Richard, *Works*, 3 vols. (Oxford, 1807).

Hooker, Thomas, *A Survey of the Summe of Church Discipline* (London, 1648).

Hooker, Thomas, "The Way of the Churches of New England," *Old South Leaflets,* No. 55 (Boston [1896]).

Hubbard, William, *A General History of New England from the Discovery to 1680* (Cambridge, Mass., 1815).

James I, *The Political Works of James I,* ed. Charles Howard McIlwain (Cambridge, 1918).

Johnson, Edward, *Wonder Working Providence of Sions Saviour in New England, 1628-1651,* ed. J. Franklin Jameson (New York, 1910).

Knappen, Marshall, ed., *Two Elizabethan Puritan Diaries* (Chicago, 1933).

Lechford, Thomas, *Notebook Kept by Thomas Lechford, Esq., Lawyer, in Boston, Massachusetts Bay,* ed. Edward Everett Hale, Jr. (Cambridge, Mass., 1885).

———, *Plaine Dealing* (Boston, 1867).

Mather, Richard [and Hugh Peter], *Church Government and Church Covenant* (London, 1643).

———, *The Summe of Certain Sermons Upon Genes: 15.6* (Cambridge, Mass., 1652).

Miller, Perry and Thomas Johnson, eds., *The Puritans* (New York, 1938).

Morton, Nathaniel, *New Englands Memoriall,* ed. Howard J. Hall (New York, 1937).

Norton, John, *Memoir of John Cotton* (Boston, 1834).

———, *The Heart of N–England Rent at the Blasphemies of the Present Generation* (Cambridge, Mass., 1659).

———, *The Orthodox Evangelist* (London, 1654).

Pagitt, Ephraim, *Heresiography, or a Description of the Hereticks and Sectaries Sprang up in these Latter Times* (London, 1645).

Plato, *The Republic,* trans. B. Jowett (New York, 1941).

———, *The Works of Plato,* ed. Irwin Edman (New York, 1928).

Preston, John, *The New Covenant, or the Saints Portion* (London, 1630).

———, *A Sermon Preached at the General Fast Before the Commons-House of Parliament* (London, 1633).

Rhode Island, *Civil and Military List of Rhode Island,* ed. Joseph Jenks Smith (Providence, 1900).

———, *Documentary History of Rhode Island,* ed. Howard M. Chapin, 2 vols. (Providence, 1916).

———, *Records of the Colony of Rhode Island and Providence Plantations in New England,* ed. John Russell Bartlett, 10 vols. (Providence, 1856-65).

Rutherford, Samuel, *A Survey of the Spiritual Anti-Christ* (London, 1648).

Saltonstall, Sir Richard, "A Letter to John Cotton and John Wilson," Massachusetts Historical Society, *Collections*, 2d Ser., 4 (1874).

Shakespeare, William, *Complete Works*, ed. W. J. Craig (New York, 1905).

Shepard, Thomas, "Election Sermon in 1638," *New England Historical and Genealogical Register*, 24 (1870), 361-66.

——, *New England's Lamentation for Old England's Present Errours* (London, 1645).

——, *The Works of Thomas Shepard* (Boston, 1853).

——, "Thomas Shepard's Memoir of Himself," in Alexander Young, *The Chronicles of the First Planters of the Colony of Massachusetts Bay from 1623 to 1636* (Boston, 1846).

Shurtleff, Nathaniel B., ed., *Records of the Governor and Company of the Massachusetts Bay*, 5 vols. (Boston, 1853-54).

Sibbes, Richard, *The Complete Works of Richard Sibbes, D. D.*, ed. Alexander B. Grosart, 6 vols. (Edinburgh, 1863).

Stoughton, Israel, "Letter to Dr. John Stoughton," Massachusetts Historical Society, *Proceedings*, 58 (1925), 446-58.

Suffolk County, Massachusetts, *Suffolk Deeds*, Liber I, ed. William Blake Trask (Boston, 1880).

Tawney, Richard H. and Eileen Power, *Tudor Economic Documents*, 3 vols. (London, 1924).

Vane, Henry, "A Briefe Answer to a Certaine Declaration," *Hutchinson Papers*, ed. W. H. Whitmore and W. S. Appleton (Prince Society, *Publications*, 2 vols. [1865]), I, 84-96.

Ward, Nathaniel, "The Body of Liberties," *Old South Leaflets* (Boston [1905]).

——, "The Simple Cobler of Aggawam in America," in Peter Force, ed., *Tracts and Other Papers Relating Principally to the Colonies in North America*, 3 vols. (Washington, 1836-46, reprinted New York, 1947), III, No. 8.

Watertown, Massachusetts, *Watertown Records, comprising the First and Second Books of Town Proceedings with the Land Grants and Possessions, also the Proprietors' Book, and the First Book and Supplement of Births, Deaths and Marriages* (Watertown, 1894).

Weymouth, Massachusetts, *Vital Records of Weymouth to the Year 1850*, 2 vols. (Boston, 1910).

Wheelwright, John, *His Writings, Including His Fast-day Sermon, 1637, and His Mercurius Americanus, 1645 ...*, ed. Charles H. Bell (Boston, 1876).

Williams, Roger, "Mr. Cottons Letter Lately Printed, Examined and Answered," Narragansett Club, *Publications*, 1st Ser., 1 (1866), 313-96.

———, *The Bloudy Tenent of Persecution for Cause of Conscience Discussed*, ed. Edward B. Underhill (London, 1848).

Wilson, John, *Handkerchiefs from Paul . . .*, ed. Kenneth B. Murdock (Cambridge, Mass., 1927).

Winthrop, John, "A Defense of an Order of Court made in the Year 1637," *Hutchinson Papers*, ed. W. H. Whitmore and W. S. Appleton (Prince Society, *Publications*, 2 vols. [1865]), I, 79-83.

———, "Reply to an Answer Made to a Declaration," *Hutchinson Papers*, ed. W. H. Whitmore and W. S. Appleton (Prince Society, *Publications*, 2 vols. [1865]), I, 96-113.

———, *Winthrop's Journal "History of New England, 1630-1649,"* ed. James Kendall Hosmer, 2 vols. (New York, 1908).

———, *History of New England*, ed. James Savage (Boston, 1825).

Winthrop Papers, 5 vols. (Boston, 1929-47).

Wood, William, *New England's Prospect* (London, 1635).

II. SECONDARY SOURCES

A. HISTORICAL BACKGROUND

Adams, Brooks, *The Emancipation of Massachusetts* (Boston, 1919).

Adams, Charles Francis, Jr., *Three Episodes of Massachusetts History*, 2 vols. (Boston, 1896).

Adams, James Truslow, *The Founding of New England* (Boston, 1921).

Andrews, Charles McLean, *The Colonial Period of American History*, 4 vols. (New Haven, 1934).

———, *The Fathers of New England* (New Haven, 1921).

Arnold, Samuel Greene, *History of the State of Rhode Island and Providence Plantations*, 2 vols. (New York, 1859-60).

Backus, Isaac, *A History of New England with Particular Reference to the Denomination of Christians called Baptists* (Newton, 1871).

Bancroft, George, *History of the United States*, 10 vols. (Boston, 1834-74).

Banks, Charles Edward, *Planters of the Commonwealth, 1620-1640* (Boston, 1930).

———, *Topographical Dictionary of 2,885 English Emigrants to New England, 1620-1650* (Philadelphia, 1937).

———, *The Winthrop Fleet of 1630* (Boston, 1930).

Belknap, Jeremy, *History of New Hampshire*, 3 vols. (Dover, 1812).

Bell, Charles H., *History of the Town of Exeter* (Exeter, 1888).

Bicknell, T. W., *History of Rhode Island and Providence* (New York, 1920).

Clapham, Sir John, *A Concise Economic History of Britain* (Cambridge, Eng., 1951).

Corey, Deloraine Pendre, *The History of Malden, 1633-1785* (Malden, Mass., 1899).

Creighton, Charles, *History of Epidemics in Britain*, 2 vols. (Cambridge, Eng., 1891-94).

Davies, Godfrey, *The Early Stuarts, 1603-1660* (Oxford, 1936).

Doyle, John Andrew, *English Colonies in America*, 5 vols. (New York, 1882-1907).

Drake, Francis S., *The Town of Roxbury* (Boston, 1905).

Drake, Samuel, *The History and Antiquities of Boston* (Boston, 1857).

Dudding, Reginald, *History of the Parish and Manors of Alford with Rigsby* (Horncastle, 1930).

Ellis, George E., *Massachusetts and its Early History* (New York, 1885).

Felt, Joseph B., *The Ecclesiastical History of New England*, 2 vols. (Boston, 1862).

Fiske, John, *The Beginning of New England* (Boston, 1889).

Green, John R., *History of the English People*, 4 vols. (New York, 1903).

Howe, Daniel Wait, *The Puritan Republic of Massachusetts Bay in New England* (Indianapolis, 1899).

Hutchinson, Thomas, *History of the Colony and Province of Massachusetts Bay*, ed. Lawrence Shaw Mayo, 3 vols. (Cambridge, Mass., 1936).

Lipson, E., *The Economic History of England*, 3 vols. (London, 1948).

Mather, Cotton, *Magnalia Christi Americana, or the Ecclesiastical History of New England*, 2 vols. (Hartford, 1820).

Morgan, Edmund S., "The Case Against Anne Hutchinson," *New England Quarterly*, 10 (1937), 635-49.

Morison, Samuel Eliot, *The Founding of Harvard College* (Cambridge, Mass., 1935).

Morris, Richard B., *Fair Trial; Fourteen Who Stood Accused, from Anne Hutchinson to Alger Hiss* (New York, 1952).

Motley, John Lothrop, *The Rise of the Dutch Republic*, 3 vols. (New York, 1853).

Neal, Daniel, *The History of New England* (London, 1720).

Osgood, Herbert L., *The American Colonies in the Seventeenth Century*, 3 vols. (New York, 1904-7).

Palfrey, John Gorham, *History of New England*, 5 vols. (Boston, 1858-90).

Phillips, James Duncan, *Salem in the Seventeenth Century* (Boston, 1933).

Trevelyan, Sir George Macaulay, *England Under the Stuarts* (New York, 1930).

Wadleigh, George, *Notable Events in the History of Dover, New Hampshire* (Dover, 1913).

Wertenbaker, Thomas Jefferson, *The First Americans, 1607-1690* (New York, 1927).

———, *The Puritan Oligarchy* (New York, 1947).

Winsor, Justin, ed., *The Memorial History of Boston* . . . , 4 vols. (Boston, 1881-86).

B. PURITAN SOCIETY AND GOVERNMENT

Allen, J. W., *A History of Political Thought in the Sixteenth Century* (London, 1928).

———, *English Political Thought, 1603-1660*, 2 vols. (London, 1938).

Bailyn, Bernard, *The New England Merchants in the Seventeenth Century* (Cambridge, Mass., 1955).

Bridenbaugh, Carl, *Cities in the Wilderness* (New York, 1938).

Brown, B. Katherine, "Freemanship in Puritan Massachusetts," *American Historical Review*, 59 (1954), 865-83.

Dow, George Francis, *Every Day Life in the Massachusetts Bay Colony* (Boston, 1935).

Dunning, William A., *A History of Political Theories From Luther to Montesquieu*, 2 vols. (New York, 1927).

Gray, Stanley, "The Political Thought of John Winthrop," *New England Quarterly*, 3 (1930), 681-705.

Greene, Evarts B., and Virginia Harrington, *American Population Before the Federal Census of 1790* (New York, 1932).

Haller, William, Jr., *The Puritan Frontier, Town Planting in New England Colonial Development, 1630-1660* (New York, 1951).

Haskins, George Lee, *Law and Authority in Early Massachusetts* (New York, 1960).

Haynes, George H., *Representation and Suffrage in Massachusetts, 1620-1691* (Johns Hopkins University Studies in Historical and Political Science, 12th Ser., 8-9 [Baltimore, 1894]).

Masson, David, *The Life of John Milton*, 7 vols., rev. ed. (London, 1877-96).

Morison, Samuel Eliot, *The Puritan Pronaos* (New York, 1936).

Morris, Richard B., *Government and Labor in Early America* (New York, 1946).

Murdock, Kenneth B., *Literature and Theology in Colonial New England* (Cambridge, Mass., 1949).

Notestein, Wallace, *The English People on the Eve of Colonization* (New York, 1954).

Osgood, Herbert L., "The Political Ideas of the Puritans," *Political Science Quarterly*, 6 (1891), 1-28.

Page, William, ed., *The Victoria History of the Counties of England: Lincolnshire* (London, 1906).

Pierce, Ebeneezer W., *Civil, Military and Professional Lists of Plymouth and Rhode Island Colonies, 1621-1700* (Boston, 1881).

Seybolt, Robert F., *The Town Officials of Colonial Boston* (Cambridge, Mass., 1939).

Shurtleff, Nathaniel B., *A Topographical and Historical Description of Boston* (Boston, 1871).

Thwing, Annie H., *The Crooked and Narrow Streets of the Town of Boston, 1630-1822* (Boston, 1930).

Weeden, William B., *Economic and Social History of New England, 1620-1789*, 2 vols. (Boston, 1890).

C. BIOGRAPHY

Adams, James Truslow, "Cotton, John," *Dictionary of American Biography*, ed. Allen Johnson and Dumas Malone, 22 vols. (New York, 1928-44), IV, 460-62.

———, "Wheelwright, John," *Dictionary of American Biography*, XX, 62-63.

———, "Winthrop, John," *Dictionary of American Biography*, XX, 408-11.

Augur, Helen, *An American Jezebel, the Life of Anne Hutchinson* (New York, 1930).

Austin, John Osborne, *The Genealogical Dictionary of Rhode Island* (Albany, 1887).

Bailyn, Bernard, "The Apologia of Robert Keayne," *William and Mary Quarterly*, 3d Ser., 7 (1950), 568-87.

Bartlett, Joseph Gardner, "Ancestry and Descendants of Rev. John Wilson of Boston, Mass.," *New England Historical and Genealogical Register*, 61 (1907), 127-33.

Champlin, J. D., "The Ancestry of Anne Hutchinson," *New York Genealogical and Biographical Record*, 45 (1914), 17-26.

Champlin, J. D., "Hutchinson Ancestry and Descendants of William and Anne Hutchinson," *New York Genealogical and Biographical Record*, 45 (1914), 164-69.

Chester, J. L., "The Family of Dummer," *New England Historical and Genealogical Register*, 35 (1881), 254-71, 321-31.

Come, Donald, "John Cotton, Guide to Chosen People" (unpublished Ph.D. dissertation, Princeton University, 1949).

Deane, Charles, "Notice of Samuel Gorton," *New England Historical and Genealogical Register*, 4 (1850), 201-21.

Ellis, George, *The Life of Anne Hutchinson* (Boston, 1845).

Ernst, James, *Roger Williams* (New York, 1932).

Fay, Anna Maria, "Some Account of the Life and Times of the Reverend Peter Bulkley," *New England Historical and Genealogical Register*, 31 (1877), 154-60.

Fish, Frederick Samuel, "Coggeshall," *New England Historical and Genealogical Register*, 73 (1919), 19-32.

Gay, Frederick, "Rev. Francis Marbury," Massachusetts Historical Society, *Proceedings*, 48 (1915), 280-91.

Gordon, Alexander, "Brerely or Brierley, Roger," *Dictionary of National Biography*, ed. Sir Leslie Stephens and Sir Sidney Lee, 67 vols. (London, 1885-1903), XI, 266-67.

Heard, John, *John Wheelwright* (Boston, 1930).

Hosmer, James Kendall, *The Life of Young Sir Henry Vane* (Boston, 1888).

Hufeland, O., "Anne Hutchinson's Refuge in the Wilderness," Westchester County Historical Society, *Publications*, 7 (1939), 3-20.

Mayo, Lawrence Shaw, *John Endicott* (Cambridge, Mass., 1939).

Morgan, Edmund S., *The Puritan Dilemma: The Story of John Winthrop* (Boston, 1958).

Moriarty, G. Andrews, "The Coggeshalls of Halstead and Hundon," *New England Historical and Genealogical Register*, 100 (1946), 14-24.

——, "President John Sanford of Portsmouth, R. I. and His Family," *New England Historical and Genealogical Register*, 103 (1949), 208-16.

Morison, Samuel Eliot, *Builders of the Bay Colony* (Boston, 1930).

Murdock, Kenneth B., "Wilson, John," *Dictionary of American Biography*, XX, 336-37.

Park, Lawrence, "The Savage Family," *New England Historical and Genealogical Register*, 67 (1913), 198-215.

Pope, Charles Henry, *The Pioneers of Massachusetts* (Boston, 1900).

——, *The Pioneers of Maine and New Hampshire* (Boston, 1908).

Preston, Richard Arthur, *Gorges of Plymouth Fort* (Toronto, 1953).

Richman, Irving B., "Coddington, William," *Dictionary of American Biography*, IV, 258-59.

Rossiter, Clinton, "Thomas Hooker," *New England Quarterly*, 25 (1952), 459-88.

Rugg, Winifred King, *Unafraid, A Life of Anne Hutchinson* (Boston, 1930).

Sanborn, V. C., "Stephen Bachiler and the Plough Company," Maine Historical Society, *Collections*, 3d Ser., 2 (1906), 342-69.

Savage, James, *A Genealogical Dictionary of the First Settlers of New England*, 4 vols. (Boston, 1860-1862).

——, "Gleanings for New England History," Massachusetts Historical Society, *Collections*, 3rd Ser., 8 (1843), 242-348.

Shurtleff, Nathaniel B., "A Genealogical Note of the Family of Elder Thomas Leverett," *New England Historical and Genealogical Register*, 4 (1850), 121-36.

Stearns, Henry P., "Bellingham, Richard," *Dictionary of American Biography*, II, 166-67.

Stearns, Raymond P., *The Strenuous Puritan, Hugh Peter* (Urbana, 1954).

Townsend, Charles H., "Richard Bellingham," *New England Historical and Genealogical Register*, 36 (1883), 381-86.

Twichell, Joseph H., *John Winthrop* (New York, 1892).

West, Edward, "Portsmouth Under the Hutchinsons," *New England Historical and Genealogical Register*, 105 (1951), 90-94.

Wheelwright, Edmund, "A Frontier Family," Colonial Society of Massachusetts, *Publications*, 1 (1895), 271-303.

Whitmore, W. H., "The Oliver Family," *New England Historical and Genealogical Register*, 19 (1865), 100-106.

——, "A Brief Genealogy of the Hutchinson Family," *New England Genealogical and Historical Register*, 19 (1865), 13-20.

Williams, Emily Coddington, *William Coddington of Rhode Island* (Newport, 1941).

Winthrop, Robert C., *Life and Letters of John Winthrop*, 2 vols. (Boston, 1869).

D. Religion and Philosophy

Allen, G. B., "Boehme," *Encyclopaedia of Religion and Ethics*, ed. James Hastings, 13 vols. (New York, 1908-26), II, 778-84.

Bailey, Margaret Lewis, *Milton and Jakob Boehme* (New York, 1914).

Braithwaite, William C., *The Beginnings of Quakerism* (London, 1912).

Burrage, Champlin, *The Church Covenant Idea* (Philadelphia, 1904).

———, *The Early English Dissenters in the Light of Recent Research*, 2 vols. (Cambridge, Eng., 1912).

Craig, Hardin, *The Enchanted Glass* (New York, 1936).

De Jong, Peter Y., *The Covenant Idea in New England Theology* (Grand Rapids, 1945).

Deutsch, S. M., "Scotus Erigena, Johannes," *The New Schaff-Herzog Encyclopedia of Religious Knowledge*, ed. Samuel Macaulay, 13 vols. (Grand Rapids, Mich., 1949-50), IX, 303-7.

———, "Eckhart," *The New Schaff-Herzog Encyclopedia of Religious Knowledge*, IV, 67-71.

Dewey, Edward H., "Shepard, Thomas," *Dictionary of American Biography*, XVII, 75-76.

De Wulf, Maurice, *A History of Medieval Philosophy*, trans. E. C. Messenger, 2 vols. (London, 1926).

Fenn, William W., "The Marrow of Calvin's Theology," *Harvard Theological Review*, 2 (1909), 323-39.

Fisher, George Park, *A History of Christian Doctrine* (New York, 1896).

Fleming, W. K., *Mysticism in Christianity* (New York, 1913).

Foster, Frank McHugh, *A Genetic History of the New England Theology* (Chicago, 1907).

Foster, Herbert D., *Collected Papers* (privately printed, 1929).

Friedman, Robert, "Conception of the Anabaptists," *Church History*, 10 (1940), 341-65.

Gilson, Etienne, *The Spirit of Medieval Philosophy*, trans. A. H. C. Downs (New York, 1936).

Harkness, Georgia, *John Calvin, the Man and His Ethics* (New York, 1931).

Haydn, Hiram, *The Counter Renaissance* (New York, 1950).

Huehns, Gertrude, *Antinomianism in English History* (London, 1951).

Jones, Rufus M., *Mysticism and Democracy in the English Commonwealth* (Cambridge, Eng., 1932).

———, *Some Exponents of Mystical Religion* (Berkeley, 1930).

Jones, Rufus M., *Studies in Mystical Religion* (London, 1923).

——, *The Quakers in the American Colonies* (London, 1911).

Jordan, W. K., *The Development of Religious Toleration in England from the Accession of James I to the Convention of the Long Parliament* (Cambridge, Eng., 1936).

Kawerau, G., "Agricola, Johann," *The New Schaff-Herzog Encyclopedia of Religious Knowledge*, I, 91-92.

King, Rachel Hadley, *George Fox and the Light Within, 1650-1660* (Philadelphia, 1940).

Knappen, Marshall, *Tudor Puritanism, a Chapter in the History of Idealism* (Chicago, 1939).

Knox, Ronald A., *Enthusiasm* (New York, 1950).

Lauer, Harold, *Church and State in New England* (Johns Hopkins University Studies in Historical and Political Science, 10th Ser., 4-5 [Baltimore, 1892]).

Levy, Babette May, *Preaching in the First Half-Century of New England History* (Hartford, 1945).

Loofs, F., "Familists," *The New Schaff-Herzog Encyclopedia of Religious Knowledge*, IV, 272-73.

Lovejoy, A. O., *The Great Chain of Being* (Cambridge, Mass., 1937).

Lyon, T., *The Theory of Religious Liberty in England, 1603-1639* (Cambridge, Eng., 1937).

McDonnell, Ernest W., *The Beguines and Beghards in Medieval Culture* (New Brunswick, 1954).

McGiffert, Arthur Cushman, *Protestant Thought Before Kant* (New York, 1915).

Mackinnon, James, *Calvin and the Reformation* (London, 1936).

McMahon, A. L., "Eckhart, Johann, Meister," *Catholic Encyclopedia*, ed. Charles G. Herbermann *et al.*, 15 vols. (New York, 1913), V, 274.

Mathews, Shailer, *The Growth of the Idea of God* (New York, 1931).

Mathews, Walter Robert, *God in Christian Experience* (New York, 1930).

Miller, Perry, *Orthodoxy in Massachusetts, 1630-1650* (Cambridge, Mass., 1933).

——, "The Marrow of Puritan Divinity," Colonial Society of Massachusetts, *Transactions*, 32 (1937), 247-300.

——, *The New England Mind: the Seventeenth Century* (New York, 1939).

——, *The New England Mind: From Colony to Province* (Cambridge, Mass., 1953).

Minges, Parthenius, "Duns Scotus, John," *Catholic Encyclopedia*, V, 194-99.

Newman, A. H., "Antinomianism and Antinomian Controversies," *The New Schaff-Herzog Encyclopedia of Religious Knowledge*, I, 196-200.

Nutter, Stephen Bernard, *The Story of the Cambridge Baptists in the Struggle for Religious Liberty* (Cambridge, Eng., 1912).

Parkes, Henry Bamford, "John Cotton and Roger Williams Debate Toleration, 1644-1652," *New England Quarterly*, 4 (1931), 735-56.

Parrington, Vernon L., *Main Currents in American Thought* (New York, 1927).

Perry, Ralph Barton, *Puritanism and Democracy* (New York, 1944).

Portalié, Eugène, "Augustine of Hippo, Saint," *Catholic Encyclopedia*, II, 84-104.

Riley, Woodbridge, *American Philosophy, the Early Schools* (New York, 1907).

———, *American Thought From Puritanism to Pragmatism and Beyond* (New York, 1923).

Sauvage, George M., "Mysticism," *Catholic Encyclopedia*, X, 663-65.

Schneider, Herbert Wallace, *A History of American Philosophy* (New York, 1946).

———, *The Puritan Mind* (New York, 1930).

Sheen, Fulton J., *Philosophy of Religion* (New York, 1948).

Spencer, Theodore, *Shakespeare and the Nature of Man* (New York, 1942).

Sterrett, J. MacBride, "Antinomianism," *Encyclopaedia of Religion and Ethics*, I, 581-82.

Stokes, Anson Phelps, *Church and State in the United States*, 3 vols. (New York, 1950).

Sturzo, Luigi, *Church and State* (New York, 1939).

Tawney, Richard, *Religion and the Rise of Capitalism*, New American Library ed. (New York, 1948).

Tillyard, E. M. W., *The Elizabethan World Picture* (New York, 1944).

Townsend, Harvey Gates, *Philosophical Ideas in the United States* (New York, 1934).

Troeltsch, Ernst, *Protestantism and Progress*, trans. W. Montgomery (New York, 1912).

———, *The Social Teachings of the Christian Churches*, trans. Olive Wyon, 2 vols. (New York, 1931).

Underhill, Evelyn, *The Mystics of the Church* (New York, 1926).

Walker, Williston, *A History of the Congregational Churches of the United States* (New York, 1894).

Winslow, Ola B., *Meetinghouse Hill, 1630-1783* (New York, 1954).

E. TECHNICAL AND OTHER COLLATERAL MATERIALS

Boyd, William, *A Textbook of Pathology* (Philadelphia, 1943).

Brett, George Sidney, *A History of Psychology* (London, 1921).

Calhoun, Arthur W., *A Social History of the American Family*, 3 vols. (Cleveland, 1917-19).

Cantril, Hadley, *The Psychology of Social Movements* (New York, 1941).

Chafee, Zechariah, Jr., *Free Speech in the United States* (Cambridge, Mass., 1948).

——, "Sedition," *Encyclopedia of the Social Sciences*, ed. Edwin R. A. Seligman, 15 vols. (New York, 1930-35), XIII, 636-39.

Cobbett, William, *Rural Rides*, 2 vols. (London, 1885).

Davenport, Frederick M., *Primitive Traits in Religious Revivals* (New York, 1917).

Davies, James C., "Charisma in the 1952 Campaign," *American Political Science Review*, 48 (1954), 1083-1102.

Dorcus, Roy M., and G. Wilson Schaffer, *Textbook of Abnormal Psychology* (Baltimore, 1950).

Earle, Alice Morse, *Home Life in Colonial Days* (New York, 1899).

Fairbairn, John Shields, "Menopause," *Encyclopaedia Britannica*, 24 vols. (Chicago, 1942), XV, 251-52.

Fromm, Erich, *Escape From Freedom* (New York, 1941).

Gatley, Clement, "Libel and Slander," *Encyclopaedia Britannica*, XIII, 995-97.

Hamblen, E. C., *Endocrinology of Woman* (Springfield, Ill., 1945).

Hartley, Dorothy, *The Countryman's England* (London, 1935).

Haynes, E. S. P., *Religious Persecution, A Study in Political Psychology* (London, 1906).

Holdsworth, William Searle, *A History of English Law* (Boston, 1922—), IV, V, VI, VIII, IX.

Holland, Eardley L., "Gynaecology," *Encyclopaedia Britannica*, XI, 34-39.

Horney, Karen, *New Ways in Psychoanalysis* (New York, 1939).

——, *The Neurotic Personality of Our Time* (New York, 1937).

James, William, *The Varieties of Religious Experience* (New York, 1902).

Kaplan, Oscar, ed., *Mental Disorders in Later Life* (Palo Alto, 1945).

King, C. Wendell, *Social Movements in the United States* (New York, 1956).

Klein, D. B., *Abnormal Psychology* (New York, 1951).

Landis, Carney, and M. M. Bolles, *Textbook of Abnormal Psychology* (New York, 1950).

Lasswell, Harold, *Psychopathology and Politics* (Chicago, 1930).

Laughlin, Clara, *So You're Going to England* (Boston, 1948).

Lecky, W. E. H., *History of the Rise and Influence of Rationalism in Europe* (New York, 1914).

Leuba, James Henry, *A Psychological Study of Religion* (New York, 1912).

——, *Psychology of Religious Mysticism* (New York, 1929).

Maslow, A. H., and Bela Mittelman, *Principles of Abnormal Psychology* (New York, 1951).

Merton, Robert K., *Social Theory and Social Structure*, rev. ed. (Glencoe, 1957).

Merton, Robert K., and Paul Lazarsfeld, eds., *Continuities in Social Research* (Glencoe, 1950).

Murphy, Gardner, and Arthur J. Bachrach, eds., *An Outline of Abnormal Psychology* (New York, 1954).

Niebuhr, Helmut Richard, *The Social Sources of Denominationalism* (New York, 1929).

Pakington, Humphrey, *English Villages and Hamlets*, 2d ed., rev. (London, 1936).

Panunzio, Constantine, *Major Social Institutions* (New York, 1947).

Pratt, James B., *The Religious Consciousness* (New York, 1926).

Pucknett, Theodore F. T., "Libel and Slander," *Encyclopedia of the Social Sciences*, IX, 430-35.

Richardson, Margaret V., and Arthur T. Hertig, "New England's First Recorded Hydatidiform Mole," *The New England Journal of Medicine*, 260 (1959), 544-45.

Rouse, Clive, *The Old Towns of England* (New York, 1936).

Schenck v. United States, 249 U.S. 47 (1919).

Thouless, Robert H., *An Introduction to the Psychology of Religion* (Cambridge, Eng., 1923).

Wach, Joachim, *Sociology of Religion* (Chicago, 1944).

Washburne, Norman F., *Interpreting Social Change in America* (New York, 1954).

Weber, Max, *Essays in Sociology,* trans. H. H. Gerth and C. Wright Mills (New York, 1946).

Williams, Robin, *American Society, A Sociological Interpretation* (New York, 1955).

Yinger, J. Milton, *Religion, Society and the Individual, An Introduction to the Sociology of Religion* (New York, 1957).

Index

SAINTS AND SECTARIES
*was designed, composed, and printed by Van Rees Press, New York.
Binding was by Van Rees Book Binding Corporation.
The text type is 11 point Caledonia, leaded 2 points.*

Anne Hutchinson's Boston

KEY TO LOCATION

1. William Aspinwall
2. Atherton Hough
3. John Coggeshall
4. William Hutchinson
5. John Winthrop
6. Meetinghouse
7. Market Place
8. John Wilson
9. William Coddington
10. Town Gaol
11. John Cotton
12. Bendall's Dock
13. Thomas Savage
14. William Dyer
15. Edward Hutchinson, Sr.